ACTING WITH STYLE

THIRD EDITION

JOHN HARROP

SABIN R. EPSTEIN

ALLYN AND BACON

Boston • London • Toronto • Sydney • Tokyo • Singapore

Senior Editor: *Karon Bowers*
Vice President, Editor in Chief: *Paul A. Smith*
Editorial Assistant: *Jennifer Becker*
Marketing Manager: *Jackie Aaron*
Editorial Production Service: *Chestnut Hill Enterprises, Inc.*
Manufacturing Buyer: *Meghan Cochran*
Cover Administrator: *Linda Knowles*
Electronic Composition: *Omegatype Typography, Inc.*

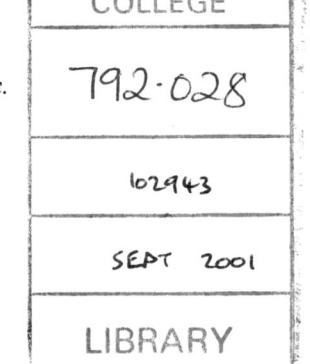

Copyright © 2000 by Allyn & Bacon
A Pearson Education Company
160 Gould Street
Needham Heights, Massachusetts 02494

Copyright 1990, 1982 by Prentice-Hall, Inc.

Internet: www.abacon.com

Library of Congress Cataloging-in-Publication Data
Harrop, John, 1931–
     Acting with Style / John Harrop, Sabin R. Epstein. — 3rd ed.
          p.   cm.
     Includes bibliographical references and index.
     ISBN 0–205–29582–7 (alk. paper)
     1. Acting.   2. Drama.   I. Epstein, Sabin R.   II. Title.
PN2061.H33   1999
792'.028—dc21   99-42664
                                                          CIP

Printed in the United States of America
10 9 8 7 6 5 4 3 2   03 02 01 00

Contents

Preface

I first met John Harrop in the summer of 1966. We were actors at the Utah Shakespeare Festival, and we quickly discovered that we were both going to Tulane University in the fall to attend graduate school in theater. We decided to share expenses and room together in New Orleans. Our friendship continued after graduate school as John finished his Ph.D. and as I embarked on a career in the professional theater.

In 1976 we began a series of discussions about acting and the actor's approach to style. We both agreed that American actors were finely attuned to the basic precepts of Stanislavski's technique but didn't have a clue as to how to approach a text of high language or "style." We decided to write a book chronicling the actor's journey from his or her first day of an acting class through the last day of rehearsal for the performance of a play of style.

Prentice Hall, in reviewing our original manuscript proposal, believed we had two books, one on basic acting, the other on approaching style. We worked on the second book first. *Acting with Style* was originally published in 1982, and the revised second edition was published in 1990. *Basic Acting: The Modular Acting Process,* the first half of our project, was completed and published by Allyn and Bacon in 1995.

John and I collaborated fully on both projects. We shared the same vision and philosophical approach to the work. However, we split the labor on the projects. John was the primary author of *Acting with Style,* while I am the primary author of *Basic Acting.* Although there is a difference in voice, or tone, between the two books, we thought they shared the same sensitivity to the needs of the actor—mainly a clearly defined, physical methodology for approaching the creation of a character by understanding how to read a text for the clues of character that could then be translated into the creation of the character mask. It was our hope that these two books, when read together, would supplement and reinforce one another in process and sensibility.

John died in September, 1995, just as *Basic Acting* was being published. In revising this third edition of *Acting with Style* you will notice a change in the voice in one section. I have added new material detailing an approach to the work of

David Mamet and the "Mamet style." In addition, I have updated and revised the text only when necessary, to make it politic with contemporary theatrical and cultural thinking.

The Mamet chapter is being used as a bridge between the American tradition of Realism and the European tradition of the Theater of the Absurd. These two sections may be cross-referenced, since they share so many basic philosophical and theatrical sensibilities. Indeed, it is my hope that you will cross-reference and use material from this book, as well as from *Basic Acting,* with creativity and imagination, since the process of discovering language is not limited to one specific time, place, or culture.

Once again, we gladly acknowledge our debt to Michael Chekhov, Rudolf Laban, and Viola Spolin as originators and codifiers of the physical approach to actor training, which we have used as the basis of our own work here. In addition I would like to thank Vicki Harrop for her valuable support and assistance in preparing this manuscript, Rod Menzies for his insightful comments, and the following reviewers of this edition: Claudia Beach, University of Central Arkansas; David Allen George, Salem State College; James Hatfield, University of Texas-Tyler; Susan Loughran, St. Edward's University; Robert McDonald, University of Connecticut; Bruce Miller, University of Miami; Chuck Richie, Kent State University; and Michael Simon-Curry, Goucher College.

Sabin Epstein

1 General Approach

Lady Windermere's Fan. *Citizens' Theatre, Glasgow. Photo by John Vere Brown.*

PROCESS

A presumption of this book is that the actor already has training in basic acting technique[1] and our purpose is to show how that personal method can be adapted to encompass the wide range of stylistic demands of the theatrical repertory. The process fundamental to all creativity is, of course, that every act of creation starts from some kind of impulse. That impulse may be an idea; it may be an image; it may spring from pure imagination, or, as is the normal presumption in theatre, it will be the actor's response to a play's text. An impulse is a movement toward action: If an actor wants to communicate an impulse then he or she must do something—play an action. So the actor's basic process is to make physical choices that will express the intention of the impulses received from the text. The interrelationship of all the choices of all the actors creates the performance—the theatrical event. This "score" of actions developed in rehearsal is essentially a constant; but the way in which it is played will vary somewhat at each performance, as the actors respond to the immediate rhythms of the occasion flowing from fellow actors and from the audience. Playing keeps vitality in performance.

STYLE AND SENSIBILITY

If performance is the playing of a score of choices, style is the way in which those choices are shaped and played. Style is choices in action; it is what distinguishes one event from another. In dictionary terms it is "a distinction or characteristic of some group or period." It is the way in which the speech, physical rhythms, clothing, and general approach to life in New York, the corporate and financial center of the United States on the shore of the cold

Atlantic, differ from those in Los Angeles, the entertainment center of the United States, on the shore of the warm Pacific. The adage "style is the man" (or woman) means that it is an essential approach to life that is manifested in active choices. Jacqueline Kennedy Onassis had a very distinctive style. It is a function of inheriting certain genes, being born into a privileged background, in a particular society, at a particular time, and being given a particular education, all of which both led and allowed her to make certain choices in housing, food, clothes, men, and general life style. The style is different from Jane Doe, who is a checkout clerk in a supermarket chain, and has a rather different sense of herself in her life based upon the somewhat different range of choices open to her. Both women have a style: the external manifestation of an inner essence, which itself is determined by a whole range of inherited and environmental responses—or given circumstances, to use the theatrical term.

Whereas style has been acknowledged in most areas of human cultural activity—art, music, architecture, etc.—it has sometimes been perceived as a problem in theatre. The young actor who would immediately recognize the difference in style between rock, rhythm and blues, and country music, and allow the difference in approach the musician takes toward them, might not as easily recognize or allow that Shakespeare, Restoration Comedy, and Tennessee Williams equally require a different approach from him or her as actor. This is a function of the domination of the acting process for the larger part of the twentieth century by a "naturalistic" methodology. This was based on the idea of the uniqueness of the human individual and the primacy of feeling. This led to the concept that the self of the actor and the self of the character had a direct one-to-one relationship, and therefore the actor's personal feelings were the touchstone of truth in theatrical performance. Anything that seemed not to be con-

---

[1]Our sense of the basic acting process can be found in *Basic Acting: Modular Acting Process* by the authors. (Allyn & Bacon, 1996).

sistent with this process was artificial and therefore dishonest. Style came to be associated with dishonesty because it made demands upon the actor outside of his or her normal behavior, and rather than being explored for its inherent truths it was responded to with facile surface mannerisms.

The imitation of the everyday behavior of twentieth-century human beings, the outward manifestation of their inner psychological processes, did create a style that is valid for the representation of Realism. But there is a vast corpus of drama that does not respond to this approach. And for good reason. The naturalistic approach tries to impose a reality upon these plays—based upon psychological interpretation of character, hidden motivations, and the engendering of emotion—that is quite foreign to the given circumstances of the texts. An actor must come to terms with the inherent truth of each text and not impose his or her contemporary sense of truth upon it. While inner process will always occur, the simple manifestation of personal feeling by an actor will not communicate the totality of a play. It is physical actions—signs and signals—that communicate, and these must take on a particular shape, create a particular style in accordance with the particular given circumstances of a text.

The given circumstances are the rules of the theatrical game. (To pursue the game analogy for a moment, it is the rules that tell us how, with the same deck of cards, to play bridge rather than gin rummy, or how, with similar implements, to play tennis rather than racquetball.) So the text not only provides the impulse to action but, through the given circumstances, also determines the shape of the actor's physical choices and the style of the event. What are these given circumstances? Most actors are familiar with given circumstances such as place, climate, dialects, and the physical type, age, and occupation of a character. These clues may distinguish quali-ties of character and situation, but they do not necessarily determine the style of a performance. The basic question is: Why do characters in a comedy by Noel Coward and a comic character in Molière require different approaches from the actor? Or, what makes a play by Tennessee Williams different from a play by Samuel Beckett and why are neither like a play by Bertolt Brecht?

The clues are in the text: given circumstances of a much more comprehensive kind than those that give information about character. They include:

> theatrical conventions of the time in which the play was written; the nature of the theatrical space, equipment, and the social manner of the time;
> the structure of the language, the use of verse or prose, verbal wit; the form of the play, classical, neoclassical, epic, comedic, tragic; character conventions such as humors or masks;
> social, political, moral attitudes of the time in which the playwright is working and by which he or she will have been influenced.

It is only by understanding these built-in clues that an actor can hope to approach a true awareness of the stylistic demands of a text. All of this we are calling the sensibility of a time—the theatrical, social, and personal values a playwright inevitably writes into a play. An understanding of the sensibility makes possible an assumption of the style. Style reflects the fact that theatre holds a "mirror up to nature." Joseph Chaikin has noted that "theatre styles are interrelated with living and thought styles—everything we see carries a recommendation to be seen within a given system of perception."[2] It is this system of perception—the reflection of a particular social

[2]Joseph Chaikin, *The Presence of the Actor* (New York: Atheneum, 1972), p. 128.

reality at a particular time—that an actor must achieve in order to avoid imposing his or her own contemporary sensibility and personal sense of truth upon a text, and thereby limiting or warping it.

CREATING THE MASK

As we have said, theatre is the creation of an illusion of reality. Lee Simonson has observed that "the reality of a performance has no inherent connection with the degree of fidelity with which it produces the facts of actual life."[3] For the actor there is a crucial distinction between simply expressing the self and using the self to express the truth of the event as found in the given circumstances. Emphasis upon honesty in acting has been taken to mean that all an actor has to do is to project his or her feelings through the role, turning every character into a carbon copy of oneself. Dion Boucicault once observed, "If actors' and actresses' minds be employed upon themselves and not on the character they aspire to perform, they never really get out of themselves. Many think they are studying their character when they are studying only themselves."[4]

An actor must take into account all the given circumstances in order to create the mask of character that the truth of the event requires. He or she must be aware that a character may be constructed as much out of the rhythms and images of its speech and its structural function in a play, as out of imagined biological or biographical data; that a playwright may deal in broad humors as much as in detailed psyches; and that the "artificiality" of manner written into some plays must be recognized as representing the physical reality of its time, and must be reproduced if the quality of the play is to be truly served. If an actor creates a mask that is a valid representation of the demands the script places on the character, then he or she is being honest with the intention of the play.

Masks have always been fundamental to dramatic representation. The use of masks may be traced back to primitive peoples who wore them in their rituals. Greek theatre adopted the practice in both tragedy and comedy, in order to define essential attributes of character. Mask continued to be part of theatrical convention through the sixteenth century where the five main characters of the *commedia del l'arte* not only wore masks but also were referred to as "masks." Molière used masks in some of his more farcical works, and ever since that time the term has been generally applied to any well-defined theatrical character type, though it may no longer wear a physical mask.

To think of a character as a mask of the action—that is, a fictive construct necessary to the plot structure—underlines the fact that theatre is not reality but an illusion of reality. As Richard Schechner has put it: "Great errors are made because performers and directors think of characters as people rather than as *dramatis personae:* masks of dramatic action. A role conforms to the logic of theatre, not the logic of any other life system. To think of a role as a person is like picnicking on a landscape painting."[5]

We are taking mask to mean everything a character is required to do physically in order to discharge its necessary function within the play. It may be based on a concrete reality as in Greek and *commedia* styles, or a set of physical choices that includes everything from hair style, vocal quality, costume

---

[3]Lee Simonson, *The Stage is Set* (New York: Theatre Arts Books, 1963), p. 46.

[4]Dion Boucicault, Constant Coquelin, and Henry Irving, *The Art of Acting* (New York: Dramatic Museum of Columbia University, 1926), p. 42.

[5]Richard Schechner, *Environmental Theater* (New York: Hawthorn, 1973), p. 165.

and physical rhythms, to kinds of shoes and manner of walk. Robert Benedetti has put it well. "Mask is a set of postures, sounds and actions performed by the actor . . . different kinds of acting, having different purposes, require different relationships of actor and character."[6]

J. L. Styan makes the point even more directly: "Voice, face, figure and how far they reveal—or obscure the personality of the player, are the surest guide to the conventions of the play as determined by mood, content, and stage conditions."[7] To illustrate more specifically how this relationship between mask and face is determined by the demands of the play, we are going to set out some rule-of-thumb distinctions among styles, which we will elaborate on in the body of the book:

1. In the most naturalistic forms of acting—film and television—the actor tends to equate his or her own psychological and emotional qualities with those of the character. The mask is the face. This is really personality acting, a form of selected "being."
2. In most realistic stage acting, the actor plays from him or herself, adjusting personal attributes to fit the character mask.
3. In Shakespeare the structure and qualities of the verse contain all the character's responses to the action of the play. The shape, rhythms, and colorations of the verse are assimilated by the actor and lead him or her to the necessary physical choices of the mask.
4. In Brechtian theatre the actor creates the mask through choices that will illustrate the socioeconomic significance of the action. He or she then plays the mask in the consciousness of the political effect it will

[6]Robert Benedetti, *Seeming, Being and Becoming* (New York: Drama Book Specialists, 1976), p. 24.

[7]J. L. Styan, *Drama, Stage and Audience* (Cambridge: Cambridge University Press, 1975), p. 160.

have on the audience. The actor is both within the mask and outside it.

5. With Samuel Beckett the mask is distinctly individual, but it is a broad symbol for larger aspects of the human situation. The aspects are selected so that the playing of them will create the metaphysical resonances of Absurd theatre. The mask is larger than the actor, but bears his or her features.
6. In theatre specifically written for a physical mask—Greek, *commedia*—the actor's face is now covered, is behind a mask, and his or her task is to play the mask in such a manner that all of its conventions are fulfilled.

There is no fundamental contradiction between the demands of mask and playing, and the need for inner process. Gestalt psychology teaches the close relationship between physical response and emotional response, and many practitioners of theatre now feel that the articulation of the physical part of the role stimulates the inner support.

FROM GIVEN CIRCUMSTANCES TO STYLE

The discovery, adoption, and playing of the right mask is, then, the actor's fundamental task. Whether the character is perceived of as "realistic" (someone you might bump into on the street) or is removed from a contemporary perspective by time or social environment, the task of approaching the style is the same. Stanley Kowalski is no less a mask of Tennessee Williams' dramatic action than is Oedipus of Sophocles', or a Restoration fop of Congreve's. Our approach in this book is to help the actor discover the clues to style in a text and to place these clues in their necessary social and cultural environment. This we have called the "intrinsic demands" of the text. Armed with this information we then show how these intrinsic demands are translated into and will determine the shape of the actor's role: the "performance demands." The connection between the understanding of the demands of the text and the physical experience of these demands is achieved through exercises that attune the actor to the playing of the style. The exercises are game-oriented, which is consistent with our belief that acting is the playing of physical actions, and thus help the actor get a concrete feeling for entering the physical skin of the style.

I Playing Tragedy

Our focus is on the physical demands that the playing of tragic drama places upon the actor. We are concerned with the aesthetics of tragedy only insofar as it will help the actor come to terms with the sensibility underlying the actor's approach. To examine the specifics of this approach we are using Greek and Shakespearean tragedy. These forms not only have their own strongly recognizable characteristics but they also will provide a good basis for the understanding of the form.

Characteristics of tragedy are: the scale and magnitude of the issues with which it deals; the elevation of the language, usually poetic, to match this scale; and the superhuman nature of the crises faced by the protagonist.

In day-to-day terms, we human beings operate in the mundane world, yet we intuit something larger and more aspiring within ourselves: a passion, a sense of eternity. These aspirations, while necessary to our spiritual existence, are also dangerous; they carry with them the sanctions of failure or death. Tragedy deals with the career of human potential as it reaches toward its highest powers, and is forced to recognize the limits of its aspiration: the inevitability of fate. It is the way in which humankind meets its fate, the fusing of grief and joy, that is the mark of tragedy; it leaves us in awe of the gods, but with a renewed sense of human possibility.

Though we may no longer live in the world of myth and legend that was tragedy's inspiration, and we are wary of heroes because our social world is too small for them, as human beings we still need and admire them, with all the pity, fear, and awe they induce. Tragedy makes a total demand upon the actor's capacity; it requires that he or she reach out to touch and embrace the inspiration that lives within us all, though we may be fearful of its destructive power.

2　Greek

National Archaelogical Museum, Athens.

BACKGROUND

Greek tragedy is our starting point for four very good reasons. It is the earliest form of Western drama for which we have texts and some evidence of its performance style. It is the most perfect example of our premise that dramatic form and performance are expressions of the culture of the society that creates it. It is the furthest removed from our twentieth-century understanding of what theatre and its relationship to reality is; as such, it is a good exercise in changing rigid mind-sets of actors brought up on "naturalistic" approaches to drama. And, in this context, although Greek tragedy is not frequently performed—because of those very differences—as an exercise in training it places vocal and physical demands upon the actor that are an excellent foundation for further work.

Origins. The drama springs from the strongest of human impulses—the drive for survival. Precivilized tribes fought nature from season to season to wrest a living from the earth. Survival required fertility: Fertile soil meant successful farmers; fertile women meant brave warriors and hunters. Forces of nature such as sun, rain, and sexuality thus determined the welfare of the tribe. In an attempt both to propitiate and control these forces the tribes made them into gods. All the seasonal facets of the tribe's life—birth, marriage, harvest, death—had appropriate gods celebrated by festivals in the appropriate season.

The Greek god of fertility was Dionysus. The myth surrounding him suggested that he was the son of Zeus, king of the gods, by Persephone. Hera, Zeus's wife, had Dionysus killed, but Zeus gave him rebirth through Semele. This death and rebirth ritual was acted out by the worshipers of Dionysus, who drank the blood and ate the flesh of a sacrificial bull and goat, believing they were therefore achieving identification with the

god: The Christian mass has a similarity to this ritual.

The spring worship of Dionysus was an intoxicating one: uninhibited dancing by torchlight to the music of drums and flutes; devotees sexually stimulated by wine. The highly physical, frankly sensual ritual was geared to the achieving of the spiritual and creative ecstasy that is at the basis of all religions and the drama springing from them.

As the Greek race became more sophisticated and moved from a tribal to an urban society, the primitive rituals became more structured and formalized. The Dionysian festival was established and took the form of a competition among poets (Aeschylus, Sophocles, and Euripides are best-known to us), whose dramatic versions of the traditional myths—the gods and heroes of the tribal history—were acted out in song, dance, and story before an audience of the entire Athenian society. Thus was born Greek tragedy. The very name *tragedy* means "goat song," thereby underlining its roots in the ritual sacrifice of the Dionysian goat. The early rituals of sustenance and survival now became more complex dramas of inquiry that looked into the fundamental moral purposes of human existence within the purview of the gods.

Thus created, Greek tragedy encompassed ritual and religion, poetry and philosophy, history and histrionics—within the dramatic event. At the very beginning of what we call drama, the organic sensibility of a people was expressed in the nature and style of its theatrical performance.

INFLUENCES

The Polis. Central to the Greek sensibility was the *polis*—the city-state. Total participation, as a citizen, in community affairs gave focus and meaning to life. Every citizen discussed and voted on all issues concerning the welfare of the state, be they military, economic, legal, or cultural. The role was not limited just to discussion, but extended to the conduct of community affairs. Any citizen could become part of the ruling body—indeed, many offices were filled by lot. All citizens were soldiers and could be called upon to defend the state. Such responsibilities were not regarded by the Greeks as onerous or vexatious but as a privilege of citizenship. Rather than the assertive individualism of modern society, the realization of the self through participation in the whole was a crucial aspect of Greek society. Certain aspects of that society such as slavery—which freed citizens to perform their public duties—and the circumscribed position of women, who were not "citizens," are morally unacceptable to us today. But this makes it even more necessary to affirm that the Greek way of life was different from ours, and this must be accepted if we are to understand the Greek drama that is rooted in that different sensibility. One of the crucial aspects of this, which we shall elaborate in future discussion, is that the focus of the theatrical event was not on the individual actor as character. Rather, it was on the impact of all the integrated elements of the performance, just as a religious service is not focused upon the priest as person, but upon the experience of the celebration as a whole.

The spirit of religion permeated the *polis* and was an integral part of the Greek life style. Religion was practical and tangible; it was not a spiritual abstraction, but a living force. And one of the major expressions of this religion—a function of the *polis* in which all the citizens were involved—was the dramatic festival of Dionysus. The central role of the drama is illustrated by the location of the festival—below the Parthenon (the city's chief temple), in the society's midst. Those who could not afford to go were paid their way by the state. Each year certain wealthy citizens were required to pay for a chorus of one of the plays. This was regarded as a privilege rather than a duty of citizenship, and any *choregus* who won the competition would raise a monument to commemorate the victory. The dramatists were not removed artists, but rather citizens in the fullest sense of the word. Aeschylus fought at Marathon. Sophocles commanded a fleet. Their work was not preciously "arty" or intellectually remote. It was active and direct, befitting their place in and understanding of society. The playwright was *didaskolos*—a teacher, not just of his chorus but of all society, in the understanding of life and the exploration of virtue. The choruses, too, were not professional but made up of the citizens themselves—one more social function to add to that of soldier, politician, and wage earner. It was citizens performing for citizens, celebrating their pride in their society and participating in a festival whose very form and sensibility exemplified the spiritual and physical oneness of that society.

Sense of Life.   We tend to view the Greek in two contradictory ways: as an Olympian being living a world of profound and tranquil thoughts in an Athens filled with statuesque, well-draped individuals pacing philosophically through life; or as a passionate pagan, dressed in horns and vine leaves and indulging with Naiads and Bacchantes in an ecstasy of abandonment to every desire and instinct of the flesh. The truth, as always—and particularly befitting the Greek sense of balance—lies in the integration of the indulgently sensual and the calmly intellectual. A moderation of behavior was part of the Greek ideal of the "golden mean." One of the major themes of Greek Tragedy is the ghastly results that attend upon excessive behavior.

A passion for physical well-being and beauty was inseparable from an energy and curiosity of the intellect in the Greek sense of the "whole." The modern mind divides, specializes, thinks in categories. Not so the Greek: It constantly attempted to look for the universals in life to find unity within the multifariousness of existence. War and peace, triumph and disaster, pain and pleasure were part of the accepted totality of life. Philosophy, dancing, drama, and athletics were all necessary to the complete human being.

The proper balancing of the physical and spiritual elements of life was attained by the reasonable exercise of the mind. Courage, for example, was regarded as a virtue, being a reasonable mean between foolhardiness and cowardice. In this scheme of things, anger found its place: If a citizen had been affronted, then he had a right to a reasonable response—not the unbridled exercise of passion such as Clytemnestra's revenge on Agamemnon, but due recourse. Turning the other cheek—the meekness of the Christian creed—was not reasonable to the Greek mind. Nor did they, like the Puritan, abjure the pleasures of the senses—only their excess, as in Euripides' play *The Bacchae.*

"To see life steadily and to see it whole" was the sensibility of the Greek. This involved acceptance of the good with the bad. The dichotomy between the pleasurable experience of life, full of striving and possibility, and the apprehension of it as subject to unalterable laws leading finally to death produces the passionate tension found in Greek tragedy. The tragic poets could see humans as both capable of free choice and yet subject to determining powers. The crime of *hubris* was to overdo the one and discount the other.

Our character is defined by striving, in the knowledge that *Dike,* the retribution of the gods, will fall upon that striving if we ever ignore their power.

This sense of life is foreign to our romantic age, which believes that science, technology, or money can achieve anything: Stop drugs, cure AIDS, abolish apartheid; and all to be done overnight.

Surprise and disillusionment follow when the desired result doesn't occur. The Greeks would have not entirely expected it to, but that didn't obviate the necessity of trying. Today, the gods and fate tend to have given way to environmental determinants and behavioral psychology. We are relieved of free choice and responsibility. The Greeks had to accept the consequences of their fate: The gods may dispose, but man was still responsible. After he has learned the truth about himself and put out his eyes, Oedipus says, "It was Apollo, friends, Apollo, that brought this bitter bitterness, my sorrows to completion. But the hand that struck me was none but my own."

All of the basic qualities that constitute the wholeness of the Greek ideal—the balance of moral responsibility, personal integrity, intellectual curiosity, spiritual passion, and physical power—are found operating within the textual and physical given circumstances of Greek tragedy.

INTRINSIC DEMANDS

We must preface our discussion of the practical nature of Greek theatre by recognizing that although there is a good deal of consensus on the physical circumstances, there are still areas of disagreement owing to the limited amount of hard evidence available. Our research, both textual and in performance terms, leads us to believe that the evidence supports our conclusions as to the nature of Greek performance style: These make good sense both in the context of Greek culture and society and in the intrinsic circumstances of the plays themselves.

Space.   The Greek theatre was built around a circular dancing area some sixty to seventy feet in diameter, called the *orchestra* and used primarily by the chorus. Two-thirds of the circumference of the *orchestra* was surrounded by an auditorium that could accommodate an audience of 15,000 people. To the rear of the *orchestra* was a scene house some fifty to sixty feet long, fronted by a somewhat elevated platform. The distance from the stage to the back of the auditorium was approximately 300 feet. On either side of the scene house was a *parados,* an entrance used by the audience to reach the auditorium and by the chorus to proceed into the *orchestra.* These specifics are important for a bald understanding of the environment of Greek theatre, but what is more important to the performer is an appreciation of how the space relates to the spirit and style of the event.

The first thing to notice is that the performance took place—as did the normal life of the Greek—in the open air, under the eye of the gods. Little artificial scenery was used; the natural environment formed the background. The largest space is given to the *orchestra,* around which the audience sits, embracing the event. This emphasis on the *orchestra* connects the drama with its past—its evolution from the choral dance within the threshing circle, a ritual thanking of the gods for the harvest. The *thymele,* the altar at which offerings to Diony-sus are made, is present in the middle of the *orchestra*—at the heart of the dramatic event.

Despite the size of the amphitheater, the relationship of the actors to the audience is very direct. The chorus was a group of citizens, not professional but trained especially for the event, who would return to their day-to-day activities when the festival was over. Thus, a body of citizens sits around a chorus of citizens, who are close to the actor/heroes, who are dealing with the gods on issues concerning the moral and spiritual life of the society as a whole. This direct line from citizens to gods, each in their place but all interconnected, was a physical manifestation both of the Greeks' hierarchical sense of life and spiritual wholeness.

Although the event was of religious origin, the audience was robust and responsive, out to enjoy itself in every way. Records tell of stones and olive pits being thrown at the actors, and on one occasion Aeschylus had to take refuge at the altar of Dionysus to escape the wrath of the crowd. Nor was the audience

Ruins of the theatre at Epidaurus.

afraid to leave during less than dynamic passages, as Aristophanes tells us in *The Birds:*

> There's nothing like wings to get fun out
>   of things;
> When you're bored with a play long
>   and tragic,
> You can fly from your seat to get something
>   to eat,
> And be back in the benches like magic.

Magnitude, both physical and spiritual; directness of approach and response; harmony, passion, and power—these are the intrinsic givens suggested by the physical environment of Greek tragedy.

Textual Structure. Tragedy evolved from two basic sources: the Homeric epic poem from which it gets its narrative structure, and the religious rituals from which derive the chorus with its songs and dances. The integration of these two elements gives tragedy its form of the alternation between acted scenes and choral interludes. Typically, a tragedy begins with a *prologue,* an expository monologue or dialogue. This is followed by a *parados,* named after the entrances on either side of the *orchestra,* through which the chorus enters singing and dancing. Next will come an *episode,* an acted scene between characters or character and chorus. Now comes a *stasismon,* a choral song and dance. The *stasismon* is itself divided into alternating stanzas—strophes and antistrophes—and a final stanza, the epode. The *stasismon* passed lyrical comment upon the action and reflected upon the issues at hand. Its music and rhythms reinforced the ritual atmosphere of the play. *Episodes* and *stasismons* alternate until the final *exodus,* which usually summarized the moral action with a pithy statement, and also served to allow the chorus to leave the *orchestra.*

The structure of the text is integrated with the physical shape of the theatre, both being evolved from ritual and religious practice. There is a valid comparison of the form of Greek tragedy with that of the spirit and rites of Christian religion—especially in its traditional Roman Catholic form. The Christian service begins with a procession of the priests and the choir. There are choral songs, there are prayers, there are invocations and responses among priest, choir, and congregation. There are readings of well-known texts from the Bible—the repository of the history and myths of the religion. There is a sermon in which the priest draws from the biblical text a moral that applies to the contemporary life and mores of the society. There is often a communion in which the priest acts out an offering and makes a ritual sacrifice in which the congregation participates. There is a final choral hymn and exit of the choir. Note too the shape of the event: The priest is usually raised above the congregation, and thereby positioned nearest the godhead, as is the Greek actor; the choir, the Greek chorus, is between the priest and the congregation—the citizens. The congregation, however, does not surround the event, which reflects the more hierarchical spirit of the Christian religion, as opposed to the more democratic wholeness of the Greeks.

But the basic similarities are very close, and the essential point for the modern actor is that an understanding of the form and spirit of an event will reveal its style.

Language. If the textual structure of Greek tragedy is organically linked to its spirit and the shape of its performance, the language is no less so: Both the action and moral purpose of the drama are wholly united to the verse form. The truths of mythology and religious experience do not submit to prose. Elevation of spirit and the magnitude of the issues require language that fits the dignity of the characters and the significance of the occasion. Gods and heroes may be accessible to mortals through religious experience, but they are not on the same level as mortals. Their style of utterance must reflect their elevated stature and the significance of the issues in which they are involved.

Apart from creating a sense of exaltation and making a direct emotive contact through rhythm, the consistent structure of verse clarifies and focuses the action. The formality and dignity of the verse does not, however, mean dullness; nor does it limit the expression of human emotions. Formality means the acceptance and use of form; it does not mean rigid and inflexible. The Greek language allowed for broad, vigorous, and imaginative emotional expression. Rhetoric becomes dull only if it is divorced from an active purpose.

In Greek tragedy, language appears in five basic forms:

1. choral odes, which have an essentially lyric function;
2. long passages of narrative description couched in active, colorful, and imagistic language often spoken by messengers as a means of expounding events from the past or an action that has taken place offstage;
3. speeches between the protagonist and antagonist dealing with philosophical issues and using language with a powerful intellectual appeal;
4. highly emotional speeches by the protagonist dealing with inner torment or conflict with the gods: the most colorful and rhetorically varied of all the language forms;
5. *stichomythia*—a series of one-line statements and responses conveying argument, anger, and sharp inquiry.

This gamut of verbal communication will enable the actor to bring out the variety in the emotive and imagistic qualities of the verse, while keeping the direct through-line intention of the action of a scene.

Costume.   The costume of Greek tragedy is in keeping with the magnitude and elevation of its space, form, and language, but it also re-

flects the fact that it is an outgrowth of everyday rituals and religious practice. Theatre garments were, therefore, grander and richer versions of everyday wear to serve the magnificence of the occasion and to create a larger-than-life impression in the large theatrical space.

The basic body garment was the *chiton,* a cool and simple tunic pinned at the shoulder and falling to the knee or ankle. Over this was worn a short cape, the *chlamys,* or a long mantle, the *himation.* The latter tended to be a mark of status, and as such it was suited to the characters of tragedy. The emphasis of these garments is upon vertical line, simplicity, and flow, all of which create a sense of dignity, substance, and authority. The *himation* especially, with its color, weight, and manner of being draped across one arm, suggests physical strength and control.

The tragic actor also wore a *kothornos,* a laced-up boot peculiar to the stage. There is some controversy as to whether or not it had a raised sole. Current scholarship tends to reject the notion of a raised-sole boot in the fifth century B.C. Obviously, a high sole would have the advantage of increasing the height and visibility of the wearer, and it is perhaps worth asking why a boot was worn at all if it did not have some such purpose. It must at least have been intended to lend a sense of importance to the actor's costume.

Two other items of costume particular to the Greek tragedy were the *onkos* and the mask. The *onkos* was an ornate headdress worn with the mask. There is some disagreement about the height and calculated artificiality of the *onkos:* It is known to have become highly exaggerated in later centuries, as did the mask. If one accepts a certain height for the *kothornoi* in the fifth century B.C., then the *onkos* is likely to have been the higher to balance this. In any case, it is fairly certain that a highly styled coiffure was worn as a means of adding to the impressiveness of the character. Further, as all

actors were male, the color and style of the headdress would help in identifying the sex, age, and status of the character. For example, the Baccantes of Euripides wore snakes and vine leaves in their hair. So, the *onkos* probably fulfilled a practical function in increasing the actor's visibility and impressiveness, and it had an aesthetic function in lending dignity, social stature, and spiritual elevation to the character.

The most significant element of costume was the mask, which had several practical functions:

1. It was a further source of identification for the audience of the sex, age, and general sensibility of the character.
2. It enlarged the features of the face, making it more easily seen.
3. It enabled an actor to play more than one part.
4. It added resonance to the declamation of the verse and probably aided audibility—

Note how line and flow of costume support dignity and authority in this statue of Sophocles. *Lateran Museum.*

Strongly delineated dominant attribute of character sculpted on mask.   *Antiken Museum, Berlin.*

although the acoustics of the Greek theatre were excellent.

More than this, however, the mask had a dramatic function; it is at the very heart of the event. From earliest times humans have, in their rituals of worship, attempted to assume the mask or attributes of the revered object (animal, god, or whatever), so that its spirit will enter the wearer: In the worship of Dionysus, from which the tragic festival traces its descent, the horns of bulls and goats were worn—attributes of Dionysus who adopted them in his flight from Hera's wrath. The mask permits that adoption of otherness while remaining oneself that is an essential quality of the actor's art.

In the Greek tragic performance the mask integrates the religious spirit with the dramatic form: the actor as character/shaman/priest with the citizen as audience/worshiper. The mask also determines the course of the action: The playwright wrote with the mask in mind, defined its attitude, and therefore the fate of the character. It is not for the actor to discover the nature of the character, but to fulfill what has been written into the mask. This does not mean that the character is one-dimensional in performance: The actor may run a gamut of emotions. But it is the dominating drive (or, to use the Stanislavski term, "through-line") that will be sculpted on the mask, determining and revealing the character's basic reaction to life and ultimate fate. The mask with its essential attitude is a strongly defined point of emotional contact for the audience in a large space in which small detail does not read.

The overall impression of the costume is one of stature, dignity, clarity, and emotional force, attributes we have seen to be present in the form, space, and language of Greek tragedy, and will now find in its action.

Concentration of Action. Dramatic action is not the same as movement or activity. Activ-

Playwright seeking inspiration from a mask. *Lateran Museum.*

ity can illustrate action: A character opening a door and going offstage may be representing a dramatic action of parting, or may simply be going to the bathroom. Lack of overt activity can contain strong dramatic action: Two people sitting silently in a room may be playing a dramatic action of sorrow at the death of a friend. Dramatic action is created by the interplay of activity and stillness, speech and silence, thought and emotion. It is the essence of what happens in a play as manifested through its total structure.

In Greek tragedy the playing out of this action is highly concentrated. Unlike romantic plays and melodramas, whose interest lies mostly in events largely peripheral to the action (such as the car chases, gunfights, drug overdoses, and abortions that permeate modern TV fare), Greek tragedy focuses upon the logical revelation of the action; anything irrelevant to that purpose is avoided. More than this, the action of the play tends to take place in one situation and within a restricted time period. Rather like in a courtroom situation, information necessary to the action of the play is brought to us by witnesses or messengers. We hear descriptions of exciting events that have taken place, but we don't see them, for the focus is not on the events themselves but on the significance they may have for the unfolding of the action. In *Oedipus Rex* we get vivid descriptions of the deaths of Laius and of Jocasta, but we do not see the deaths, for our concentration is meant to be upon Oedipus. This play is, in fact, the classic example of the Greek method of logic and condensation. Its action may be said to be to find and expel the guilty party, or, in terms of ritual, to seek and purge. As such, it follows the logic of a detective story, but it only shows the final scene, when the detective calls everyone into the parlor, recapitulates the events and evidence, and points to the guilty party. We do not—as we tend to in plays by Agatha Christie—see all the events leading to the murder: the creation of false motives, the footprints in the flower beds, the shots in the dark. We simply see the detec-

Statue of Poseidon shows clarity, strength, and extension of gesture.   *National Archaeological Museum, Athens.*

tive gathering facts, cross-examining, and letting the logic of the evidence lead him to the culprit, which in *Oedipus*, with splendid irony, turns out to be the detective himself.

This concentration (which is sometimes called the *unity of time, place, and action*) puts the characters in an extremely intense relationship with one another. Like boxers in a ring, they cannot escape each other. The action is "to win," and there is no place for activity not geared to that end. The action is contained, economic, and direct, and nothing distracts the attention of the audience from its playing out. There are no cheerleaders to distract from the action of the game, as it were. In Greece this concentration was further enhanced by the space in which the action took place. The embracing amphitheater with the play at its center was the very hub, in fact, of the Greek world: It was compressed between heaven and earth, between gods and citizens, between past and future.

Issues.   At the heart of the action of Greek tragedy lies the question as to how human beings are to live out their lives—not whether it is preferable to be a rock star or a television personality, but what it means to be human in the fullest sense of that word. To the Greek mind "goodness" was all-encompassing—the property that enabled a person to live as a virtuous citizen in harmony with his neighbor, and in accordance with the gods' laws.

It is not surprising, therefore, to find a religious issue having political significance in the tragedies, or both being involved with the making of moral choices. Nor is it surprising that the punishment of hubris should be a theme in almost every Greek tragedy. Humankind must never forget that it is mortal and vulnerable: It is subject to laws that have meaning and purpose even though it may not understand them. A necessary humility must temper necessary pride.

Oedipus is the classic illustration. Through no conscious fault of his own he killed his father and slept with his mother. But these sins transgressed the laws of the gods, and his pride blinded him to his sin. He lacked self-knowledge. Only by blinding himself to the outer world, therefore, could he gain knowledge of the world within.

Antigone deals with the conflict between the laws of the gods and those of society, and the moral choice this involves. In contemporary terms this issue would be expressed as the rights of the individual versus the power of the state. *The Bacchae*, a play based upon the very worship of Dionysus in which the tragic festival originated, is concerned with the balance between passion and reason and, again, with the necessity of self-knowledge—that understanding of what it means to be human that teaches humility, compassion, and moral goodness.

The essential point is clear: The issues dealt with by Greek tragedy have great magnitude, directness of impact, a powerful effect upon the emotions, and a central significance for society. These qualities are equally manifested by the space, text, language, costume, and action of the theatrical event: They are a reflection of Greek sensibility. The performance style of Greek tragedy is that sensibility expressed through the physical givens of the theatrical event.

PERFORMANCE DEMANDS

Movement and Gesture.   Size, simplicity, and selectivity are basic qualities required by Greek tragedy performance. Basic technical reasons exist for this as a response to the costume:

1. The *onkos* and mask prevent sharp or sudden movements and require the head to be held upright.
2. The mask restricts peripheral vision, which suggests that movement involved full body turns.
3. Movement is further refined by the holding of the *himation* across the arm.

These technical reasons suggest that the physical presence of the actor is upright and controlled. There will be no shuffling of the feet; moves will be made strongly with clearly defined strides. The large space will require long strides to give the impression of normal pace: Size of movement on stage is always relative to size of space. The upright posture of the actor's head shows the *onkos* and mask to best advantage, elevating and dignifying the character. It also facilitates direct communication with the gods and audience, both of whom are situated above the actor. The modern actor should remember that direct communication is achieved by the forceful projection of the action through space—by voice, gesture and emotional power. It does not require leaning toward the audience or any other attempt to make physical contact.

Gesture is the most flexible part of the actor's body movement. But there is no place for fidgeting or individualistic mannerisms. The frequent small gestures we observe in modern daily life are meaningless in Greek tragedy and lessen the strength of the character and the impact of the situation. Not only are large gestures needed to communicate meaning over a large space, but the size of the emotion requires them. Large gestures must be highly selective; however, they can still be varied, and one of the demands upon the actor's imagination is to discover meaningful gestures emanating from the differing emotional forces of the action.

The emotional idea should catalyze and lead the gesture, which should flow from the center of the body—the actor's emotional core—and not just extend from the shoulder. Gestures should have a clear beginning, middle, and end, and the actor should not be afraid to hold a gesture as long as it is filled with active meaning. An incomplete or abrupt gesture weakens the force of the theatrical moment and disrupts the flow of the rhythm. Flow is important. There is the danger of becoming stiff and mechanical when attempting to put on a formal posture and assume dignity. But Greek tragedy has a strong continuous flow of action with virtually no scene changes or other intervals. The processions, dances, and flowing costumes add to this full unbroken rhythm.

The actor must flow with the rhythm of the event. This doesn't mean the casual lack of definition of the modern sense of "going with the flow." It means working comfortably within a disciplined formality. This will come to the actor through understanding, familiarity, and concentration on the action. Playing the action, here as in any theatrical style, relaxes and releases the actor so that concentration is not upon moving in a stately manner, or remembering to extend gestures, but rather in engaging inner emotional force to achieve an outer practical objective.

Mask. Greek tragic characters are archetypal: They are personifications of a set of human values or attributes. The plays are not written to depict human beings but to illustrate actions of human concern: issues not people; not the person but the *persona*, which is the Latin term for mask. This suggests the connection between the portrayal of an archetypal character and the use of mask. By definition, an archetype is highly focused and magnified for clarity of impact. This is what the use of mask produces: The mask enables the audience to see the facial characteristics, which define the part the character is to take in the action, over the large space of the Greek theatre where, in any case, small changes of expression would be lost. More than this, the mask has the effect of investing the event with a superterrestrial quality; you simply can't put on a mask and then go about your ordinary daily business.[1] The actor who accepts this fact and does not fight the mask will find that

it does much of the stylistic work, and will gradually eliminate nonessentials.

As the actor's body accepts the mask, a further important effect takes place: A direct relationship develops between the physical identification required by the mask and the interior emotional response. The mask takes over not only the body but also the feelings of the actor. This gives the actor a strong purchase upon the spine, essential characteristic, or active through-line of the character. The actor need look for no more than this. Psychological and personal detail is not only irrelevant but distracting. The character has no life outside the play; for the purposes of Greek tragedy, heroes never had indigestion or went to the bathroom. The mask delineates all the characteristics the situation requires; character "drawing" for its own sake is not a virtue. For example, when Hippolytus, in Euripides' play of the same name, expounds upon the virtue that prevents him from responding to Phaedra's passion, we might today regard him as a prig or a nerd. But this would be to misunderstand his function in the play. Greek characters were not "characters" as we understand the word, but tragic figures. Hippolytus's purity is the basis of his tragic function. An actor who tried to play him as a prig, or even a homosexual, would be quite wrong in doing so. The mask of Hippolytus is chasteness, and his tragic function is to maintain chastity and be destroyed for it.

Again, with Medea, the actor is playing the human capacity for pride and jealousy and its consequences, not giving a well-rounded depiction of a woman scorned. Oedipus illustrates the consequences of lack of self-knowledge, not a libertine who has been duped. The actor must play what the playwright has given: the dominant trait or passion, the mask which, because of its incredible stillness, idealization, and clarity of outline, tends to charge the surrounding space with the electricity of its presence. It is

---

[1] We are indebted here, and in the section on Neutral Mask, to *Behind the Mask* by Bari Rolfe, from which we have quoted.

Power and fullness of gesture in this 1993 production of *Antigone*. *American Conservatory Theatre. Photo by Larry Merkle.*

Intensity and clarity of focus created by masks in the Guthrie Theatre Company production of *The House of Atreus*. *Courtesy of the Mark Taper Forum, Los Angeles.*

a dynamic theatrical artifact for the actor who can fulfill its purpose without imposing upon it.

Voice. As the action of the tragedies is communicated not so much by activity as by language, the voice attains special significance as an actor's tool. With an audience 200 feet to 300 feet away, the actor would need not loudness so much as good breath support, strong and precise enunciation and clarity of projection. Clarity requires less rapidity than in everyday speech, just as we saw that movement is full and strong rather than brisk. The rhythms and structure of the verse are guides to delivery. "Naturalistic" breaking of hythms, deliberate working against the verse, introduction of verbal mannerisms for "character" definition—all have no place in Greek drama.

Voice delivery takes essentially three forms:

1. declamation, which is nearest to "normal" speech, but distinguished by the structure of the verse meter;
2. recitative; often accompanied by a flute;
3. singing; essentially a choral form.

These may usefully be compared with the forms of modern opera, with its arias, recitative, and chorus ensembles.

Unmasked actors create attributes of mask with the intensity and stillness of their focus and concentration in Yale Reportory Theatre's production of *The Cure at Troy. Photo by T. Charles Erickson.*

The language can span the entire human emotional and descriptive palette. There is nothing dull or restricted about it if the actor discovers, assimilates, and responds to the emotional action of the language. Vowel sounds are very important as they carry the emotional energy and coloration of the breath; but the actor should avoid one of the traps of the rhetorical mode, overly extending the vowels and turning every word into a keening howl—oooooo!, aaaaaa!—with rising and falling inflections unrelated to the sense of the speech.

Sense of Occasion. By way of summation and to underscore again the sense of integration and wholeness we have stressed as a crucial part of the Greek sensibility, we should emphasize that all the performance choices are inspired in their playing by a strong sense of occasion.

For the Greeks, the dramatic festival was a momentous occasion. More specifically, it was a religious occasion: A ceremony descended from ritual, it celebrated the history of the race, discussed its moral purposes, and praised its continuance, all played out within the sight of the gods. To create an equivalent sense of occasion today, we would have to combine the qualities of a Roman Catholic Mass, a football game, a rock concert, and a session of the Supreme Court.

Actors must be aware of this; they must be willing to rise to the occasion. In general, we contemporary actors are used to underplaying. We choose and judge in terms of what we see around us: small persons performing small tasks. Contemporary dramatists, mirroring contemporary life, mistrust the large gesture, the blatant assertion. They see "honesty" in terms of everyday actions: The men and women of the stage must seem to behave and speak like their audience where everyone is ordinary now, or, as Andy Warhol put it, "everyone is famous for fifteen min-

utes." But Greek heroes were descended from the gods, or at least significant enough to suffer their wrath. The fate of the tragic hero caused cosmic reverberations, and the actor's gesture, voice, and passion must live up to this occasion.

EXERCISES, GAMES, TECHNIQUES

Isolation/Plastique. This is an exercise in body control and body awareness. The essence of the exercise is to work upon one part of the body at a time while the rest is relaxed but focused.

Stand in a comfortable, balanced, and centered position, and move the top of the head in all directions; continue with the nose, the jaw, each shoulder, each elbow, and so forth down the body until all parts have been worked upon separately. This is not simply a warm-up exercise, although it serves that purpose; the intention is not just to roll the jaw or shoulder, but to move it in as many ways as possible, isolating the part and extending its potential. The mind should be focused in the part of the body that is being worked upon. Do not let the mind drift off into thoughts of this morning's breakfast or tomorrow night's date. The parts of the body should follow their own course, with the mind supporting the activity.

An extension of this exercise is to allow the body to follow one specific part with complete plasticity through 360 degrees of space. Start, say, with the shoulder and move it in any direction, leading the rest of the body with it. Then transfer the leading point to the head, the pelvis, the hip, the knee, and so on. The body follows, and the center of balance is constantly adjusted to remain the fulcrum of whatever position is taken up from moment to moment. The exercise should never jerk; the body should never overbalance; all parts of the body should lead at some time, and a full 360 degrees should be explored.

This is an exercise in moving and controlling energy flow from the center.

Space Walk. This exercise gives players a consciousness of filling space with their body. Start by having the players simply walk around the workshop area in a neutral manner. Coach the players to make the space concrete. Let them discover where it supports them—the chin, the underarms, the crotch, and so forth. Coach them to lean on it; let it fill their body. Then throw images at the players and coach them to explore each one fully. For example, they are wearing stilts that make them ten feet tall. Take the stilts away and coach the players to remain ten feet tall with all parts of their body in proportion. Coach them to experience the body rhythms of this situation: There will be a greater sense of size, and movements will be fuller and slower. Ask players to add sounds and words while they are moving and to note the distance the sound travels in their body and the fullness with which it is projected. Other images may be used to achieve this effect; for example, the players have their heads in the clouds; the players are working on top of a high mountain.

A further image must be used with care as there is a danger that the players may adopt a stiffness of movement, which is to be avoided. The players are coached to become an oversized puppet with the gods controlling the strings. A string from the top of the head is essential, as it will tend to extend the posture, and strings to the arms—shoulders, elbows, wrists—legs, and so on, should lead to extension and control in those areas. Being controlled by the gods is a useful image for players to have as they explore the sensibility of Greek tragedy, and not just its physical style.

Explosions. Players should begin as in the space-walk exercise—by becoming conscious of their bodies in the workshop space. On a signal (a hand clap or a drum bang) they explode out of themselves, fill the 360-degree space around them, and remain completely still in whatever position they land. Have the players hold the position for a few moments, and then coach them to release slowly from the fingertips and toes back to the center. Repeat this three or four times, coaching players not to think about the position they are going to adopt (that is, "how" they will explode), but to let it happen spontaneously upon the signal and to fill the 360-degree space around them. Initially, players will tend to use just their arms and legs and either adopt a standing explosion with arms burst into the air or land flat on the floor. Both ways avoid a full commitment to the exercise. Coach for a total explosion from the center.

Once the players are committing themselves fully to the exercise and discovering interesting positions, after the explosion, have them hold their position for a few moments and then coach them to begin a simple rhythmical movement suggested by that position. Let this movement continue until it is well established, and then coach the players to turn it into any simple activity it suggests. For example, a movement of the spine up and down could become digging with a pick, chopping wood, casting a fishing rod, or picking apples and putting them in a basket. Coach players to let the movements develop out of the position and the activity out of the movement without imposing a thought process. Coach them to make their movement strong, simple, and extended. This exercise focuses upon dynamic flow from the center and, once again, upon economy, extension, and control.

Neutral Mask. Work with the neutral mask requires an open space and mirrors and chairs enough to comfortably accommodate the players. It has a general validity in the training of actors. Some of the qualities it encourages are, however, especially useful to the player concerned with Greek drama. Use of the neutral mask focuses the players upon whatever is necessary to execute a given task, and only that. By dispensing with all personal mannerisms and irrelevant responses, use of the neutral mask reinforces what is communal among human beings and identifies the essence of their actions. It emphasizes the expressiveness of the whole body by removing the expressiveness of the face, and it leads the player to the simplest, minimal physical ways of dealing with activities and situations. The mask demands only what is necessary to perform with highly focused energy and economy. This combination of economy and energy gives an experience of size and clarity that we have suggested is part of the performance of Greek drama. The neutral mask helps the player to discover this experience organically, and not impose magnitude by an attempt to play "nobly" or "grandly."

Put on the mask as though it were a sacred object. Focus upon this act, aware that something is about to happen to you. Once the mask is in place, do not touch it or relate directly to it as an object, except to remove it from your face. Do not relate to another person as yourself while wearing the mask. With the mask in place, look at your entire body in the mirror until you feel the neutrality of the mask informing your whole body—this will start with the face and work down. The relaxed, serene, neutral features of the mask will help the body to achieve a neutral posture—one neither sloppy nor stiff, but well balanced and centered with a relaxed but powerful energy ready to be discharged in a highly focused way into whatever activity is asked of it. This is positive neutrality, player's neutrality. It is a neutrality that puts the wearer in touch with the universal in yourself: your inner core.

Exercises may be done in the mask, such as mirror exercises with a partner—copying gestures as a mirror would do. Individual exercises are best geared to the performance of simple activities such as lifting and carrying; picking a flower and smelling it; making a bed; building a fence. Coach players to avoid naturalistic cliches and any stylistic imposition upon the activity, such as mime. Players should let the mask respond simply to the physical demands of the object, action, or situation.

Psychological Gesture.[2]   This is one of the most useful exercises for a player approaching Greek tragedy. It is based upon the principle that the more you repeat any simple gesture, the stronger it will become and the more it will induce supporting emotion in your body. The strength of the movement activates the emotion.

To put the principle into practice, choose any strong quality—greed, lust, pride, despair—and explore it physically until you discover some configuration of the body that communicates your sense of the quality. Work for strong gestures and total involvement of the body; avoid small detail. Once you have discovered the gesture, repeat it both to clarify and strengthen it and to encourage the supporting feeling that will have developed in your body.

In working on a character, determine the main desire of the character—in Greek drama this will be its mask—and use that as the starting point for the psychological gesture. Start very simply with the foot, hand, or arm—note the connection here with the isolation/plastique exercise—and let your discoveries extend to involve the whole body. For example, your character may have a defiant, arrogant mask, and you might start with

[2]We are indebted to Michael Chekhov, who originated this exercise on the basis of Stanislavski's theory of physical actions. Those who wish to go into the exercise in more detail should refer to Chekhov's book, *To the Actor* (New York: Harper & Row, 1963), chapter 5.

sweepingly dismissive or strong punching gestures. For a character who is more humble and submissive, a downward movement of the head or an imploring, open-palmed gesture might be a useful starting point. The important thing is to start simply with a strong focus upon the mask.

Having discovered the psychological gesture that communicates the main desire or mask of the character, you may refine it by working to encompass other attributes. For

Psychological gesture as illustrated in Michael Chekhov's To the Actor.   *Drawing by Nicolai Remisoff. Copyright 1953 by Michael Chekhov. By permission of Harper & Row, Publishers, Inc.*

example, prideful ambition may be a dominating characteristic, but the character will at times be subject to other emotional states—uncertainty or despair. These may be explored in the context of the basic psychological gesture, which will influence the way in which the other emotions are manifested. A psychological gesture is like a charcoal sketch done broadly and simply with the least possible number of strokes.

Explosion-Emotion.   This is an extension of the explosion exercise; here it relates to the psychological gesture. Begin as in that explosion exercise, moving fairly quickly so that players are exploring a physical action suggested by the position they fall into after the explosion. Coach them to extend and strengthen their action until it produces some emotional response such as pain, anger, despair, or futility. Have players make any adjustments necessary to clarify the action and strengthen the relationship between it and the emotion. Have them return to neutral by concentrating upon lessening the action until the emotion drains away, and then relaxing the gesture back into the center. Repeat the exercise several times, then extend by coaching the players to support the action/emotion with enough given circumstances to give it a real focus—to create a reason for the despair, an object of the anger. Coach players to keep the action strong, clear, and simple; do not allow unnecessary detail to creep in with the given circumstances.

Emotional Mask.   Start from a floor alignment and have players concentrate on their breathing. Ask them to think of a sentence expressing a strongly emotional attitude such as "I hate people" "I want to be alone," "Nobody loves me," or "I refuse to give in." Have players repeat this quietly to themselves and then more strongly until a facial expression develops that epitomizes the attitude. When this becomes established, coach the players to stand and walk around the space, concentrating upon the phrase and the facial mask. Coach them to let the mask inform the body rhythms, so that the facial expression is absorbed into the entire body, and the posture and rhythms of movement become one with the facial mask. When this has become well established, coach players to repeat the original phrase more and more strongly, and to develop a single gesture that expresses the emotional idea that the body now also contains. Coach them to repeat the gesture as strongly and fully as possible. Gradually reduce the gesture and allow emotion to drain away; return to the center and rest.

Animal Dance.   Choose a speech with strong images. Either of the messenger speeches in *The Bacchae* would be suitable, as would the messenger speech or some of Medea's speeches from Euripides' play. Work with the images in the manner of the psychological-gesture exercise, having the players discover strong physical gestures that communicate the essential quality of the images. Gradually build up the momentum and rhythms of the gestures until a dancelike movement has evolved. Concentrate upon the physicality of the dance and the emotional rhythms now produced. Coach to develop more intense, primitive, and animalistic gestures and rhythms. Throw animal images to the players; make the animals strong or predatory. Allow the dance to reach a peak of intensity, then bring players to rest by giving relaxing images of evening, sunset, cooling breezes, and so on. Now have the players go back to their original speeches and perform them with no movement other than the absolutely necessary gestures. Players will find that their vocal range and their gestures are now strongly supported by a physical emotion emanating from the images kinesthetically implanted in their body memory.

Domestic Activity.   Choose a domestic activity that is not too complex—for example, making a sandwich, shaving, brushing your teeth, or painting a door. Pantomime it as a normal, everyday activity. Repeat the exercise, this time clarifying the activity—that is, removing unnecessary movements. Repeat the exercise again, this time performing the clarified activity for a special purpose—shaving before going out with a special girl; painting a door because you want to sell the house, making a cake for someone's birthday. Repeat the exercise with the added dimension that there is to be a prize for the best baking, painting, or shaving. Repeat the exercise a final time, competing for a prize with the judges sitting fifty yards away from you. Starting from personal experience, the exercise moves toward clarifying and strongly focusing an action, investing it with a larger significance, and finally bringing the size of the action to match both its significance and a large acting space.

Operatic Scene.   Players pair off and decide upon some simple situation with a potential for conflict, such as playing cards, ending an affair, or arranging furniture in a room. Then they create a simple improvisation upon their theme. Repeat the exercise as if the situation were part of an opera. Initially, the players will tend to impose their idea of operatic style upon the exercise and lose touch with the basic reality of the situation. Coach them to focus upon the reality they discovered in the realistic improvisation, but to project it through an operatic event. Repeat with groups of three players.

   This is one of the very best exercises for coming to terms with the demands of a Greek style—indeed, any style that has presentational demands. It is an exercise that players can have a lot of fun with, and it leads to high energy and dynamics. The game re-creates all the necessary qualities of playing in a large manner—economy, clarity, getting to the essence of the action without unnecessary detail. More than this, the whole quality of approach changes, in speech as well as gesture: "Sure, man, I'll do it" becomes, without coaching, "It shall be done," because that is what now feels right to the player. The players gain a strong sense of language as a major part of the event—the cadence, rhythm, and weight of the line, which convey meaning as much as the words. They learn a very important lesson; namely that "truth" is what is right for the given situation, and what is right will also be comfortable to the player. The style begins to feel both right and necessary to them. Players discover that the "truth" of the realistic improvisation is projected through new dynamics to create a different but equal truth for the new event. This is an essential lesson for understanding the playing of style.

Verbal Coloring.   Start with a simple mirror exercise: players in pairs opposite each other mirroring movements. Throw images for the players to explore: "yellow," "ice cream," "peaches," "rough blanket," and so on. Coach players to move out of the mirror relationship while continuing to explore individually and adding sounds that the images and movements suggest. Continue the exercise, presenting more potent images taken from the Greek tragedies—again, the messenger speeches from *The Bacchae* could be used, but all the tragedies have extremely dynamic images. At the end of this part of the exercise, have the players come to rest on the floor, align themselves, and concentrate upon breathing.

For the next part of the exercise, use excerpts from any heroic or patriotic songs or speeches, "The Battle Hymn of the Republic," "The Gettysburg Address," "The Preamble to the Constitution," and "Jerusalem" are all suitable. Give sentences to the players as they are at rest and have them voice them on their outward breaths. Have them gradually deepen

their breathing and voice the sentences with more power. Bring the players to their feet and move them around the space chanting sentences. Introduce music of a heroic mode— organ music is excellent, or Beethoven or Handel—and have the players continue chanting in the rhythms and the emotional atmosphere of the music. Finally, bring all the players together and chant verses in unison to the accompaniment of the music. Have them return to rest in their floor alignment. Now go back to work on the speeches from which the Greek images and phrases were taken. The players will now be inspired by the physical sense of the imagery they have gained, the vocal range they have discovered in exploring the images with sound alone, and the sense of size and occasion the exercise encourages.

Ritual.   This is an excellent culminating exercise, bringing elements together and creating a sense of occasion. Start with an "orchestra" exercise: Players are in a loose circle; one player in the center is the conductor. Start a rhythmical beat on a drum. The conductor starts a movement expressing the rhythm and the players in the circle pick up the rhythm and movement and explore it further. After a minute the conductor goes up to another player in the circle and takes his or her place; that player now becomes the conductor. Change drum rhythms and tempo frequently. The exercise continues until most players have been conductor. Build up the tempo and rhythm to an intense level and coach the players to close in on the conductor. The conductor now becomes the victim and is pressed to the ground. Change the rhythm and tempo to a steady, gentle beat. Darken the space. The victim is now raised on six players' shoulders and carried around the space. The drum leads with a solemn beat, followed by two players with lighted candles. The rest of the players follow the victim. All chant. The players process for a few minutes and then return to the center of space and place the victim on an altar (made of boxes or levels). Candles are placed at the sides of the altar, and two players bless wine and bread, offer it to the gods, and then place it at the victim's feet. Players return to the original circle and the chanting ceases. There should be a period of absolute silence. Now a new, dynamic drumbeat begins and the players begin an ecstatic chant. This raises the victim, who takes the bread and wine and gives it to each player in turn while embracing each one. As the victim-become-priest moves around the circle, it closes and players put arms around each other's shoulders. The chanting and singing continue. When the victim has given wine and bread to all the other players, he or she stands on the altar and proclaims to the gods the opening of the festival. At this moment bring up the lights once again as dawn breaks. The players now return to their places and the festival begins.

This exercise works extremely well when the players commit themselves to it. At first there is the danger of camp and of surface reaction. Strong coaching can remove this and establish an emotional response to the situation. There will be a tendency to be overly primitive and aggressive after the killing of the victim. Coach for a sense of the religiosity of the occasion—the total significance and atmosphere of the ritual. Note how the citizen becomes victim and then priest and then player. When the exercise is played seriously it gives a strong sense of the ritual roots as well as the religious and dramatic power of the occasion.

PLAYING THE STYLE

The Chorus.   We have left a discussion of the chorus to this section because, whereas everything we have said about an actor's approach to Greek tragic style can be applied to chorus work, the chorus is an integrated unit whose performance choices are manifested in ensemble playing under the guidance of the director or choreographer.

The chorus is believed to have originally numbered fifty; then it was reduced to twelve and finally settled at fifteen for much of the drama. This pattern reflects the evolution of Greek tragedy from its early beginnings in ritual and dance with a strong choral focus, to the later emphasis upon dramatic action with an increase in actors to three. The chorus had three basic functions:

1. It retained the atmosphere of ritual and religiosity in the dramatic event; a chorus was present at all Greek ceremonial occasions—weddings, funerals, victory celebrations, etc.;
2. It set a lyrical mood or tone, and it reinforced the passions of the acting with song and dance. In this the rhythms of the choral work were often as important as the content of the lines;
3. It was a unifying element. The permanent presence of the chorus provided a visual thread to the performance. It also connected the audience with the actors both literally—in that they were between the audience and the actors and dramatically in standing for the audience, asking questions of the actors, and making responses.

A major performance choice is whether the chorus should be regarded as a collective character with a part in the dramatic action, or impersonally like a modern choir or corps de ballet. Certain plays support the idea of collective character. In *Oedipus Rex*, for example, the chorus represents the people of Thebes, a permanent reminder of the presence of the plague and underlining Oedipus's responsibility to the society. Again, in *Agamemnon*, the chorus represents the city elders, and in *The Bacchae* it carries the central action of the play in representing the maddened followers of Dionysus. In other plays where the function of the chorus is not personified, it is likely that the full impact of its function will only have force in performance, where the singing and dancing will add enormously to the dramatic impact, even if they do not directly further the action. Thus, chorus playing may range from rhythmical dance and singing, to chanting and movement patterns, to simple use of collective gesture and the dramatic rhythms of the verse, depending upon the demands of the text.

When an actor in the chorus is part of a collective character, his or her approach to playing the style will have the same determinants of size, clarity, economy, as if he or she were an individual character. The further demand will be that of working in unison with a group. As choral gestures and movements done in unison will have a powerful impact, the actor must listen for and accept the music of the verse that, with its inherent rhythmical discipline, greatly assists the unifying process. There are certain guidelines for choral work:

1. The work of the chorus should be consistent with the style as a whole.
2. Movement and gesture should arise, as far as possible, from the textual circumstances, in the form of patterns illustrating the persona of the chorus and its function in the action.
3. Movement may run the gamut from dance to walking patterns; and singing, chanting, and speaking may all be employed. Movement should be consistent with the givens of the circumstances: It is probably inappropriate for stately and dignified elders to dance around like young nymphs.
4. It is desirable not to improvise rituals unrelated to the text and then impose them on the action. However, modern icons can sometimes be successfully integrated. In one production the chorus performed

a dance for peace and employed the pattern of the international antinuclear sign—an inverted Y within a circle.

Choral Exercises.   All the exercises previously set out may be used by chorus actors. The ones below are particularly adapted to the ensemble nature of a chorus.

Getting Together.   Basic ensemble games such as "Machine" (Chapter 11), and "Conductor" (Chapter 12) are useful starts for chorus work. Tag games in which players join hands when tagged until all players are in a connected line make players aware of joint physical rhythms. These games can be varied with added demands such as hopping on one leg, putting one arm behind the back, or moving in slow motion.

Passing Rhythms.   Rhythms are developed and passed around the group with voice, hands, drums, pieces of wood, and so on. This may be done in various ways:

1. A leader begins and other players join in, in any order.
2. A rhythm is passed from player to player, each adding an adaptation.
3. All players start together and by listening to the person on either side players gradually adapt their own rhythm until a group rhythm is evolved.

The exercise may be done with pure rhythms, or a coach may give ideas or provide a theme to the group as a basis for rhythms. Such rhythms may be of a joint character: the rhythms of the elders of Thebes or of the Bacchantes, or of a more abstract quality, such as despair, hope, or joy.

Follow My Leader.   Players sit in a circle (they may stand when they are more adept), with one player outside, back turned to the group. The players in the circle agree upon a leader, who begins a rhythmic movement with some part of the body. All players follow until the entire circle is performing the movement together. From time to time the leader changes the movement and rhythm and the other players adapt. After a couple of minutes the outside player turns toward the circle and tries to identify the leader. The trick is for the players in the circle to follow without looking directly at the leader—they come to develop a 180-degree sense of connection and rhythmical flow. Coach the leader to use large, expansive gestures. Play the game several times with different leaders. Players get a real sense of pleasure and achievement at being able to defeat the observer with the unity of their movements.

Melting Sculptures.   Players stand in a circle and number off. Numbers are then called and the numbered player runs to the center and adopts any physical posture with a strong energy. Other players, as called, attach themselves to the developing group until all players are in contact and form a dynamic but immobile sculpture with their bodies. Numbers continue to be called, and each player must adjust position, keeping in contact, so that the sculpture is constantly melting and reforming. The game may be played with a theme for each sculpture, which will give players a stronger sense of focus. This exercise trains players to be aware of others while working physically in a group, and to become part of a larger physical pattern.

Group Mirror.   Two players face each other and begin a simple mirror exercise. Each player is joined by two more players standing slightly behind and to each side. The mirror exercise continues. Each group of three is joined by two more, again slightly to the rear, and so on until all players are involved as two equal groups facing each other. The mirror game continues with each group keying off its leader.

Expanding Explosion.   This is an elaboration of the explosion exercise presented earlier in this chapter. Start as for that exercise, with players exploding 360-degrees out of their centers, and adopting frozen positions. Players explore their position and begin a simple rhythmical movement suggested by it. Now each player turns to a partner; and by a process of offering and taking, the two players adapt their individual movements into a joint movement that incorporates part of each. When these joint movements are well established, each pair turns to another pair and offers/takes once more until a joint four-way movement develops. The process is continued—four, eight, sixteen, and so on—until the entire group has developed one united rhythmical pattern of movement. The coach can elaborate the exercise by introducing a theme as a basis for movement once the explosion has taken place.

Cheering Chorus.   Players divide into two even groups and occupy areas at different sides of the workshop space. Set up a small platform in front of each group. The groups agree on a theme that has social, political, or moral overtones. As a simplistic example, if the groups are one of men and one of women, the theme may be the battle of the sexes. The idea of the game is for the men to propound male superiority and the women female superiority. First, a male player mounts his platform and declaims an assertive phrase—for example, "Men are physically stronger" or "Men are more intellectual." At the same time, he performs a strong physical gesture that illustrates the point. His chorus picks up the gesture and joins him in declaiming. The opposing chorus denies the proposition: One of the female players mounts her platform and makes a gesture and declamation asserting female superiority: "Women sustain the race," "Women are more artistic," or whatever. When this happens the male player rejoins his chorus, which discovers a gesture denying the female proposition. And so the game continues male and female players making assertions and denials in turn.

Strong coaching will be needed at first to keep a joint focus upon idea and gesture, and to encourage each chorus to work as a unit. Energy runs high in the exercise, which gives players a strong sense of the demands of the group gesture and vocal rhythms. The exercise also acquaints players with the dynamics of give-and-take present in the strophe/antistrophe choral structure, and with the relationship of chorus to both protagonist and antagonist.

Protagonist. We are using Oedipus from the tragedy *Oedipus Rex* as our example of an actor's approach to the playing of a protagonist's role. A thorough examination and understanding of the play, in the perspectives we have discussed earlier in this chapter, will be crucial for an actor undertaking the role. What we will do here is to point out some salient features to support our discussion. Oedipus was fated to kill his father and marry his mother. He attempted to avoid his fate but was unable to. The action of the play concerns humankind's necessary recognition and acceptance of the dictates of the gods. Structurally, this takes the shape of a process of self-discovery and a seeking and purging ritual. This process is integrated with the mask (character) and through-line of action of Oedipus himself. Thebes is polluted because of the presence of a criminal; citizens are dying and both the earth and women are barren (see p. 9 for how this connects with the earliest ritual roots of tragedy). It is Oedipus's responsibility as ruler to discover and drive out the criminal and save his people. His through-line of action is very much like that of a detective: to cross-examine witnesses, gather information, make deductions. This he does in a direct, determined, and intelligent manner. He is proud of his intelligence, of his

position as ruler, of the responsible way in which he goes about the exercise of his authority. This prideful belief in himself, a useful and necessary attribute of a ruler, does, however, make him refuse to accept the logic of some of his discoveries. He believes that his mother and father are King and Queen of Corinth and, as he had left Corinth behind, he cannot accept evidence that suggests they were not his true parents, and that he had killed his father in an altercation just before reaching Thebes and was now married to his mother. The possibility of this situation is so appalling to him, and his belief in his false understanding of his own identity is so strong, that he at first behaves in an arrogant and dismissive manner toward those witnesses who are trying to tell him the truth.

As enlightenment dawns upon Oedipus during the process of the play, his fears become ever darker until the final flash of truth coincides with his dashing out of his own eyes and a final darkness of the soul. Apart from the suffering inflicted for his moral blindness and belief that he could avoid the gods' dispensation, the final metaphor suggests that human self-awareness cannot be achieved if our focus is rigidly fixed upon a fickle external reality rather than the inner truth that comes with humility and the acceptance of our own blindness.

In the context of this physical and emotional journey that Oedipus makes through the action of the play, his mask will denote the salient features of character that catalyze the journey and ultimately lead him to his fate. The basic features of the mask will be intellectual energy, pride in achievement, sense of authority, and belief in his own judgment and rightness. Oedipus is not a wicked man; he believes he is acting as a good ruler should—to discover and purge the cause of his people's suffering. He is not a foolish man—he goes about the inquiry with energy and intelligence. He is not basically an arrogant or angry man: But he is blinded by a belief in his own (limited) understanding of life's vicissitudes, which leads him at times to respond with arrogance and anger to those who threaten his understanding.

The playing of these salient features of the mask will give the actor a strong hold upon Oedipus's through-line of character, and the responses he makes to the obstacles he meets in pursuing his intention: to be a good ruler and to seek out and purge the cause of the city's blight. The emotional build of Oedipus's action moves from a firm and determined belief in himself and his authority through an angry and dismissive response to challenges to this, to a gradually dawning apprehension and fear as an appalled understanding overtakes him.

There is an absolute consistency throughout the play: The structure is that of a seeking and purging ritual; the emotional tension is created by a discovery of self-knowledge and the suffering this entails; the moral function is to underline the parameters of human action—we are free to discover that we are subject to the gods' laws. This consistency is present in Oedipus. He sets out to discover the source of the plague and to drive it from the city. This he does. He applies to himself the justice he intended for the criminal. He acted with integrity as a good ruler should. Both the power of his self-disgust and the extent of his suffering reinforce the moral values of the society.

The qualities of the mask the actor has been given to play, and the emotional energy supporting them, are completely reinforced by the play's language. To illustrate this we are going to look at a section of a speech by Oedipus after he has discovered the enormity of his circumstances and has blinded himself:

1392

> Cithaeron, why did you receive me? Why
>   having received me did you not kill me
>   straight?
> And so I had not shown to men my birth.

> O Polybus and Corinth and the house,
> the old house that I used to call my father's—
> what fairness you were nurse to, and what
>   foulness
> festered beneath! Now I am found to be
> a sinner and a son of sinners. Crossroads,
> and a hidden glade, oak and the narrow way
> at the crossroads, that drank my father's
>   blood
> offered you by my hands, do you remember
> still what I did as you looked on, and what
> I did when I came here? O Marriage,
>   marriage!
> you bred me and again when you had bred
> bred children of your child and showed
>   to men
> brides, wives and mothers and the foulest
>   deeds
> that can be in this world of ours.

1407

Here we have the destruction, or obverse side, of the original mask. Pride and belief in Oedipus's own rightness have become despair and humility. It is this change in circumstances that is calculated to produce the effect of sympathy and awe in the audience: sympathy at the suffering of a fellow human; and awe at the power of the gods that even the most powerful and seemingly fortunate of human beings cannot escape. To help achieve that effect Sophocles makes Oedipus flagellate himself with the memory of all the circumstances that have brought him to his present condition. The actor is given a speech that is highly compressed to increase its emotional charge. In seventeen lines Oedipus recalls his childhood, his parents, the killing of his father, and his incestuous marriage. Pain, self-hatred, despair, and remorse are all contained within the brief compass of the speech whose language rains down like blows upon Oedipus's head.

Together with this active function of the speech, there is a ritualistic sense of invocation. Oedipus calls upon the memories and the events of the past as if they were the godheads responsible for his doom, as indeed they were: "O Polybus and Corinth;" "O Marriage, marriage!" The image in lines 1400–1401 of the earth drinking his father's blood offered by his hands has a strongly sacrificial and ritualistic quality. The lines "you bred me and again when you had bred/bred children of your child" (lines 1404–1405) have a rhythmical quality strongly evocative of the casting of a spell.

The very nature of the language is geared to the character's situation. Lines 1396–1397 oppose fairness and foulness—the two sides of Oedipus's mask. In the same lines "foulness festered" is a succinct metaphor for the whole action of the play. Line 1398, with its alliteration of sibilants, "sinner and a son of sinners," spits out the hateful words from the actor's mouth.

In all these ways the playwright has integrated the emotion, the action, and the form of the language so that the actor who plays the full range and force of the language will, at the same time, encompass the mask of the character and the emotional dynamics of the play's action.

In approaching and creating the playing of Oedipus's character mask, an actor might consider the use of the following structure of exercises that start from a physical base and finally incorporate the language of the text.

Neutral Mask. This is a fundamental exercise for neutralizing and energizing the body, which will enable the actor to approach the building of a character mask from a firm, centered base with no personal mannerisms.

Psychological Gesture. This exercise will discover a strong physical foundation for the character's mask. In the case of Oedipus we have suggested that pride, sense of authority, and belief in his own rightness are fundamental qualities of the mask. After working strongly with these characteristics they might be tempered by a sense of justice and desire to

act as a good ruler. Having worked on this aspect of the mask, which will have given the actor a whole range of gestural possibilities, the actor may turn to discover the converse side of the mask—the Oedipus of despair, disgust and humility at the end of the play who, however, acts with the same integrity and sense of justice as his happier self. A psychological gesture discovered here, incorporating, yet in tension with, the earlier discovery will give the actor a dynamic range of possibility for the physical characterization of the mask.

Emotional Mask. This exercise may be used to explore the spectrum of emotional change that Oedipus's intentions go through during the passage of the play. The movement from "I want to find and punish the criminal," through "I don't want to believe what I am hearing," and "I must go on even though I fear the outcome," to "I cannot bear to look upon the world I have corrupted," is an integral part of the structure of the play, and by working on each intention as a separate emotional mask the actor will bring strength and clarity as well as variety to the part.

Verbal Coloring. This exercise moves into the language of the play by starting with powerful imagery, working with emotive music, and then exploring significant phrases from the text. In working on Oedipus, some suggestions might include regalness, power, control, denial, self-righteousness, pollution, murder, and incest as images.

Music might range from Beethoven's *Emperor Concerto* through Elgar's *Pomp and Circumstance* to Tchaikovsky's *Pathètique* and Penderecki's *Dies Irae*. Phrases could include: I Oedipus whom all men call the great (1.8); who would not feel his temper rise (1.339); you are the land's pollution (1.353); I am full of fears (1.767); I must be ruler (1.628); do not seek to be master in everything (1.1523); I am now hated by the gods (1. 1518).

These exercises, selected from those on pp. 22–26, seem to be particularly appropriate to work upon Oedipus, creating a structure of exploration that supports and enhances the givens of the mask while introducing the actor to a variety of possibilities in choice of gesture, movement, and emotional structure. Each individual actor will, of course, use that structure of exercises and discover those choices that seem appropriate to his sense of the role.

The Messenger.   Along with the chorus and the protagonist, the messenger is the other distinctive mask the actor may have to construct. The function of the messenger is to report events, usually of a highly active and colorful nature, and the approach to his speeches will make demands upon the actor different from both the chorus and the protagonist. We are going to examine part of a messenger speech relating what took place after Oedipus had learned of his sins, and Jocasta, his mother/wife, had killed herself:

1253
He burst upon us shouting and we looked
to him as he paced frantically around,
begging us always: Give me a sword, I say,
to find this wife no wife, this mother's womb
this field of double sowing whence I sprang
and where I sowed my children! As he raved
some god showed him the way—none of
    us there.
Bellowing terribly and led by some
invisible guide he rushed on the two doors,—
wrenching the hollow bolts out of their
    sockets,
he charged inside. There, there, we saw
    his wife
hanging, the twisted rope around her neck.
When he saw her, he cried out fearfully
and cut the dangling noose. Then as she lay,
poor woman, on the ground, what happened
    after,
was terrible to see. He tore the brooches—
the gold chased brooches fastening her robe—
away from her and lifting them up high

dashed them on his own eyelids, shrieking
    out
such things as: they will never see the crime
I have committed or had done upon me!
Dark eyes, now in the days to come look on
forbidden faces, do not recognize
those whom you long for—with such
    imprecations
he struck his eyes again and yet again
with the brooches. And the bleeding eyeballs
    gushed
and stained his beard—no sluggish oozing
    drops
but a black hail and bloody rain poured
    down.
So it has broken—and not on one head
but troubles mixed for husband and for wife.
The fortune of the days gone by was true
good fortune—but today groans and
    destruction of death and shame—of
    all ills can be named
not one is missing.
1286

As always with verse, the way in which the speech is constructed helps the actor discover how it should be performed.[3] It is full of actively descriptive and onomatopoetic words. "Bellowing," which if given full value by the actor, suggests that very sound; "wrenching," "dashed," "gushed," "oozing,"—all are active, colorful words that suggest, through their sound, the concept they are depicting. The actor should be aware of the function of these words; their choice is not accidental. The actor should also be aware of the rhythms and construction of the speech as a whole. The first half of the speech builds upon the three highly explosive words "burst," "rushed,"

[3]It should be mentioned here that the actor is very much at the mercy of the translators. The best translations are those that convey the active spirit of the play, and actors and directors should be aware of this when selecting a text. The Grene and Lattimore edition, published by Chicago University Press, from which we have quoted by permission of the publisher, has the virtues of being close to the original, poetically valid in its own right, and highly actable.

and "charged." The forward power of the speech is then suspended with the inward breathtaking pain of "hanging" and "dangling." There is a quietus in the middle of the speech with "Lay, poor woman, on the ground," which enables the speech to build again through the description of Oedipus blinding himself. Then, with "so it has broken," the speech philosophically and reflectively examines the consequences of the terrible action just described, as if they were pieces of a broken life scattered about the stage.

The active description in the speech also gives the actor strong images to assist the choice of gesture. Though much of messenger speeches will be narrative and not call for physical embellishment, such images in the above speech as "struck his eyes again and yet again" certainly offer gestures to the actor. There is perhaps no better example of the language, the gesture, and the sense of the line being one than in "he struck his eyes again and yet again." The rhythm of this line is *di da di da di da di da di da*—a series of iambs—which is the rhythm of lifting and striking. It is the only line in the speech with such short, sharp rhythms.

As for the "character" of the messenger, as much as is necessary is contained in the speech. We are not concerned about who the messenger is, whether he is married, or even whether he has any particular concern for the events he is describing. What the playwright wants us to know of him he has given us. The messenger's functions define him. He plays his part in the action and that is enough. The last thing the actor should be concerned with here is embellishing his mask in "character" terms—like the bit actor described by Michael Green who, for a walk across the stage, assumed a limp, an eye patch, an arm-sling, and a toothless grin.[4]

We are not suggesting that an actor play generalities; but that he should play the specifics given to him rather than those of his own invention outside the play. When approaching the mask of the messenger, the actor has the following information:

1. the given circumstances of the situation: where the messenger is, where he has come from and whom he is addressing;
2. the objective: to ensure that the king receives and understands the information;
3. the information: an eyewitness account full of highly charged detail to engage both the king and the audience in the account.

All of this gives the actor powerful material with which to play the action of the messenger—the reporting of the information. But the actor neither needs to know nor to convey more than the situation and the action demand. The general quality of the speech is descriptive. It does not directly communicate the emotions of the character. There is no conflict implied in the speech, no personal passion. The messenger who is speaking has no direct emotional involvement in the speech; it has no effect upon his life. This is quite different from the protagonist, who is directly and emotionally connected with a personal outcome.

Messenger speeches in general contain narrative. They report events, actively describing them in colorful terms. There may also be an element of personal comment, sometimes a philosophical reflection upon the event, and, in exceptional cases, a direct conversational remark to a character on stage. The main functions, however, are to provide information necessary to the action but not available to the other characters and the audience, and to evoke a strong response in them. The purpose of the messenger speech we have quoted is quite clearly to evoke part of the pity and terror, the cathartic effect, that

---

[4]Michael Green, *Downwind of Upstage: The Art of Coarse Acting* (New York: Hawthorn, 1966) p. 44.

is the purpose of the action of this play and of Greek tragedy as a whole.

An exercise structure for the messenger mask will concentrate more upon coloring of the language and vocally commanding the audience than upon emotional connection or gestural display. The neutral mask exercise will again be a foundation and the verbal coloring exercise an important culminating point of the process: We have already drawn attention to the powerfully emotive images contained in the messenger's speech, which this latter exercise could build upon. Between these two exercises, such exercises as *Passing Action* and *Domestic Activity*—rather than work on emotional connection—will assist the clarity and simplicity of outline and focus upon the projection of language that is a particular demand of the messenger mask.

What we have tried to do here is suggest a short structure of exercises from among the entire range we have set out, which might be specifically appropriate to the building of cer-

tain masks of Greek tragedy. All of the exercises are useful in achieving an approach to the style as a whole, and each actor will discover and use what is most helpful to him or her in a particular situation. We have tried to suggest structures without being prescriptive. Finally, however, it is the language that is the foundation of all work on Greek tragedy. Within the discipline of the verse form, the structure, rhythms, and imagery of the language span the entire human emotional and descriptive palette and are both a tremendous challenge and fruitful foundation for the actor's work.

CONTEMPORIZATION

What happens to the actor's approach if a modern production of a Greek tragedy wished to perform it without masks? Some of the tragedies, especially *Antigone* and the *Electra* and *Medea* of Euripides, tended to explore character actions in more personal detail and might appear to lend themselves more to the realistic approach of the twentieth century. But what must always be kept in mind is that Greek tragedy was written for the mask in the all-encompassing sense in which we have described this artifact. The issues were still more important than the individual; the characters were still archetypes and not descriptions of well-rounded psyches; and it is in language, not in activity, that the fate of the character, as defined by its mask, is integrated with the play's action and communicated to the audience.

Economy, clarity, and strength in a modern production of *The Trojan Women*.   *Alley Theatre, Houston.*

If the mask is not used, and some form of stylized facial makeup (as is the case in some Oriental drama) is not used, the actor's face will inevitably be more plastic and expressive. The absolute, determined formality will be reduced and the nature of gestures will reflect this. However, the fundamental nature and structure of the play will not have changed: It will not suddenly have become "realistic," dealing with the minutiae of daily life and the psychological detail of character. The concerns of Greek tragedies were with larger social issues, with gods and fate, not with the daily round, common task, individual self-interest, and make-your-own-fate psychology of realistic theatre. The issues determine the structure and the structure supports the style. The idealization of the mask will inform facial and physical gestures: no grimacing or twitching through the vocabulary of modern mannerisms, but strong, selected, economical gestures, and clarity of purpose written large upon facial features; more plastic, more fluid than if working iconographically in a mask, but without the "busyness" of naturalistic playing, which would obscure and undermine the scale and significance of the issues in Greek tragedy.

What is true for the actor approaching a major character is equally true for the actor in the chorus in an unmasked production. As we have suggested, the Greek chorus represented a set of ideas or values rather than a group of characters. These ideas might be vested in a group—such as the elders of Thebes—but they thought and spoke as one: The function of the chorus was to represent the view of the *polis* or the gods. Differentiation is not then an issue. Even without masks it would probably still be preferable to have the chorus in similar costumes—there is a visual as well as musical rhythm that the chorus brings to the event. But, even with costume differentiation, in no sense should an actor attempt to individualize the choral action and illustrate a separate psyche. The chorus is structurally created to function as one. To be consciously different, to be individual, to stand out is to distract from and weaken the impact of the chorus in the play's terms.

Extended, clear, firmly-purchased gesture of actor Patrick Stewart in a modern dress production of *Hippolytus.*   *Royal Shakespeare Company.*

What we have been trying to emphasize here is that, even if the actor does not concretely have to use a mask in Greek tragedy, there are fundamental and structurally integrated elements that constitute the play's style and must be respected if the total impact of the play is to be communicated to an audience.

SUGGESTED READINGS

Anderson, M. J., ed., *Classical Drama and Its Influence.* New York: Barnes & Noble, 1965.

Arnott, P. D., *Greek Scenic Conventions in the Fifth Century B.C.* Oxford: Oxford University Press, 1962.

Bieber, Margarete, *The History of the Greek and Roman Theatre.* Princeton, N.J.: Princeton University Press, 1961.

Brooke, Iris, *Costume in Greek Classic Drama.* London: Methuen, 1962.

Hope, Thomas, *Costumes of the Greeks and Romans.* New York: Dover, 1962.

Kitto, H. D. F., *Greek Tragedy.* London: Methuen, 1961.

———, *The Greeks.* Chicago: Aldine, 1964.

Pickard-Cambridge, A. W., *The Dramatic Festivals of Athens.* Oxford: Oxford University Press, 1953.

Rolfe, Bari, *Behind the Mask.* Oakland, Calif.: Persona Books, 1977.

Taplin, Oliver, *Greek Tragedy in Action.* Berkeley: University of California Press, 1978.

Vickers, Brian, *Towards Greek Tragedy.* London: Longmans, 1973.

Webster, T. B. L., *Greek Theatre Productions.* London: Methuen, 1956.

———, *The Greek Chorus.* London: Methuen, 1970.

Williams, Raymond, *Drama in Performance.* New York: Basic Books, 1968.

3 Shakespeare

Vanessa Redgrave and David Harewood as "Cleopatra" and "Antony" in the Joseph Papp Public Theatre/New York Shakespeare Festival production of Antony and Cleopatra. Directed by Ms. Redgrave. *Photo by Michael Daniel.*

BACKGROUND

The work of William Shakespeare was the finest cultural manifestation of the English Elizabethan period. This age equalled that of fifth-century B.C. Greece in dynamic and distinction but, whereas in Greece the drama had reflected a society in a "classical" harmony of balance and proportion, in England Shakespeare's drama expressed the vigorous interplay of the contradictory elements of a "romantic" sensibility. Much of the power of Shakespeare's work is contained in the dynamic balance he explores in reflecting the social, political, economic, and spiritual forces at work in the Elizabethan period, and the tensions they created between the necessity of order and the questing energies of life; between the aspirations of the individual and the structures of a social system.

Elizabethan Age.   The coming of Elizabeth to the throne brought England a significant degree of political solidity. During the sixty years before Elizabeth became queen, England was racked from within by civil war—the Wars of the Roses—and threatened from without by Catholic Europe—a result of Henry VIII (Elizabeth's father) breaking with Rome. Just before Elizabeth became queen, her sister, Mary, a closet Catholic, caused further instability by conspiring with Spain to return England to the Roman Church. Elizabeth's accession brought political stability to England and confirmed the independence from Rome of the newly founded Protestant Anglican Church. The defeat of the Spanish Armada in 1588 is the political high point of Elizabeth's reign, for it confirmed in one blow the military security, political integrity, and religious independence of England.

In a sense, England became a prototype of the values of independence and vigorous effort associated with Renaissance humanism. Breaking with Rome was an assertion of individual rights in the face of old traditions. Eliz-

abeth, as head of both state and church, was no longer, in political or moral terms, indebted to any foreign power. This was, of course, a disruption of the medieval sense of a hierarchical religious order based on the concept of the *chain of being:* The chain stretched from the foot of God's throne to the meanest of inanimate objects. The angels were nearest to God, followed by humans and the lesser living creatures—the pope, of course, being at the head of this class. Then came vegetables and finally inanimate objects such as metals and liquids. The function of all classes was to come nearer to God, but without disrupting the given progression of the chain.[1] Elizabeth not so much disrupted a natural order as refocused it. She simply replaced the pope's authority and place in that scheme of things with her own. Thus, past traditions were not so much broken as reoriented, or subsumed into a new sense of life's purposes. New social structures were built upon old foundations, which were not obstacles to progress but provided a firm base for it.

Integration of Medieval and Renaissance. This flexible sense of the integration of the past with the possibilities of the future was typical of the Renaissance and of the reign of Elizabeth, and was present in Shakespeare's work. The balancing of the tensions between medieval roots and modern attitudes brought political and religious security as well as a dynamism that created great economic and cultural wealth.

The period saw the establishment of the commercial base that in the eighteenth and nineteenth centuries was to make the middle

---

[1]Shakespeare asserts this sense of life in a speech by Ulysses in act 1, scene iii of Troilus and Cressida:

> The heavens themselves, the planets and this centre,
> Observe degree, priority, and place,
> Insisture, course, proportion, season, form,
> Office, and custom, in all line of order.

class the power center of England and England itself the commercial, industrial, and colonial power center of the world. There was a new spirit of commercialism and profit incentive at home, and the securing of the seas to English ships, a result of the defeat of the Spanish Armada, led to an expansion of trade abroad.

Capitalist entrepreneurship was also supported by the new spirit of Protestantism. Humility on this earth and trust in the priest to intercede for oneself in the better life to come was replaced by material self-reliance. The counting of sheep and money replaced the counting of rosary beads and the lighting of candles. One could buy one's way to heaven as well as enjoy material goods on this earth. When the merchant of London looked into his heart he found that God had planted there a deep respect for the principles of profit and private property.

The Elizabethan period was also one of dynamic conflict in its philosophical outlook on life. A God-oriented sense of life whose rewards were in eternity was opposed to a man-oriented, humanistic outlook stressing achievements on earth. Humanism suggested that man could define his own nature: "What a piece of work is Man. . . ." Hamlet's words express the humanism of the day, in which the dignity rather than the humility of man is paramount. The hierarchical and unchangeable sense of religious and social authority was giving way to secular individualism. But the earlier traditions died hard. They formed part of the vocabulary and sensibility of Shakespeare's time while providing a framework upon which the new ideas of the Renaissance were grafted.

Humor and Personality.   Medieval concepts of the universe and of man himself are part of the stuff of Shakespeare's work. The medieval world was God-oriented and earth-centered. The sun, the planets, and the rest of the known universe moved around the earth[2] and produced the "music of the spheres." It was an age of "belief" not only in God but in the magical, mystical, and alchemical. The medieval world was made up of four elements: earth and water, which were personalized as having a tendency to fall; and air and fire, which were given a tendency to rise. These elements also became the humors of living bodies: Earth was cold and dry and corresponded to melancholy; water, cold and moist, corresponded to phlegm; air, hot and moist, gave rise to a sanguine temperament; fire, being hot and dry, was choleric in bias. Because a harmonious balance of the elements was necessary to the world, so balance of humors was necessary to the functioning of the human body. The humors were related not only to the general health of a person, but also to the personality traits. Overbalance of a particular humor was thought to determine basic sensibility. The four elements entered the body as food, went to the stomach, and then journeyed to the liver, which was regarded as the seat of the humors, or personality.

The concept of a dominating personality trait was a fundamental principle of medieval thought, and it persisted well into the eighteenth century. The behavior of an individual was determined by his or her predominant humor—phlegm, melancholy, and so on. This attitude went hand-in-hand with the concept of the seven ages of man, which forms the basis of Jaques' speech in act 2, scene vii of *As You Like It*. People were expected to behave, as their humor, station in life, age, and gender dictated. The "lean and slippered pantaloon" would not be expected to play tennis or go jogging with his wife.

Character "Typicality."   It cannot be overstressed in our age of individualism and self-determination, where everyone is to be

---

[2]As we saw from Ulysses' speech in footnote 1.

regarded as a separate and unique "person" in his or her own right, that a sense of "typical" behavior—mined by such variables as class, race, gender—was common in the Elizabethan period. Nor should we make value judgments about this if we wish to understand the sensibility of the time. Such concepts were not regarded as antidemocratic, sexist, racist, or any of the other terms we would now apply to them. They represented the social and intellectual structure of that time. Not only were they perfectly acceptable but they were also a way of looking at life and understanding people that the playwrights of the time inevitably reflected in their work.

Two other concepts of the Renaissance tended to reinforce the idea of typicality: decorum and verisimilitude. Decorum dictated that behavior should be appropriate to rank, place, gender, and other qualities. Verisimilitude required that actions be true to life. But the truth was not a private and individual one—it was an ideal or universal truth. Kings should be "kingly"; they should behave in a formal manner, carry an air of authority, be brave and honorable, and never, certainly in public, be seen to pick their noses, belch, or appear to be capable of any of the coarser bodily functions that are the appropriate actions of lesser mortals.

A book of the period on the art of rhetoric set down some of the received character determinations of the time: A man of good years is sober, wise, and circumspect; a young man is wild and careless; a woman, babbling and inconstant; a soldier is a great bragger and vaunter of himself; a scholar is simple; a courtier is flattering. The English are known for feeding and changing apparel, the Dutch for drinking, the French for pride and inconstancy, the Spaniards for nimbleness and disdain.

Lest we be too quick to dismiss this simple view of character, we might remember that in our day certain generalizations are held about national and ethnic identities: Latins are regarded as hot-blooded, emotional, and sexually dynamic; the British as phlegmatic and aloof; Germans as proficient technicians and heavy beer drinkers. One could go on. The point is not how true this is of any individual, but that it is a received attitude based in very generalized observation and truth. It serves as a reference point if one wishes to characterize a people or group as a whole. This is what many playwrights regarded as the function of character before the nineteenth century. Their main concern was not individual or psychological but for action and events, and a recognizable shorthand of character saved a good deal of time that could be devoted to the main purpose of the play: dramatic action.

Verbal Society.   Elizabethan England was predominantly an aural and verbal society. Less than 50 percent of Shakespeare's audience would have been able to read or write. But it would not have regarded itself as deprived by this inability, for reading and writing were yet to be general expectations of society. Communication was geared more to the tongue and ear and to broad visual panoramas than narrowly to the printed page. Remember, Shakespeare was not concerned that his plays should be printed—this was not completely done until some seven years after his death. The people of his time were used to listening. It was a time of long speeches, sermons, stories told on winter evenings. The town crier, the night watchman, and the itinerant tradesman all added their sounds to a daily life that included church bells and bird song as part of its music. People were accustomed to listening and glad to hear. Education had a verbal tradition. One of the basic principles of instruction in the grammar schools and universities of the day was learning by heart and repeating aloud. The teaching of rhetoric supported this sense of performance. Students were taught to recognize and understand the emotional function of many poetic structures: how the quality of certain words and the nature of their arrangement in particular images and structures—alliteration, onomatopoeia, apposition—can produce a particular effect upon the ear and upon human emotions. The aim of rhetorical speaking was clear enunciation, fitting modulation, and the conveying of proper emotions. Language was not just a means of conveying information, but for stimulating effect.

Ritual and Rowdiness.   As well as being verbal, the Elizabethan period was an age of activity, color, and enormous contrasts. A time of ritual, ceremony, and processions saw the formal dignity of the Mass side-by-side with the celebration of pagan festivals such as May Day, with its Morris dancing, phallic maypole and "country matters" in the woods. Elizabeth's "progresses" through the country, surrounded by her court, from one dignified mansion to another—in itself an enormously theatrical act—took place next to country fairs with their bear-baiting, exhibiting of cretins, and tooth breakers who removed teeth with pliers, to the great amusement of the crowd. It was an age of rugged physicality; it was closer to its pains and its passions. Criminals were not only hanged in public but also cut into quarters. It was not uncommon to see the heads of traitors on the spikes of city walls. The poetry and the physicality, the formality and passion, the blood and thunder, the perfume and music, the folklore and the classical rhetoric: All the colorful diversity of the society of the day found its way into Shakespeare's work.

A Popular Theatre.   Theatre itself played an important part in the social life of Elizabethan people. Fynes Moryson, a sixteenth-century traveler and writer, after confirming the tremendous number of games and sports played by the Elizabethans, goes on to say:

> All Cittyes, Townes, and villages swarme with Companyes of Musicians and Fidlers, which are rare in other Kingdomes. The City of London alone hath four or five Companyes of players . . . they all play every day in the week but Sunday, with most strange concourse of people. . . . There be, in my opinion, more Playes in London than in all the partes of the worlde I have seene, so do these players or Comedians excell all other in the world.

Theatre had always been a part of the social tradition of England. Mystery plays flourished in the streets of medieval cities such as Coventry and York. Troupes of itinerant actors—still regarded on a level with "vagabonds and sturdy beggars"—presented morality plays and interludes in market squares and the halls of country mansions. A whole tradition of popular theatre was alive in England in the sixteenth century, when the cultural influence of the Renaissance and the economic prosperity of Elizabeth's reign led to the professionalization of theatre and the development of permanent audiences. The rediscovery and teaching of classical playwrights such as Plautus, Terence, and Seneca in schools and universities provided for a greatly expanded repertory of plays. These neoclassical models were integrated, especially by Shakespeare, with conventions, characters, and forms taken from the native stock of farces, religious plays, and moralities to create the unique quality of the Elizabethan drama.

The Elizabethan theatre was not a break with, but a continuation and sophistication of, a popular tradition. The audience at the Globe would be socially, economically, and educationally heterogeneous, made up of every rank and class of society—artisans, craftsmen, shopkeepers, petty gentry, nobility, and respectable women in company with whores, pickpockets, students, and apprentices.

There was something for everyone in the plays. Middleton's prologue to his *No Wit, No Help Like a Woman's*, asks:

> How is't possible to suffice
> So many ears, so many eyes,
> Some wit, some in shows
> Take delight, and some in clothes;
> Some for mirth they chiefly come,
> Some for passion—for both some.

The appreciation of different elements—wit, passion, blood and thunder, perfection of poetic form—was obviously at different levels for different parts of the audience, but the involvement was total—the audience participated in the event.

It was in a sense a secular festival, to be compared with the religious festivals of the Greek theatre. Tracing its descent from the popular tradition of the mystery and morality plays, and incorporating many of their conventions, the Elizabethan theatre is a celebration of humankind and its attempt to define itself, discover a moral structure, and come to terms with its own nature. God was still present, but the heroes were of this world, dealing with each other in human terms. As with the Greek theatre, the themes of Elizabethan drama ask large questions as to how humans should deal with the challenges of living—but the answers were to be found more in the woods, heaths, and throne rooms of England than upon Mount Olympus. Again, in common with the Greeks, pride and curiosity in the historical evolution of the race are significant elements in the drama. Shakespeare's chronicle plays trace the history of England from the time of Henry IV through the Wars of the Roses to the accession of Elizabeth's ancestors, the Tudors. This, for Shakespeare and England, was equivalent to the Greeks' use of the Homeric legends in their tragedies. Both bodies of drama reflected a dramatic use of the historic mythology of the race to underscore its achievements, create pride in ancestral roots, and place a heroic mantle around rulers.

Dynamic Contrast.   The Elizabethan era was, then, a period of flux, flexibility, and contrasts. The conflict between the old and the new, in every area of life, produced dynamic accommodations, a creative fervor in which curiosity, ambition, private enterprise, and initiative abounded, but always with a rooted sense of continuance, structure, and popular form. Ambition was given scope but absorbed into existing structures, in this way ensuring social stability without inhibiting the upward mobility of talent. Shakespeare's own social ambition was to buy a small estate and carry the title of "gentleman"—which he achieved.

Popular tradition and new values crosspollinated, jostled each other, and found expression in the drama. The theatre was a union of classical control with a romantic sweep of energy, color, and exuberance; of classical verbal form with romantic insistence upon action.

Embracing and juxtaposing the contradictions of his age, Shakespeare made an artistic virtue of this dialectical dynamic. The integration of contrasting ideas gives the clue not only to the understanding of the Elizabethan period and the theatre it produced but also to the style of Shakespeare's drama and how it should be acted. Contrast informs Shakespeare's dramatic structure, which is compounded of accepted conventions yet allows for an experience of the crosscurrents, whirligigs, and "mingle-mangle" of life. Contrast is in the nature of his language, where poetry and prose, elaborate imagery, and simple, active speech all find their place. Contrast is at the heart of his characters, where "typical" attitudes and a conventional core support the more subtle and sophisticated actions and emotions of unique individuals. And, finally, however elevated may be the emotion or idea, the superhuman is always firmly anchored in the everyday.

Shakespeare combines classical plots, rhetoric, moralizing, and blood and vengeance with his native tradition born of Christian religion, morality types, clowning, pagan dances, royal processions, and the virile and acrobatic physicality of a passionate age. His own life typified the contrasting values of his time. He embodies Renaissance drive and medieval structure. His ambition and his success in London did not lead him to sever his connections with his native town. Nurturing his roots, he brought the profits of his talent back from the dynamic activity of London to the earthy solidity of Stratford, where he died. He was a poet with a strong sense of everyday reality. Though his head may have been in the clouds of inspiration, his feet were planted firmly on the ground. All the dynamic variety and energetic curiosity of his time went into his theatre and its acting style, as we shall discover in our detailed inquiry.

INTRINSIC DEMANDS

Space. The theatre where most of Shakespeare's plays were first performed was the famous Globe, home of the Lord Chancellor's (later renamed the King's) Company, of which Shakespeare was a shareholder. In some respects we have even less concrete evidence of the Globe than of the original Greek theatres. When the Puritans came to power in the 1640s they banned play performances and razed the public theatres. However, some evidence remains: a drawing of the Swan Theatre; contracts for the building of other theatres; and references found in property lists of the time. This, together with intelligent conjecture from references found within plays, and the inherent staging demands of the plays themselves, has given us a very good sense of what the Elizabethan public theatre must have been like.

The prologue to *Henry V* speaks of an "unworthy scaffold," a "cockpit," and a "wooden O." And it is reasonable to presume that the Globe Theatre, as befits its name, was round in shape, or at least octagonal, with the acting space, as confirmed in the Swan drawing, a raised platform thrusting into an audience that surrounded it on three sides. Here, immediately, we find a connection with the tradition of popular entertainment. The "scaffold" is

Elizabethan architecture: Bramall Hall, Cheshire.   *Countrylife, Reproduced by permission.*

directly descended from the cart or platform upon which itinerant players acted in town squares, and from the *platea* of the medieval theatre. The circular shape of the theatre recalls the pits where bearbaiting and cockfighting took place, which, together with the yards of inns, were the first homes of professional companies, before the building of permanent threatres. Like the bear pits and inn yards, the Globe Theatre was open to the sky, and the performance took place in daylight. The platform is calculated to have been about forty-three feet wide, twenty-seven feet deep, and about five feet high. At the back of the platform was a permanent facade at least two stories high—to accommodate such action as the balcony scene in *Romeo and Juliet*—which may have looked like an Elizabethan mansion. At all events it remained a constant background to the play and was not used as

a changeable scenic device. At either side of this facade was an entrance, and there is some evidence that in the center was a curtained recess called the "study" or "inner below," which may have been used for intimate interior scenes such as bedrooms. The second story may have contained a balcony over this lower recess—an "inner above"—and balconies and windows over the side doors, providing flexible acting areas in the facade itself. There may have been a third-story room used for musicians or storage of certain properties. It seems certain that a canopy, known as the "heavens," stretched out from the upper level of the facade (also known as the "tiring house," probably because the actors dressed—"attired"—there), supported by two pillars rising up from the stage. There was certainly one, and possibly more trapdoors in the stage—allowing for such scenes as the grave-diggers' scene in *Hamlet*. So, the whole concept of the stage can be seen as a metaphor for the universe, with heaven above, earth on the *platea*, and hell below. At the same time, the facade of the stage was a concrete, if neutral, reminder of everyday reality: The metaphysical was firmly anchored in the mundane.

The Globe Theatre. Reconstruction by Richard Southern. *Theatre-Museum Munich.*

In front of the stage platform, within the open yard of the theatre, stood the groundlings, or "stinkards," the poorer and possibly less educated members of the audience (though students from the Inns

Modern reconstruction of an Elizabethan theatre outdoors. *Utah Shakespeare Festival.*

Little stage furniture, scenic elements, or properties were used for the staging of Shakespeare's plays.[3] Although certain actions and locales were loosely defined by free-standing scenery—trees and walls are found in property lists of the day—the emphasis is essentially upon the actor, the verse, and the audience's imagination. As the prologue to *Henry V* says, "Let us . . . On your imaginary forces work." The broad unlocalized stage was a fluid and flexible area that, through interaction of the actor and the audience's imagination, could represent whatever the playwright wished. A situation could be specific, loosely defined, or unlocalized. Eighty percent of Shakespeare's scenes simply require actors and a bare stage—not even a stool is called for in the text. In several plays, Shakespeare tells

of Court and apprentices would also be there). The wealthier citizens—shopkeepers, professional people, and petty nobility—sat in the galleries within the surrounding walls of the theatre. A potential audience of two thousand people has been conjectured for the Globe, with no one member more than fifty feet from the stage—an incredible potential for intimacy with such a large audience: The audience was visible and indeed palpable to the actors.

us where we are—the forest of Arden, Illyria, Troy—and in many instances where the next scene is moving to. The beginning and ending of scenes are demarked by actors entering or leaving the stage. The fiction of a scene is created by the actor, and when he leaves, the

[3]In comparison with ours, Shakespeare's world was uncluttered with objects: A room furnished only with a chair and table would not have seemed particularly bare.

"verbal scenery" dissolves with him "into air, into thin air." as Prospero tells us, "like the baseless fabric of this vision."

Shakespeare's theatre is a "vision" of life, for it is founded in inspiration and imagination. Yet because it is created by humans and is compounded of their deeds, it is firmly anchored in a tangible reality. The stage is a metaphor. It stands for rather than represents a situation. Can one put Illyria, Cleopatra's Egypt, Othello's Venice, or Lear's world upon an "unworthy scaffold"? They are too large to be encompassed: Concreteness would minimize them and limit the scope of Shakespeare's action. So he says "imagine," and "suppose," and in the blinking of an eye the audience is transported from England to France, from Egypt to Rome. All this magic is, of course, the responsibility of the actor. Without the help of Prosepero's staff but with the aid of Shakespeare's language, he or she must draw the given circumstances for the audience, playing with the tongue upon the eye of their imagination.

Shakespeare's stage is a platform from which to tell a story. The action presses on swiftly—the "two hours traffic"—to its climax. There is in Shakespeare's work a constant forward sweep that requires an unimpeded presentation. The flexible unlocalized stage and the essentially neutral facade is the perfect environment. The world of Shakespeare's plays is compounded one-half of the life of man, one-half of the presence of God, one-half of

Modern reconstruction of an Elizabethan playing space indoors.   *Stratford Ontario Shakespeare Theatre.*

history and legend, one-half of fantasy. The result is a vision of reality twice as large as life itself. But if it could be spacious enough to imitate the universe, the stage could equally be as intimate as a conversation between two people. An actor talking to the audience from the limit of the thrust could reduce the space, the whole world, to the simplicity and directness of one-to-one communication.

What has been called the "unlicensed geography" of the Shakespearean stage allows actor and audience to traverse the world and be wherever and whatever the imagination presumes. It is a space to tell, excitingly and vigorously, "sad stories of the death of Kings." The unity we find in Shakespeare's work is a poetic unity, not a spatial and temporal unity that attempts (again in the service of verisimilitude—truth to "nature") to equate the use of time and space on the stage with that of "reality." Poetic unity is a unity of action; the totality of impression makes the event whole.

It is important for an actor to accept the diversity of impressions the playwright has unified by his total vision. He or she will not, then, make the mistake of applying too rigid a logic to the role, but will see himself as part of the all-embracing sweep of the play. At the same time, the actor *is* the primary focus of the Shakespearean theatre. The bare stage works as the unadorned walls of an art gallery, to isolate the essential thing—the actor. It requires him or her to encompass and manipulate many contrasts. There is a pattern of vigorous, fluid movement: from exit to entrance; above to below; locale to locale. The doors, windows, recesses, traps allow for and demand a diverse and dynamic use of space. As opposed to the central focus of the Greek stage, or the two-dimensional quality of the picture frame proscenium stage that succeeded the Elizabethan stage, it was open to the audience on three sides—an arena for action to please an audience that enjoyed bear-baiting and cockfighting. It allowed the actor sweeping yet direct confrontation both with fellow actors and the audience itself. The dynamics of the space with its potential for flexibility, continuity, and intimacy demanded an energetic, fluid, and diverse quality of playing from the actor to fill both the space and the very nature of the plays themselves.

Form.   In keeping with the sensibility of the age and the dynamics of the space, the nature of Shakespeare's plays tends toward open rather than closed forms. The Elizabethan period had an upwardly thrusting sense of life: a world bursting outwards from its core. This led to a nuclear rather than linear form, unified by action but with a fine contempt for limitations of time or space. It was pre-Cartesian sensibility, and we must beware of expecting it to be logically sequential or intellectually explicable. It is intended more to be experienced than analyzed. Stanislavski, whose linear and analytic method was splendidly useful for the proscenium-oriented, neo-Aristotelian realism of the late nineteenth and early twentieth centuries, confessed himself defeated by Shakespeare's plays, which illustrate the varied possibilities of human experience and may not mean any one thing. Imagery, symbolism, thought, action, character are all interrelated and cannot be viewed in isolation. Character, especially, must be seen in the context of the whole play, not as a psychological integer. There is no time, nor is there the necessity for things to be fully and minutely explored.

The Shakespearean form, then, is a swiftly flowing coherence of contrasts. The apposition of opposing qualities—movements and soliloquy, humor and suffering, violence and tenderness, verse and colloquial speech, formality and physical energy, philosophy and clowning—creates a sense of tension and conflict that is the heart of drama. Lacking the coolly intense compression of the best of Greek tragedy, the all-embracing unity of Shakespeare's work reflects the multiplicity, the reinforcing contrasts of Elizabethan life, integrated by the poet's own idea of human action. The form is related to the experience and finds a perfect environment in the theatrical space.

Language. Shakespeare's language is poetic—mostly blank verse, some rhymed verse, and some prose—but the total effect is a poetry of the theatre. Theatrical poetry is active and functional, not simply decorative. Cocteau has said that it should not be tenuous like gossamer, but thick like the rigging of a ship and visible at a distance. Poetry, while able to express the nature of human existence, is not limited by the details of everyday reality. Poetry both simplifies and gives sophistication to the portrayal of human conduct. It strips away day-to-day irrelevancies like indigestion and dandruff—if there are bathrooms in tragedy, they are for Agamemnon to be murdered in. At the same time, Poetry extends the range and quality of human comprehension, expressing and defining patterns of thought and feelings otherwise inexpressible and indefinable. The use of verse gives the world of tragedy a certain distance from the audience. It invests characters and actions with a special magnitude. Royal and heroic characters are higher than mere mortals in the chain of being, and their style of speaking reflects their elevation. Kings speak in verse; common mortals reply in prose.

The actor must be aware of the total shape of poetry, and how that shape is constructed. It is not enough just to understand what the verse "means"—a comprehension of the text—but to have an apprehension of the verse, how the patterns of sound, rhythms, images, and texture go beyond intellectual understanding and are filled with clues to character and the larger meanings of the dramatic action.

Technical Structure. The fundamental feature of Shakespeare's poetry is his use of blank verse written in iambic pentameter. This is where each line breaks down into five "feet," and each foot has two syllables of which the second is stressed. To take a well-known line from *Romeo and Juliet:* "Bŭt sōft./ Whăt līght/ thrŏugh yōn/dĕr wīn/dŏw brēaks?"

This is a perfect iambic pentameter, but you will note that "yonder" and "window" are split to achieve the meter of the line. It is only infrequently that the meter and integrity of the word will coincide, as this produces a somewhat oppressively regular effect. The playwright consciously creates a tension between the syntax of the line and its metrical beat to set up a particular effect or emphasize a particular quality of what is being said. Here, for example, "soft," "light," and "breaks" are the words stressed by the meter and have a lot to say about Romeo's breathless anticipation of this electrifying moment in his life. Opposite to the iamb is the trochee, where the stress falls on the first of two syllables. Lear's line upon discovering the dead Cordelia is a perfect trochaic pentameter: "Nēvĕr,/ nēvĕr,/ nēvĕr,/ nēvĕr,/ nēvĕr./" Here, the oppressive regularity of the line is calculated by the playwright. It is a mournful, falling meter, like the sound of a tolling bell at a funeral.

Both the iamb and the trochee relate to basic rhythms of the human body. The iamb is the even, lively beat of the human heart—*di dum.* The trochee is the fuller, more reflective rhythm of our breathing—the long drawing in of breath and the quicker exhalation. English speech falls naturally into iambic pentameter. You may well speak the meter in your daily communication without realizing it—just as Monsieur Jourdain, Molière's Bourgeois Gentilhomme, did not realize he had been speaking prose all his life! A simple sentence such as "You came home in the middle of the night" does, in fact, scan into an iambic pentameter.

That the natural rhythm of the English language reflects the rhythm of the heartbeat gives it a swift, strong, flowing quality that has an immediate and direct effect upon the listener. It is a romantic and visceral rhythm that befits the sensibility of Shakespeare's England. In contrast, the principal verse rhythm of the French language is the *Alexandrine*, which is a longer line, perfectly balanced with a rational, logical structure. This reflects the more neoclassical quality of the French sensibility. In both instances it is important to note how much the rhythms of verse, as opposed to the flatness of prose, are a reflection of and have a strong emotional impact upon human rhythms: The very sound of verse can tell us much, even when we do not understand the intellectual meaning. This is a point of fundamental significance to the actor performing Shakespeare.

Apart from the iamb and the trochee, there are four other foot structures the actor is likely to come across in Shakespeare's verse. The *pyrrhic*, which has two unstressed syllables, ∪ ∪, and is the weakest foot; the *anapest*, which has two unstressed and one stressed syllable, ∪ ∪ —; the *dactyl*, which is opposite the anapest with one stressed, then two unstressed syllables, — ∪ ∪; and the *spondee*, the strongest foot of all, with two stresses, — —. Scansion is not an exact science: One actor's choice will lead him or her to stress words or syllables that another might underplay. Again, stress is relative: The amount of stress will vary from foot to foot. Readings would tend to be monotonous if this were not the case. Actors should develop an instinct for reading verse, if they have not already done so. They will then feel the inherent rhythms; the line speaks to them as much as they speak to the line. The more one reads verse aloud, the more this instinct will grow. It is certainly not necessary, formally, to scan every line in every part—to say, "'Ah yes, that's a spondee," or an anapest, or whatever.

Verse and Meaning. The basic iambic pentameter flows easily off the tongue. But the more sophisticated and subtle the character, the more Shakespeare deviates from the iambic norm. To take as an example perhaps

the most famous line in Shakespeare: "To be, or not to be, that is the question" (*Hamlet*, act 3, scene i). This line scans into five feet.[4] *To be,/ or not/ to be,/ that is/ the question.* Each foot should have two syllables, and, for the line to be a perfect iambic pentameter, the stresses would be marked as follows; "To be, or not/ to be,/ that is/ the question."

However, the line is not perfectly iambic, as it has eleven syllables. "Question" has two syllables, not one as marked above, and is a complete foot in itself. This gives the fourth foot of the line three syllables: "that is the," with stress on "that." This foot is called a dactyl (see above). The fifth foot, "question," will now scan "question," marking the scansion of the whole line "To be,/ or not/ to be,/ that is the/ question." There are several reasons for this. This sense of the line is Hamlet framing an existential problem for himself. He is working something out and has put his finger on it—which leads to a stress on *that* (what I have come to realize) is the question. In technical terms, "that" is in apposition to the phrase "to be or not to be," and balances it. It is also the fulcrum of the line, balancing "to be or not to be" and "question." "Is" performs neither of these functions; being a slight word, it lacks the weight to balance the line. "That" also comes after the natural break in the line—the *caesura* (of which more below). Thus, stress falls rhythmically upon the word, emphasizing the whole phrase. To stress "is" would be an artificial imposition upon the natural rhythm of the line, as would stressing "the." Either choice would disrupt the flow and balance of the line as it illustrates the weighty, reflective quality of Hamlet's action. The fifth foot of Hamlet's line—"question"—has become a trochee. This inverted iamb is the most common form of variation in Shakespeare's verse.

---

[4]Scansion is the term given to the analysis of verse, to discover the meter—the number of feet per line and stresses per foot.

Punctuation.   We have already mentioned the caesura. This is a major pause in the line of verse. Unlike the French Alexandrine, it will only infrequently come in the middle of the line, more often at the end of the second or third foot, but it may come anywhere. In some instances there is no major pause, as in "Never, never, never, never, never," whose regularity and pounding monotony is the effect the playwright wants. The placement of the caesura gives shape to the line. The caesura also indicates where rhythmical pauses should be taken—thus giving emphasis to particular parts of the line—and is a possible place for the taking of a breath.

The caesura is, of course, a form of punctuation. Punctuation in the Shakespearean texts is often a tricky business. The Elizabethans had a somewhat more cavalier approach to punctuation than did later ages, and this, together with inaccuracies, ambiguities, and corruptions in the early editions of Shakespeare's work, has led to much controversy. The punctuation given by scholars in the major editions of Shakespeare's plays is an intelligent guide to the actor, but, as with the caesura, sense, syntax, and rhythm are the best guide to the shaping of the lines. In considering punctuation we notice that not all of Shakespeare's lines are end-stopped, or concluded by some kind of punctuated pause—comma, colon, period, or whatever. Often the sense and rhythmical nature of one line runs into the next. This run-on effect—*enjambement*—will occur very readily when lines have a "feminine" ending: The last syllable of the line is unstressed, which gives a bounce from the second-to-last syllable of one line straight into the next line.

Elision.   Sometimes syllables are given very little or no stress, and are not voiced at all. This process is known as *elision*, and it is used to keep the rhythmical meter of the line. For example, a speech by Macbeth (which we will use more fully below to illustrate some of the technical qualities we have discussed) has the line "Who should against his murderer shut the door." Giving full value to all syllables, we would scan this: "Whŏ shōuld/ ăgāinst/ hĭs mūr/dĕrĕr shūt/ thĕ dōor." This would give the line one more syllable than the ten syllables of the pentameter form, make the fourth foot an anapest, and break the rhythmical flow of the line. It is possible to argue that Shakespeare wanted to emphasize "murderer," and thus employed the "hypermetrical" (more-than-ten-syllable) line. But the anapest seems to hold up the line and interrupt the flow of Macbeth's argument, and it seems preferable to elide one of the syllables in "murderer," making it "murdrer," and the fourth foot of the line a normal iamb. In the opposite case, there are occasions in our normal speech where we would elide syllables that in Shakespeare's verse structure must be given a full value to complete the meter. An example of this comes in a famous speech by Mark Anthony in act 3, scene ii of *Julius Caesar.* The speech contains the line: "The good is oft interred with their bones." In order for this line to become an iambic pentameter, "interred," which today would be pronounced "interd," must be given three syllables so that the line will scan: "Thĕ gōod/ ĭs ōft/ ĭntēr/rĕd wĭth/ thĕir bōnes."

Scansion and Sense: An Example.   To pull together and illustrate the use of the technical attributes of blank verse, we offer below a scanned and annotated passage from *Macbeth,* act 1, scene vii.

> Ĭf ĭt/ wĕre dōne/ whĕn tĭs/ dŏne thĕn/
> twĕre wēll

(Attack upon the speech seems to demand emphasis upon "if," which gives a trochee in the first foot. Emphasis upon "when" also makes the third foot a trochee. The caesura will come in the middle of the fourth foot, laying especial emphasis upon "then.")

> Ĭt wĕre dōne/ quĭcklÿ./ Ĭf th'as/ sāssĭ/
> nātiŏn

(This is a hypermetrical line with either eleven or twelve syllables. It seems to flow better with eleven which is achieved by eliding "the" in the third foot and making "th'as" into one syllable. The first foot works as an anapest, reemphasizing "done." The caesura comes with the period before "if" and emphasizes that word again. The line is mostly trochees and has a feminine ending, with "-tion" running into the next line.)

> Coŭld trăm/mĕl ūp/the cōn/sĕquēnce/
> aňd cātch

(an iambic pentameter; caesura before "and")

> Wĭth his/sŭrcēase/sŭccēss; / thăt bŭt/ thīs
> blōw

(The fifth foot seems to call for a spondee, "this blow"—once and for all—being the crux of Macbeth's thinking. The caesura comes before "that.")

> Mĭght bē/ the bē-/ ăll and/ the ēnd-/
> ăll hēre

(We scanned this as an iambic line, but there are possible variations: The first foot could be read as a trochee with stress upon "might"; the last foot could become a spondee, which would give three stresses at the end of the line—"end-all here." The latter variation slows down the line and deemphasizes "here," which Shakespeare reemphasizes in the next line. So although it is a conceivable choice, we think the iamb at the end of the line, with strong emphasis upon "here" [which is reinforced by the caesura before "here"] is the better reading.)

> Bŭt here,/ ŭpoň/ this bank/ aňd shōal/
> ŏf tīme

(It seems that "here" and "this" are in apposition and should both be stressed, giving a spondee in the third foot. The caesura is after "here," lending it further stress.)

> Wĕ'd jump/ the līfe/ tŏ cōme./ Bŭt ĭn
> thēse/ cāsĕs

(This is another hypermetical line with a feminine ending. The fourth foot could be a dactyl, which would mean deemphasizing "these," and seems to go against the sense of the speech. We cannot emphasize both "but" and "these" without throwing away "cases": The scansion would have to be "Bŭt ĭn/ thēse căsĕs." This is a good example of the necessities of scansion telling us where the emphasis must be.)

Further Technical Effects.   The speech continues, and we will deal with it again more fully in the section on performance demands. It remains here to mention a couple of further aspects of Shakespeare's use of verse: the employment of rhyming couplets and the splitting of lines between characters. Rhyming couplets are by definition more formal and less subtle and flexible than blank verse. The couplet is usually found at the end of a speech, and particularly at the end of a scene. Act 1, scene vii of *Macbeth*, from which we took our preceding example, ends with a couplet spoken by Macbeth:

> Away, and mock the time with fairest show.
> False face must hide what the false heart
>   doth know.

Couplets such as this sum up or emphasize important points of action, give a strong completion as the actor moves to exit, and also indicate to the audience a change of scene.

Shakespeare frequently shares a pentameter line with two characters. This happens consistently in the *Macbeth* scene from which we are quoting. There is an urgent discussion, not to say an argument, going on between Lady Macbeth and Macbeth. The completion of one character's line by the other character gives an impetus, an almost stichomythic quality to the scene, despite the length of the speeches. A particularly good example is:

LADY MACBETH: And dash'd the brains out
       had I
    so sworn as you
    Have done to this.

MACBETH: If we should fail?
LADY MACBETH: We fail.

The last three lines are one complete pentameter shared over three speeches. The lines must be taken as one; the build shows tension, excitement, anticipation. Lines such as these and half lines completed by another character required no pause—being one line. Divided lines usually call for quick, overlapping delivery. However, when a half line at the end of one speech is followed by a complete line at the beginning of another, a pause seems to be indicated. The incomplete line is marked by silent beats that complete the pentameter. There are examples of this in *Othello*, act 3, scene iii, where Iago is laying seeds of jealousy in Othello's mind. Othello has such short lines as "O misery," and "Dost thou say so." These are followed by complete lines from Iago, and the nature of the scene suggests that Iago lets Othello stew in his juice of uncertainty before replying. Othello's lines are completed by short pauses in which he can be seen to be thinking, worrying over what Iago is saying.

Summation of Structure.   Everything Shakespeare does with his verse has a purpose in furthering action and delineating character. The sense is revealed by the sound and shape of the lines. This applies equally when Shakespeare shifts from verse to prose, which we will deal with in the section on character. To sum up, the technical characteristics of Shakespeare's verse that the actor should identify include the following:

1. the scansion of the line into metrical feet, and the determination of the nature of these feet;
2. the distinction between word divisions and foot divisions, and the dynamic tension this creates;
3. the caesura in the line, with the emphasis this places upon words and phrases;
4. such properties as elision and enjambement, which affect the rhythm of the line, and the grouping of lines into larger patterns;
5. the use of rhyming couplets;
6. the distribution of a pentameter line over more than one character or speech.

Figures of Speech.   For the preachers, lawyers, teachers, politicians, and playwrights of the Elizabethan period, speech was an affirmation of man's dignity, his superiority over the beasts. It was the great civilizing force, and beauty in discourse was calculated to win people over to virtuous actions. Rhetoric was the core of humanistic education and Shakespeare had an enormous vocabulary of rhetorical figures that he incorporates into his verse. It is not our purpose to give a lesson in rhetoric, but the ability to recognize some of the major figures of speech is useful to the actor.

Various forms of repetition is one of Shakespeare's main devices. Repetition of words at the beginning of sequential sentences is a common form of emphasis. This may be taken further, in a form known as *parison* (remembering the name is not important, unless it helps to identify the function), where there is an almost exact correspondence between two sentences:

> Was ever woman in this humour woo'd?
> Was ever woman in this humour won?

These lines from *Richard III*, act 1, scene ii, emphasize by repetition and add an irony by the antithesis of the last words in each line. *Antithesis* is another figure of speech, which by opposing words and images balances them, lets each emphasize the other, and can show calculation and an ironic sensibility.

There is also a form of punning repetition, which repeats a word but with a change of meaning. This figure often reveals a sad irony, as with Othello's line in act 5, scene ii:

> Put out the light, and then put out the light.

The repetition of "light" referring to Desdemona's life.

Finally, there is a very active form of repetition, which is illustrated by the lines that Henry V speaks after the Dauphin has mockingly sent him tennis balls:

For many a thousand widows
Shall this, his mock, mock out of their dear
    husbands;
Mock mother's from their sons, mock castles
    down; (act 1, scene ii)

The repetition of "mock" gives it the feeling of a riposte, a blow. It creates the rhythm both of a tennis match and the firing of a series of cannonballs. "Mock" is also used here in an onomatopoeic manner, whereby the sound of a word suggests the sense in which it is used: "mock" becoming the sound of a ball striking a racket. *Onomatopoeia* is a figure of speech often used by Shakespeare, as in Juliet's famous line "Gallop apace, you fiery-footed steeds." The word "gallop" creates the sound of horses galloping, which is reinforced by the repetition of "p" in "apace."

The use of "fiery-footed" in Juliet's line is yet another rhetorical device—*alliteration*. This, again, is a form of repetition: of the initial sounds of words in close proximity. It is used for emphasis and gives a rhythmical reinforcement to the words. In our example it also has an onomatopoeic value in that the repetition of the "f" sounds creates, in itself, the breathy attack of fire.

A very calculated rhetorical form that employs repetition is climax. Claudius, in act 5, scene ii of *Hamlet*, has this speech:

And let the kettle to the trumpet speak,
The trumpet to the cannoneer without,
The cannons to the Heavens, the Heavens to
    the earth,
Now drinks the King to Hamlet.

There is a climbing ladder of degree in the speech: The picking up and repetition of "trumpet," "cannon," and "Heavens" builds the splendor of the ceremonial, and the hyperbole indicates the somewhat hollow pomposity of Claudius. There is a calculated formality in the speech, which indicates the sentiment is not deeply felt. Indeed, the king believes he is drinking to Hamlet's death. All of this illustrates Claudius's character in action.

The last rhetorical figure we will mention is technically known as *paronomasia*. It occurs when two words are used in apposition and the sense is radically altered by a change of letter or syllable. The most famous and sophisticated example is in *Hamlet,* act 1, scene ii, in which Hamlet's stepfather calls him "son," and he replies: "A little more than kin, and less than kind." "Kind" here being used both in the sense of "like" or "relative," and "sympathetic" or "good-willed." This figure of speech either lends itself to irony or draws attention to opposing feelings within a character, as when Iago employs it in act 3, scene iii of *Othello:*

But, O, what damned minutes tells he o'er
Who dotes, yet doubts, suspects, yet strongly
    loves.

Our intention here is not to get the actor to emphasize heavily Shakespeare's figures of speech, but simply to be aware of their presence and function. They go together with the rhythms and imagery of the verse in helping the actor create character and action.

Imagery.   Imagery is painting with words. This is probably the best description of a poet's use of imagery. Whereas a journalist might have said that "Cleopatra's barge shone brightly as it sailed down the Nile," Shakespeare, through Enobarbus, tells us: "The barge she sat in, like a burnish'd throne Burn'd on the water. The poop was beaten gold." The appeal of imagery is total. It is not just to our intellect, but to our rhythms and emotions—the whole inner vocabulary of seen and intuited experience.

The presence of imagery is recognized more easily than are figures of speech, so we will illustrate its use only briefly with a further example from *Macbeth,* act 3, scene ii:

> Come, seeling night,
> Scarf up the tender eye of pitiful day,
> And with thy bloody and invisible hand
> Cancel and tear to pieces that great bond
> Which keeps me pale.
> Light thickens, and the crow
> Makes wing to the rocky wood:
> Good things of day begin to droop and
>   drowse
> While night's black agents to their preys
>   do rouse.

The speech is a personification of night in imagistic form: "night thickens" perfectly creates the feeling of the mellowing, opaque, less distinct light of dusk. It also has the resonances of "the plot thickens," which is what is happening to Macbeth, now plotting to kill Banquo and gradually sinking into the "darkness" of sin. The image of night seen as sewing up the eyelids of the tenderer-hearted day gives us the feel of Macbeth's desire to keep his actions secret and the brutal manner in which he must constantly kill to achieve this. The night is also the night of Macbeth's soul; he is lost to the light of goodness—good now "droops and drowses" while he pursues his prey like an animal. The experience of the speech gives us the feeling and the understanding that Macbeth has become habitually brutalized; that he almost welcomes the darkness into which he is sinking as a way of forgetting that he once had a conscience. It would take a great deal of exposition to convey all of this. It would also lose force in the telling, and be more limited in its appeal to our senses than the total, or "holistic," effect achieved by the verse images.

Shakespeare's imagery, though it certainly embellishes his verse, is not there for that purpose alone. It plays a direct part in delineating character, establishing situation, and furthering the action of the play. The imagery is the more impressive because much of it is taken from life in Elizabeth's time and, recognizably, our own. In the passage from *Macbeth* the references to crows, woods, and sewing are everyday and countrified. Wilson Knight, in illustrating Shakespeare's use of daily experience, tells of meeting two countrymen in Shakespeare's own county of Warwickshire in the 1950s. The men were repairing hedges. Knight asked them what they were doing, and was told: "Well, I roughhew the branches, while he shapes the end." This country expression found its way four hundred years ago into Shakespeare's verse: "There's a Divinity that shapes our ends, roughhew them how we will" (*Hamlet,* act 5, scene ii). Perhaps the most wholesale and perfect unity of idea, action, and imagery comes at the end of *The Tempest,* "probably" (that is, to take into account those who argue for *Henry VIII*) Shakespeare's last play. Prospero has a valediction in act 4, scene i:

> Our revels now are ended. These our actors,
> As I foretold you, were all spirits and
> Are melted into air, into thin air;
> And, like the baseless fabric of this vision,
> The cloud-capped towers, the gorgeous
>   palaces,
> The solemn temples, the great globe itself,
> Yea, all which it inherit, shall dissolve
> And, like this insubstantial pageant faded,
> Leave not a rack behind. We are such stuff
> As dreams are made on, and our little life
> Is rounded with a sleep.

Here we have an extended image of the stage as a metaphor for life itself. What actors create is ephemeral, as is man's life; the play comes to an end, as must man's life. Man can no more grasp his own reality than the fantasy illusions of the stage. This was Prospero's swan song, as it was Shakespeare's own. Shakespeare lived upon the stage, as did Prospero, but, for an equally little life. Here, on this globe (which was the theatre's name), on this earth, on this stage did we once live, and were illumined and aware. Now there is nothing to come but dust and sleep. There could hardly be a better example of integrated and active images.

Shakespeare's language is lyrical, dynamic, and flexible. Based in the iambic pentameter, a rhythm close to that of everyday speech. It is essentially an active language in which shape, structure, and rhythm combine to make the required impression of character and action upon the audience. The language contains transcendental poetry and vernacular prose; formality and colloquialism; soliloquy and stichomythia; rhetorical forms and coarse humor; poetic imagery and direct information. As in sensibility, structure, and space, so we now find in speech that dynamic integration of opposing forces that typified the Elizabethan period and informed its theatrical style.

Costume.   Such evidence as we have from sketches, contemporary references to performance, and the plays themselves suggests that the Elizabethan actor was the "glass of fashion," wearing clothes from the everyday wardrobe of the time. There were two basic principles of Elizabethan stage costumes. First, though based in the everyday, costumes were more splendid than it. Second, close attention was paid to decorum and verisimilitude: Costumes should be seen as fitting the rank and station of the character. But, as we have already suggested, the verisimilitude of the day was not detailed or precise; it was geared more to a typical expectation. Thus, although care was taken to fit the richness and splendor of a costume to the rank of the wearer—royalty would wear purple velvet, ermine, and satins; friars, the simple brown habit of their calling—little attention was paid to historical accuracy or geographical variety. Julius Caesar would wear Elizabethan costume with possibly a toga over it; Othello,

Elizabethan clothes with perhaps a Moorish headdress. Such emblematic identification was the furthest concession to "realism" made by the Elizabethan stage.

However, the audience was not concerned about realistic detail; it accepted the conventions of the day. What the audience did expect was that the costumes should be evidently rich and expensive. This was part of the show. It was an age of splendor in dress, and this had to be outdone upon the stage. Costumes were the heaviest expenditure in an acting company's budget. It has

The foursquare dignity of Sir Walter Raleigh and his son in Elizabethan clothing. *National Portrait Gallery, London.*

been suggested that members of the nobility either gave their castoff clothing directly to players, or to their servants, who then sold them to the actors. In any event, the costumes were frequently trimmed with gold and pearls, and three layers of velvet were often used for a slashed doublet. Remember, the audience was close to the stage, and the performance was given in the light of day. The modern costumer's art of using cheap fabrics that can appear costly under lighting was not available to the Elizabethans.

The male dress generally consisted of a shirt with fancy cuffs that were pulled out to trim the sleeves of the overgarment—the doublet. The doublet emphasized the shape of the male upper body, padded in the shoulders and chest and narrowing down into the waist. This gave a sense of strength and dignity that was furthered by the ruff, worn around the neck, which meant the head was held high with a certain arrogance. Breeches were either full, like a pumpkin, or worn tight on the thigh (in which case they were known as Venetians). Beneath these were close-fitting hose, and flat-heeled shoes or boots for riding and rough activity. There was a strong emphasis upon the leg that suggested virility and sexual potency. Hats were decorative as well as utilitarian (in a cold, wet climate). Embellished with feathers, they added to the rakish arrogance of the set of the head. The Elizabethan male was something of a peacock in his sense of dress, but it was to emphasize a pride in showy masculinity. Because Sir Francis Drake wore earrings it should not be forgotten that he pirated the Caribbean or sank the Spanish fleet. The time of Raleigh, Essex, and Sydney put English ships around the globe, gained military influence in Europe, and laid the foundations of the future British Empire. The elaborate costumes and heavy jewelry showed anything but a lack of masculine force.

We are, of course, essentially dealing here with the "gentle" or upper-class characters

The portrait of Queen Elizabeth's sister Mary shows the ornate heaviness of female clothing and the erectness it gave to body posture.   *Isabella Stewart Gardner Museum, Boston.*

who predominate in Shakespeare's work. The "base" or lower classes were dressed more simply in smocks, or breeches, shirts, and the aprons of their trade. As would be expected in a hierarchial society, the splendor and richness of dress related to the position of rank and authority within the society.

Female dress was as heavy and ornate as that of the male, but much more binding and constricting. The lower part of the body was the freest, though covered by layers of petticoats and skirts over a farthingale—a hooped construction that gave a bell shape to the body below the waist, extending the hips well beyond the normal body line. This gave the impression, when the woman moved, of a procession rather than a sense of body movement. The upper body was bound from below the breasts to the lower stomach by corsets and a "stomacher." The latter was a triangular piece of wood that pushed up the breasts and pointed down toward the crotch. The gown, which went over all this, was usually highly ornamented with pearls and other gems, and of rich material. It revealed the upper breast, had large puffed sleeves, and was often slashed at the front to show the fancy petticoats. With the gown went a large ruff or a high wing-collar. Headdresses were high, encrusted with jewels, and often topped with a small ornamental hat.

Thus, the formality, dignity, and pride of the male was repeated, but without his freedom of movement. The woman was bound into a masculine sense of uprightness (as a "good" woman should be). She showed a strength, but one that befitted her place in society. Shakespearean women who attained a certain freedom from formality are to be found in the comedies, not the tragedies. They did this by adopting masculine clothing and wearing it with the kind of pubescent virility that might be expected of the boys who played them.

In general, the Elizabethan dress worn on Shakespeare's stage was costly, dignified, and ornate, and it emphasized an essentially masculine pride and strength. Note that even the feminine ideal—Queen Elizabeth herself—showed a masculine force, and was childless. The dress reflected both the sensibility of the age and the nature of Shakespeare's language: Rooted in the everyday but heightened and embellished, formal yet flexible, forceful and flowing, it filled the stage with powerful and colorful images of poetic life.

PERFORMANCE DEMANDS

We cannot, finally, *know* how the actor performed Shakespeare's work. But the clues gathered from the areas we have just discussed can help us to make a reasonably accurate reconstruction. The evidence from the nature of the theatrical space, dramatic form, language structure, and costuming identifies certain consistent qualities: dynamism and formality, simplicity and embellishment, muscularity and lyricism. These seemingly contrasting properties are a result of the confrontation of deep-rooted popular traditions with newly discovered Renaissance values. This created the dynamic tension of the Elizabethan period, which will inevitably have been reflected in the actor's approach to Shakespeare's plays, which were themselves a product of the same energies.

Formality and Energy.   The physical nature of the Elizabethan stage emphasized the actor as the prime element in performance. The actor moves the audience with his or her body and voice, and, technically, the costume will have a significant influence upon the actor's movements. The male costume emphasized broad shoulders, full chest, strong legs, creating a formal sense of self-display with a strong erect carriage. The way in which Elizabethan people carried themselves was undoubtedly upright and aspiring. It was an age of ambition and upward thrusting energies; the spine would be uplifted and erect. The wearing of the ruff around the neck would give a further strong, upright emphasis of body movement, as it would eliminate small head movements and lead to full body turns.

The heavy breeches and free, exposed legs indicate wide-legged stances, strong stage purchase with the feet, and long, firm strides. The actor would be very solid in his possession of his stage space, and when he moved it would be definite, with purpose—no shuffling of feet, or shifting of weight from leg to leg giving a weak, uncertain air. Muscular legs were a part of male physical attraction, and consciousness of the leg would mean the adoption of deliberate positions for both standing and sitting. Elizabethan chairs had tall, straight backs, an indication of how people were expected to sit: once again, in an erect, dignified manner with the male leg well displayed—one leg forward and slightly turned out, the other back with the knee bent, and a hand possibly resting on the thigh. This posture communicated a sense of purposeful ease, a man dignified yet ready to move quickly into action.

The corset, stomacher, and ruff gave the women an even more erect, contained, and formal stance than the men. Small movements were not possible. Turning the head necessitated turning the body, and turning the body meant manipulating the large expanse of far-thingale and skirts. The farthingale also prevented the arms from being held loosely at the sides of the body. Rather, they were held forward, the lower arms and hands curving down toward the point of the stomacher. Walking was a smooth, even "process" so that awkward swaying of the skirts could be avoided and the corset and stomacher prevented any forward bending from the waist, further emphasizing the upright carriage. This meant women had somehow to back into chairs and sit on the forward edge to prevent the skirt from billowing up and revealing the leg. Although some of this might sound awkward for both men and women, it should be remembered that it was their everyday dress and manner and would be comfortable to the

Formality in posture and stage picture: Joseph Papp Public Theatre/New York Shakespeare Festival Production of "Antony & Cleopatra." Directed by Vanessa Redgrave.   *Photo by Michal Daniel.*

Athletic geometry in action.   *Citizens' Theatre, Glasgow.*

wearer. The style of movement is precisely the physical adaptation to the nature of the costuming so that it does appear natural in both its formality and its impression of strength.

If the costuming lent an air of formality and strength to the performance, the stage space called for dynamism in movement. It was a fairly deep, wide, open stage thrusting into the audience, with entrances at the rear. The structure of the plays called for a continuous rhythm of playing. Scene followed upon scene with a rapid flow; actors often entered in mid-speech. There was no stopping for change of scenery; there may, indeed, have been no intermissions whatsoever. The space, then, was filled with a continuous activity: entrances and exits taken at different sides of

the stage, and upper levels engaged in the action. This "athletic geometry" of Shakespeare's work required dynamic, bold, and compelling movement from the actor. The directness of much of Shakespeare demands that the actor get down front to contact the audience. There is a lot of distance to cover and the audience must be held while it is being covered. On an essentially bare stage the actor confronts the audience with his or her own resources. The audience shared the same daylight and was aware of the ever-present distractions. To impress and control such an audience required an alert, quick-witted, powerfully energetic physical and vocal presence. The raised stage did give the actor a certain immediate dominance over the audience;

but this had to be justified: The actor had to take the stage and fill it with the powerful passions of Shakespeare's work.

The necessary physical energy was combined with the formal tradition of the Elizabethan period. It was an age of ceremony. The ritualistic sensibility of the Middle Ages was still present in church, at court, and in the minds of much of the population. Elizabeth's "processes" through the country capitalized on this. Greetings and leave-takings were ceremonious. Bows, curtsies, hat removals, arm clasps, and "God be with you" had not yet been replaced by the offhand "Hi" of the casual present. Shakespeare's plays incorporated ritual and ceremonial entrances, which impressed the audiences by their dignity and were recognizably a part of everyday social manner. With violence and speed of action went nobility of character and elevated situa-

Nimble footed, powerfully alert physical presence of Antony Sher in *Richard III.*   *Royal Shakespeare Company. Photo by Reg Wilson.*

tion. It was a function of the time. Shakespeare's actors could integrate physical and formal qualities, just as they could dance the lively jig, the nimble galliard, and the stately pavane. There was no uncomfortable contradiction in this; it was all a part of the dynamic formality of the physical style.

Selectivity and Directness.   As with movement, the nature of gesture will be related to costume demands. In this we find women more restricted than men. The fullness of the women's sleeves and the fitted nature of the bodice across the shoulders limit the movement of the upper arms and tend to emphasize the hands and lower arms. Such smaller, more delicate, and contained gestures would, of course, be perfectly in keeping with what society regarded as women's place. Men were less restricted in this way, but the heaviness of the doublet's shoulder makes it likely that gestures did not extend the upper arm above the head. High gestures were probably made with the upper arm parallel to the ground and the lower arm extended upwards from the break at the elbow.

Size of gesture is related to space and the scope of the drama. The Elizabethan theatre is smaller than the Greek and the manner of performance is therefore more direct. Although aware of human relationship to heavenly powers, it is not as directly God-oriented. The space of Shakespeare's theatre is less and the tempo is quicker: Time flows swiftly rather than standing still, and the rhythms of the plays reinforce this. Thus, the tendency will be for quicker gestures with a powerful thrust, taken more directly to other actors and the audience. Shakespeare's characters, though elevated, are more human than the Greek; gestures will carry meaning in more everyday terms, but at the same time must fill the poetic time and space in which they are operating.

Perhaps we should affirm here, although it is implicit in what we have said, that we do not subscribe to the view that Shakespearean acting is a form of recitation with a specific vocabulary of gestures based upon accepted rhetorical forms of the day such as found in Bulwer's *Chirologia* and *Chironomia*. It is certainly possible that the actors were aware of and did in fact use some of these conventional gestures. However, if such gestures were used, they would become a part of the actor's own reality. They would be made dramatic by actors—who were not preachers or speechmakers but performers. That Shakespeare's players did use gesture and physical activity is confirmed by our Elizabethan traveler Fynes Moryson: "Stage players came out of England into Germany, having neither a complete number of actors, nor any good apparell, nor any ornament of the stage, yet the Germans . . . flocked wonderfully to see their gesture and action." So, without costumes or any set pieces, the actors could make the performance live by their physical presence.

There was a certain amount of recognizable "domestic" business. Pulling of beards and playing with codpieces is called for in the plays. Then there is putting on and off of clothes, gloves, and armor and the handling of swords, food, drink, etc. But for the most part, gesture will illustrate action and character, and here we should mention the importance of selectivity: "Suit the action to the word," as Shakespeare tells us in his famous acting lesson in *Hamlet*, act 3, scene ii. But, as he also tells us, if this is overdone it will make "the unskillful laugh" and "the judicious grieve." An important fact to remember is that Shakespeare has done a great deal of the actor's work for him with language. Let the line do the work when it can. Tyrone Guthrie's comment "What do you want, a **pink light**?" given to an actor discussing Horatio's speech in act 1, scene i of *Hamlet* ("the morn, in russet mantle clad, walks o'er the dew of yon high eastward hill") aptly makes the point about the descriptive capacity of Shakespeare's verse. This was further confirmed in a production of *Romeo and Juliet* in which the

otherwise competent actor playing Mercutio seemed to find it necessary to illustrate physically every image in the Queen Mab speech. Leaping, prancing, mincing, swashbuckling, he managed to so overburden the speech that the audience reeled away from it like a beaten boxer, and a brilliant piece of verse was reduced to a molten mass of gestures and images. Selectivity is a watchword of all good acting, but never more so than in Shakespeare.

Selectivity and directness go hand in hand. The Shakespearean actor was strongly aware of the audience's presence. He could hardly have avoided it. The audience closely surrounded the stage in broad daylight and came to the event not with sepulchral reverence but with delighted awe. The whole popular tradition reinforced the element of direct

Strength and formality of manner in a modern dress production of Hamlet.   *Yale Repertory Theatre. Photo: T. Charles Erickson*

communication between actor and audience. It was present in the street shows, mysteries, and morality plays and carried over into the professional theatres. Modern actors sometimes have a problem with this concept. Unless we are very fortunate, our first contact with "theatre" today will be either filmic or through television—totally passive forms in which no audience response is possible. Contact with "live" theatre is likely to be some form of "fourth-wall" realism in a darkened theatre where the actors are doing their best to make us believe that they are not actors at all but "real" people. Thus, the idea of being aware of the audience's presence, and even addressing it directly, is immediately foreign to a young student's sensibility. Raymond

Williams probably made the definitive comment: "It is as natural when on a stage before people to address them, as to pretend to carry on as if they were not there." It must certainly be seen as natural to the actor playing Shakespeare.

It must also be remembered that if Shakespeare's work does not call for a naturalistic approach in the sense of using a vernacular language and recapitulating the minor details of everyday life, it is still entirely "real" in requiring the actor to pursue real intention and react to real stimuli.

Playing the Verse.   The vocal qualities required in Shakespearean performance match those of physical movement. There is an energy, directness, strong sense of action, and a certain elevation. Modern speech often tends to be downward in inflection and inner-directed —we are concerned for our psychological responses. Verse is much more active;

Dynamic, contained and direct gesture. Donald Sage Mackaye as "Mad Tom" in King Lear.   *A Noise Within Theatre Company. Directed by Sabin Epstein.*

More contained than the Greek, but powerfully expressive gesture: Anthony Hopkins as King Lear. *British National Theatre. Photo by Nobby Clark.*

the beat moves it onward and upward with the energy of its highly compact imagery. Because of this compression it is important to keep the thought-line of the speech very clear. Do not elaborate. Clarify. This is particularly true whenever the poetry declares itself and becomes deliberately rhetorical. Play against this—go for the sense and intention. There is a danger with Shakespeare that actors adopt a "tune"; they play the emotional effect they believe the speech should have on the audience. This creates a monotonous, unvaried tone that has nothing to do with the sense of the language. Playing the language not the emotional tone will engage and convince the audience.

Conversely, beware of over-logical analysis that can lose contact with the flavor of the words. While avoiding vocal attitudinizing and over-elaboration, the actor must also observe the fact that it is poetry that is being spoken. While controlling the speech, gathering it rather than scattering it—speaking as it were from the seat of one's pants—do not lard it with pauses or interjections in the cause of "naturalness." Shakespeare has included his pauses in the verse where he wants them. Avoid the modern acting habit (most prevalent in television soap opera) of taking "thought" pauses before speaking. In Shakespeare the thought is on and with the line; the fact of thinking and reflection is continued in the rhythmic pattern of the speech. Do not add words—they will adversely affect the meter. Robert Lewis, in *Stanislavsky and America*, tells of an actor who added "Y'know" to almost every speech. When Lewis asked him why, he was told that it made it more "natural"; that was the way the actor spoke. To this Lewis responded: "Well, you aren't going to be able to say 'Y'know, to be or not to be.'" As Peter Brook has put it: "That line exists and it helps you; it doesn't change—you change."

While respecting the meter, don't get sucked into it (you won't if you go for the sense of the line), stressing the ends of each line in a rhythmical monotone. Yet it is verse not prose the actor speaks, with all the values of rhythms, imagery, and figures of speech. Think of the verse as being there to help the actor. To the Elizabethan actor it was a natural medium. Shakespeare did not write it as an obstacle course, but as a powerful means of theatrical communication. The actor must look at these lines as the only possible ones for his or her character in the situation. Through the agency of the lines the actor must make choices about the intentions and concerns of the character so that the lines as written are the only possible means of expressing them. Thoughts and feelings are explicit in the lines, and emotion is revealed through the structure of the speech. The actor must find the reason to express the sense of what the character is saying through the poetic elements of the verse.

Soliloquy. The soliloquy has special problems of focus for the actor. It can have different qualities and serve various functions, but it is likely to fall into four categories, each of which calls for a slightly different technique. There is what might be termed the introspective or contemplative soliloquy, in which the character is trying to resolve an issue or is reflecting upon the situation in philosophical terms. Hamlet's famous "To be, or not to be" falls into this category, as does Macbeth's "Tomorrow, and tomorrow, and tomorrow" (act 5, scene v). Here it is likely that the actor's focus will be inward: He will see images in his mind; there is less likelihood of any direct external focus, even in space.

Other soliloquies might be described as more actively reflective. There speakers are basically persons of action who are being troubled by a conscience. *Macbeth* has two examples of this: "If it were done when 'tis done," from which we have already quoted, and the dagger speech (act 2, scene i). In these the images will be placed in space; they are out in front of the actor, beckoning or driving him on, or forming obstacles for him to stumble over. Thus, the focus will be shifting, but directly fixed upon images the character sees outside himself.

The most direct form of soliloquy is that given to the audience. Iago frequently does this, most obviously, perhaps, with his "And what's he then that says I play the villain," (*Othello*, act 2, scene iii). Richard III also enjoys taking the audience into his confidence: The first speech of his play is almost a prologue, except that it establishes character as well as situation. *Lear's* Edmund (and indeed most of Shakespeare's villains) likes to get down and talk to the audience, telling them of his misfortunes, cunning, and witty knavery. Nor is this surprising when one remembers that the villains are the descendants of the medieval Vice characters, whose function, in the popular theatrical tradition, was to amuse the audience as much as disconcert the "good" characters. Speaking directly to the audience does not mean transfixing one poor soul in the eye, but talking to the audience in general as participants—other actors—in the play.

The last soliloquy technique is the use of an *objective correlative*. Shakespeare provides Hamlet with one in act 5, scene i, in what is more of an apostrophe than a soliloquy (he is not alone on stage). The objective correlative here is the skull of Yorick, which Hamlet addresses. If the playwright does not provide one, it can be useful to the actor to create one for himself in order to give a more direct purchase on or focus to the speech. Sometimes it may be an object on the stage, sometimes simply the actor's hand that seems to contain the image. A sword, or the sword hilt (which forms a cross) may also be used in appropriate circumstances. The actor's imagination and sense of the speech must be the guide here. Nor will the techniques described above be discrete. The actor may wish to employ more than one in a given soliloquy. We don't wish to dogmatize, simply to show possible approaches from which the actor may determine what best suits the needs of a particular speech.

Character and Humor. Actors who come to Shakespeare from work in modern, realistic drama often have problems coming to terms with the creation of character. They find lack of motivation, or inconsistency, or lack of biographical or physical detail on which to "build" a character. Some of these elements are, indeed, facts of Shakespeare's work, but they are problems for the actor only if he or she approaches the plays from the wrong perspective. Actors sometimes fail to recognize motivation because of ignorance of the Elizabethan approach to human psychology, or of Shakespearean dramatic conventions. Shakespeare was communicating an essentially imaginative and poetic, not literal, interpretation of human action. Character is not important in and of itself, only in furthering the action of the play and illuminating the passing of the human soul. It is this soul rather than psyche, passion rather than personal feeling, with which Shakespeare is concerned.

The theatrical space and the form of Shakespeare's plays create a continuous, swift, forward-flowing sweep of action. This is developed quickly: The story is always moving toward its climax, and there is little time for complex psychological exploration of character. Shakespeare does not stop to examine character; he displays it in action.

Nor would Shakespeare's actors or audience have understood what we mean by character today. It was not until the mid-eighteenth century that dramatic characters were listed in a play; before that time it was simply a list of actors. And even in the mid-nineteenth century the idea of character as a set of inner qualities was quite new. The Elizabethan actor presented the appropriate performance of his or her text, to serve the total living illusion of the play. Character analysis in psychological terms would have been completely mystifying: A character was defined by his or her function in the dramatic action. The audience was still steeped in the morality play traditions and would not ask why "Good Deeds" were good, or the Vice figure evil. That was their function.

The playwrights and the sensibility of the time dealt in opposing values of good and evil, personifications of God and Devil, the seven deadly sins, and the four basic humors. To take a simple example: Jaques in *As You Like It* is melancholy. No one in Shakespeare's theatre would waste their time asking, "Did he have an unhappy childhood?" "Is he a frustrated artist?" "Was he rejected by his first and only love?" It was his humor; it had to do with his liver. He would be expected to act in a certain way and have a particular view of life. To be melancholy was also his function in the play. He was part of a total pattern; he lent a particular poetic coloring that Shakespeare wanted. It is to these factors—his function, place in the larger pattern, and poetic coloring—that the actor must look when preparing to play Jaques, and not to his genes or childhood environment, which in any case we can know nothing of.

There is a certain relationship between the "essence" of a Shakespearean character and the mask of a Greek. The Greek mask, being physical and unchanging, is much more specific and concrete than the Elizabethan. But "essense" can serve the actor in a similar way, as a handle, a purchase, a starting point for his character. For the Elizabethan there was a direct correspondence between character type and character action, and between external appearances and internal qualities. Young men will be rash. Don't ask why Romeo falls in love: He is young, unstable, emotional; that's what young men do. A deformed person will be evil—look at Macbeth's witches and Richard III.

The four basic character humors worked in permutations with the passions. Love, pride, lust, ambition, envy—all were accepted human temperaments whose existence in a character the Elizabethans would take for granted, without asking for specific reasons

(a)   (b)

Essential attributes of character strongly but economically played in (a) Hamlet   *Yale Repertory Theatre. Photo by T. Charles Erickson* and (b) The Merchant of Venice.   *Shakespeare's Globe. Photo by John Tramper.*

or motivations. Unpromoted men would be given to envy, as Italians to revenge, and women to lust. These passions would be expressed in a recognizable fashion, not repressed or internalized. Feelings and behavior were on the surface; the Elizabethans had yet to hear of Freud or Stanislavskian subtext. They were interested in what the character did, how the passion moved him to action, and this is what gave typicality variety.

If we are ever in danger of trying to impose a twentieth-century conception of "realism" onto Shakespeare's work, we have only to remind ourselves that his women were played by boys. An audience that happily accepts such a convention would have no trouble with Iago's "motiveless malignity" (as Coleridge called it) or Othello's sudden jealousy. That the female characters were played by boys often seemed to give them a certain masculine authority and strength. Their sexuality is boyish; they love poetically, not physically. It is well to remember this, for too much emphasis upon the physical details of love can reduce and demean the larger qualities of Shakespeare's love relationships. The women in the tragedies are masculine in sensibility—Lady Macbeth, Reagan, Goneril—or have the strength to disobey the proprieties of a male-dominated society—Juliet, Desdemona, Cordelia. They are unusual, interesting women, whose mask of character owes not a little to their boyish players.

There is, then, a tangible essence to Shakespeare's characters. In a simple sense Macbeth is ambition, Lear is pride, Othello jealousy, Falstaff both the Roman braggart warrior and the medieval Vice, and Henry V nobility and right kingship. This gives a strong, central definition to character and ensured quick recognition by the audience.[5] But, of course, Shakespeare went much further than this. He created recognizable and complex human individuals from the medieval form. He was touched both by the humanistic sense of human uniqueness and by genius. He brought his own intuition and observation of human passions, motives, and actions to his characters and transmitted these through language, action, and form. Once again we have that integration of traditions, of seeming contrasts that typified the age: a strong central character trait given individuality in action. Shakespeare's characters are "complete" because he gives them traits that act well. The character is built to accord with the demands of the action, so every trait is necessary and actively expressed. This gives the impression of fully rounded characters, but their human definition is only what is required to further the action and passion of the play. The actor's prime task is to find the intention of the character, and how that character pursues it in action as defined by the structure, rhythms, and imagery of the text.

If we have heavily stressed the idea of psychological typicality, and motivation inspired by the necessities of the action, it is not because we do not recognize the sophistication of Shakespeare's characterization, but rather to shake the actor out of the modern sensibility that acting can be "real" and "honest" only if based upon detailed psychological analysis, personal "feelings," and subtextual motivations. "Typical" human behavior was perfectly real to the Elizabethans, and Shakespeare's drama is entirely real if it is taken as a theatrical event, with its own integrity, consistent conventions, and totally believable illumination of the human condition. If we look too hard for psychological motivation and ignore the demands of the poetic structure, language, and action, we will get a rather limited, pseudomodern character who has a problem

[5]Compare the way television news, interested in action, identifies persons it interviews: Joe Doe, "hostage"; Ann Smith, "victim"; Willie Jones, "stranded." It is the essence of the part played by the person in the action that is being reported.

with arcane speech. It is false to treat Hamlet as a living man rather than an element in a dramatic composition. There is no Hamlet outside of the play. It is equally invalid to ask how many children Lady Macbeth might have had. "I have given suck" must be taken at its value in the play: She has experienced maternal love, which lends greater force to her statement that she would dash out her child's brains before being as vacillating as Macbeth. Shakespeare does not bother to motivate when it is irrelevant to the action. In what has been described as "superb effrontery," he has Portia say in *The Merchant of Venice* (act 5, scene i): "You shall not know by what strange accident I chanced on this letter." It doesn't matter how she got it; the important thing is she did. Finally, everything we are saying is in the hope that no actor reading this book will ever remark, as a famous actor once did, "I could never play Othello, as I wouldn't have killed Desdemona"—a perfect example of the "naturalistic" fallacy of putting one's own emotions or psychological makeup before the action of the play.

Shakespeare has given the actor all that is needed in order to stimulate the imagination. If we look for subtext that isn't there or become involved with minutiae, we are in danger of reducing the stature of the characters to our own petty size and diminishing the impact of the tragedy. The characters are recognizably human, but through dramatic structure and poetic expression.

Character and Verse.   As we have suggested, a character is not just defined by what is said but how it is said: Why the character employs that particular structure of words and sounds. If we trace back the derivation of our term "personality" we find the Latin term *persona*, which was the name of the mask in classical drama; and *persona* itself means "through sound," giving the clear connection between the production of sound, from the language in

the text, and the delineation of the mask or character. We are briefly going to illustrate how the clues to character and performance are found in the language by looking at short speeches by very differing characters, and then look at some length at a speech from *Macbeth*.

In the play *Hamlet*, if we look at the language Shakespeare has given Hamlet himself, we are immediately struck by three things: significant use of soliloquy, complex nature of verse rhythms, and frequent use of prose. This would indicate a self-questioning, somewhat solitary individual who operates on many levels and in his use of prose deviates from the expected norm of a royal prince. And this is precisely what we find. Hamlet's basic humor would be melancholy, which tends to solitariness and introspection. Note, too, that he is dressed in black—the "typical" costume that might be expected of a melancholy humor. In the play, Hamlet adopts the mask of madness and, while wearing it, adopts prose speech, which becomes part of that mask. Madness is a deviancy, and Shakespeare deviates from the norm of verse to give it active force. Hamlet also adopts prose when speaking to Polonius, Rosencrantz, and Guildenstern—the gulls of the play. He does this at times to ridicule and demean them, at other times to show familiarity—which adds to the levels of his character and illustrates the use of language in depicting relationships.

In the same play, we have already suggested that Claudius's speech "And let the kettle to the trumpet speak," which comes at the end of the play, shows qualities of hyperbole, pomposity, and hollow sham. If we look at his very first speech in this play we find a structural consistency:

> Though yet of Hamlet our dear brother's
> death
> The memory be green, and that it is befitted
> To bear our hearts in grief, and our whole
> kingdom
> To be contracted in one brow of woe,

Yet so far hath discretion fought with nature
That we with wisest sorrow think on him
Together with remembrance of ourselves.

This is the first sentence, and the speech goes on like this for some forty lines. It is tortuous, flatulent, calculated, filled with sub-clauses—exactly the kind of speech one hears from politicians when their position calls upon them to pay empty homage to a situation—kiss babies and pat cows. There is an elaborate formality, a hyperbole that is geared to fooling people with sound. It is full of rhetorical figures: antinomes, alliterations, oppositions. The actor will find the character's intention in this situation quite clearly defined in the rhythm, shape, and sound of the speech.

Turning to quite a different character, we next look at part of the Nurse's first speech from act 1, scene iii of *Romeo and Juliet*:

Come Lammas Eve at night shall she be
    fourteen.
Susan and she, God rest all Christian souls,
Were of an age. Well, Susan is with God;
She was too good for me. But as I said,
On Lammas Eve at night shall she
    be fourteen;
That shall she, marry, I remember it well.
'Tis since the earthquake now eleven years,
And she was weaned—I shall never
    forget it—
Of all the days of the year, upon that day.
For I had then laid wormwood to my dug,
Sitting in the sun under the dovehouse wall.
My lord and you were then at Mantua.
Nay, I do bear a brain.

Again the speech goes on for some forty lines and the rhythm of it gives us an immediate sense of character. It is disjointed; full of short phrases, repetitions, stops and starts. It is a busy speech, which suggests a busy person—even if we don't go so far as to say busybody: a chatterbox. It is flat, not colorful in a rhetorical way, suggesting someone who is of the earth, living in the everyday world. A simple person whose life is demarked by festivals and events of nature, and with an equally simple faith in God, and acceptance of her status in this life. Somewhat scattered, a rag-bag of memories, wrapped up in a familial and mothering world.

Finally, we examine Lear's last speech, from which we have already quoted:

And my poor fool is hanged. No, no, no life.
Why should a dog, a horse, a rat have life,
And Thou no breath at all. Thoul't come
    no more,
Never, never, never, never, never.
Pray you, undo this button. Thank you sir.
Do you see this. Look on her. Look her lips,
Look there, look there.

We have already drawn attention to the fourth line with its trochees creating the funeral sound of a tolling bell. There is also the repetition of "no" in the speech adding to the sense of inevitability and emptiness. The building of mournful repetition is the feature of the rhythm of the speech through the first four lines. The second line probably starts with a trochee to emphasize "why," Lear's existential question that informs the whole play, and then it is strongly iambic to set up dog, horse, and rat in apposition to Cordelia's life. After the ritualistic sound of the "nevers," the fifth line becomes conversational. Lear is now simply a man. He is polite; "pray you" and "thank you" are in apposition and enclose the simple humility and need to which he has come. The two final lines have the quality of a moan: the repetition of "look" with its two open vowels "oo." The "looks" are further emphasized by the caesura in the sixth line, and the fact that they demand spondees, two stresses in a foot, in the final line: "Look there,/ look there." The total quality of the dramatic action of this speech is carried by the structure of the lines.

We are now going to look at Macbeth's speech from act 1, scene vii, the scansion of which was partly discussed in the section on the technical structure of language. First, here is the complete speech with suggested scansion:

Ĭf ĭt/ wĕre dōne/ whēn tĭs/dŏne thēn/ 'twĕre wĕll
Ĭt wĕre dōne/ quĭckly./ Ĭf thᵞ as/sāsŝi/ nātiŏn
Coŭld trām/mĕl ŭp/ thĕ cōn/sĕquēnce,/ aňd cātch
Wĭth hĭs/ sŭrcēase,/ sŭccēss;/ thăt bŭt/ thīs blōw
Mĭght bĕ/ thĕ bĕ-/ăll ānd/ thĕ end-/ăll hēre
Bŭt hēre/ ŭpŏn/ thĭs bānk/ and shōal/ ŏf tĭme
Wĕ'd jūmp/ thĕ lĭfe/ tŏ cōme./ Bŭt ĭn these/ cāsĕs
Wĕ stĭll/ hăve jūdge/mĕnt hēre;/ thăt wē/ bŭt tēach
Blōody ĭn/strŭctĭons,/ whĭch bĕ/ĭng taŭght,/ rĕtūrn
Tŏ plāgue/ thĕ' īnven/tŏr; thīs/ ēvĕn/ hāndĕd/ jūstĭce
Cŏmmēnds/ thĕ' īngre/dĭents/ of oŭr/ poisŏn'd/ chālĭce
Tŏ oūr/ ōwn lĭps./ Hĕ's hēre/ ĭn dōub/lĕ trūst:
Fĭrst ăs/ Ĭ ăm/ hĭs kīns/măn aňd hĭs/ sŭbjĕct,
Strŏng bŏth/ agaĭnst/ thĕ dēed;/ thĕn ăs/ hĭs hōst
Whŏ shŏuld/ agaĭnst/ hĭs mūr/dĕrer shŭt/ thĕ dōor
Nŏt bēar/ thĕ knĭfe/ mўsēlf./ Bĕsĭdes,/ thĭs Dŭncăn
Hăth bōrne/ hĭs fāc/ultĭes/ sŏ mēek/ hăth bēen
Sŏ clēar/ ĭn hĭs grēat/ offĭce/ thăt hĭs/ vĭrtŭes
Wĭll plēad/ lĭke āngĕls trūm/pĕt-tōngued,/ agaĭnst
Thĕ dēep/ dămnā/tĭon ŏf/ hĭs tā/kĭng-ŏff
Aňd pĭ/tў, lĭke/ ă nā/kĕd new/bŏrn babe,
Strĭding/ thĕ blāst,/ ŏr heav/eň's chĕr/ŭbĭm, hōrsed
Ŭpōn/ thĕ sĭght/lĕss cŏur/ĭers ŏf/ thĕ aīr
Shăll blōw/ thĕ hŏr/rĭd dēed/ ĭn ēv/erў eye,
Thăt tēars/ shăll drōwn/ thĕ wīnd./ Ĭ have/ nŏ spūr
Tŏ prĭck/ thĕ sĭdes/ ŏf mў īn/tĕnt, bŭt/ ŏnlў
Vaŭlting/ ămbĭt/ĭon, whĭch/ o'ĕrleaps/ ĭtsĕlf
Aňd falls/ ŏn thĕ/ ōthĕr.

In simple words, Macbeth wishes to kill Duncan and become king, but he is afraid of being found out. His ambition wrestles with his fear, to create vacillation and uncertainty. This desire for action versus fear of consequence is clearly shown in the structure of the first line and a half. There are three sets of equivalents: the repetition of "done" is active, falling like a blow, but this is qualified by "if," "when," and "then," and by "were," "twere," and "were." Thus, the balance of the line sets up the nature of the problem. This is then extended by the use of imagery and rhetorical devices. We have the antithesis of "assasination" and "consequence," and the repetition of "trammel up" by "catch," and the paronomasia of "surcease" and "success." To catch the consequences, bind them up would be to catch success, to tie up the deed neatly.

Macbeth returns to a series of active words in "blow," "be-all," and "end-all," but the consequences are still on his mind and he goes into a long examination of them. This has the effect of frustrating his direct action. The extended images that follow seem to "trammel up" his own ability to take action. The active words are being caught in an imagistic web of uncertainties.

Macbeth's main concern is that justice might catch up with him in this world. We have the repetition of "here" four times in the space of six lines, and the "even-handed" nature of justice means that it is likely to catch him. Duncan deserved justice, but justice to Duncan means justice to his murderer too. Once again Macbeth gets caught up in antitheses (which are, by definition, even-handed): "Host" balances "murderer," and "shut the door" equates with "bear the knife myself." The balanced nature of the argument is displayed in the structure of the line.

Macbeth's fear of the consequences takes over for the next ten lines. There is a complex, hectic imagery that shows Macbeth's mind running away with him as he tries to come to grips with his confusion. Images of innocence—angels and children—are mixed with images of headlong, screaming rush to destruction—riding a storm of keening, howling, swirling winds. The speech ends with a riding metaphor, but with a rhythmically declining fall, broken only by the image of "vaulting ambition."

Essentially Macbeth comes full circle in the speech. He starts by being unable to act quickly because of fear of earthly consequences; he finishes still anxious to kill Duncan, but even more afraid of the consequences. The images also come full circle, from "jump the life to come" to the ambition that "o'erleaps itself." "Jump" and "leap" suggest the man of action that Macbeth is.

However, he is a man of action afflicted with a fearful imagination. Thus, his will to action is opposed by imagined obstacles. The imagery and structure of the speech reveal this. It moves strongly and actively up to line 7, but is unable to complete the course of action because of the obstacles set out at lines 7, 12, and 17. To follow up the inherent riding imagery of the speech: The rider sets out wanting to complete the course but, unsure of himself and having had to clear three obstacles, presumes that he is likely to fall and decides not to go for the finish.

All of this reveals Macbeth's character. He is ambitious but uncertain of himself, a man of action whose fears affect him through his imagination—later he imagines both a dagger and the ghost of Banquo. Note that the images of fear in the speech are Christian, not Freudian. The speech embodies that sense of contrast that we have suggested is typical of the Elizabethan period and of Shakespeare's work. Humanistic, human ambition is opposed by medieval Christian ethics.

Another way of looking at the shape of a speech is to phrase it as seems indicated by the demands of breathing cadences, caesuras, punctuation, and scansion emphases. With

Macbeth's speech we would get something like this:

> If it were done
> When 'tis done
> Then 'twere well it were done quickly.
> If th' assassination could trammel up the
>   consequence
> And catch with his surcease
>   Success;
> That but this blow
> Might be the be-all and the end-all
> Here, But here,
> Upon this bank and shoal of time,
>   We'd jump the life to come.
> But in these cases we still have judgment
>   Here;
> That we but teach bloody instructions,
> Which, being taught, return to plague th'
>   inventor;
> This even-handed justice
> Commends th'ingredients of our poison'd
>   chalice
>   To our own lips.
> He's here in double trust:
> First, as I am his kinsman and his subject,
>   Strong both against the deed;
>   Then as his host
> Who should against the murderer shut the
>   door
>   Not bear the knife myself.
>   Besides,
>   This Duncan
> Hath borne his faculties so meek,
> Hath been so clear in his great office,
>   That his virtues
> Will plead like angels, trumpet-tongued,
>   against the deep damnation of
>   His taking-off;
>   And pity,
> Like a naked new-born babe, striding the
>   blast,
> Or heaven's cherubim, horsed upon the
>   sightless couriers of the air,
> Shall blow the horrid deed in every eye,
> That tears shall drown the wind.
>   I have no spur
> To prick the sides of my intent,
>   But only

Vaulting ambition,
Which o'erleaps itself
And falls
On
The other.

Setting out the speech this way will give the actor a strong physical sense of its shape and impress the phrasing and rhythms upon him. The shape of Macbeth's speech shows the strong through-line of thought carried by such words and phrases as "If 'twere done," "success," "here," "even-handed justice," "besides," "pity," and "falls." It also illustrates the obstacles, in the shape of larger phrases, to the through-line—particularly the largest phrase of all, which climaxes the confusion of the speech before the declining fall from "I have no spur" to "The other."

We have by no means exhausted the many ways of approaching Shakespeare's language, but we have tried simply to illustrate the point that the clues to Shakespeare's characters lie mainly in a broad understanding of the rhythms, structure, imagery, and verbal melody of the characters' speech. Sound equals sense; melody equals mask; character is displayed through language and in action.

Playing the Occasion.   Shakespeare's theatre was an occasion. We tend to have lost the sense of occasion today; in fact, we almost consciously work against it. We don't understand the social function of ceremony. We regard it as an unnecessary formality, and dressing for an occasion is seen as some form of "dishonest" mask behavior. Because of this we have lost a feeling for eloquence, life seen as poetry. Belief in life's colors, passions, faraway places, the forces of the imagination— witches, ghosts, the irrational—has been taken away from us by science. Electric light has removed many of the fears and fantasies from life and replaced them with television. Watching television is not an occasion. We must be aware of this suprahumanity in Shakespeare's work and not be afraid to manifest it. It is largeness not so much of manner as of spirit.

Yet for all its poetry, Shakespeare's theatre was still a rootedly popular one. It may have been conscious of heaven and hell, but it happened on this earth, in broad daylight, and between people. A direct chemistry could flow from actor to audiences—a robust, curious, imaginative people eager for physical and emotional experience, and for adventure. The theatre was intimate and epic, immediate and removed. Poetic imagination was linked to physical vigor. We must, as actors, be aware of the richness and variety of the occasion and let it inform our approach to performance.

The actor in performance had to match both the expectations of a vigorous, virile, and somewhat violent age, and the demand of the sweeping, onward drive and powerful passions of the dramas he was performing. A

Direct, virile approach to Midsummer Night's Dream by LaJolla Playhouse.   *Photo by Ken Howard.*

direct, robust, foursquare physical approach seems the obvious response. The actor was of humankind yet more than this. Firmly on this earth, yet halfway to heaven, the characters were touched by fate and drawn by the genius of a poet. The language the actor spoke, though rooted in human action, had transcendental power and lyrical grace.

It was a romantic form of acting—not extreme and decadent, but lively, brawny, passionate, direct. The actors were not afraid to project the stature of their characters, to deal in archetypal vices and virtues rather than peccadilloes and idiosyncrasies. There was power, poetry, and passion; there was a lyrical physicality that was derived from the sensibility of the age, inherent in the dramatic form, reinforced by the physical setting, and communicated through language and action.

EXERCISES, GAMES TECHNIQUES

Courtesies. Although we firmly believe that the performance of external manner is useless if not informed by both an understanding of why it is required (the sensibility of the period), and a strong sense of character mask, the character does work within a given social form. Therefore we are starting this section with a few specifics of Elizabethan social manner.

The Bow. Draw the left foot backwards, slightly turned out. Bend both knees, keeping the heels on the ground. At the same time the body bends forward from the waist with a straight spine and neck. The body weight moves partially onto the back foot, and the back knee is slightly turned out. If the bow is deep the back knee may touch the ground. At the end of the bow, the body comes erect, the weight moves onto the front foot, and the back foot is drawn in.

The Curtsy. Starting with feet together, draw the left foot back a few inches behind the right, keeping the foot flat and the body straight. Bend the knees and incline the body slightly forward with straight spine and neck. The knees turn outwards slightly and the left heel rises. At the end of the curtsy rise slowly and smoothly and replace the left foot beside the right.

Other major courtesies were as follows:

When doffed, the hat was swept down to the side during the bow (inside of hat to the thigh) or, in the presence of a superior, held under the arm.

The kissing of a woman's hand was done with a bow. The hand was never actually touched with the lips.

An informal greeting, kissing lip to lip, was quite frequent among the Elizabethans.

The kissing of one's own hand, which was then held out toward the person saluted, was used only for extreme reverence; it became more commonplace in the later-seventeenth-century court.

Arm clasps and strong physical embraces were common among men.

Exercises. The first few exercises are of a strongly physical nature, and they emphasize the necessity of leg purchase. They may be played as robustly and vigorously as the ensemble of players wishes, but they must always bear in mind that physical contact is not the purpose of the game but the necessary means to the achievement of the objective. The games are also good warm-up exercises and achieve high energy levels.

British Bulldog I. Players line up at one end of the space and have to walk as quickly and purposefully as they can to the other end; they may not run. There is one player in the middle who has to intercept them and take prisoners by lifting the walking players until both legs are off the ground. The captured player now joins the player in the middle. The game continues until all the crossing players have been

Elizabethan bow and curtsey.   *Drawing by Janis Martin.*

taken prisoner. When intercepted, players may not drop to the ground but should remain upright and try to keep both feet on the ground for as long as possible.

British Bulldog II.   Once again players line up at one end of the space with one player in the middle. All players fold their arms across their body. Now players have to hop on one leg to the other end of the space. They may change legs, but only one leg may be in contact with the ground at any one time. The player in the center has to intercept by knocking the crossers off balance. This is done with the folded arms. The center player must also hop when intercepting. The game continues until all players have been intercepted.

Shark Island I.   Draw a chalk circle in the middle of the space. The circle should be just large enough to accommodate all the players with a one-foot margin all around. The players all stand within the circle. They are castaways on an island, with just enough water for one person. The sea around is full of sharks. Players must try to jostle and push each other off the island. The game continues until just one player is left standing in the circle. There is an elaboration on the game whereby all the people pushed into the sea become sharks and from outside the circle try to pull the remaining castaways into the sea.

Shark Island II.   Draw a chalk circle somewhat larger than for the first exercise. All players inside should have learned one of Shakespeare's more active soliloquys—any of the chorus speeches from *Henry V* work well. Players try to jostle each other out of the circle with chests or shoulders—no arm pushing this time—while all are reciting the speech. The voice becomes jostled with the body and will be pushed into and come from interesting places. Also, the dynamics of the speech will be felt physically.

Shark Island III.   This time players form a circle by linking arms. The speech should be spoken again with each half of the circle pulling in opposite directions. The halves can be demarked at different points so every player gets to work with or against all other players. This helps to achieve an ensemble sense of the dynamics of language.

Cockfighting I.   Two players are within a chalked circle with hands clasped behind their backs. The circle should be no more than eight feet in diameter. The object is for a player to push the other player out of the circle using only one's chest—no other contact may be made. The game adds nimbleness of foot and strong-chestedness to leg purchase. The game may not be suited for women, but women might play it using their backs instead of chests—this would give a sense of the upright but not forward-thrusting strength of Elizabethan women.

Cockfighting II.   Same circle. Two players are holding a three-foot piece of wood between them, and are in a squatting position. Each player must now try to push the other out of the circle by thrusting with the stick. This puts an even stronger pressure upon leg power and agility.

Cock o'the Midden I.   Players should have an energetic speech at their command. The chorus in *Henry V* would do again or Henry V's "If we are marked to die we are enow," from act 5, scene iii; Hamlet's "O, what a rogue and peasant slave am I," act 3, scene i; Cassius's "Why, man he doth bestride the narrow world," act 1, scene ii of *Julius Caesar.* Place a solid six-inch plank across two levels about eight inches above the ground. The players are armed with rolled-up newspapers and, while saying the speech, try to knock their opponent off the plank. The exercise is good for focus, concentration, and physical use of language.

Cock o' the Midden II.   This time three or four eight-inch platforms are placed about eight feet apart in the space. A player stands on one of these levels and begins a speech. He or she is armed with a rolled-up newspaper. Two or three other players approach and, while saying a different speech, try to knock the first player off the level. If they succeed the first player retreats to the next level. The game goes on until the first player finishes the speech or is driven off the stage. While defending the space the first player must keep the sense and flow of the speech going: If the thread is lost the player must retreat and start over. The exercise gives a strong sense of occupying one's space on stage as well as the physical occupation of the language.

Letters.   Take a speech that is addressed to someone in the play and write it out as if it were a letter one were sending. It takes more thought and effort to write than it does to speak. The player should gain a strong sense of why the letter is being written (that is, why the speech is made), and why the particular words of the speech were necessary.

Telegrams.   We stressed that no matter how important it is to be aware of the structure, imagery, figures of speech, and other elements of Shakespeare's verse, it is still of primary importance that the through-line of thought be maintained. The intellectual sense of the speech must be clear to the audience. This won't happen unless the actor has gotten a strong purchase on it. There are a couple of ways actors can clarify the speech in their own mind. One is to write a synopsis of the speech in one's own words. The other is to write out the speech as if it were a telegram. The purpose of this, of course, is to reduce the speech to its absolute essentials, so that if one more word were removed it would lose meaning. Macbeth's speech in act 1, scene vii, which we have already worked on in different ways, would look something like this in telegram form:

> If done when done then done quickly. This blow end-all here jump life to come. But judgment here. He's here double trust. Kinsman host. Besides Duncan virtues plead pity. Every eye tears. I no spur but ambition. Which o'erleaps falls.

It might just be possible to remove another couple of words—"besides" or "o'erleaps," but not much more. It's an interesting exercise to decide which word you would delete if you couldn't afford the whole telegram. But the point of the exercise is that the sense is reduced to an absolute skeleton and becomes very clear to the speaker. Now, of course, the actor must go back to the entire speech and give it full value, but with a clearer sense of spine to guide him or her through it.

Poetic Palette.   Write out a highly imagistic speech and physically color the images. Use crayons or paint and let the feel of the images influence your choices. Avoid literalness. Forest images aren't necessarily green, nor are sea images blue. Be aware of the effect the image is trying to produce. When you have colored the whole speech see what kind of pattern has been created—it will look like an abstract painting. Look at the whole effect of the speech in visual terms. See whether the shades and tones blend, or whether there are images that stand out from the rest. This exercise, combined with the speech shaping discussed on page 72 and the telegram exercise, will give an actor a very strong and clear sense of the dimensions of a speech.

Verbal Circle I.   Players sit in a circle. Some familiar lines from Shakespeare are chosen, known to all the players or quickly learned by them. One player begins the speech by saying the first word. The player on the right continues with the second, the next player with the third, and so on around the circle. The object of the first reading is to pick up the quality of the speech received from the player before you, and carry it on. Repeat the exercise, this time attempting to change the quality of the speech when it reaches you. This may be done by altering pitch, volume, coloring, rhythm, or stress. Repeat several times, mixing up the circle or starting at different places so that all players get to handle different words and to use all the many possibilities of altering the line readings. Discuss the exercise in the following terms: which verbal qualities were most difficult to alter; what qualities, when changed, most significantly altered the speech; how far a player was swept into the rhythm of the speech as it came to him or her; what in the group's opinion became the optimum reading of the speech.

Verbal Circle II.   Repeat the exercise, this time illustrating your word with a gesture—even prepositions and conjunctions can be made physical. Then do the speech again with gestures alone. Discuss what gestures are unnecessary to the speech and what seem most appropriate in communicating the sense.

Body Language I.   Scan a speech and then beat it out with the feet as a dance, finding the rhythmical stresses of the feet with the feet, and consequently throughout the body.

Body Language II.   Again use a scanned speech. Now beat out the rhythm of the foot scansion on your own body: rub, pat, beat as the weight and rhythm suggest. This can also be done to a partner as he or she is saying the speech.

Body Language III.   Say a speech while carrying out aerobic exercises or any similar physical activity.

Body Language IV.   Two teams have a speech each. Mark out a basketball court in the space—any size will do. The teams now play a game of basketball, and each time a player has the ball he or she begins a line of the text and ends it as the ball is passed or a shot is taken. The rhythm of the line should be determined by the running, passing, or shooting. A whole physical range of vocal dynamics can be explored with hard passes, faking opponents,

touch shots, three-pointers, dunks, etc. When a pass is received the player must pick up and continue the line.

Kinetic Images I.   Players pair off and begin with a simple mirror exercise—performing physical gestures exactly copied by the partner. When concentration and fluidity are established, the game leader should throw some simple images at the pairs, such as birch trees, waving flags, fountains. The pairs now use these as a basis for the mirror exercise. When this is working, coach the pairs to split up and give the individuals more abstract or complex images to perform—yellow, Monday morning, vanilla ice cream with butterscotch topping. Allow the players time to explore and establish an image before moving on. When the players are committing themselves fully to the exercises and exploring with the whole body (this will need some coaching), start to introduce some literary images and images from Shakespeare's plays. Keep coaching players to avoid literal interpretation, to go for the poetic meaning of an image; they should let the image speak to their body, not to their mind. The point of the exercise is not to discover physical gestures for the specific communication of images, but to experience the images, so that the physical sense of them will inform the actor's speech, although he or she may well not use a gesture at all to illustrate an image in performance. This is an intense exercise, physically and emotionally, and should probably not be played for more than twenty minutes at a time.

Kinetic Images II.   Take a short speech and work through it silently moving around the space. Now voice the speech. Without sound, convey the speech to another player, to the roof of the building, to the back of the building. Choose a physical image for each sound. Create image groups and demonstrate them physically with the entire body. Add sounds, not words; create sound groups and work through speech with sounds and physical images. Now work the speech with its own words. Finally, communicate the speech to another player; the roof of the building; the back of the building. This is an exercise for the connection of vocal and physical images and the filling of space.

Kinetic Images III.   Create a dance out of a speech. Players use a Shakespearean speech that might take two or three minutes to speak. Choose a dance style—classical ballet, modern jazz, Spanish, disco. One player now reads the speech while the other players interpret it according to the chosen style. Repeat the exercise in different styles of dance. Make sure the players stick fairly close to the form of dance chosen and don't go off into abstractions—the fact of the dance form gives a structure and discipline to the exercise. Finally, let the players interpret the speech with any combination of the dance forms that seems appropriate. When each player has choreographed the speech, have him or her perform it to the other players while speaking the lines. This gives the players a tremendous experience of the physical shape, rhythms, and dimensions of the speech.

A Day in the Life of . . .   This is a soliloquy exercise. Players should sit in a half circle. In the middle are a few props, such as a chair, table, pen, paper, pipe, and cigarettes. Each player in turn goes into the middle of the half circle and tells an amusing anecdote about something that has happened to him or her. This will be much in the manner of the stand-up comedian. Now each player in turn gives a two- to three-minute synopsis of the previous day, in the following different ways:

1. as a report, as if a witness talking to a jury;
2. as if thinking aloud about the day's events;
3. as if writing a letter to a distant friend;
4. as if concerned by the events and actively visualizing and considering them;
5. as if musing upon the events, telling them to the dog or a glass of whiskey.

The players may sit, stand, lean on the table, move around, or adopt any other manner, but they must keep their focus upon the events, be consistent in their chosen manner, and retain an awareness of the players sitting around them. Finally, players should do the exercise using whatever mode of delivery seems appropriate to the nature of the events being related. Thus, several modes may be employed in one synopsis. It is often useful to follow up the exercise by doing a Shakespearean soliloquy. In doing so, the actors will find themselves more aware of the variety of ways it may be approached.

Everyday Shakespeare I.   Players sit comfortably in a circle and hold a conversation by passing sentences around. Each sentence must scan as an iambic pentameter, but it must be completely prosaic in its content. For example:

A: How would you like another cup of tea.
B: Why yes. That's very kind of you to ask.
C: I take mine black so don't add any milk.
D: Where did you spend last Summer? At the beach?

And so on. As the exercise continues, players will get more comfortable with the ease of speaking the verse, and more sophisticated in their use of it, in sharing lines and continuing thought patterns.

Everyday Shakespeare II.   While speaking a piece of verse, the actor performs some mundane tasks such as making coffee, shaving, mending a fuse, washing up, etc. This should be done in three ways:

1. By performing the task casually as counterpoint to verse.

2. The task is the prime action and the verse fits in.
3. Find every opportunity in the speech to combine the active nature of the verse with the physical actions. For example, if one were mending a fuse to "Now entertain conjecture of a time" chorus, "creeping murmur" and "poring dark" illustrate the tentativeness of the approach. "Fire answers fire" could suggest testing the fuse, "piercing" the use of a screwdriver to fix it, etc.

This is a further exercise in taking the mystery out of verse speaking, and it is a comfortable way of discovering how sense and active image combine.

Humor Game.   As we have already suggested, Elizabethan psychology was based upon a set of humors, the balance of which determined the basic way in which an individual was likely to act. This was also used as a core of character or a basic mask for *dramatis personae*. The humor game accustoms actors to using the humor qualities as a foundation for the creation of character. Players should begin by walking in space, concentrating upon a good, easy body alignment. They should then be coached to perform simple domestic activities—sweeping the floor, washing windows, making a bed, and so on. The coach now suggests particular humors: melancholy, phlegm, sanguinity, choler. The players continue the domestic activities, but the work is now affected by the nature of the humor. Coach the players to become aware of how the humor is affecting their rhythms and how those physical rhythms affect the way they feel about the situation. Keep the exercise simple at first so that players gain a quick experience of the quality. Now set up a simple situation: a hotel where a party arrives to find there has been a mistake in booking and no rooms are available. Let the players draw from cards that have the names of the humors on them.

They must now play out the situation in a character based upon their humor. The basic humors might manifest themselves as follows:

MELANCHOLY: We might have expected this.
PHLEGM: O well, let's make the best of it.
SANGUINITY: There's probably a better place just down the road.
CHOLER: Where's the manager? I'll wring his neck.

As the scene develops so will the character. And the players will make discoveries about how a person with a basic humor will act in the situation. They will develop certain rhythms and responses to the other characters in the situation. As they make choices and decisions they will be developing much fuller characters. However, the characters will be based upon the original humor and the actor will not need to know more about it than demanded by the situation. The character will be a function of action within the situation. When the exercise is concluded, it should be discussed in terms of the discoveries made by the players about their characters' rhythms and responses, and in terms of just how much they needed to know about the character to operate within the scene. Probably the choleric players discovered abrupt, fast rhythms and quick-tempered responses. The phlegmatic players may have found steady, flowing rhythms (the element associated with phlegm is water) and a somewhat easygoing manner. Having made these discoveries, the players may test their developing character in other situations with gradually fuller and more sophisticated responses. The entire function of the exercise is to examine how the assumption of a particular humor will produce a set of physical responses in a situation. These responses will themselves produce feelings that will influence physical action. This is an economical approach to the development of Shakespeare's characters—through an understanding of their humors, their objectives, and the part they play in the action pattern of the drama.

PLAYING THE STYLE

We are going to look at the characters of Othello and Iago from *Othello* to show how the actor can employ the above discussion and techniques in approaching a Shakespearean character.

Othello. We are not given a lot of facts about Othello. We are told he is black, a Moor, which is not a territorially specific definition in Shakespeare's time. Nor is he given a specific age, although he suggests he is past the sexual heat of youth, and the fact that he is the general of the Venetian army indicates the prime of middle life. He is a warrior, claims royal lineage, and has been a man of action rather than a politician. He is much traveled, which obviously impressed the young white girl he has married.

He sees himself as a noble man of action; he is aware how much the state needs him, speaks of "My parts, my title and my perfect soul"; and he takes pride in these facts as well as the fact that Desdemona chose him to wed.

Only Iago has negative things to say about him, and these are related to the fact that he is black. This is equally Brabantio's concern in not wanting Desdemona to marry him. It is not his personal qualities but his strangeness. This is an important fact for the actor; it may seem redundant to stress it, but the most immediate thing about Othello's physical mask is that it is different from everyone else. He is different in look, background, and sensibility. He is referred to as "The Moor," a curiosity.

If strangeness is one quality of Othello's mask, pride must be added to this. He is a noble egotist. This is not necessarily bad. He has every right to be proud of his background, his achievements, his soldierly success, and, strange though he is, Desdemona's choice of him as husband. But Othello's egotism borders on the edge of vaingloriousness; and this makes him vulnerable, because he believes he is invulnerable. As a type, or humor, he could be traced back to the Braggart Warrior, whose pomposity and false egoism is pricked in many comedies. As this is a tragedy, Othello is a "noble" egotist, and the undoing is much more cruel and fatal.

It is when the simple nobility of his pride comes into conflict with the uncertainty inherent in his strangeness that Othello's vulnerability appears. And it is at this seam that Iago picks so cleverly. Othello's through-line might be said to be "to live as if he were the same or better than the aristocracy of Venice." His major obstacle is, very simply, that he is different.

When we examine Othello's language we get a clear sense of both strangeness and pride. The first thing one notices about Othello's speech is its highly colored, rhetorical nature. This is not a man who uses small words or simple iambic pentameter. His syntax has an architectural stateliness to it. There is an extravagant baroqueness that makes him seem to be orating even in simple situations. He uses the vocative *O* a great deal, as well as words containing the vowel o—the fullest vowel in the English language—of which there are two in his name. This gives his speech a full-chested resonance, a sonorous sound. On the one hand, this is consistent with a man of large emotions and open mind. On the other hand, it draws further attention to his strangeness. Words such as "Anthropophagi," "Propontic," "Hellespont," all containing "o's," make him sound like a stranger, a man from different and mysterious climes. To Iago, Othello's language is full of "bombast circumstance," which may reveal his sense of egotism, or be the excessive deliberation of someone speaking an unfamiliar tongue while wishing to assume a formal equality with his listeners.

For all the orotundity of Othello, the simple sweep of his language has an almost childlike ingenuousness. He is innocent of any political machination and works on instinct and direct response. He does not intellectualize, or try to reason things out. He is credulous; he trusts, and then just as easily mistrusts when Iago undermines his innocent instincts with villainous thoughts.

It is interesting that when under Iago's pressure, Othello breaks down in act 4, scene ii, so does the nature of his speech. The architecture of his speech is shattered into short phrases, small words, and abrupt rhythms. Then, when he recovers his self-image and pride at the end of the play, his language recovers its romantic imagery and reinforces the isolated nobility of his death.

Othello is clearly a man of size and stature with a strong forward energy center in the chest: the seat of the heart and the lungs from whence comes his sonorous rhetoric. There are probably lesser centers in the shoulders—important to a warrior—and the legs that support his stately carriage but finally collapse, as does his language, under the pressure Iago brings to bear upon the vulnerable strangeness of Othello's "perfect soul."

Iago.   Turning to Iago we find he is almost everything Othello is not. This contrast between them is, of course, both the conflict in and crux of the play. Despite the fact that he is more devious, we know more about Iago than we do about Othello. He is a professional soldier, twenty-eight years old, and married to Emilia. He is Othello's Ancient—third in command—having been passed over as second in command. Because of this he harbors a grudge against Othello. He tells us he doesn't like "arithmeticians," educated men who prattle without practice: This refers to Cassio, who became second in command. He is consciously devious, a mask wearer: "I am not what I am"; "Show out a flag and sign." He does not hold

human life in high esteem, and he has a cynical view of human nature: "Preferment goes by letter and affection"; "Virtue, a fig." He is equally cynical about women's lusts and fidelity: "Go to bed to work"; "A thing for me—it is a common thing."

One of the crucial facts about Iago is that no one mistrusts him. The terms most characters use of him is "honest." This is repeated countless times in the play by most of the other characters. He is also seen as "just" and "kind." The actor must obviously present this facade to the world: no sly and insinuating villainy in the public eye. Iago tells only us, the audience, he is a villain, which adds to the irony and humor in our watching him go about his business on the stage. By getting us on his side, or at least into his confidence, he makes us examine our complicity in the consequences of his deeds.

In language, the very quality of Iago's speech is differentiated from Othello's by every means. Except for the soliloquies he speaks almost entirely in prose: simple, easy, acute, and cynical. His language is direct and filled with images of "poison," which he uses four times; "plague" and "pestilence." With these images go animalistic and sexual expressions: snorting, scurvy, tupping, hot, prime, act of sport. He also employs images of catching or ensnaring in a "web" or "net." Shakespeare gives Iago a fascinating oath, "By Janus." Janus is the Roman household God with two faces—an instructive expression for a mask wearer.

As we have noted, Iago has a good deal of direct address to the audience. This gives us a clue to one part of his character typicality: he belongs to the Medieval Vice tradition, a figure part rogue, part clown who faced the audience with the dangerous attractiveness of evil. This accounts for the humor in Iago; the bluff, good-natured soldier, about whom the images of sex, wine, and fighting are not more than to be expected of the man who has made his way through the ranks and has deserved his promotion. This easy relationship with the audience has the dramatic function of letting them see both his faces. The other face is that of the calculating Machiavel who holds life cheaply and revenge dear, and who uses sex and wine to commit mortal sin in a cold, unrepentant manner. The two masks fit well together and allow Iago to draw both the audience and Othello into the net of deceit that brings about the play's tragedy.

His energies would seem to be centered in the head—a calculating energy—and the legs—a nimbleness seems to be one of his qualities. A secondary center might well be in the groin, supporting his sexual prurience.

Rehearsing. In building the character masks of Othello and Iago in a rehearsal situation, both *Cockfighting* exercises would be a good starting point. Not only are these highly physical and, therefore, both good warm-up exercises and suited to the martial profession of the characters, but they also allow the actors to explore the physical tensions that come to be manifested between the characters during the play. Just how hard does Iago push or pull, and how does Othello respond? Equally, the *Cock o' the Midden* exercises explore this physical tension in the relationships and add the maneuvering for territory in space.

Added to this the *Telegram* and *Poetic Palette* exercises would be useful to Othello— the first to clarify the through-line of his speeches and to see what their direct intention is beneath the rhetoric. The second exercise will show the color/shape of the speeches and provide indications as to Othello's character through size, shading, and grouping of the images he uses. The actor will find a considerable number of sea and water images, which fits the sense that he is from distant parts, and the swelling rhythms of his speech.

Iago, on the other hand, with his directness will probably find the *Letter* exercise most

Locked in their immortal struggle: Othello and Iago in a production of *Othello* directed by John Harrop.

useful. It is a more personal self-expression that will encourage the actor to examine the nature of Iago's self-disclosures and the intentions behind his choice of words.

All of the *Kinetic Images* exercises will help the actors to explore the physical nature of the language. *Kinetic Images III* especially should get the actors in touch with the basic rhythms of their own character, and to appreciate the other characters' rhythms and how to respond to them. In this connection it could be interesting to have actors read each other's speeches from which the dances are created. This will give actors a sense of how each character affects the responses of the other.

A Day in the Life of . . . will help Iago to deal with the various levels of his speeches to the audience, and both actors could benefit from *Everyday Shakespeare II*. Othello might play this with Desdemona, and Iago with Emilia, to gain a sense of the domesticated nature of their relationships.

The *Humor Game* is fundamental to this approach to playing Shakespeare's characters. Actors shouldn't approach the game by feeling that they have to be right the first time in choosing the exactly appropriate humors for their character. One of the virtues of a game-playing technique is that discovery comes through physical exploration and imagination. Actors may try opposing humors in the same situation, especially with Iago, who is a dissembler: How true and comfortable does an honest and optimistic through-line feel, and how does it fit with a more choleric and mean-minded intention? The function of the humor approach is not to create a one-dimensional character, but to take a clear and direct attack upon the role; an energetic starting point based upon how the character's intentions are revealed in the language of the play and the patterns of their action. Actors take the discoveries they make in simple physical terms by playing the game and testing them against the text; finding how and where they fit, and where adjustments have to be made so that the rhythms of the language and the physical rhythms of the character become one.

The physical approach to playing style lends itself well to the two crucial scenes in *Othello*, act 3, scene iii, and act 4, scene i, in which Iago is first sowing uncertainty in Othello's mind as to Desdemona's fidelity, and then encouraging him to take revenge. In the first scene Iago is tempting; in the second he is goading. Both of these intentions may be turned into physical exercises. In the first scene Othello is being played like a fish on a line: Iago can have a piece of cord tied to Othello with which he tests the dynamic in his speeches. When does he tug? How does Othello react? When does Iago move

away or pull in on the line? The energy of every line and its intention will be physically felt by both players. They cannot get away from each other and hide behind empty line readings; the intention of every line must be physically manifested. The language can be tested and played with until a pattern evolves, which satisfies the actors in terms of their characters' intentions in the scene.

The second scene has more the shape of a bullfight. Iago is the toreador and Othello the increasingly maddened bull. Here Iago could use a cape and a padded stick to test the rhythms and intentions of his lines. When is he literally goading Othello and how hard? When is he simply trailing his cape? How does Othello escape and respond to this attack? When does he evade; when does he charge? At whatever level the game is played, the actors finally return to the language. The language shape of the scene has provided the basis for the game, and when the cords, capes, and padded sticks are put aside it is the language that will contain the energies discovered through the practical means. The language contains the style; the style must manifest the language.

Here, at the end of the chapter, let us briefly reaffirm that the actor's process is an understanding of those aspects of the period that influenced the spirit, thought, and practice of the playwright and that became intrinsic elements of the playwright's text. With this understanding, actors discover the clues contained in the images, rhythms, and shape of the language, which reveal the character's intentions, as they play their part in creating patterns of action in the scenes, and the scenes build the structure of the play's action. Actors should always bear in mind that they need do no more than discover and play fully what is given. Shakespeare wrote well-rounded plays; and his characters exist only to serve that intention.

SUGGESTED READINGS

Aykroyd, J. W., *Performing Shakespeare*. New York: Samuel French, 1979.

Barton, John, *Playing Shakespeare*, New York: Methuen, 1985.

Berry, Cicely, *The Actor and His Text*. New York: Macmillan, 1988.

Bertram, Joseph, *Acting Shakespeare*. New York: Theatre Arts Books, 1960.

Brown, John Russell, *Discovering Shakespeare*. New York: Columbia University Press, 1981.

David, Richard, *Shakespeare in the Theatre*. New York: Cambridge University Press, 1978.

Sher, Anthony, *Year of the King*. London: Chatto and Windus, 1985.

Styan, J. L., *Shakespeare's Stagecraft*. Cambridge: Cambridge University Press, 1967.

Thomson, Peter, *Shakespeare's Theatre*. London: Routledge & Kegan Paul, 1983.

II

Playing Comedy

The comic viewpoint is as necessary to our social well-being as is the tragic to our spiritual life. It brings a heightening of our social vitality. Comedy does not concern itself with the grand passions, with humankind striving with the gods, but rather with the details of everyday existence; men and women in conflict with other men and women in their more earthy and mundane circumstances. Comedy rejoices in the wearing of human masks, in playing with human posturings and shortcomings. Its focus is the upsetting and recovering of the protagonist's equilibrium; his or her triumph by wit, luck or strength; or acceptance of mischance by philosophical or ironical humor. Comedy ranges from the broadest, most knockabout form of physical humor to the most elegantly turned shafts of intellectual wit: low comedy to high comedy, farce to comedy of manners. The gradations along the spectrum are not discrete; the ingredients tend to become mixed in the middle. But whatever the mixture, the immediate sense of life force is its underlying rhythm, which gives it a common sensibility and organic form.

We are going to examine the two ends of the spectrum, comedy of manners and farce. Within farce we are going to include a discussion of *commedia del l'arte*, perhaps the purest and most atavistic expression of the comic mask. From *commedia*, farce draws its dynamic physicality, and comedy of manners its strong definition of social types.

There are certain fundamental conventions and techniques that will be found in any comedic script: exaggeration, aggression, incongruity, automatism are but some of them. They may be expressed in verbal or physical form, and just as the building of comic structures is carefully contrived, the playing of comedy is dependent upon a high level of technical expertise. David Garrick is credited with saying, "Any fool can play Hamlet, but comedy is a very serious business." Comedy tends to flirt with the potentially painful, and the need to keep the necessary balance, the right distance from the reality of pain—a light-footed, playful, yet absolutely serious approach—makes the playing of comedy perhaps the greatest test of an actor's ability.

4 Comedy of Manners

Colley Cibber as Lord Foppington.   *Courtesy of The Garrick Club, London.*

BACKGROUND

Historical. As its name suggests, *comedy of manners* is concerned with the social manners and attitudes of groups or classes of people who define themselves as superior, or at least different, by the following of very particular life styles based upon strict codes of behavior and taste. The most distinctive and complete expression of it occurred in England after the restoration of Charles II to the throne in 1660. Exiled during the period of the Commonwealth, Charles had been brought up in the French court, and when he returned to England he brought with him the code of manners of that court, as well as its sense of theatre as being a court entertainment. So, the two Restoration theatres that Charles allowed to operate in London—under William Davenant and Charles Killigrew—were geared to the taste of the small coterie of aristocrats who patronized the theatres and who expected to see their own life style portrayed on stage for their amusement while they displayed that life style as members of the audience.

Life and art precisely mirrored each other. The comedy reflected the court's concern for the presentation of the accepted social mask by which people were judged, and it dealt with the mores, patterns of behavior, and values of the self-involved aristocratic society.

Although the details of the mask of accepted social behavior have changed over time, the underlying sensibility remained constant. To take a simple example: The lace cuffs of the seventeenth century and the starched cuffs of the nineteenth century have a similar function; the flicking of the lace and the "shooting" of the starched cuff illustrate a similar sense of pride and self-display. The spectrum of comedy of manners from the Restoration through Sheridan, Wilde, and Coward is based in this common sensibility while reflecting the shifting of social power and privilege. In the eighteenth and nineteenth centuries the aristocracy was obliged to share its position first with the prosperous bourgeoisie and then with the professional middle class as portrayed by Noel Coward. Although the specifics of the external manner of these groups was affected by changing physical environments, the inner attitudes and sense of values remained remarkably similar over nearly three hundred years. Once the actor understands the nature of this manner beneath the mask, his or her task becomes the adaptation of the social mask—the shooting of the cuff rather than the flicking of the lace—to fit the different conventions of different periods.

Living as an Art Form. This is an aristocratic attitude that dates back to the Age of Chivalry and knighthood. It must be understood and accepted if the actor is to achieve the ease and comfort that go with the physical style of this form of comedy. The actor must not resist or comment upon the values of the social groups being portrayed because they seem to be unacceptable to a democratic age. If this occurs the style becomes either an empty, supercilious posing, which bores the audience through its lack of human identity, or a jaded pseudo-Brechtianism that completely destroys the humor in the play.

The aristocratic outlook was fundamental to the court society of Charles II. It is based in the divine right of the king to rule and, by extension, of the aristocracy to support him in this mission. In the hierarchical structure of a God-given social order it was the function of the lower classes to serve the upper classes, whose divine right it was not to work for a living. Thus, if a courtier did not inherit an estate (for land was the only acceptable source of income), it was important either to marry into one, to marry a fortune with which to purchase one, or to have one given by the king's favor.

The necessity of marrying an estate or a fortune is one of the principal plot devices of

Restoration comedy. As with kingship, so membership in the aristocracy was conferred by birth, and a gentleman's breeding was his major asset. He might cheat (though not at cards), run up debts, borrow, or even kill without losing claim to gentility, but he must not be seen to work for a living. As breeding was conferred by divine right, so the evidence of it—comporting oneself according to the accepted code of manners—must be displayed with effortless ease: "as to the manner born." To be seen to ape or copy a manner was a sure sign that one was not born to it. Thus, one of the main distinctions in Restoration comedy was between the true wit, who managed life with an effortless air of urbanity, and the false wit, who tried too hard to be

thought one of the charmed circle and became a butt of laughter.

The acceptable manner of the polite code had, of course, to be learned: the art of sitting a horse, lolling in a coach, dancing a minuet, writing a poem, paying court to a woman. But it had not to appear learned, for that would give a stiffness or an extravagance, and any form of excess was to be abhorred. The art of living had to be absorbed through the pores, as by osmosis, which could only come to one born to it. Sincerity, indulgence in emotion—these were not regarded as virtues. The inner man was judged by the outer manner, which was above all to show the controlled and polished mask of the gentleman. Sir George Etherege was known as "Easy," a

1888

THE HEIGHT OF MASHERDOM

'Well, ta-ta, Old Man! My People are waiting up for me, you know!'

'Why, don't you carry a Latch-key?'

'Carry a Latch-key! Not I! A Latch-key'd spoil any *feller's* figure!'

The importance to the gentleman of not spoiling the line of his clothes is satirized in this late-nineteenth century cartoon. *Reproduced by permission of* Punch.

(a)

(b)

The air of urbane, effortless superiority which distinguished an upper-class manner seen here from the seventeenth to the twentieth century in productions of: (a) *The Misanthrope* by the Mark Taper Forum, Los Angeles; (b) *She Stoops to Conquer* by the British National Theatre; (c) *The Madras House* by the British National Theatre; (d) *Design for Living* by A Noise Within directed by Sabin Epstein.   *Photo by Craig Schwartz.*

great compliment of the day. Congreve let it be known that he would rather be remembered as a gentleman than a playwright. To write plays was a way to court preferment, but it was to be regarded as the exercise of gentlemanly wit—an amusing hobby rather than a profession, which smacked too much of work.

Even among those for whom work has brought success, the acceptance of the superiority of the gentlemanly way of life was a major social force and, in Britain, the nineteenth century saw a large expansion of the public-school system[1] as a result of the desire of successful industrialists to turn their sons into gentlemen. Just as the educational system in the United States is responsible for turning the sons and daughters of immigrants into good Americans, with the sense of values that

entails, so the British public school took up, preserved, and spread the gentleman's code derived from the seventeenth century.

The "amateur" gentlemanly sensibility of the British upper class continues down through the twentieth century. [2] Professionalism was associated with having to work at something, as opposed to the assumption of being able to do it by divine right. The ruling classes had to evince effortless superiority in order to assure themselves of their God-given ascendancy. Until the middle of the twentieth century the English international cricket team was captained by an amateur, who did not need to be paid to play but made it a gentlemanly hobby.

[1]The public school is the equivalent of the American prep school, a private, fee-paying institution.

[2]*Upper class* is taken to mean the group that exercised social power and adopted the aristocratic tradition of manners and sensibility. By the nineteenth century, however, many of the group found their origins in successful entrepreneurs of the Industrial Revolution.

(c)

(d)

The gentlemanly manner had such significantly trivial manifestations as the wearing of a pocket handkerchief—it should have a slightly careless appearance not too precisely achieved—and the leaving undone of the bottom button of the waistcoat to give the look of correct casualness—not too contrived, not too exact.[3] Only deep-red carnations were worn with a dinner jacket; pens should never be seen in the breast pocket of a jacket (this would suggest that work was more important than the line of the clothes), and a gentleman was never seen carrying a parcel—the presumption being that there were servants divinely ordained to do this.

There are a myriad of external expressions of this code of cultivated ease, urbanity, and indolence, but the important fact for the actor is to understand and assume the sensibility. This will enable him or her to display the essence of the manner rather than attempt to imitate the ideal.

Social Mores and Attitudes. Certain specific values tend to be common to all comedies of manners and reveal the prime concerns of the social coterie. The importance of the ownership of land has already been mentioned. It was first a source of income at a time before commercial interests predominated, and then it became a mark of social standing for the successful merchant. However, if it was important to own land, it was equally important not to live entirely in the country. In the seventeenth century, society was essentially court-oriented, and to live in the country was by definition to be an unfashionable clod. One of the most famous Restoration come-

dies, *The Country Wife,* deals with an old rake, who has retired to the country because he can no longer stand the competition of London society while his innocent, country-bred wife is quickly captivated and corrupted by the lascivious manner of the town. Again, in act 4 of *The Way of the World,* Millamant tells us: "I nauseate walking; 'tis a country diversion; I loathe the country."

As both communications and facilities improved, the country gradually became acceptable as a place of weekend retreat. However, London remained the center of the social season. The interview between Lady Bracknell and John Worthing in act 1 of Oscar Wilde's *The Importance of Being Earnest* bears witness to the consistency of the attitudes still operating in the upper-class society of the late nineteenth century. With regard to land, Lady Bracknell acknowledges the position it still affords, but this is tempered by the difficulties

Artificiality and Nature seen together in a production of *Jacques and His Master.* *Los Angeles Theatre Center.*

---

[3]This was a later development, said to have been an imitation of Edward VII, who, ironically, became too corpulent to do up the final button. Another royally induced convention was the wearing of wigs in the seventeenth century, said to have been in imitation of Louis XIII, who adopted one when he lost his hair.

created by the land and death duties imposed by a gradually democratizing society.

Though Lady Bracknell first deals with the economic matters that had priority in society matches, she soon turns to birth. The satire here is so broad as to reach farce proportions when John Worthing admits to being found (in a handbag) rather than born, and he attempts to compensate for this by specifying the particular railway line where it happened. Lady Bracknell thunders that "the line is immaterial." Again, a fine piece of comedy of manners by Wilde; in society marriages, the particular "line" of a family was often very important.

Land, town versus country, marriage and birth are still the concerns of comedy of manners after more than two centuries. The amateur sensibility is equally evident. Lady Bracknell does not approve of anything that tampers with natural ignorance, a satirical comment on the upper classes' divine right to govern by instinct rather than knowledge and effort. Although the play contains some satire on the idea of love in marriage—Gwendolen being able to marry John only if his name was in fact Ernest—both it and Sheridan's eighteenth-century play *The School for Scandal* (which otherwise takes a similar perspective on upper-class society) have a sentimentalized attitude toward male-female relationships, compared with that of the seventeenth-century comedies.

The court society of Charles II took a somewhat Hobbesian view of life: The human was a creature of animal passions and instincts, the amoral pursuit of pleasure was the true aim of existence, and the person who could laugh at life most wittily was the winner of life's ephemeral and somewhat cynical stakes. Thus, carnal pleasure was highly prized, and the sexual chase was the great sport of the day.

Part of this attitude came as a strong reaction to the Puritan morality that had held Britain in thrall for the previous twenty years and had severely repressed all physical appetites: Of the Puritans it was said that they opposed bearbaiting not because it gave pain to the bears, but because it gave pleasure to the spectators. Part of it was also a reflection of a major philosophical issue of the day. The period was on the cusp of the Age of Reason, and Cartesianism was to lead to a new scientific perspective on the human being, which challenged the values of the Christian morality. There was opposition between humankind perceived as a superior moral creature, and as an animal born to the amoral pursuit of carnal appetites. The Restoration mind-set was, then, full of tensions: faith versus reason; soul versus animal nature; ethics versus science; courtly love versus physical passion. The easiest tension to resolve was sexual. Sexual license supported the sense of liberation from a Puritan moral structure; but that freedom also locked the individual into a world that had no meaning beyond hedonism and self-interest.

To some degree the court circle might be likened to the situation of young students when they first enter a university. They don't have to earn a living, they are freed from parental restrictions, and they are suddenly set free upon the sexual cookie jar. It may be some time before, amid the delights of the new-found irresponsibility, they have to come to terms with themselves and discover values that will outlast the ephemeral—however varied—thrills of the sexual chase. There was *some* feeling in the Restoration period that love and caring should be a part of the human condition and that there should be values superior to the satisfaction of sexual appetites. But, caught as it was upon the cusp of new ideas, it was an age that was uncertain of values and mistrustful of the differences between reality and appearances. The emphasis upon masking throughout the period represents this sensibility. The stronger was the sense that humankind was merely a creature of lusts and appetites; the greater was the need to keep up a ceremonious external manner to prevent the world falling into an anarchy of sensuality. Civilized appearance had to mask brute desire.

The greatest tension surrounded the idea of marriage. Marriage was necessary to most young aristocrats in order to increase or protect their estates and to continue the line of their family name. It was necessary to most young women as the only future open to them: to free them from parental tutelage and give them some position in society as wife and mother. But, especially in this period, marriage was regarded as a necessary misfortune that marked the end of the sexual adventures that seemed to bring the major satisfaction in life. Hence, marriage became an economic contract and love was not of the essence. Nor was there the real possibility of divorce. So, under the necessary mask of marriage, both men and women pursued each other sexually for amusement and cursory gratification. It was a game, like cards, horse racing, or going to the theatre. Whoever won with the least effort and most wit was the model to be respected.

If women were for company in bed, and a witty woman more prized than a dull one, for companionship a man sought the company of his fellows: at cards, in the hostelries, and in other social situations in the male-dominated society. The values of comedies of manners reflect this sensibility well into the twentieth century, where the first breakdown of these presumptions may be seen in the plays of Noel Coward, written when women had achieved some measure of social and political emancipation after World War I. The society Coward depicts and satirizes is attempting to reject the manners and mores handed down to it and to discover some way of navigating in the shifting social seas of its time. In many ways the general sensibility was a throwback to the seventeenth-century Restoration period. A hedonism was abroad that, though neither as savage nor as urbane as the court of Charles II,

placed a frenetic emphasis upon indulging in earthly pleasures and throwing off the restrictive moral mask of the Victorian period. The social ambit was now essentially professional middle class, still desperately clinging to a gentlemanly manner while dealing with drugs, divorce, and homosexuality. The surface gloss hid unease; the casual manner betrayed uncertainty. Comedy of manners would in the future have to reflect a different kind of social mask—the faceless face of an increasingly classless society.

Realism of the Day.   Possibly the most difficult problem today for the actor approaching comedy of manners is the presumption of artificiality that has grown up around it. All too often performances replace manner with mannerism, and style with affectation. Actors impose a superficial gloss upon the play to compensate for their inability to recognize the textual clues to the style. Actors tend to make judgments from their everyday circumstances and condemn the plays for lack of truth and reality because they demand behavior different from the actors' own. There is, however, more than one possibility of natural and truthful behavior—it can be a question of perspective. Truth for the actor must be that of the event in which he or she is involved. An actor is not required to present truth as he or she feels it, but to motivate action truthfully in terms of the demands of the characters represented. With comedies of manners the external attitudes are a true reflection of social reality. Before we dismiss them as having no reference to our understanding of reality we should remember that the frank acceptance of the sexual chase is just as real as disguising it with other conventions: Courtship in the Restoration theatre and the singles bars of the late twentieth century are both grounded in the same human truth. The use of stage conventions such as asides, and the frank acknowledgment of the audience's presence is just as real as "realism's" fourth wall. The assumption of a polite manner and the use of elaborate social courtesies are just as real as the adoption of an offhand manner and ignoring the world behind the aural mask of a Walkman.

Comedies of manners are great theatrical games made out of ever-present human truths. Actors should embrace and revel in the artifice, the conventions, the language, and the wit that, while displaying the reality of another day, create a dynamic theatricality in our own.

INTRINSIC DEMANDS

Space and Social Settings.   The Restoration stage made no pretense at being other than il-lusionistic, a painted theatrical reality, but a reality nonetheless. The raked stage with its perspective of painted flats leading up to a backdrop to represent St. James Park would have seemed as much a miracle of realism to the audience as Antoine's use of real sides of beef on stage was to seem two centuries later. The use of this groove-and-shutter technique had the further advantage of quick set changes allowing for a continuous flow of the quick-paced comedy.

The perspective effect kept the actor downstage—the closer the actor is to the backdrop the more the illusion is destroyed. This gave a central focus to the action, which was reinforced by the apron stage that allowed close contact with the audience and put the

Raked, perspective space of the Baroque stage seen in the Operhaus, Bayreuth.   *Verlag Georg D. W. Callwey.*

actor in the best light. The sense of pictorial realism with a central thrust toward the audience was completed by the proscenium arch that framed the scene and created the effect of a picture of the times. The downstage focus and use of apron facilitated both direct address and asides to the audience whose presence was accepted as part of the event.

The settings depicted on stage further added to the sense of reality—they were the locales where the audience spent the rest of their day: boudoirs, eating houses, and outdoor promenades and parks—"natural" settings where the true nature of the mating game could be played out. There was a strong sense of space and spaciousness. Not only did the size and sweep of the costumes demand this but the formal patterns of the social encounters needed room for their choreography. Even in indoor settings the furniture was sparse and formally placed, throwing the focus upon language and the physical manner of the actor.

This sense of space, elegance, and simplicity is fundamental to the comedy of manners. Although the apron disappeared in the eighteenth century and the sparse perspective stage gave way to the more fully realized elegance of the Victorian drawingroom (as the nineteenth century imposed its heavier and more opulent sensibility), comedies of manner were still highly pictorial and audience-focused. The theatrical space of such drama must always allow for easy and elegant movement. There must be room for the sweep of costume and the formality of manner that demands a certain social distance between characters. The space should be light, bright, and uncluttered, providing scope for the curving flow of action and the total, effortless command of both social and stage space the actor must achieve.

Costume.   What an actor in a comedy of manners now calls his costume was simply everyday clothing to the society of the time.

Formal and open eighteenth-century living space. *Countrylife. Reproduced by permission.*

The relationship becomes more exact if it is appreciated that the costume the actor adopts as part of his character mask was, in its time, just as much of a mask for the individual who wore it. Our clothing is probably the most immediate and obvious manner in which we present ourselves to others. It is our social mask with which we define our external self and conceal what we do not wish to reveal.

In the Restoration period the clothing mask was influenced by the discrete opulence of a wealthy leisured class, the sexual acquisitiveness of the time, and the concealment of both physical blemish and emotion. The emphasis was upon bodily adornment—silks and laces, frills and curls—and the female bosom and the male leg were titillatingly revealed for carnal attraction. Specifically, the man wore a long coat with wide cuffs and pockets, from which a handkerchief would dangle. The coat would be heavily embroidered and the shirt beneath would be trimmed with lace and ribbons. Breeches reached only to the knees, revealing the leg in stockings and the feet in red-heeled shoes and drawing attention sexually to that part of the body. A shaved head was covered by a large wig on which was perched a large plumed hat. To carry a sword was the mark of a gentleman, and added to this would be a tall cane, gloves, and a muff. A snuff box completed the appurtenances. To manage all of these objects with skill was the ideal—to be a perfect peacock, yet not draw attention to the way in which perfection was achieved. To be clumsy was the mark of the country clod; to be affected denoted the false wit and the fop. The demands upon the actor's dexterity are even greater than the handling of the cups and saucers, cigarettes and cocktail glasses of later periods.

Women wore a bell-shaped full-skirted gown in lace, brocades, and satins, falling to the ground, but sometimes caught up to show the petticoats beneath. The bodice was cut low to reveal the upper part of the breasts,

Seventeenth-century male costume. Note high heels, muff, and snuff-taking attitude.   *Victoria and Albert Museum, London; Crown copyright.*

Seventeenth-century female costume. Note peeping toe, fan, and mask.   *Victoria and Albert Museum, London; Crown copyright.*

and a corset kept the spine very straight and pushed the breasts up further. The hair was adorned with hats, ribbons, and scarves, and the lady carried a fan and used a mask to enable her to pass unrecognized at a play or outdoor rendezvous. The Restoration theatre, while mirroring the image of the times, went further in titillating the sexual appetite. If propriety allowed only the women's breast to be revealed, the theatre invented "breeches parts" for women, enabling them to show the legs and thighs which the social mask required them to conceal.

As cleanliness was not a particular virtue of the age, it was compensated for by powder and makeup used by both men and women. This had the further advantage of disguising the ravages often caused by smallpox and the other "pox" of the time. A perfect mask sensibility is shown by the use of beauty patches, first to conceal pockmarks and then simply for adornment's sake. The heavily made-up face tended, of course, to be somewhat inexpressive—a dispassionate mask that revealed little emotion. This concealment of emotion continued to be a hallmark of the upper-class Englishman long after the male had ceased to wear makeup and is testified to by the expression "stiff upper lip" associated with the stereotyped English character down into the twentieth century.

Clothes, as both mask and mirror, have always reflected social attitudes and needs. Men's clothing has become less formal and more functional as pure idleness has given way to professional occupations. Women's clothing took a great leap into equality in the 1920s when political emancipation brought social emancipation with it. This led Cole Porter to remark that a glimpse of Victorian stocking had been shocking but "Now anything goes." Today, the further physical and moral emancipation of women is indicated by the second skin of aerobic clothes and the universal bikini. Far from being shocking, revelation now no longer presumes titillation.

1922
GLORINDA

Artist's impression of female posture and clothing in the early 1920s.   *Reproduced by permission of* Punch.

In the 1920s the cigarette holder became a popular affectation. It was, of course, just as much of a prop as the fans of the earlier centuries. It allowed for elegant gestures and betrayed its mask function in keeping the unpleasant smoky reality of the cigarette away from the smoker's face. The contemporary vogue for dark glasses is the equivalent of the seventeenth-century vizard mask. The padded brassieres of the 1940s, the bustles of the 1880s, and the padded male calves of the Restoration all show the continuity of the costume mask in indicating the sensibility of a time.

Group Identity.   Social groups that define themselves by attitude, manners, and costume provide the material for comedy of manners. Privilege, leisure, a sense of social or moral superiority, and a distinctive set of behavior patterns seem to be necessary qualities of such groups. But no longer, in a democratic society, is this the preserve of an upper-class elite. The student revolutionaries of the late 1960s—the "flower children"— were imbued with many of these qualities and, in their attempt to react against the restraints of a bourgeois society, adopted clearly recognizable costume and manners. The long hair (interestingly the longest since the eighteenth century), the faded denim, the patches, the granny glasses, the special handclasps, the use of drugs to liberate the senses and to help "make love not war," were all intended to show that the students were members of a select or "alternative" society.

The flower children were followed by the "Punks" of the late 1970s. Deliberately outrageous in dress, punk began as a working-class movement in Britain, once again in protest at the structure of bourgeois society. The dress and manner had the purpose of assaulting the sensibility of that society, and finding support from a clearly defined community of like-thinkers. It is an interesting comment upon the power of fashion in society that the extravagant dress of the Punks was taken up by youth culture everywhere, not with the original sense of social protest, but as part of the human need to personalize and define oneself, which goes back at least as far as the ornaments worn through the noses of some primitive peoples—which, of course, the Punks adopted!

One could go on to point to the "Yuppie" culture with its designer jeans, BMWs, cappucinos, Perrier water, and no offspring. Our repeated concern is to make the actor aware that the sensibility behind comedy of manners is ever-present. Although the sense of values of the late twentieth century may seem far removed from the Restoration courtier, the determined adoption of a set of values by any exclusive group will always create a sensibility that finds the need for external manifesta-

Flower children of the 1960s.   *San Francisco Chronicle.*

tion in a very distinctive social mask and manner. An awareness of the ongoing sensibility will help the actor to understand and adopt the mask and manners of comedy from the seventeenth through the twentieth centuries.

Character as Social Type.   The individual character was important to the playwright only insofar as he or she represented the manner of the social group and played a part in moving the plot forward. Before the age of Realism, characters were regarded as *dramatis personae:* masks of the drama. They were there to serve the action of the play, not to be analyzed. The playwright was not interested in character detail or psychological development. Characters were the vehicle for the plot; and the plot was an excuse for the display of wit and manner, and the consequences of the sexual chase. All of which was to be done as interestingly, cleverly, and amusingly as possible.

The playwright took pleasure in making a "bright dance of life" with what were essentially typical characters. Frequently the very name of the character underlined his or her principal personality trait and function within the play. The audience easily recognized the Prigs, Tattles, Sullens, Petulants, Sir Courtly Nices, and Aimwells of the time. The actor's task is not to make the character unusual or different, but to play the expected function (spine of character) as brilliantly as possible. The coterie societies that the comedy of manners illustrates are made up of recognizable social types—that is part of their attraction for the playwright, and pleasure for the audience in recognition. The playwright shows us the wits and fops, the lounge lizards and flappers doing what was expected of them: going their inevitable way in the social world of their time. The playwright's concern was for a social truth. The truth of the character is the way in which he or she partook of that truth: the part that his or her mask played in creating the total social mask of the group. It is not psyche that is the issue for the actor, but a larger theatrical life made up of social mask, physical manner, and verbal wit.

Wit and Language. Conversation is the principal means of human communication, and in a leisured society it is refined into an art. In the seventeenth century much of the social round—at court, in the theatre, and eating houses—depended upon the exercise of language. A person would be judged and accepted as much by the ability to turn a phrase as by the turn of the calf, the arrangement of a cravat, or the handling of a teacup. Conversation was a medium for intellectual flirtation and display. It facilitated the exercise of supe-

riority of mind and could show sexual interest while retaining emotional distance.

Brilliant conversation led to preferment at court and invitations to the dinner tables of the aristocracy. Before radio, television, or film, the theatre was the principal medium of social entertainment. And what better arena for the display of verbal wit. The seventeenth-century courtier went to the theatre to see and hear the manner of his society wittily displayed; and in his turn the witty playwright would be accepted in court circles.

Wit in language was, then, a crucial part of the structure of the comedy of manners, and that language tended to have an epigrammatical form. The epigram was essentially formalized by the Roman poet Martial into a short poem ending in a witty or ingenious turn of phrase that pithily sums up its substance. The wit or ingenuity of phrase was usually a function of punning, paradox, or antithesis, and the form of the language was carefully balanced. The following concluding couplet would be an example:

Treason doth never prosper: what's the
      reason?
Why, if it prosper, none dare call it treason.

Here we have the antithesis of treason and reason; the balance of *prosper* as the fulcrum of each line; and the satirical paradox that if treason prospers it then becomes legal and is no longer considered treason.

Compare this formal verse epigram with a line from Congreve's play *The Old Bachelor:* "Lay by that worldly face, and produce your natural visor." This is to a lady who is wearing a mask. The line is one of ironical antithesis and perfect balance. "Lay by" is balanced by "produce," "worldly" by "natural," and "face" by "visor." All of these are opposed concepts. The irony is produced by the switching of expectations: natural face and worldly visor would have been normal expectations. The speaker is passing a witty comment upon the

Punks of the 1970s.   *Whiteway Publications.*

fact that in this woman it is impossible to tell reality (natural face) from false appearance (worldly visor). Epigrammatical language as used in comedies of manners had the rhythmical flow and concise energy of its verse ancestry, but was speakable as prose to give the necessary dramatic feel of real conversation. As we saw with Shakespeare, his blank verse differed from the rhyming verse of the French neoclassicists, giving the sense of the normal rhythms of speech rather than the formal rhythms of verse. It was the same with the British comedy. Where the French was written in rhyming verse, the English playwrights took the structure and function of the epigram—concise, witty and pointed—and put it into a more conversational form. It was still balanced and antithetical and filled with rhetorical repetitions, but not as consciously contrived and artificial as formal verse.

The antithesis used in the epigrammatical form was a reflection of the turn of mind of the seventeenth century that was trying to come to terms with contrary perspectives on life: love versus physical passion; faith versus reason, as we have already suggested. The antithetical form of the epigram was a contrasting of propositions in order to create laughter out of life's tensions. To respond to life's enigmas with intellectual and verbal games can, for a time, seem preferable to the emotional pain caused by dealing too closely with its contradictions.

The epigrammatic tradition is consistent throughout comedy of manners. In the late nineteenth century we find Oscar Wilde using the same structure of antithesis and reversal. A famous example of this is Lady Bracknell's reply to John Worthing when he reveals that he has lost both of his parents: "To lose one

A strong sense of social typicality: Baroness de Champigny and Viscount de Rosalba in *The Italian Straw Hat.   Guthrie Theatre Company.*

ents we mean they are dead, but we mask that reality with the euphemism "lose." The tension between mask (that is, appearance) and reality is a consistent source of humor for the writers of comedy of manners.

Wit, though most evident in the epigrammatical language, was in fact an attitude toward life as a whole. It implied a superior way of dealing with life that was evinced equally in turning the jeweled phrase or amusing oneself with someone else's wife or husband. Horner, in *The Countrywife,* is a fine example of this active wit. He achieves his aim of sexual conquest by pretending to be impotent and therefore no sexual threat. This is, of course, itself an antithetical posture: He turns the going sensibility against itself and makes it work for him. The wit was the man who came out on top because of his innate abilities. No effort was involved in this; it was part of the amateur sensibility of taking life as a game to be played with consummate ease.

PERFORMANCE DEMANDS

Verbal Facility.   Witty language and a particular manner of speech are distinguishing features of comedy of manners. The physical mask of a character was supported by manner of speech. Rhythms, structure, and choice of words gave a clear indication of both social class and character type, from the breathless Sir Harry Wildair through the quickfire Sir Jasper Fidget to the blunt and direct verbal manner of Farquahar's recruiting sargeant. Handling of lines, therefore, places a double demand upon the actor. The manner in which the line is spoken is an important part of character mask, and the content of the line must achieve its comic impact.

Verbal repartee was not as fatal an exchange as fencing with rapiers, but it could destroy reputations, and the idea of fencing with the tongue suggests some of the qualities required by the actor: quickness, agility, variety

parent, Mr. Worthing, may be regarded as a misfortune; to lose both looks like carelessness." Here the sentence is balanced by the apposition of "lose," and the fortune" with "carelessness." The humor is based upon the reversal of expectation contained in the pun on "lose." Interestingly what Wilde is doing here is to point up the way in which we mask reality. When we speak of losing a parcel we mean mislaid; when we speak of losing par-of stress rhythm, and pointing. Intellectual ability is measured by speed of response, the display of quick verbal reflexes. The actor must be able to speak lines quickly but, equally, the words must be distinct if the wit is to score its points. Lip and tongue agility and the use of a variety of head tones to give the correct stress are necessary, as is an awareness of the shape of lines so that its rhythm sets the audience up to laugh at the right moment. This is achieved by timing. The actor builds the tension of a line so that the audience feels the need of release, that is, knows a laugh is coming. The audience must have enough time to understand the humor, but not too much time to analyze it. The audience is poised, breath held expectantly as the actor hits the audience with stress on the crucial point of the line—hence "pointing."

Verbal fencing is a good metaphor for early comedies of manners, but as the sharpness of satire moderates in the nineteenth century the simile of a tennis match could be used. We are going to look at a short passage from Oscar Wilde's *The Importance of Being Earnest:*

JACK: When one is in town one amuses oneself. When one is in the country one amuses other people. It is excessively boring.

ALGERNON: And who are the people you amuse?

JACK (AIRILY): Oh, neighbours, neighbours.

ALGERNON: Got nice neighbours in your part of Shropshire?

JACK: Perfectly horrid! Never speak to one of them.

ALGERNON: How immensely you must amuse them!

To examine the tennis image, notice that Jack's first line is a winding up and serving; that is, setting up the comedic ball for it to be played with. Algernon blocks the ball back, and Jack's line about "neighbours" has a casual air about it—it is a defensive lob. Algernon keeps it in play with a full top-spin return, Jack tries to finish it off with a hard drive, but Algernon cuts it off and wins the point with a short, sharp volley. The game structure is a useful way to examine the shape of comedic repartee. The entire exchange is, of course, built upon antithesis and the reversal of expectations that we have seen to be fundamental to the linguistic structure of comedy of manners.

In comedy the actor is playing as much with the audience as with his or her fellow actors. The convention of the *aside* in Restoration and eighteenth-century theatre underlines this. There is no pretense on the actor's part that audience members are not watching actors

The upright yet relaxed physical bearing of the eighteenth-century British nobleman. Note especially the leg position, the hands, and the childs recapitualtion of the adult manner. *Courtesy of the Earl of Mar and Kellie.*

imitating people like themselves. The actor comes in and out of the play, taking the audience into his or her confidence just as if the audience is another actor. In comedy the actor needs the audience response, and the verdict is immediate—the audience either laughs or it doesn't. In a comedy of manners much of the response will be to what an actor says (as opposed to farce, where it will be mostly to what the actor does), and the actor must pay heed to that response. Just as it is pointless for an actor not to deliver humorous lines clearly, so it is pointless for him or her not to allow the audience to have its laugh. Whereas the audience can watch comic action while laughing, it cannot hear further lines, and this places a

particular demand upon the actor in manners comedy: The actor must have very fast verbal brakes. The pace of the dialogue is brisk. An actor may expect, but must not anticipate, laughter; must take the line full tilt, then hold when the laugh comes, keep the brakes on until it just begins to fade, and then accelerate away through the end of the laugh into the next line.

If this all sounds somewhat technical—it is. But it is a technique that is part of the necessary truth of the comic event. The skills are used not for the display of technique but to manifest the manner, the sensibility, and the wit of social groups that were themselves very conscious of the necessity of these social

The calculatedly casual bearing of the eighteenth-century gentleman. *Tooth Galleries, London.*

(a)

Sophisticated ease and languorous elegance in the nineteenth and twentieth centuries, as seen in (a) a production of *She Stoops to Conquer* and (b) a portrait of Compte Robert de Montesquieu.   *(a) British National Theatre; (b) Musée de Louvre, Paris.*

skills to being a successful player in the game of life.

Physical Flair.   One of the actor's principal skills will be the achievement of the studied but effortless grace and ease of physical manner with which the men and women of comedies of manners presented themselves in society. It might be equated with the confident yet unselfconscious flair of the high-fashion model, who is there to be looked at but quite comfortable in the courage of the sartorial mask. Uprightness of stance and posture is a basic feature. Standing upright is a learned behavior for the human being. Slouching or standing loosely is perhaps closer to an unmasked manner. The distinctive upright posture of the upper-class physicality has certain functions: It inhibits emotional display; shows elegant clothing to the best advantage; betrays the assumption of looking down upon, and therefore manifests superiority; and bears witness to particular kinds of training given to an

(b)

upper-class person—from the poise needed to dance in the French manner of the seventeenth century, to the military officer drill given to public-school boys in the nineteenth.

The physical manner was, of course, reinforced by the clothing. The wig dictated that the head be held high; full cuffs and lace trimmings required the hands to be held away from the body; moving the weight of the full-bottomed coat required a swinging stride, and the high-heeled shoes threw the energy forward. Sitting required the coat tails to be lifted, the fall of the sword to be correctly placed, and the body lowered, with eyes up and back straight, on to the front edge of the chair while one leg was displayed forward and the other took the weight of the body.

Standing was an elegant pose with emphasis upon the leg: the least clothed part of the male body and a focus of sexual attraction. To "make a leg" the male stood with the weight essentially on the back leg, while the front leg was advanced and turned out at about ninety degrees, the heel of the front foot pointing to the instep of the rear. This is, of course, the third position in ballet and bears witness to the fact that movement was taught by ballet and dancing masters. The hands, meanwhile, would either be on the hip or between the flaps of the coat if unbuttoned. The head would be turned slightly to one side to complete the picture and display the profile.

The main distinction in male attitude in the eighteenth century was that it lacked the precise courtly formality of the preceding age. A leg was still made but with less sexual consciousness, and the arms and hands were never allowed to hang at the sides of the body—that posture was fit only for merchants and servants. So, the gentleman rested his hand on his sword, on his hip, or tucked inside his waistcoat, the top of which was left unbuttoned.

In sitting, the eighteenth-century male adopted a pose of elegant nonchalance. Chairs were used as props, and to avoid formality asymmetrical positions were taken: The gentleman seldom sat erect in the center of a chair but reclined to the left or right on the arm, one leg resting lightly on the other knee. If the chair had no arms the male might straddle it with arms resting on the back.

We cannot overemphasize the quality of ease with which the manner was carried off. To a young man today, with his jeans, T-shirt, tennis shoes, and loose hair, flopping down in furniture is natural and comfortable. For an eighteenth-century gentleman this would be not only painful but expensive: His silk stockings would run; his bodice stiffening would cut into his body; his breeches would split; his cravat come undone, and wig was pushed awry. Precisely in order to be comfortable and feel at ease he had to adopt an attitude that seems uneasy and artificial today. It is the actor's task to make that attitude look absolutely natural.

The sense of gentlemanly nonchalance and studied ease carried down into the nineteenth and twentieth centuries. Though clothing became less elaborate in a more work-oriented society, it was still well tailored and gave a strong contour to the body. Starched collars ensured the head was held high, continuing the attitude of aristocratic deportment handed down through the centuries. Within this frame the gentleman still carried himself with careful carelessness—flicking the wrist to display a flash of cuff and jeweled links; hitching the trouser to prevent bagging at the knee; carrying a handkerchief in his jacket sleeve, and casually in the breast pocket; cigarette held negligently between index and first finger as he lolled cross-legged in sofa or armchair.

The female manner was equally a reflection of its sensibility and time. In the seventeenth century, women walked as if doing a small-stepped dance. Dresses had stiffly corseted bodices cut low to reveal the breast and shoulders. This display was heightened by the deep curtsies of the time and coyly concealed by the fans, whose function was equally to provoke. The management of the dress was an art. Just as the men, the women had to ma-

Bowery Rose in *Diamond Lil*.   *American Conservatory Theatre. Photo by Marty Sohl.*

side a sea of petticoats, subordinate in a male-dominated society and locked within a moral code that regarded sex for women as, at best, a rather unfortunate method of procreation. Stiffly correct, she displayed the demure manner expected of the weaker sex. Far from the flirtatious prop of the seventeenth century, her fan is now a security blanket to ward off the fetid air or glances of overheated males.

Following World War I, the emancipated woman strode out of her petticoats into the freedom of shorter skirts and male trousers. She could now cross her legs and ape the lounging manner of her male friends while elegantly smoking a cigarette. As the final breakdown of aristocratic and neoclassical attitudes is approached, the underlying social presumptions of the upperclass are now manifested in a manner much more equal for men and women: The feminine ideal is now much closer to the masculine.

Playing the Costume.   While not minimizing the work involved for the actor in coming to terms with the period costumes so that the ease in wearing may look as if no work is involved, the actor should, however, regard the costume not as an obstacle but as a great opportunity for using the imagination to discover those choices of playing the costume and props that will add interest to his or her character. Even within the limitations set by observing the necessary decorum of a period, the women can get a lot of mileage out of the dressing and toilette scenes, for example. This was not only a ritual, but one performed to increase one's sexual attraction. The use of combs, paint pots, and powders galore; the decision whether to push up the breasts an extra inch; where to put on beauty patches for the best sexual advantage—all these actions afford splendid opportunity for the comic actor. Moreover, the playing of the decolletage itself: how far to reveal when curtsying; how far to cover with the fan; how far

neuver their dress forward as they sat poised upon the front edge of a chair. In movement the dress made sweeping curves as it was held just off the ground, and settled into elegant poses with the women's arms in graceful ballet curves, the hands held demurely at the point of the bodice—the hint of license always present beneath the air of formal reticence.

The eighteenth-century woman partook of a somewhat more consciously cultivated manner. Affected by bourgeois wealth and a more sentimental than sexual mask, she moved as a ship in full sail, balancing elaborate hair styles. Fans were large and more exquisite, used for display of wealth as an adjunct to dress, as much as for flirtation. The nineteenth-century woman had to swim into show with the eyes that one is aware the man is looking: a concealing/revealing coquetry that led to the writing of letter-concealment scenes, to draw further attention to the breast—all these opportunities, plus those given by such breeches parts as Margery Pinchwife, and Silvia in *The Recruiting Officer*, place a tremendous premium upon playing flirtation and sexual provocation. The women of the Restoration reveled in disguising as a male in order to succeed as a female, and the moment of revelation was played to the hilt. In this connection it is interesting that today when women frequently wear overalls and hard hats, television advertising has capitalized on this by creating the convention of the woman dressed as a man taking off the hard hat and shaking out her long hair—thus revealing herself as female. This is a *coup de théâtre*, which makes the same point as it would have done three and a half centuries ago.

Of all the opportunities afforded to the actor, the use of the fan is the most varied and dynamic. In one sense the fan is to the woman of the seventeenth and eighteenth centuries as much a weapon as the sword to the man: not to kill a rival but to capture a lover. The rhythms of the fan are written into the language of comedies of manners. Snapping it to show rejection, fluttering it to show passion, deftly touching parts of the body to draw sexual attention—there was a whole vocabulary of gestures that could say more than words were allowed to convey. The tip of the fan touched to the lips meant "hush"; to the right cheek, "yes"; to the left cheek, "no"; and to the nose, "I do not trust you." Yawning behind the fan meant "You bore me"; pointing the fan horizontally to the heart, "You have my love"; hiding the eyes behind the open fan also conveyed love; brushing the open fan toward a person was dismissive. While none of these specific gestures would have conventional meaning today, the manner of their performance by the clever actor can give them just

as much meaning in the theatre. And a lot of amusement, both for actors and audiences, can also be had by experimentation with the fan and the creation of a contemporary set of conventions, based upon the rhythms of the language and action of the plays.

The male actor has just as many opportunities to personalize the wearing of his costume and props as does the woman: the strong but graceful handling of the sword; the elegant posing with the cane; a flick of the head to keep the hair off the shoulders; a flick of the wrist to keep the lace off the hand; a flick of the handkerchief to keep snuff off the coat. All of these afford the actor a vocabulary with which to reveal his "parts," as the Restoration gentleman would have said. The taking of snuff, especially, was a highly distinctive male ritual. It is performed essentially in the following manner: The snuff-box is held in finger and thumb to display its jewels; the top is tapped to get the snuff off the inside lid—it is too expensive to waste; it is inserted with finger and thumb to get well up the nose; any spill is dusted off the costume with the handkerchief to prevent stains. There are perfectly good economic or practical motivations for each of the actions. The way in which these actions are performed makes snuff taking part of the social manner of the day, and an element of mask upon which judgments are made. Excessive display denoted the fop; sneezing afterwards denoted the unskilled clod. The only change in the eighteenth century was that the snuff was put in the indentation behind the thumb on the back of the hand, and sniffed into the nostril. This was regarded as less coarse than sticking the thumb and finger up the nose.

All the airs and graces may be played with to illustrate social manner and the part any character plays in the society. Fops, particularly, afford opportunities for imagination. Their essential quality was that they overdid the manner and betrayed themselves by exaggeration or ineptitude. We have al-

Strong delineation of character masks in the Glasgow Citizens' Theatre production of *The Impressario from Smyrna.*   *Photo by John Vere Brown.*

ready suggested how this may be done with snuff taking, which can be personalized according to the social situation or mood of the character: the sniff aristocratic, the sniff licentious, the sniff supercilious, etc. Every aspect of costume and manner gives opportunities for character business: The bow can be over-flourished with a handkerchief; the head can be tossed too mincingly, to make the curls bounce; ribbons may be toyed with, and, as an extremity, swords can always get caught between legs. Even normative characters can have their own foibles; indeed, the playwrights frequently suggest these manners in the names of their characters. The actor should take the use of costume as far as it will go to discover where his or her character finds its place in the balance of the production. Style should be consistent, but it doesn't have to be blandly homogeneous, and, always keeping within the accepted conventions, the way in which any character sits, walks, bows, or plays with a fan will be at the discretion of the actor.

Playing the Mask.   The relationship between the creation and playing of a physical mask of character and the "truthful" performance of that character is often a problem for the young actor. The source of this problem is a confusion between the truth of the character as discovered in the text, and the private truth of the actor's own feelings. To restate a point already made, theatre is the communication of a fabricated truth—a mask of truth. In comedy of manners this becomes part of the reality-appearance tension that is fundamental to the form. The mask is, of course, founded in the absolute validity of a character's intentions; but it does not involve a deep exploration of the truth behind them. Arthur Miller, although a psychologically oriented playwright, has allowed: "It is destructive to delve too deeply into a character that is essentially a series of lines crafted to address a situation."[4]

[4]Arthur Miller, *Timebends* (New York: Grove Press, 1987), p. 423.

To take the character Horner in *The Countrywife* as an example, what we need to know is that he partakes of the sensibility of the court society of Charles II and has a dominating sex drive that reflects an aspect of that society. The final definition of his mask is the way in which he responds to the drive within the constraints of the sensibility, and, as would be expected, it is an active and witty response. Any deep psychological motivation is irrelevant—it was neither the concern of the playwright nor the interest of the audience. The social motivation, however, is vital and based in complete truth.

Playing a mask doesn't limit an actor's physical and social imagination, because he or she isn't looking to reveal psychological depth. The actor not only has to assimilate the truth of the period sensibility but must also appreciate the comic intention of the playwright in selecting certain aspects of the social situation. The playwright, while reflecting the manners of society, is also passing comment upon them and taking a particular perspective in the creation of the comic masks. The nature of the comment is always to arouse laughter, even when treating the potentially painful. The actor must be aware of this and not search for deeply felt and painful psychological responses. He or she should play the mask according to the playwright's truth, so as to reveal the necessary attitudes in the necessary proportion.

The comic comment, however severe, is always good-natured. To take the example of the "testy-old-gentleman" mask, such as Pinchwife, Sir Peter Teazle, or Sir Anthony Absolute, whose social function it was to be cuckolded or thwarted—these characters are all easily angered and fly into rages that are perfectly truthfully motivated—they have good reason from their standpoint. But the rage is never "real" with any deeply emotional effect upon the audience. It it were it would undermine the comic point of the action,

which is to reveal the ridiculous unreasonableness of the character. The rages are exaggerated. These are repressive characters who deserve to be thwarted. They have set themselves up for it, the audience knows this, and it is properly amused when they get what they deserve. The laughter itself is, naturally, not without sympathy and recognition of certain human foibles of which the audience could be equally culpable.

The actor must maintain the comic balance and, while understanding the human truth of a situation, reveal through the mask the perspective that leads to laughter rather

Costume, wig, posture, and facial attitude combine to create a strongly integrated sense of character mask in *The Relapse.* *American Conservatory Theatre, San Francisco.*

than tears. What is emphasized is the exaggerated nature of the obsession. The total balance of truth is tilted toward the side of comedy, and this disproportion becomes the new truth, the comic reality of the event—the mask. The actor shares this truth with the audience, plays with them within the mask. Both are aware of its exaggeration, that it contains the comic perspective, and there is conspiracy between them to enjoy the game—to share the agreed reality.

Playing Tension between Mask and Appetite. One of the chief ways in which an actor's choices are determined is by the degree of tension between the assumed social mask of the character and the reality of its face. Comedy of manners deals with the mask of a particular social group and the way in which each character relates to the norm and displays a certain aspect of it. Part of the social mask of Restoration society was an elegance yet ease of social manner. Thus, much of the humor surrounding the fops or false wits was created by affectation—overdoing the manner—and the lack of self-knowledge that allowed them to assume a superiority that their actions denied. Their mask doesn't quite fit; it is out of balance with the convention of the time, and the actor creates comic tension by the way in which he or she reveals this solecism.

The playwright may draw the audience's attention to the gap between the assumptions of a mask and its reality by direct verbal comment from another character, or may condemn the character out of its own mouth by failed attempts at wit. More usually, however, the comic tension is revealed in action, which emphasized the significance of the physical choices an actor makes—the exaggeration of a flourish, the false coyness of the predatory matron.

Comedy tends to deal with human appetites, and comedy of manners deals with the polite veneers with which we cover them. One of the less dangerous appetites, perhaps, is that for food. In *The Importance of Being Earnest,* Wilde has invested Algernon Moncrieff (Algy) with an excessive urge in this direction. He first consumes all of the cucumber sandwiches prepared for Lady Bracknell, and he later does the same with John Worthing's muffins. This latter scene contrasts Algy's gluttony with the imperturbable elegance of his manner. He consumes the muffins "calmly," which, as he says, is the only way to eat muffins; otherwise, the "butter would probably get on my cuffs." This is an amusing juxtaposition of the necessity for keeping up the outer mask while satisfying the inner appetite. In this particular scene the comic effect is heightened by the emotional crisis that surrounds it, which Algy ignores with superb, self-centered urbanity.

However this is achieved, the tension between the assumption and the appearance is one of the principal comic devices of the comedy of manners. The degree of a character's deviation from the social norm established on the stage—a lack of self-knowledge or lack of wit—will create the level of humor surrounding a character. This is as true for the "silly asses" of Noel Coward's day as for the false wits of the Restoration. The actor, through his or her choices, creates the correct degree of comic tension for the truth of the character mask.

Playing the Occasion. Comedy of manners made a theatrical occasion out of social occasions. In the Restoration it was the court, theatre, royal parks, and eating houses of the day that were the forum for seeing and being seen. The salons, coffee shops, and spas of the eighteenth century performed a similar purpose. This social round became even more institutionalized in the nineteenth century with the development of the "season." In England this included racing at Ascot, rowing at Henley, sailing at Cowes, tennis at Wimbledon, and balls both in London and at the great country houses.

The season would start with the presentation at court of the daughters of the upper classes. This was followed by dances at which they and specially selected (for birth, money, and prospects) young men would be allowed to perform ritualized mating ceremonies. The ceremonies would continue through the social round of the season, and each occasion would require a special costume, the correct mask for the event: morning dress at Ascot; white suits and blazers at Henley; flowered hats and dresses at Wimbledon. Thus would the nature of the occasion be defined and its ritual celebrated with strawberries and cream at Wimbledon and champagne picnics at Oxford for Eights Week (the annual university rowing races).

A sense of occasion, then, surrounds all the relationships of the social groups with which comedy of manners concerns itself. It is the unspoken affirmation of the fact that a function of the social round is to confirm the values and sensibility of that particular class structure—to check, as it were, the correctness of the mask. The fact of being on parade, of displaying the right mask, is not denied by the pretense of not wearing a mask at all. It is the same kind of art disguising art that is fundamental to the actor's craft. This particular demand of comedy of manners gives the actor a double opportunity—to play at playing—which makes it a theatrical exercise of great potential. It stages, theatrically, the dance and mating game of the real social season. The entertainment is based upon the nonsentimental view of sexuality where the winner was he or she who played the most cleverly, and one's immortal soul was not at issue. The game is fast and furious; it is a sexual chase done up in the splendid costumes and formal patterns of a dance, but driven by a tremendous sexual vigor underneath. Comedy of manners for the actor is in the balls of the feet, the tip of the tongue, and the urgency of the groin.

EXERCISES, GAMES, TECHNIQUES

Courtesies.   While we recognize that probably no one in the audience will be able or concerned to judge the precise correctness of the courtesies we describe, the correct use of them is a crucial part of the physical style and social form of comedy of manners. It is a basic task of the actor to be able to perform them with ease and flair, out of an understanding of what they reveal about the sensibility of the society of their time.

Seventeenth-Century Bow.   The hat is swept off with the right hand and transferred to the left. The right foot slides forward a step, feet turned out, both legs straight. The body inclines forward from the waist, spine and neck straight. Both knees bend outwards, the front leg kept straighter than the rear, which takes most of the body weight; feet stay flat on the ground. The right arm sweeps forward and down on the ground. Upon rising, the hand is kissed to the person saluted, the weight comes onto the front foot, and third position is adopted.

Eighteenth-Century Bow.   Variations on bows began to proliferate. A general-purpose bow is as follows: The right foot is taken to the side, with the weight on it, leaving the left foot resting on the toe. The hat is removed and taken to the side, and the back is inclined. As the body comes up, the left foot comes behind the right into fourth position.

Later Bows.   Just as the eighteenth-century bow is simpler than the bow of the earlier century, so the bow becomes more and more simplified through the nineteenth century to the early twentieth. The bow was taken with both heels together and the body bent from the waist. The degree of bend lessened throughout the period until, in the comedies of Noel Coward in the 1930s, it is barely more than an inclination of the head, together with a handshake.

Seventeenth-Century Curtsy.   A step is taken to either side, to draw attention to the curt-

Detail of seventeenth-century bow and curtsey.   *Drawings by Janis Martin.*

sier; the foot is then brought back to the other foot, heels touching. The knees are bent smoothly and slightly outwards, the body inclined a little forward with arms falling naturally to the side. Depending upon the depth of the curtsy, the heels remain on the ground or are raised slightly.

Eighteenth-Century Curtsy.   As with bows there were variations of curtsies. The most

Detail of eighteenth-century bow.   *Drawing by Janis Martin.*

respectful was similar to that of the seventeenth century. A more everyday curtsy, somewhat lighter in feeling, was made by sliding one foot forward into fourth position, bending the back knee, then without bending the body rising onto the front leg. This curtsy could be oriented to right or left, and taken without pausing in a walk.

Later Salutations.   In formal society the curtsy continued to be used until the early twentieth century, with more or less formal use of the eighteenth-century curtsy. After World War I the emancipated woman began to shake hands and incline the head like the male in his salutation. Variations on this were the giving of both hands, the extending of one hand palm down, or the directly outstretched hand as the male—depending upon the formality of the occasion, the degree of friendliness, and the level of emancipation of the woman. Whereas a man would always shake hands standing, a woman could remain seated to give her hand to a man, or to a woman who was younger or her social inferior.

Elegance of manner while taking refreshment. *Residenzmuseum Munich.*

Taking Tay. The drinking of chocolate or coffee, and later tea, was one of the new social rituals of the eighteenth century. Served in delicate china from the newly developing ceramics industry, taking tea became an exercise in effortlessly artful poses: saucers cradled in the palm; cups enfolded with all five fingers, or taken by the handle with thumb, index, and middle finger and raised to the lips with little finger delicately extended. Above all the cups should never be seized, or the impression given that drinking was a serious matter.

Exercises

Patterning Space I. Use furniture or blocks to create various ground plans within your space. This will demand particular patterns of movement from the players, who are asked to move through the space at different speeds. Start with slow speeds and build up to a swiftness that is just short of running. Players must not touch any of the furniture as they move on their toes, glide, skate, walk with a rhythmical stride, and so on. As the speeds and types of movement can be varied, so can the shape of the space be altered to provide different patterns. The exercise can be extended, with teams entering from different sides and avoiding each other as well as the physical objects. Ultimately the space can be filled with players performing the task in any combination of speeds and movement.

Patterning Space II. To the above basic exercise may be added any number of elaborations concerned with control and balance. The players can be asked to move with books on their heads; balancing tennis balls in teaspoons; as waiters in a restaurant with trays of crockery and dishes. Extensions can be attached to the players' waists to make their judgment of space more acute, or some may wear rehearsal skirts. The exercise may be turned into individual and team competitions as long as the emphasis does not fall upon the competition rather than the objective of the exercises: controlled, balanced movement combined with ease, agility, and awareness of spatial relationships. To win is not simply to arrive first, but to do so having fulfilled the demands of the exercise.

Conversations in Space I. This extends the previous exercise into making statements with patterns of physical movement. Again, use furniture or blocks to create different spaces. The players are now required to communicate with each other through their movement. The exercise is best begun in pairs, but it may be developed to include several players. Although the exercise lends itself to any number of situations (such as quarrels and outwitting), a good starting point for a pair is the flirtation—the mating dance often found in comedy of manners. Players must express this without speaking or touching the partner. The various encouragements, avoidances, carnal desires, and distastes are communicated by movement alone.

Conversations in Space II. Play the above exercise, now allowing the players to express their intentions in any physical manner they wish. Physical contact and full expression of feeling are encouraged—including vocal noises, but not words. After this the original exercise is repeated, and players will feel a much greater sense of the physical tension between their desires and emotions and the mask of social form through which they must express them. The space may be adapted to the different environmental demands of the comedy of manners, ranging from the open spaces and sparse furnishings of the Restoration, to later comedies, where players are likely to sit more and adopt positions relating to furniture.

Plumage I. This is an exercise related to posture and mask, and it is based upon the adoption of bird physicalities. The player is asked to choose a bird of brilliant plumage and to experiment slowly with the adoption of its posture and manner of self-display. This is first done individually and then developed into an aviary situation in which birds display themselves to each other. The exercise may be extended into courting dances, and a whole range of attractions and responses can be developed.

Plumage II.   Now the objectives of the exercise become discovering the pecking order and also attracting a satisfactory mate in competition with the other birds. A range of levels may be introduced into the workshop space to provide perches and enable positions of dominance to be taken up. Although this exercise is concerned chiefly with projection of the physical mask, it also introduces the idea of differing postures—those of individual birds—and social superiority within the central notion of self-display. All birds may display their plumage equally well, but the nature of the bird will determine the individual manner and success of the performance.

Preening I.   This exercise is done in front of a mirror. The player first removes outer clothing, returning to a close approximation of a "bare, forked animal," and takes a moment to become acquainted with his or her own fundamental physicality and the possibilities of movement it allows. The player then slowly adopts the costume mask of, say, the seventeenth or eighteenth century. As each item is put on, the player carefully examines what it does to the body, both in restricting or restructuring movement and in embellishing appearance. What is the function of each item, and why is the player wearing it—both as an actor and as a seventeenth- or eighteenth-century individual? What, for example, constitutes a well-tied cravat, and what is it meant to say about the wearer? Slowly the player

builds up, understands, and assimilates the costume mask, aware of the impression it is intended to make.

Preening II.   Once an understanding has been gained of what a normative wearing of clothing entails, the player may adopt different attitudes toward self-presentation: judicial, military, foppish, etc., to explore how this would affect the wearing of clothes. The exercise may be done with another player assisting in the dressing—most upper-class ladies and gentlemen would have valets and maids to assist them. The second player can also help the first to examine and understand the self being built.

Preening III.   Players form two ranks, down the center of which each passes in turn, acknowledging the others by means of a bow, curtsy, or other salutation such as kissing hands. The player saluted should respond. Canes and hats should be used in the exercise, which may be extended to include an attitude with the salutation. The salutation is performed correctly, but with it a particular feeling is shown toward the other person such as respect, distaste, love, or boredom.

Model Show.   This is a good early workshop exercise for dealing with the mask and movement demands of comedy of manners. It is not geared to achieving any specific period manner, but generally to helping the player get out of a "normal" physicality and enjoying the idea of dressing up and display. Gather together as many extravagant pieces of clothing and costume props as possible—scarves, hats, boas, bits of colorful cloth, shoes, ornaments—from which the players will improvise costumes for a "high-fashion" show. Set up a situation with a ramp along which models parade to display their costumes, and around which sits the audience of those players not modeling at that moment. Have a commentator describe the nature and utility of each costume—players can take turns at this—and encourage the audience to ask questions of the models regarding the costumes, examine them, and generally express approval or disinterest.

The exercise usually generates a high level of interest, enthusiasm, and imagination. The generic style of the costumes is likely to be eclectic and contemporary camp, which is fine, for its main purpose is to break the actor out of a sweatshirt, jeans, and flat-shoes sensibility. The players must be encouraged to take their costumes, however outrageous, quite seriously and to use as a presentational image that air of languidly dynamic cool that is the hallmark of the high-fashion model.

Party Time.   This is an extension of the previous exercise. It is based on setting up a series of parties that allow the player to discover both the common sensibility beneath the external manner of upper-class societies and the different detail by which that manner is manifested. It is best to start from the player's own experience. Dress up for a contemporary party, and examine why certain clothing was adopted and how that clothing and the fact of being at a party made the player alter social manner. From here move back in time to, say, a cocktail party in the 1920s, a nineteenth-century reception, an eighteenth-century salon, and finally a court levee in the Restoration period. Use as many costumes and prop simulations as are available, and let the player choose whatever is necessary for the specific occasion. It is also useful to let the players change the settings for each new occasion, making them directly confront the physical demands of the environment.

The exercise should be done twice. First, hold a discussion at the end of each party, analyzing the discoveries the players made about each new physical mask and its rela-

tionship to the physical manner. The second time the exercise should be allowed to flow as much as possible, one party leading into the next with no definite break. Final discussion should focus on the way the manner of each period was adjusted to the particular environment while the underlying social attitude remained the same.

A Day in the Life of . . .   This exercise examines any one of the periods dealt with in "Party Time" in greater depth and detail. Though of necessity selective, it simulates a typical day in the life of a principal character of comedy of manners. It will give players a more complete flavor of the time and the experience of continuously presenting a social mask in different situations. Here is one possible outline of a day in the life of a Restoration gentleman:

11 A.M.	Rose. Performed toilet, assisted by valet. Received fencing master (or dancing master, shoemaker, etc.). Wrote, read poetry.
12:30 P.M.	Received friends and repaired for dinner to Sun Tavern in the City. Traveled by hackney coach. Ate stewed carp, a chicken, tansy pudding, neats' tongues, and cheese.
3 P.M.	Went to the play; sat in pit or on the stage; spent time ogling the ladies in the boxes and talking back to the actors. Or went to a cockfight, played bowls, or real tennis.
7 P.M.	Walked down the Mall through St. James's Park, bowing to the ladies. Drank sillabub and ate cheesecake at the gate.
8 P.M.	Supper at Locket's on lamb, pigeons, anchovies, and tarts. Drank burgundy; then brandy later while playing cards at

friends' lodgings in Whitehall—
whist ombre basset.

1 A.M.   Took chair to mistress's house.
Retired.

Again, the precision of the detail is not as important in this exercise as the sense of life style—the social round, the pursuit of pleasure, the sense of occasion, the incestuous nature of relationships in a small elite circle.[5]

Instant Character I.   This is a useful general exercise based upon the immediate assumption of a physical mask. Many of the characters in comedy of manners have a strong obsessive trait, which is suggested by their name and provides the basis for their mask. In this context, players concentrate upon an attitude and allow this to become a strong, one-dimensional relationship of emotion and physicality. This may be done in two ways. The mental attitude may be the catalyst, as in the case of such characters as Petulant, Sullen, and Sparkish. Here the player, by concentrating upon the idea of petulance, sullenness, or whatever, will discover a facial attitude that matches it. This can be taken further into a posture, a walk, and finally a complete physical mask derived from the mental image. In the opposite case, with such characters as Fidget, Snake, and Clumsy, it is the physical manner that is given, and by playing a strong physical identity the player will be able to discover a corresponding inner attitude. The exercise is, of course, simply a tool to encourage physical imagination and the playing of

a strong physical mask with clarity and attack. In performance such a character mask will be informed by all the understanding of social manner and sensibility the player's background work will have given him, which will add subtlety and variety to the mask.

Instant Character II.   This is a contemporary version of the above game. All players choose a well-known celebrity and adopt his or her manner: posture, gestures, physical rhythms, etc. Players now have to collect celebrity autographs; but the twist is that other celebrities sign your book with who they think you are. Whoever collects the most autographs has created the most successful mask. It is useful to discuss afterwards what precise aspects of the manner led to easiest identification.

Verbal Fencing I.   Players are given light sticks with padded tips. They then pair off and take a piece of repartee dialogue from any of the works of the comedy of manners writers: Etherege, Wycherley, Congreve, Farquhar, Sheridan, Wilde, Coward. The players now fight a duel with their sticks as they go through the lines of repartee. This will help the players feel the thrust and parry of the lines, the weight and delicacy of the rhythms, and the literal "pointing" of the wit. The exercise also gives players a physical sense of the aggression behind verbal repartee combined with the formality and lightness of touch with which it is expressed. For playwrights such as Noel Coward, whose wit is not quite as sharp as the Restoration playwrights, balloons make an interesting substitute for sticks. This use of balloons also works for the joshing one-liners of Neil Simon.

Verbal Fencing II.   While women can also use the sticks in the above exercise, fans are the most appropriate weapon. Here the dueling isn't by contact with the fans but by use of fan rhythms to emphasize the phrasing and point-

---

[5]Worth noting here is the relationship with servants. This was usually civil, and sometimes familiar. Indeed, in the nineteenth century the nanny or butler was often better-known to the child than was the parent. This always presumed an unspoken sense of knowing one's place. As a Victorian hymn put it:

The Rich man in his castle
The poor man at his gate
God made them high or lowly
Each born to his estate.

ing of the line. Essentially, tapping gestures with the fan closed were used to emphasize remarks. The tapping could be of the other hand or parts of the upper body. Occasionally, if the witty opponent were a man, the women might tap him with the fan, but not another woman. All fan gestures made to men have sexual implications, the slower ones being more overtly sensual. Two things to remember: Fan gestures should be used sparingly and to make a point; fans should never be wildly waved about unless the character is of a lower social status.

Tongue Twisters I. A few verbal exercises may be useful in sharpening the lip and tongue agility so necessary for the playing of comedy of manners. First, speak them as rote exercises, concentrating upon the absolute clarity of each syllable and then of each word. Then gradually increase the speed of speaking without sacrificing clarity, until your optimum combination of speed and clarity is reached.

> In Tooting two tutors astute
> Tried to toot to a Duke on a flute.
> But duets so gruelling
> End only in dueling,
> When tutors astute toot the flute.
>
> The actuary's honorary secretary showed her
>   extraordinary
> literary superiority by working literally
>   solitarily in the
> library particularly regularly during
>   February.
>
> With blade, with bloody blameful blade, he
>   bravely broached his
> boiling bloody breast.
>
> Peter Piper picked a peck of pickled peppers,
>   a peck of pickled
> peppers Peter Piper picked. If Peter Piper
>   picked a peck of pickled peppers,
> where's the peck of pickled peppers Peter
>   Piper picked?
>
> She sells sea shells on the sea shore; the
>   shells she sells are

sea shells for sure. If she sells sea shells on
  the sea shore,
I'm sure she sells sea-shore shells.

> Julia was actually due to be married to the
>   Duke of Turin on the
> first Tuesday in June, dressed in her superb
>   jewels. When the day
> duly arrived, Julia's mature duenna could
>   not produce the jewels.
> Julia felt suicidal, for the Duke, persuant to
>   his promise, had
> dutifully started a ducal serenade with a
>   superfluous but celestially
> tuneful Tudor tune played on lutes and flutes.

Tongue Twisters II. When the players have gained some skill with the individual tongue twisters, interest may be added by using them as the basis for group work:

> Players pass the exercise around a circle,
>   taking a word each.
>
> Two players hold a conversation with the
>   exercises, taking up the words when
>   they wish.
>
> Two or more players use the exercises to
>   hold conversations based upon a
>   particular situation—for example, a love
>   scene, a quarrel, or selling insurance.

Other useful verbal exercises may be found in the prologues from Restoration comedies, such as Congreve's *The Old Bachelor* and *The Way of the World,* and the patter songs from Gilbert and Sullivan operas, such as "Commander of the King's Navy" from *H.M.S. Pinafore* and "Model of a Modern Major-General" from *The Pirates of Penzance.*

PLAYING THE STYLE

We are going to look at the character of Millamant from Congreve's *The Way of the World* to see how our approach may be applied in practice, particularly in the context of the "contract scene" (act 4 scene i), from the same play.

As might be expected from the masked quality of comedy of manners, we find very little personal information about Millamant in the play. What we know of the character is gained from her social and verbal manner. The nearest Millamant comes to revealing an emotion—let alone any psychological motivation—is after the contract scene when she says: "If Mirabell should not make a good husband I am a lost thing, for I find I love him violently."

Millamant's first entrance is highly indicative of her character. We are told she is in "full sail, fan spread with her streamers out." She is also compared to a "whirl-wind," and there is a strong sense that she is almost always in motion, deftly tripping through life. Her verbal rhythms confirm this impression. They are full of little trills and sallies; short sentences tumbling over one another in quick succession. She is also full of little contradictions, advances, and denials, although none of them seriously put. She treats the idea of love wittily and whimsically: She uses love letters to put up her hair and finds that only poetry works—her hair never looks good in prose!

All of this is consistent with her name, Millamant, "a thousand lovers." But all of them are distant and dispensable: "One makes lovers as fast as one pleases, and they live as long as one pleases: and if one pleases, one makes more." There is a sense of an assumed coquetry about Millamant. It is assumed as a mask of safety, just as there is safety in a number of lovers, which keeps anyone from coming too close. Millamant plays the flirtation sexual game of the day better than most in order to stay in control. Behind the verbal coquetry is an intelligent woman who wants more from life than becoming victim to the sexual and social forms of the day. She has a large power of giving but won't be undervalued, and she knows that in the sexual and social fencing of the day "When you part with your cruelty, you part with your power." She is always in motion and defending herself with shafts of wit, so that she may choose whom she will allow to catch her.

Mistrustful of the restrictions of marriage, yet unwilling to treat it as a shallow mask of appearances, she is fleeing from it until she can find an honest relationship. Until then she states her intention thus: "I'll fly and be followed to the last moment." This is to get full value out of the chase and to prove the worth of the hunter: She doesn't want simply to "dwindle into a wife."

Images of Millamant that come to mind are "flighty," which has to be tempered by the fact that she is looking for a perch. Also "animated," in the sense of a young filly, fully dressed for a show, whose friskiness is just controlled by the formality of the paces she has to go through. In any terms there is a clear indication of strong energy in head and feet.

All of Millamant's qualities come together in the contract scene, in which she and her suitor, Mirabell, agree to marry, but on terms that will make their relationship different from and more honest than the marriages of economic and social convenience that were the norm in the late seventeenth century. In many respects it is a very modern scene, based upon the classic Restoration conflict between external appearances and natural reality. Millamant and Mirabell are trying to reconcile the sexual chase with emotional stability, and social form with personal honesty. The scene has the classic structural antithesis of comedy of manners, but it is unique in examining the need for some humanity that is broader than animal lust and deeper than the shallow mask of social manner.

The scene was written on the cusp of the Age of Sentiment in which sincerity of emotion was to replace superiority of social manner as the mark of gentility in polite society. Mirabell, although of the stock of the Restoration rake, is imbued with sentiment, and he is a splendid antithesis in manner to Millamant. Where she is flighty, he is serious; where she is instinctive, he is legalistic, his rhythms more solid and earthbound. This leads, in the contract scene, to the classic verbal and spiritual fencing of two vulnerable and mistrustful persons who need to test each other's sincerity and affirm their love.

A structure of exercises for work on Millamant's character might be as follows.

Instant Character. This is a useful starting point for an approach to Millamant's physical mask. *Only* a starting point, however, for she is not simply an obsessive character, and one of the tasks for the actor playing her is to reveal her true needs beneath her social manner. The manner may be approached from the image we have already suggested of a spirited filly. This would be a way of exploring the lower body energies and the sense of shying away from too close emotional encounters. A "flighty" or bird image could be added to this, and concepts such as "impulsive" and "bewitching" might be fruitful in encouraging the actor's physical imagination toward the discovery of Millamant's basic rhythms and physical manner.

Verbal Fencing. This exercise is not only an introduction for the actor to the physical structure of epigrammatical language, but it will also be a good way for Millamant to approach the contract scene. One of the problems of the contract scene is the weight of language, which can at first seem static and almost oppressive to the actor because of the way in which the characters seem not to be making contact. Use of the fencing sticks to explore and point out the physical energies that have led to the scene being played will help the actor to break the scene down into a physical shape that represents those energies, and to feel the caring, the uncertainty, the need, and sexual desire beneath the verbal mask. It will also be a way for Millamant to approach working with Mirabell on the scene.

Patterning Space I. This is an especially useful exercise for Millamant, for movement is such a fundamental part of her character mask. A vocabulary of movement rhythms and patterns, which lend both a consistent shape and variety to her flirtatious manner of attracting while retreating, is a basic necessity for the actor in the part.

Conversations in Space. This exercise, which leads directly from the previous one, can be played again with the actor who is Mirabell. It is an excellent exercise for continuing work on the contract scene and expanding the energies and rhythms found in language in the "Verbal Fencing" exercise into larger physical patterns. The intention of both actors in this scene is to win the other on his or her own terms. The tactics are somewhat different. To take further the image of Millamant as a spirited young filly, the scene can become a kind of a delicate horse-breaking scene. In the early part of the scene Millamant shows her mettle and exactly how she must be handled, how much license she must be given, if she is to be taken at all. She is not going to "dwindle." She is going to back into the bridle, tossing her head and kicking up her heels. And that is the shape of the scene. Millamant has two long early monologues in which she lays down the conditions, that is, bucks, kicks, and tosses her head, and then the rest of the scene is Mirabell's responses—allowing her some rope while he slips on the bridle—which is punctuated by short sentences from Millamant, which are the final tosses of the head and kicking of the heels as she gains confidence and allows herself to be tamed. The "Conversations in Space" exercise lets the actors explore the movement patterns of this mating dance, to discover how the shape as suggested above translates into the formality of the period, and yet keeps the strong sense of physical dynamic beneath the formality of the epigrammatical language in which it is couched.

Plumage. The contract scene may also be explored through this exercise, which places greater emphasis upon the use of costume mask and physical manner both to attract and to assert superiority. Both actors may explore how and where they display themselves through the process of the scene, and whether the self-display alters in response to the attraction-rejection dynamics of the scene. To pick up on the first costume image we have of Millamant in full sail with streamers flying, this exercise could be played with Millamant bedecked with ribbons, which stream out as she moves. In the context of the contract scene a game could be played with Mirabell trying to catch the ribbons—a metaphor for catching Millamant. The actors could explore how this is done: quick moves, slow moves, forcefully, delicately. It also allows Millamant to determine how she allows this to be done; when she cooperates, when she denies, and what is her emotional response to being stripped of her free-flying identity.

Verbal Fencing II.   We started this structure of exercises with a verbal fencing exercise that enabled the actors to get a strong physical sense of the dynamics of the language of the contract scene. These dynamics have been further explored and expanded in the intervening exercises, and now Millamant can channel all of that experience into the use of the fan. What we called the kicks of the heels and tosses of the head in the *Conversations in Space* exercise will, in performance, become fan gestures supporting the intentions of the language. The advances and retreats of the *Plumage* exercise will also be assisted by the use of the fan in defensive flourishes and the sensual motions of flirtation. In this way the language and manner and movement of the character become one, in an integrated pattern of rhythms that both define the character and illustrate the character's intentions in action at the same time.

Pictorial Sources.   Extremely useful in understanding the external manner of a period are the pictorial sources. The portraits of the seventeenth and eighteenth centuries, by Gainsborough, Lely, and Knellar, together with the engravings of Bosse, Hogarth, and Boucher give an active sense of the physical manner of their time. The cartoonists of the nineteenth century such as Spy (Leslie Ward) continue this representation and, in the late nineteenth and twentieth centuries, society magazines such as the *Tattler* and the *Illustrated London News* show the *beau monde* performing its social rituals.

SUGGESTED READINGS

Bryant, Arthur, *The England of Charles II.* London: Longmans, Green, 1935.

George, Kathleen, *Rhythm in Drama.* Pittsburgh: University of Pittsburgh Press, 1980.

Henshaw, N. S., *Graphic Sources for a Modern Approach to the Acting of Restoration Comedy.* Doctoral dissertation. University of Pittsburgh, 1967.

Holland, Norman, *The First Modern Comedies.* Cambridge, Mass: Harvard University Press, 1959.

Loftis, John, ed., *Restoration Drama.* New York: Oxford University Press, 1970.

Seyler, Athene, and Stephen Haggard, *The Craft of Comedy.* New York: Theatre Arts Books, 1946.

Styan, J. L., *Restoration Comedy in Performance.* Cambridge: Cambridge University Press, 1986.

Wildeblood, Joan, and Peter Brinson, *The Polite Society.* New York: Oxford University Press, 1965.

5 Farce

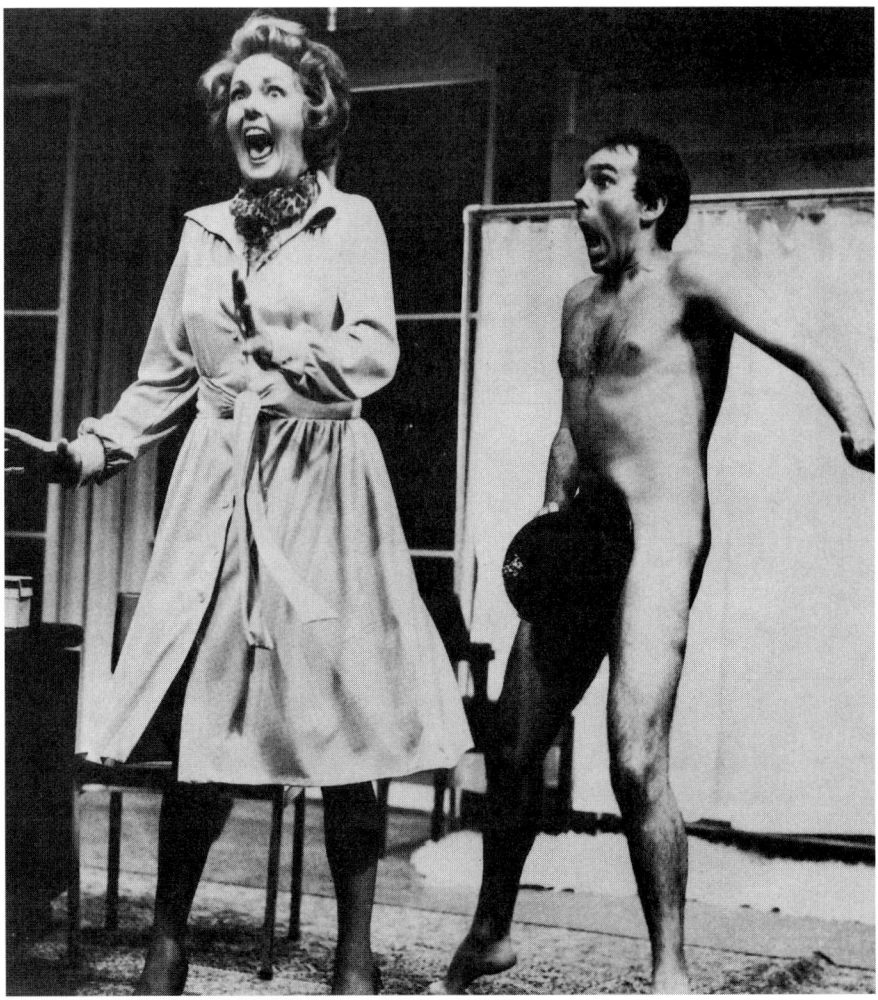

What the Butler Saw.   Royal Court Theatre, London.

BACKGROUND

General.   Farce is a particular expression of or perspective on life that at times finds itself fully fleshed out in dramatic form as a play. At other times it may appear as part of a dramatic event; for emotional or rhythmical contrast in a serious drama or tragedy (the porter's scene in *Macbeth*, for example); as a more robust and physical element in comedy (the watch scene in *Much Ado About Nothing*); or as a short event in any forum of popular entertainment, from fairgrounds to circuses and vaudeville shows.

Farce probably gets it name from the French *farcir*—to stuff: As a dramatic form it was used as a fill-in, a stuffing at other theatrical performances (also, as a form, it is itself stuffed full of business and comic ingenuity). The term came into use in France in the fifteenth century. From that time farce gained increasing significance as a dramatic genre until it achieved a peak in nineteenth-century France—with Labiche and Feydeau—and in England with Pinero. However, as a popular form under other names, farce goes back to the very roots of Greek dramatic performance and shows markedly consistent features throughout the long history of drama.

Popular appeal and physical activity are probably the two distinguishing features of farce. This could also be said of public hangings in the eighteenth century, so it must be added that farce was intended to entertain and provoke laughter. (Alas, this might also be said of public hangings, which suggests that one of the sources of human laughter is the discomfort of others—a point to which we shall return.) We are, briefly, going to trace the development of farce from its popular roots in order to identify some of its salient features. Special attention will be paid to a form of drama called *commedia del l'arte*, which was essentially farcical in perspective and structure and thus provides a useful skeletal basis for an understanding of farce playing.

Historical.   The roots of farce are probably to be found in the kind of mimic plays with which primitive people celebrated the return of spring, with all its associations of seed sowing, fertility, and renewal of life. Eating, drinking, playing, and copulating are expressions of fundamental human needs—representations of the life force at its most primitive level. Early revelers in this manner were the Dorian Greeks, whose burlesque playlets may well have been a source for the later, more sophisticated comedies of Aristophanes in the fifth-century-B.C. Athenian celebration of the Dionysia.

Whether Aristophanes consciously imitated the Megarean farces, as they are now called, or whether similar human drives gave rise to similar responses is irrelevant for our

Bawdy physicality of Old Greek Comedy actors.
Antiken Museum, Berlin.

purpose. What is significant is the use of masks and phallus by both playwrights and the similarity of human types and attitudes they depicted. Although Aristophanes' comedies were much more sophisticated in plot and in their satirical, political comment than were the Megarean farces, they still involved a good deal of physical and sexual humor and included, among a wider range of characters, doctors, soldiers, comic slaves, old men, and old women—the very masks that were found in the early farce plays.

Greek New Comedy tended to take over the masks of its predecessors and add a sentimental love interest in the form of a young man and young woman; the humor became less physical and intrigue more significant. But when we move on to Rome we find early sexual energies combined with sophisticated form in Plautine farces, which are based upon love intrigue, seduction, and money, and whose character types include young lovers, miserly and impotent men, pimps, swaggering soldiers, and both stupid and cunning slaves—all the consistent elements of farce's historical evolution.

After Plautus the actor in the Roman theatre became highly unpopular with the moralistic, nascent Christian church. As we have suggested, there is a certain phallic energy at the root of all farce, and pagan peoples, however sophisticated, were willing to accept the fact and expression of sexuality, with its attendant bawdiness and vulgarity, as a necessary part of human experience. But in the Christian church sex somehow became bound up with original sin, and immaculate conceptions were preferred to fertility rites. So out went the actors into the wilderness of excommunication, to be classed with thieves and sturdy beggars for the next millennium.

It is difficult for tragedy to survive in the wilderness, but popular theatrical forms such as farce can. Based on stock characters and human foibles that are common to any geographical situation, farce requires mainly physical skills and improvisation, and it thrives upon the fairground arts of juggling, tumbling, singing, and dancing. It can also be performed on the back of a cart in any marketplace; on an inn-room table; or in the great hall of a medieval mansion. Thus it was that small groups of itinerant actors under many names—clowns, skops, jongleurs, goliards, minstrels, farceurs, cabotins—kept popular drama alive for a thousand years. The drama itself took many names—mummings, sotties, drolls, interludes, and "farces"—but however performed and under whatever name, popular drama was based upon similar situations dealing with stealing or hiding money, sexual intrigue, deception, trickery, and practical joking of all kinds. The characters in the dramas took local forms, but were all some variation of a cunning or stupid peasant or servant, tricky lawyer, voluptuous priest, clever and sexually potent young man, randy matron, impotent and miserly husband. They were all thrown together and mixed up in a bawdy physical intrigue or romp. We still find them today, less robust, watered down, geared to the needs and sensibility of a late-twentieth-century bourgeois, capitalist society, but little changed in stock situation and type—on television, in situation comedies.

After its wanderings through the Middle Ages, the spirit of popular drama and its farcical instinct next found a permanent form in sixteenth-century Italy. Here the *commedia del l'arte* developed—performed by troupes of about ten actors and based upon a stock set of characters and situations. The characters were identifiable by a facial mask and costume, which hardly varied from troupe to troupe or place to place. The plots were equally defined in structure, and the art of this form of theatre lay in the improvised changes the actors could ring within the givens of their character and the set nature of the plot. It was essentially an actor's theatre: There were no literary overtones. It found its roots and expressed itself through the popular, farcically oriented sensibility that we have shown to be a consistent form of human communication.

It is no surprise, therefore, that the stock characters, or masks, of the *commedia* should closely resemble those found in the earliest Greek farces, and in Plautus. There is an academic discussion as to whether this shows the continuation of a tradition passed on over a thousand years from the Romans to the Italian Renaissance, or whether it is the self-contained revival of a popular instinct, which found expression in recognizable forms because of the consistency of human nature and its concerns. Either reason suits our purpose, which is to identify certain qualities of the form and character of popular drama as the continuing essence of farce.

The basic *commedia* masks are an impotent, lecherous, miserly old man—Pantalone; a pompous, lecherous old pedant—Dottore; a swaggering, cowardly, amorous soldier—Capitano; and a couple of tricky servants known as Zanni, who went by various individual names, but usually Arlecchino and Brighella. The troupes also contained young lovers of either sex and the occasional serving maid or older female confidante. The basic plots are young lovers trying to get together, helped by servants but hindered by the older men—who either forbade it, wanted the girl themselves, wouldn't give the lovers money, or wanted them to marry someone else. The interest is not whether the lovers would make it—they always do—or whether the older masks would be fooled—they always are—but how the servants would trick the old men, and how the old men would be made fools of this time. The characters and plot situations are very similar to those used in the Roman farces. They were simply given the external appearance of an Italian social type of the sixteenth century: Pantalone was recognizably a Venetian merchant; Dottore, a graduate of the University of Bologna. But as misers, lechers, fathers, and so on, they are recognizable as

Commedia masks in action.   *Dover Publications Inc., by permission.*

Hume Cronyn, as Harpagon in *The Miser*, creates a Pantalone-based mask.   *Mark Taper Forum, Los Angeles.*

universal human types going back to humankind's earliest social relationships. As Gertrude Stein might have said: A lecher is a lecher is a lecher; a miser is a miser is a miser.

The *commedia del l'arte* lasted the best part of two hundred years and influenced the work of Molière, whose plays, written in seventeenth-century France, are sometimes called comedies of character. However, Molière's work spans a wide spectrum, from satirical plays of considerable literary merit to plays that are unashamedly and brilliantly based upon the tradition of farce characters and intrigue plots. At the simplest level, his plays such as *The Doctor in Spite of Himself* and *The Knavery of Scapin* are full of tricky servants, mean and lecherous old men, mistaken identities, young lovers, and all the paraphernalia we have come to associate with farce intrigue. Even somewhat more sophisticated plays such as *The Miser* and *The Imaginary Invalid* have a similar formula, and *Tartuffe,* often regarded as Molière's most brilliant comedy, is not above having a wife seduced on a table beneath which the husband

is hiding, or a sassy servant who engages in farcical backchat with her master.

We will look more closely at Molière's farcical genius in a later section. Here, in order to complete our review of farce, we have to move on a couple of centuries to Labiche, Feydeau, and the great French farces of the later nineteenth century. Just as the *commedia* and Molière, while keeping the inherited stock characters and situations that typified popular farce through the ages, invested the characters with recognizable qualities of their own day, so in the late nineteenth century farce took on the characteristics of that Victorian and bourgeois period.

It is the drawing rooms, the salons, and particularly the hotel bedrooms of the late nineteenth century that are the environments for the intrigues of Labiche and Feydeau. Theatre was now in the period of realism, and the farceurs used entirely recognizable domestic

Highly physical seduction of Elmire with Orgon beneneath the table; from the Oregon Shakespeare Festival's *Tartuffe.*   *Photo by Henry Kranzler.*

backgrounds for their farcical situations. But if the physical backgrounds and the characters' costumes would not have been familiar to a Roman audience at a play by Plautus or an Italian audience at the *commedia*, plots and the machinations of the characters would have been instantly recognized. Sex, marriage, and money were the motivating factors of the plot, and the members of the *haute* bourgeoise—lawyers, physicians, civil servants, and others with a certain authority and position in society to uphold—were the characters doomed to being made ridiculous. Young lovers did not appear to the same degree in this rather sophisticated and somewhat decadent society: circular intrigues, with everyone chasing everyone else's wife, and the occasional *cocotte* thrown in for good measure, were the order of the day. But the complications, frustrations, and all the fun of man, the buffoon, chasing his own tail (or phallus) are there. Beneath the now elegant mask of clothing, the stiff collar, and the starched shirt front still beats the heart of the comic satyr, bursting his buttons to get out.

Essence and Function. Why do the same characteristics, the same intrigues, the same situations, the same responses to the same stimuli, keep repeating themselves to maintain the consistency of farce structure over more than two thousand years of theatre history? Essentially because farce takes a particular perspective upon certain unchanging qualities in humankind and its relationships. The qualities are the most basic human drives, and the perspective is essentially physical. Farce goes for the belly and the backside. It makes us laugh at the fact that we look funny, or at a disadvantage, with our pants down. Yet three of the five basic human physical functions—shitting, pissing, and fucking—can only be performed with the pants off. We have deliberately used the Anglo-Saxon terms, which our dictionary tells us are "usually considered

vulgar," because that is part of what farce does—it removes polite masks to show the primitive realities beneath, and asks us to laugh at the discrepancy between what we show and what we are.

Ever since Adam and Eve discovered original sin and tried to cover it with fig leaves, humanity has been constantly caught with its pants down. Farce relies upon both the literal and metaphoric sense of this statement: the literal, because farce has been concerned with the most primitive of all drives—phallic sex—ever since the fertility rites from which it traces its roots; metaphorically, because of farce's concern to debunk all forms of human pretension—to reveal the urgent, primitive reality beneath the most supercilious and sophisticated of human masks. However dignified the human soul, however aspiring the human spirit, both are trapped within and must express themselves through a body that is basically geared to ingesting and excreting through various orifices in a very down-to-earth manner. The romantic tends to become melancholic at the conflict of flesh and spirit; the tragedian kills the body to release and magnify the soul; the farceur makes us laugh at our pretensions so that we may accept ourselves for what we are in the most physical sense: fools of mortals, fated to repeat the comic pattern inherent in human existence, and doomed never to give up trying to escape it. The characters on this human-created carousel are all pursuing either basic human wants or those that social structures have made desirable: love, sex, food, money, power, glory. They also suffer from the corruptions that the pursuit or possession of these aims has given them: greed, lechery, avarice, vainglory, undue self-esteem, intellectual pomposity. The merry-go-round spins within a closed system of values—social, moral, and economic—that tend to favor those with power and authority.

Farce goes for all pretensions, all masks, and tends to attack in the simplest way, with the kick in the backside or the knock on the head. In the world of realpolitik that farce inhabits, all usually get their just deserts. The power structure of society must be renewed—there is always a need for new virility to preserve the race. Those who get in its way must be outwitted, put in their proper place. To the young and the bold goes sexual fulfillment; to the old and incompetent, frustrations; to the clever and agile, an advantage. Factors that tend to become obstacles must be reduced to size and reconciled with society's needs.

Farce deals with the most basic social irritants: interfering relations, shrewish wives, impotent husbands, pompous teachers, miserly merchants, arrogant bankers, soldiers, government officials. It pits against them the underdogs, those who have less power but equal human needs; young people in love who can't afford to get married and are forbidden by the social structure to go to bed with each other; servants and others who have to perform the menial functions in life; the poor; the disadvantaged, who have to live by their wits alone; any worthy but socially oppressed figure.

Arrogance always comes before a fall in farce—usually a pratfall. This is normally engineered by the clever underling. Farce has been on the side of the "little man," from the Roman slave to Charlie Chaplin. Chaplin's art in many ways embodies the farce sensibility. He is the downtrodden little Everyman, alone against a usually unkind world, who survives on his wits and agility. He is constantly up against the bigger and more powerful—the authority structure in its many forms. His outwitting maneuvers are usually physical, and just when he believes himself to have gained the advantage, his naive pleasure at his cleverness leads to his own downfall. The advantage gained by all the tricky servants

Chaplin's "little tramp" confronts authority.   *The Academy of Motion Picture Arts and Sciences.*

throughout the history of farce is usually short-lived. When they overreach themselves the joke turns on them—any unjustified human pride tends to come before farce's fall. Farce tends to preserve the social balance: It brings both the high and low alike back into line when they get above themselves. But Chaplin, like all the clever servants and the eternal resilience of man himself, "picks himself up, dusts himself down, and starts all over again." If tragedy pays tribute to man's indomitable spirit, farce embodies his physical resilience—his enduring capacity to keep on trying. Just as long as he doesn't get too clever for his own good, for then he will assuredly trip over his own feet.

The little man, however, is more usually seen tripping up authority, which practice, together with the ridiculing of sexual taboos, forms the two principal subjects of farce.

Breasts, buttocks, phalloi, underwear, bedpans, enemas—all the social "unmentionables" are fair game for farce. Sexual organs and the sexual act are the fundamental human force and the fundamental human taboo. We try to conceal them behind moral strictures and masks of clothing. The "beast with two backs" is the physical reality of the cherubic Cupid (the only word in English that rhymes with "stupid")—a subject for laughter as we hide a sexual function behind a mask of childlike spirituality. If we didn't try to romanticize the sexual act or pretend it doesn't exist, it wouldn't be a subject for laughter. If we didn't have such moral phobias about the body and its functions there would be no need for "throwing moons" or other acts of aggression ("cocking a snook") against the social mores that draw the response of laughter.

Elmire saves a pratfall but loses her dignity and her skirts in this Los Angeles Theatre production of *Tartuffe*.   *Photo by Chris Gulker.*

If the conscious revealing of the body's sexual and excretory organs is an attack on the moral structure, the unconscious revealing is an act that produces laughter through the embarrassment caused to the victim. Pants falling down, skirts blowing up, and underwear up or down have all been perennial sources of amusement—the revealing of what we try to keep hidden, the slipping of the mask of moral propriety.

Farce uses laughter—the belly laugh, not the intellectual snicker of less robust forms of comedy—to confront us with the reality of our sexual drives and taboos, and of our social power structures. Laughter has been described as the sudden release of repressed energy that has been performing the function of restraining forbidden desires—keeping antisocial elements away from consciousness. This energy is often sexual and potentially aggressive. It goes back again to the orgiastic joking of the Dionysian fertility rites. These festivities gave play to two human impulses—to pleasure and self-indulgence, and to aggression and hostility.

There is, indeed, something orgiastic and destructive about the nature of farce, but in this sense it is a kind of safety valve for the survival of society. Freud, whose theory of laughter as the release of repressed energy was mentioned above, suggested in his *Civilization and Its Discontents*[1] that humans buy social and cultural structures at the price of frustration. Dreams, fantasies, and farces are the means by which humans live with frustrations, acting them out, and purging them before they lead to madness and anarchy.

[1]Sigmund Freud, *Civilization and Its Discontents,* trans. James Strachey (New York: Norton, 1962).

Sex and agression meet in this Los Angeles Theatre Center production of *What the Butler Saw.*   *Photo by R. Kaufman.*

Marriage, for example, is a necessary social mechanism—providing emotional stability and a secure environment for bringing up children—but it may be said not to satisfy human sexual curiosity or need for variety. Thus the inevitability of dirty jokes, bedroom farce, and mother-in-law gags. Playing out one's fantasies or empathizing with them on stage is a form of imitative magic, a wish fulfillment like that of primitive man, who wore the mask of the animal or enemy he wished to kill or keep away from him. And the wearing of masks has long been associated with the playing of farce. The very dynamic of farce may be said to be the interplay between the facade—the mask of civilization—and the face of the primitive instinct beneath. In the playing of farce the primitive energy must always be present beneath the sophisticated facade.

From the Roman theatre through the Feast of Fools to the Marx Brothers, farce has led the revolt against oppressive reason and the attack upon society's sacred cows. It has incorporated the urge to destroy what we cannot understand or operate within. In a Marx Brothers movie, Groucho is asked why Harpo is tearing up a book. His reply: "He is angry because he can't read." We are often angry because of things we cannot do, or because of our insecurities at the difficulty of functioning in a complicated world. So farce lets us enjoy a fantasy of breaking things up—it often involves the destruction of everyday artifacts. It also reassures us by letting us laugh at the comic antagonist. We feel superior to him, are amused by his misfortunes, congratulate ourselves upon being less stupid—indeed, vicariously associate with the clever character who seems to be able to win out against the world. But we aren't allowed to feel too superior. The tricky servant often gets caught by his own cleverness, and the custard pie, after having made the rounds, comes back to land in our own face.

Farce is sometimes criticized for pandering to our "baser" instincts—for encouraging

our hostility and indulging a pleasure at the humiliation and suffering of others. But the moralizing sentiment misses the point that farce is essentially amoral. It neither seeks to pass moral comment nor deliberately attempts to avoid it. It is an improbable game based upon probable premises. It shows us how humanity contrives to escape after being caught in predicaments of its own making. It does this so the world may continue safely upon its way, as it did before the outburst of primitive energy caused the disturbance. This is not the moral solution sought by comedy and tragedy. Farce is a somewhat conservative form that affirms and accommodates to reality.

Being conservative in essence, farce displays few conversions. The characters may be sobered by misfortune, but they leave pretty much as they came in. There is loss of face and embarrassment, but they are not permanent defeats and disasters—death is not a serious threat. Farce is a holiday, a celebration, a day off from responsibilities, that enables us to put up with the rest of the year. And no one really gets hurt. That is one reason we can afford to laugh with impunity at the misfortunes of the characters—we know it's a game. Dogs in films, when they are "attacking," give the game away by wagging their tails—they are "playing" at being fierce and hurting someone. So is the farceur.

Certain elements of farce are sometimes called *slapstick*. The essence of the slapstick is the essence of farce itself—exaggerated noise and effect, but no real pain.[2] Farce has the appearance of reality, but is distanced from the audience by the manner of its performance. It mustn't be allowed to come too close to the audience's feelings, or become a subject for intellectual appraisal. That is why it goes for the direct, physical response—the belly and the backside. In farce the comic butts are meant to

---

[2]The slapstick is a kind of paddle split down the middle so that the two halves come together with a sharp noise when used to strike someone.

(a)

(b)

The aggression of farce is well illustrated by (a) Laurel and Hardy, and (b) in a production of *A Flea in Her Ear* by the Goodman Theatre.   *(a) The Academy of Motion Picture Arts and Sciences; (b) Photo by Charles Osgood.*

be laughed at. We may sympathize with their predicaments as we laugh, but we can never pity them, or the play is lost. The playing of farce is a robust exercise, but at the same time very delicate. The farceur treads a fine line.

INTRINSIC DEMANDS

Form.   Farce celebrates the eternal, ritualistic contest of men and women. Not far beneath farce's civilized or sophisticated surface it is still primitive in its quest for self-preservation, in its aggressive self-assertion. A *"gifle,"* a small slap in the face, is what farce is all about—an involuntary act of aggression or trespass delivered at the moment when instigation, personal desire, and opportune situation meet. Farce ritual requires no real belief. It moves inexorably through layers of situation, achieving a successful whole without essential meaning. Played well and furiously, it draws us into its own logic, creates for us its own sense of truth. It is an essentially theatrical form truly experienced only in performance.

Even a fully developed farce script is still something of a scenario. The outcome will depend a great deal upon the actor's invention within the series of situations given by the author. The English actor Donald Sinden was once having problems working in farce. He mentioned this to Edith Evans, who replied, "Of course. You see, in a farce you don't have a play to help you." A farce plot is a thread linking comic situations. It is a pretext to pull the strings of human puppets. The playwright raises storms of banter and arrays of traps so that men may be cheated of their desires and revealed in their folly. The basic principles and qualities of farce structure are:

1. *Situation:* It is given and not overelaborated. Brevity is a feature of farce—set up a skittle; knock it down; set up another one. Don't ask questions. The situations are basic human and domestic problems:

young lovers, marriage, money, parents at cross-purposes with children, servants at cross-purposes with masters. The situations are compounded and create a snowball effect. This is because decisions are made on impulse, not by reflection. The snowball effect is also a form of repetition and exaggeration, two important comic qualities: Father hits boy, boy hits servant, servant kicks dog. To round this one off, dog would bite father.

2. *Physical action:* The situations and the snowball effect lead to chases, avoidances, pratfalls, beatings—hectic physical movement usually ending in some form of disequilibrium: the reduction of dignity or a bringing down to size.

3. *Outwitting:* Again a function of the situation, which brings about such maneuvers as disguising, hiding, impersonations, mistaken identities—all different forms of mask play.

4. *Obstacles:* These are the reasons for the outwittings, and they are usually authority characters who have either social, political, or economic power. These characters are reduced, ridiculed, frustrated, reconciled to the necessary social situation, but do not suffer permanent or serious harm.

5. *Devices:* Farce employs, in physical form, the gamut of comic devices. We have already mentioned repetition and exaggeration. Then there is inversion—servants dominating masters—a reversal of the norm. This is part of the topsy-turvy world of farce—the holiday from reason. Incongruities are a prime farce device: small hats on large heads; too tight trousers, and almost any kind of physical abnormality—especially large noses, cross-eyes, and missing teeth.

Form at Work.   To put some flesh on the above outline, and to show both how the structure works in practice and how consistent it has been over the history of farce, we are going to look briefly at plays by Plautus, Molière, and Feydeau, and a *commedia* scenario. Plautus's *The Pot of Gold* concerns a poor old man who finds treasure, then gloats over it in a miserly fashion while still pleading poverty. He has a daughter who, unknown to the father, has been seduced by an impoverished young man. The plot involves getting the young man married to the girl before she has the baby. Obstacles to this are the young man's poverty, the father's miserliness, and a wealthy neighbor (who just happens to be the young man's uncle) who wants to marry the girl.

The play is essentially a pretext on the absurd lengths to which the father goes to conceal his pot of gold. He is constantly running back into the house to make sure it is still there, or moving it to ever more ridiculous hiding places. He constantly believes his servants are cheating him, which leads to chases and beatings and "miser" gags from the servants: "He ties a bag over his mouth at night so as not to lose this breath"; "He had his hands manicured, collected the nail clippings and took them home." But most often the humor is manifested in physical terms—such as the miser, suspicious that a servant has got his gold, asking to see his "third" hand just to make sure. Repetition and exaggeration are the main comic devices.

The "third-hand" gag was, in fact, used by Molière in his play *The Miser*, which is based upon the theme by Plautus. Molière elaborates the idea by doubling the number of lovers and putting them at cross-purposes. He also has the miser, Harpagon, as a suitor for the girl, Marianne, whom his son wants to marry. A couple of comic servants cause Harpagon endless trouble by such "extravagances" as wanting food for his horses and money to buy food for his guests.

The play is again a series of comic confrontations based upon the situation that Harpagon is an obstacle to all the lovers getting together—through being a rival to his son and not wanting to part with money for his daughter's dowry. The play is set in late-seventeenth-century France, and the characters are recognizable as Frenchmen of their day. But beneath their periwigs, beneath Harpagon's attire as a bourgeois merchant, and the servants' rig as seventeenth-century coachmen or cooks lie the same human types with the same reactions to the same situations that form the eternal "stuffing" of farce: Sex and money provide the stimuli to comic action. Only adultery is needed to complete the unholy trinity of farce action, and adultery provides the dynamic of the last two plays whose structure we are now going to examine.

Leon Katz has taken a *commedia* scenario, *The Three Cuckolds,*[3] and fleshed it out into a farce play, using the kinds of devices, comic business and development of situation that might have been expected of *commedia* actors. The plot outline has three simple premises: One is a sexual *ronde* with three old men after each other's wives; the second is a young man after one of the old men's wives; third, there is a comic mask of the tricky servant type, who will do anything for anyone for a meal. The play is full of set pieces—which would have been improvisations in the original. The tricky servant is, at one time or another, a doctor, a dentist, and a woman—all in the cause of getting the women the lovers they want and, the servant hopes, food as his reward. There is a running gag about the breath of one of the old men (Pantalone), which sets up a farcical tooth-pulling scene. This does nothing to advance the action, but is simply there for its coarse, physical humor and to bring discomfort to Pantalone. The

[3]Leon Katz, *The Three Cuckolds*, in *The Classic Theatre,* Vol 1. (New York: Doubleday, 1958).

doctor scene is at the expense of the other old man, who is impotent and is told by the "doctor" that his wife is to have a baby. This is all to enable a lover to be smuggled into his house in the baby basket. And so it goes. The outcome is that all the men discover that their lust and pretensions have rebounded upon their own heads—they have all been made fools and cuckolds—and they are better off accepting things are they are, trying to live in peace with their own wives.

Feydeau's farce *Le Dindon* (*Sauce for the Goose*)[4] is also predicated upon the oldest game in town—the quest for illicit sexual adventure. Set in elegant bourgeois surroundings in late-nineteenth-century Paris, it starts with a bang—a married woman is pursued by a would-be seducer into her own drawing room. Unknown to the seducer, the woman is married to a friend of his, and, sure enough, in comes the husband. (Feydeau has been quoted as saying that a basic principle of his structure is that when any two characters should on no account come together, he throws them at each other as soon as possible).

Essentially the plot convention is that the women are trying to remain chaste—the moral double standard has them in its grip—although they do have a lot of inner urges. But they agree that if they find their husbands in the act of being unfaithful, they will pay them back in kind. Hence the play's title: What is sauce for the goose is sauce for the gander—inverted as befitting a farce. In the second act, set in a hotel bedroom, all the plot complications come together. By this time Feydeau has managed to achieve three pairs of potential infidelities, all obligingly going to happen in the same room. He then adds to the melee a *cocotte*, who has been the mistress of the one unmarried man in the play, and an old couple who are celebrating their wedding anniver-

sary and have been given the wrong room. The old couple have essentially nothing to do with the plot—they are there to provide extra physical humor and comic business. The old lady, for example, is deaf. She can "hear" people only when they don't speak aloud—then she seems to be able to read their lips. The old man is an ex-army officer who is pompous, lecherous, and gets hold of the wrong end of every stick. By the time Feydeau has finished with the bedroom scene he has bells under the mattress to ring when the adulterous couples are in bed; husbands and wives, who constantly just miss seeing each other, hidden behind every door in the room; and the wrong people getting into bed with each other. Finally, he contrives to have the police arrive, and the scene ends with everyone chasing after and struggling with everyone else, round and round the room.

The play ends with no one actually committing adultery at all. The only couple who sleep together are the unmarried man and the *cocotte*. Everyone has been made to look foolish, but all are reconciled. The only one who really loses is the original seducer, who describes his situation in a speech at the end of the play that is worth quoting because of the way it illustrates Feydeau's genius for arranging complicated relationships:

> I'm in the most appalling mess. Two cases of adultery—which I didn't commit. Caught by a husband I don't know, with a wife I don't know. Caught by my own wife, with the same woman I don't know. . . . A quarrel with my wife. The woman I don't know arrives this morning and tells me in a German accent I owe her reparation, complicated by the man I don't know taking the law into his own hands. Worries, lawsuits, scandals, the lot.

Nothing really has changed at the end of the play. The social balance has been restored and a lot of prosperous citizens—lawyers, soldiers, merchants—have been made to look foolish, which is probably good for their souls. One

---

[4]Georges Feydeau, *Sauce for the Goose*, trans. Peter Meyer (London: British Broadcasting Corporation, 1974).

Incongruity creates farce out of elegant manner in *The Importance of Being Earnest.   Arena Stage, Washington.*

question of whether this is farce and that is comedy, but instead this situation, these rhythms, this set-piece structure requires this approach rather than that one. As a rule of thumb, farce will have more intrigues per minute than will comedy. It will have fewer metaphors, less symbolism, and fewer literary artifacts in general. In farce the situation tends to control the characters. Comedy allows characters a rapport with the audience in unfolding the situation for them. Comedy characters are thus more developed; they have some insights and feelings. The audience has more time to involve itself with the characters in a comedy; it is not just the detached observer of a farcical strategy. Whereas farce gives people a day off to help reconcile them to things as they are, comedy will try to expose shortcomings in the hope of a better possibility. The hymen—young lovers marrying at the end of comedy—has a romantic potentiality for living happily ever after. Farce knows they probably won't live happily ever after but will help them make the best of it. Farce is more improbable, aggressive, exaggerated, mechanical, and physically oriented. It moves shallowly across the surface of human reality. It avoids cynicism and sentimentality. It is always festive, playful; it has made a compact with the audience to make fun of the world.

might presume the play to suggest obliquely that if one sets out to commit adultery, one will end up looking foolish and infinitely complicate one's life, so it probably isn't worth it. The play doesn't say, "It's wrong." The original seducer may have learned a lesson and taken pause for a while, but one doubts whether he will entirely give up his lecherous ways. Anyway, whatever he does or doesn't do is, finally, irrelevant to the play—once the game is done and the joke over. Fantasies are best left as fantasies and laughed at from the comfort of a darkened auditorium.

Before leaving the discussion of farce form we should say a final word on the difference between farce and other forms of comedy. We have suggested that there is a comic continuum and there are no hard-and-fact distinctions. In *The Importance of Being Earnest* we have a mixture of farce situation with a veneer of witty manner. Sheridan and Goldsmith also used farce techniques within comedies of manners. So it is not always a

Character Masks.   We have already traced the evolution and consistency of character types, or masks, from farce's earliest roots to the sophisticated expressions of Feydeau. Now we are going to underline the essential characteristics of these types so the actor may have a simple and clear idea of how character operates in farce.

Character is stated, not examined. It is illustrated by an abundance of verbal gestures or physical actions that show different aspects of the same character traits. The character is motivated by basic human drives—sex, food, self-preservation—not by subtle and individual psychological qualities. Farce is not remotely concerned with why a character happens to be a miser or a lecher. It deals with the surface facts and relies upon its audience's recognition and understanding of basic human motivations. Farce also moves too quickly for the audience to be concerned with subtextual implications or complex psyches. The character is to a great degree the author's puppet, whose strings are pulled according to the requirements of the situation. The characters tend to be blinded by self-conceit, unaware of their deficiencies, one-dimensionally motivated; often resourceful and ingenious, they produce only immediate and temporary solutions to their problems. Lacking in both insight and foresight, the characters have their shortcomings exaggerated for comic purposes.

A character's responses to a situation will be as mechanical as his attitudes are rigid. Lack of flexibility will prevent him or her from adapting to changes in circumstances in any other than an impulsive way. Because they don't examine the result of their actions, the characters are trapped within the improbable logic of extreme solutions. Acting and reacting blindly, they are swept along by the impetus of events. But their mental fixation produces its own logic so that the character, in however exaggerated and abandoned a manner, will always behave consistently within his or her improbable world. Because of this consistency, and the fact that the character mask is based, however remotely, in observed human truth, the audience will accept the improba-

bilities and exaggerations as part of the logic, the "reality" of the event.[5]

Farce characters are what they seem and do what they are expected to do. The interest lies in the situation and the number of ways the playwright and actor can physically illustrate the quality of the mask. To take the *commedia* masks as an example: Pantalone, in whatever form, will have all the contradictions of senility. He is an impotent old man who has economic power and authority in the community, yet he chases after young women and throws childish tantrums when thwarted by his servants. He is miserly yet loves display, crafty but rash, old yet lustful, benevolent yet irate. It is these qualities the audience will expect from the Pantalone figure, and it is these qualities upon which the actor must exercise physical imagination to create the character. The Dottore is basically pedantic, pompous, loquacious, and a muddler. The same exercise may be done for all the *commedia* characters. How the qualities are manifested in any given situation is up to the actor.

In many ways the basic principle of farce is two-person confrontation: he who kicks the backside and he whose backside is kicked. This, of course, is also the basis of the eternal comic artifact—the double act. The comic servants, or Zanni, in *commedia* are part of this tradition. One tends to be clever, sharp, the trickster; the other, pleasantly dull-witted but with a kind of native cunning. They are constantly in confrontation with one of the other masks, either kicking backsides or getting their own backsides kicked. The tradition has had some notable representatives in the twentieth century: Laurel and Hardy, the Marx Brothers, W. C. Fields, and Charlie Chaplin. Each of these has his mask: unchanging clothes,

---

[5]It is interesting, in the context of the reality an audience will accept, that the most farcical characters on TV in recent years have been nonhumans: 3rd Rock from the Sun. This is so that absurd behavior may be acceptable in a highly realistic medium.

(a)

(b)

(c)

(a) Maccus, a Greek farce character, (b) a Commedia Zanni, and (c) a servant from a modern production of *The Miser*, show the continuity of comic masks over three thousand years.   (*a*) *The Metropolitan Museum of Art, Rogers Fund, 1912; (b) Dover Publications Inc.; (c)* The Miser, *Mark Taper Forum, Los Angeles.*

character traits, reactions. What changed were the situations and circumstances. And so it has always been with the characters in farce, whether in Greek mime form, the *commedia*, silent movies, or the fully developed, sophisticated plays of Feydeau.

Modern farce, such as written by Feydeau, tends to have a patina of realism over the mechanical structure. This is because its settings are of a recognizably middle-class nature, and the characters are evidently members of contemporary social classes and professions. The masks are not as rigid as in *commedia*, but the essence is the same. Beneath the urbane, everyday manner of the characters in a Feydeau play lie the obsessive and frenetic drives that have catalyzed the masks of farce from the beginnings of drama. Characters may not get chased with slapsticks, but they get boxed on the ears and hit with umbrellas and canes. And although nobody's backside actually gets kicked—being too improbable in the sophisticated environment—many ways are found to reduce the dignity and upset the equilibrium of the foolish char-

acters. To give a very simple example: In *Sauce for the Goose* the wife gives the would-be lover, kneeling in supplication before her, a push and, sure enough, he lands on his backside on the floor—just as the husband comes in.

They may be dressed differently, they may adopt a different social manner, but not far beneath the surface of the magistrates, bankers, lawyers, lechers, and buffoons of modern farces beat the hearts of the Pantalones and Dottores of the *commedia*—and all their forefathers stretching back to the small Greek town of Megara two thousand years before.

Costume/Properties.   Costume is always a form of mask, and seldom more so than in farce. We have already mentioned the physical masks that formed part of farce conventions from the Greeks through to the *commedia*. These costume conventions, such as the *phalloi,* can both show the connection with the orgasmic roots of farce and enable the audience immediately to recognize a character: They originate in some kind of human social truth. Pantalone's traditional *commedia* costume derives from the dress of a sixteenth-century Venetian merchant. Dottore wore the academic dress of a graduate of the University of Bologna. Perhaps the best example of truth becoming tradition is the costume of Arlecchino (Harlequin). As a poor ser-

Frenetic physicality in Feydeau.   *Mark Taper Forum, Los Angeles.*

vant he could not afford decent clothing, so he wore rags with many patches. Over a period of time this was conventionalized into the costume with its multicolored lozenges that is so recognizable today.

Costume and manner become synonymous. The phallus may no longer be visible but the lecher is immediately identifiable by his actions and reactions, and he fulfills his expected function in the structure of the farce. In fact, the great modern descendants, both of the classical tricky slaves and the *commedia* Zannis, wore an easily identifiable costume mask that is equally a part of their character.

The Bourgeois "mask" of W. C. Fields. *The Academy of Motion Picture Arts and Sciences.*

Chaplin's tramp outfit and the unchanging clothing worn by Laurel and Hardy, W. C. Fields, Harold Lloyd, and the Marx Brothers are totally identified with the consistent character of their wearers. It's interesting to note that the costumes of most of these characters are based upon the accepted wear of the successful bourgeois, from the end of the nineteenth century up through the middle of the twentieth: top hat or bowler hat; frock coat or shorter black jacket; waistcoat, collar, and tie; plain gray or striped trousers; gloves, walking sticks, umbrellas. The costumes, of course, don't quite fit the farceurs; they are shabby or worn incorrectly. Such incongruity reinforces the fundamental farcicality of finding upper-class costumes on deadbeat characters. The characters pretend a dignity they don't have. The mask has a double effect: It tells us what they are and how we may expect them to react. Because we associate a particular manner with the costume, it defines the character—Chaplin *is* the tramp. At the same time, the faded or ill-fitting dignity of the clothing reminds us of what the character would like to be, or sees himself as. This creates the comic gap between mask and reality.

This comic gap plays its part in the effect of modern farce plays. Feydeau's characters wore the proper clothing for persons of their rank in the late nineteenth century. These costume masks set up a series of identifications and expectations—dignity, propriety, authority—that farce sets out to break down and reveal the truth beneath. As with the *commedia* masks, it is the difference between what "ought" to be expected of the character—given his age, social position, and so forth—and what "is" to be expected of the character when the pressure of farce situations makes the masks slip—or lets the pants fall down.

There is always a tension between mask and appetite, between what the clothing allows and what the character wants. Collars are too high and too tight to allow the characters, comfortably, to chase in and out of doors. Trousers are too tight to allow them, comfortably, to climb out of windows. Hats and ties begin to slip under pressure of physical activity. Shoes or socks get lost or put on the wrong feet; shoelaces get tied together and trip one up. Trousers get put on back to front, and articles of ladies' underwear find their way into gentlemen's pockets in mistake for handkerchiefs. The elegant mask of the dignified bourgeois must constantly be readjusted, as it slips to reveal the impulsive child or instinctual animal below the well-dressed facade.

Incongruity is, then, one of the chief characteristics of farce costuming—either because the costume doesn't fit the character or the character doesn't live up to the costume. If the costume isn't too big, too small, too tight, too loose for the character, then the character will be too manic, too childish, too weak, too lecherous, or too stupid for the costume.

Before leaving costuming we should mention the function of properties in farce action. Here, another fundamental comic quality comes into play—exaggeration. Unusually large properties are standard in farce. They sometimes serve to reinforce character traits; such are the miserly Pantalone's overlarge keys or the Dottore's voluminous books or the braggart warrior's double-size sword. Often they are geared to human discomfort or organic functions—huge enemas, enormous syringes, vast dental instruments. Everyday artifacts of discomfort, or items we would like to hide, are made larger and more visible. Medical pills become the size of golf balls, or, if one is trying to keep within the bounds of "reality," an improbable number of "normal"-size pills are stuffed down a patient's throat. Surgical operations take place with carpentry saws, hammers, chisels, and an incredible amount of intestinal tubing, and lurid-looking organs are "removed" from the sufferer. The very first exaggerated farce property was probably the Greek phallus, which outdid in size even the most optimistic male fantasy. Exaggeration, like incongruity, is comic in its improbability and serves to distance discomfort or pain. We know no dentist would use such pliers, no surgeon such a syringe, no nurse such a needle, so we can laugh at the victim's discomfort while the action lances our own fears of such things happening to us.

Language.   If the basic function of language is to inform and communicate, the basic function in farce tends to be to achieve misunderstanding. Communication requires three things: a sayer, a sayee, and a convention that is accepted by both. Comic use of language involves a breakdown of this structure. It is essentially the way in which the Double Act works:

1. the comic sets up,
2. the straight man responds,
3. the comic tops off.

This can be illustrated:

COMIC: How's your boy doing?
STRAIGHT: Not so good; I took him to a psychiatrist who says he has an Oedipus complex.
COMIC: Don't worry, he'll be all right as long as he's a good boy and loves his Mommy.

Here two conventions are clashing. The reasonable assumption that if a boy is good and loves his parents other matters are less important; this clashes with the specific assumptions of Freudian psychiatry.

A joke is, then, the collision of two incompatible logics that produces a flashpoint—a surprising result that releases laughter. The joke depends upon:

1. Convention: the assumptions must be known and accepted;
2. Originality: the outcome must be a surprise;
3. Simplicity: the tension must be built directly; over-elaboration defuses tension;
4. Emphasis: the use of verbal rhythm to hit the crucial information.

Physical incongruity in Shakespeare's Commedia-based farce, *The Taming of the Shrew. The Guthrie Theatre.*

The 1-2-3 structure can probably be related to the Hegelian dialectical form:

Thesis: setting up a proposition
Antithesis: a response within the same logic but incompatible
Synthesis: a new way of looking at the logic that is surprising or funny.

When dealing with wit or epigrammatical language the collision of expectations appears in the form of balanced antithesis—as we saw in the section of comedy of manners: "I'd no more play [cards] with a man that slighted his

ill-fortune than I'd make love to a woman who undervalued the loss of her reputation." Farce takes a more robust approach; its thesis and antithesis, its collision of opposites, tend to be illustrated in physical ways: Wish fulfillment versus moral convention appears as pants off for adultery versus not being caught with one's pants down, and this leads to all those chase scenes with people hobbling around trying to pull their pants up. Farce doesn't have the time to stop for literary conceits or wordplay. Its language also tends to work physically in structures and rhythms. The joke is contained in the way the verbal situation is built, not in the content of the language. It functions in terms of character and situation by illustrating character in action rather than describing it, and by creating verbal traps in which the character reveals its foolishness.

The basic rhythm of farce tends to be stichomythic. Short, sharp sentences create a strong, vigorous pace and a sense of confrontation. Occasionally there will be longer set-piece speeches, sometimes for the purpose of exposition, or to let the audience watch the thought process of a comic victim as he or she tries to think a way out of a situation and invariably becomes more entangled in the web of deceit.

As we have suggested, misunderstanding is one of the principal verbal structures of farce. This can be seen in the Lazzi of the *commedia:* Hearing the Dottore say "Rumpe moras [Put an end to delay]" Pulcinella translates this as "Your ass hurts!" We find the same conceit in Molière, set up in 1-2-3 Double Act form in *The Miser:*

HARPAGON: . . . you are just the sort of man to spread the rumor I have money hidden.
LA FLECHE: You have money hidden!
HARPAGON: No, you rogue, I didn't say that.

Molière contains further examples of verbal structures used to illustrate masks of characters. Again in *The Miser* there is a situation in which Harpagon is going to marry off his young daughter to an old man she doesn't want, because the old man will take her without a dowry. Another character is trying to dissuade him from this, but to every argument Harpagon makes the same response: "But, without a dowry." He says it five times in succession, and he is clearly incapable of hearing any argument to the contrary. This is an illustration of his obsession with money—his mask of miserliness. The comic device used is that of repetition, and the humor is contained not in the content of what Harpagon says, but in the structure of his responses. Somewhat later in the same play there is an example of the set-piece speech. Harpagon discovers someone has run off with his cash box. His reaction is completely exaggerated, but totally in keeping with his mask as an obsessive miser. In his frenzy he tries to arrest himself, claims he has been murdered, and threatens to hang the entire audience unless they confess.

Under the pressures to which farce subjects its characters, the ability to communicate tends to break down, the logic of speech disintegrates, and the ensuing incoherence is often more truly revealing of basic desires. The force of emotion becomes too much for words, but farce's characters still try to communicate in normal social terms, which sets up all kinds of comic situations. Harpagon is so overcome with the thought of not having to pay a dowry that all he can do is repeat the phrase—revealing himself for the miser he is. He is so overcome with the loss of the money that all logic leaves him; he can only shout out the first and most extravagant threats that come to him.

Incoherence, the breakdown of the logic of communication, leads to incomprehensibility and misunderstanding. And this is the stuff of further farcical situations. We have already mentioned the deaf character in *Sauce for the Goose*, who could hear only when her husband mouthed silent words at her. Feydeau also introduced a character with a cleft palate into his play *A Flea in Her Ear*. The breakdown of the normal means of communication helps to throw social relationships into chaos. In the middle of chaos we often truly reveal ourselves for what we are. By using language in this way farce thus achieves two of its chief aims: to keep people in touch with the human reality behind the social mask, and to laugh at their attempts to keep the mask in place.

Space/Settings.   As farce belongs to no specific historical period, it has not been written with a particular space or setting in mind. It uses pretty much what it finds and ties its antics to the stage conventions of a given time. Because it usually deals with middle-rank authority figures and their families, it has a domestic environment, taking place in or in front of some form of house or home. Roman farces used the conventional set structure of their time, and they usually took place on a street in front of two or three houses, with further exits leading to the town and to the country. *Commedia* tended to have similar settings, either in its more primitive and portable form on a platform stage in front of a curtain or, later, in the proscenium-oriented stages of the Italian and French sixteenth and seventeenth centuries. Molière used stages with settings both in front of and inside houses, and Feydeau used the nineteenth-century proscenium stage in which to set his salons, restaurants, and hotel bedrooms of the French *fin de siècle*.

More important than the details of the particular settings are the demands made upon space by the structure and sensibility of farce. What environment does it need to work within? It needs room for physical action yet a sense of compression and intensification. As the shape of farce tends to be both circuitous and erratic, the space must allow for chases and in-and-out movements—it must channel the actor's physical efforts by providing exits and obstacles. There must also be opportunities for the characters to hide from one another, to avoid one another, and to surprise one another.

The Roman stage provided its farces with up to five different exits: plenty of scope for "shell games" and the mazelike pursuits of farce activity. In keeping with this tradition, the modern farce is unlikely to have fewer than four or five doors in a set, plus windows that may be looked in, jumped out of, or gotten stuck in halfway. The doors are, of course, a kind of mask. They conceal what is going on: Characters hide their presence and their illicit intentions behind them. Doors are also to be escaped through—the most dynamic form of concealment is disappearance. Initially, *commedia* stages were smaller and simpler: exits behind each side of the curtain and, possibly, off the side of the stage platform. But the stage was essentially a base for the activities of the actors—and their one-to-one confrontations, their individual-set-piece improvisations, their tumbling and acrobatics. The plots of *commedia* were less complex, the environments less sophisticated, and the world a simpler place than in a modern farce.

The compression and intensity created by the small size of a *commedia* stage is achieved by the clutter of a modern farce set. We live much more in a world of things, an age of technology, and as farce is a game, there must be paraphernalia for play: traps, obstacles, objects—the adult variation of the children's playground and sandlot. Thus, appurtenances form a part of the realistic environment of a modern farce, and they provide much of the opportunity for farcical action. We are trapped not only by the physical world we have created but also by the physical desires we have inherited. The acrobatic tricks of the *commedia* Zannis, which were exhibited for their skill alone, have today become falls out of chairs, over sofas, through windows; trips over rugs, our own feet; slips on banana skins; the essential physical function is the same but trans-

lated into a modern environment. In the farce of the silent movies and the mid-twentieth-century drama, horseplay includes motorcars, conveyer belts, electrical equipment—all the clockwork "slapsticks" of a modern technological society that can go berserk themselves or drive us crazy through our inability to control them. Computers are the ultimate authority figure.

The farce writers of the nineteenth and twentieth centuries use recognizably everyday settings in which the totally improbable takes place. These normal social arenas—drawing rooms, restaurants, bedrooms—become the scenes of the downfall of their inhabitants. The mask slips, the private act becomes public: The pants, metaphorically and sometimes actually, fall down. The cluttered, tightly constructed, space-limiting nature of modern farce settings force confrontations that might not otherwise occur. Characters may frequently hide, but they seldom escape altogether, and it is a platitude of psychology that confined creatures become frustrated and consequently more aggressive. The furnishings themselves create a tangled web that entraps the victims. Doors won't open, windows won't shut, ties or coattails catch in cupboard drawers, rugs slip from under us, beds collapse on top of us. All of this plays its part in the chaotic working of a seemingly normal environment: that cross among an obstacle course, a maze, and a children's playground that is the physical world of farce.

PERFORMANCE DEMANDS

Movement.   Farce is full of a restless vigor. The jokes are physical, revealed in activity. Acting in farce requires the energy and fortitude of a laborer combined with the physical agility of a tap dancer. The primitive energy at the very roots of farce, which catalyzed the sexual rites from which it sprang, is constantly there beneath the civilized facade. It drives the action at a manic pace. The pace is fast for many reasons: the impulsive drives just mentioned; the characters' constant attempts to avoid disaster (danger either lurks behind every door, or one must get behind a door to avoid danger); the fact that the characters are always either avoiding or trying to catch up with something—like uncertain jugglers, they are constantly toppling forward to keep up with the balls. Farce characters are creatures of the moment, of the body's impulses, not the active intellect—they do not think out consequences. The fast pace also distances the situation—no "real" human being acts like that—and leaves the audience no time to reflect upon the improbabilities.

The fast pace heightens the seemingly uncontrollable chaos, adds a sense of frenzy, daring, and danger, allows more disasters to happen per minute. There can be no gaps in farce action or the actors will be left hanging in midair. There is no infrastructure to support them, only the energy of the moment, which must be kept coming—like hot air keeping up balloons. The devil himself is in farce rhythm. The actor seems to be dragged along behind a runaway horse, but must, in fact, be keeping a tight rein. The physical space and structure of farce requires discipline, control, agility, precision. The actor must be able to move at speed through physical clutter: in and out of doors, around furniture. He or she must be able to turn on a dime and change one's manner in the wink of an eye to match a new situation. Chaos is always highly organized to produce the appropriate comic effect—chaos per se is not funny. Without discipline chaos could produce physical injury. Actors must seem to take and give physical punishment; the hitting, the falling

The light, fluid energy of farce in *The Inspector General*.   *Los Angeles Theatre Center.*

over furniture, and the bumping into each other have to be carefully controlled. Equally, the freedom to improvise in farce must be within a carefully respected set pattern. Finally, farce is a clockwork mechanism that requires as strong ensemble playing as individual imagination.

Movement is, then, quick, light, balanced, flexible. It contains more energy and is exaggerated more than its "real"-life equivalent. Movement always tends to be in conflict with the character's attempt to keep up the mask—retain dignity, elegance, or whatever—and with intelligent response to a situation. The character's body moves more quickly than the brain. Acting on unthinking impulses, the body often seems to want to go in all directions at once.

The impulse to escape, to find any solution, sends arms and legs in different directions. The French farceur Jacques Tatti is a splendid example of this technique. In films such as *M. Hulot's Holiday* he is always look-

ing in one direction and moving in another; legs seem to go in opposing directions and arms somewhere else again. This extends to all he does. He plays table tennis like a ballet dancer, exaggerating and conventionalizing the reality of table-tennis movements into a curious, comic dance.

Such use of exaggerated gesture is another fundamental element of farce movement. Gestures are quicker, larger, more frenetic than the life gestures upon which they are based. Running will be done with elongated strides; beating with large arm movements; expression of surprise can send the eyebrows through the hat brim, or the chin down to the chest. But none of these is sustained. Brevity, as much as speed, is a quality of farce. The gesture or expression makes its point and then the action moves on. There is no time allowed for consideration of the situation or for emotion or feeling to take over. Gesture is based upon a human response, expresses a feeling, but does not contain emotion. The incongruous

Exaggerated gesture in a production of *Flea in Her Ear.*   *American Conservatory Theatre.*
Photo by Beeber and Associates.

juxtapositions, mechanical confusions, staccato repetitions, brisk reversals, and violent directness of farce all call for short, sharp, quick rhythms punctuated by laughter, not thought.

We have been talking as if all farce movement is the same, and indeed the basic principles are universal. But, perhaps as a footnote, we should mention the particular qualities of *commedia*. Because of its use of actual mask and its highly improvisational nature, *commedia* is the most physically oriented, free wheeling, and broadly played form of farcical theatre. *Commedia* does not have to keep up the realistic patina of modern farce. Based in a distant reality, the masks now exist in a historical vacuum; they are there to play their part in the comic game of human greed, lust, aggression, pomposity, cunning, and romance that *commedia* presents in all its absurdities. Each mask can be played to its comic hilt. Pantalone may be old and impotent, but he is still capable of extraordinary physical feats in defense of his money. His speed and agility do not have to take into account his age. Part of the farcical humor is to see what the old decrepit can do when his fixed interests are threatened. And this sets up more opportunities for exaggerated pantings and wheezings when the frenetic chase is over.

Motivation is even less important in *commedia* than in other forms of farce. The mask is all. Arlecchino will tumble and perform acrobatics because that is expected of him—he doesn't need a chair to fall over. The servants will be beaten and return beatings with the slapstick, because that is what happens when *commedia* masks confront each other. Business can be improvised to whatever level and length the audience will accept. As long as they are consistent among the members of the troupe, gestures and movements may be exaggerated as the relationship with the audience demands and allows. The difference between the physical performance of *commedia* and more modern forms of farce is a question

Exaggeration farcifies elegance of manner in a production of Molière's *The Learned Ladies*, directed by John Harrop.

of degree. The essential farce qualities are common; it is the level of exaggeration, improbability, and physical emphasis—given the differences in costume, setting, and so forth—that demarks the form.

Verbal Manner.   The qualities required by farce movement apply equally to speech. Energy, speed, agility of vocal delivery are as much a part of the clockwork mechanism of situation and character as is the movement to which it must be related.

Responses are quick, stichomythic. Characters blurt out unthinking replies—there is no pause for thought process. A pause in farce is physical—a gesture of astonishment or speechlessness. The concern is not with subtext, but with direct action. Verbal manner can be a part of the character mask. The playwright may call for a particular character to have a harelip, a stammer, or a cleft palate in order to use incomprehensibility to complicate a situation. The actor may discover that a lisp, an accent, a plummy voice, or a squeaky voice fits the mask of character he or she is creating. The physical rhythms and mannerisms of a character are likely to be reflected in his or her pattern of speech.

Whatever the verbal mask, it will have to communicate the linguistic structure of the play. Farce relies little upon verbal wit. Jokes in farce tend to be direct. The gassy stuff is given a quick shake, the cork pops out of the bottle, and is quickly stuffed back in again. There is no slow escape of air such as might be found in a comedy of manners. It is not the content of the lines that produces humor, but rather the structure.

The actor must be very aware of how lines are built—the development of a verbal gag may take place over several shared lines. The actor is frequently either setting up or completing a verbal structure. We have already used the example of the exchange between Harpagon and Valere in *The Miser* over the question of Harpagon's daughter's dowry. While Valere is giving Harpagon all kinds of reasons why she shouldn't be married off to a rich old man, all Harpagon can do is say "But without a dowry" five or six times. Here Valere is setting up and Harpagon topping. Harpagon must discover changes in inflection and intensity so that each identical line is slightly different in delivery, while rising to the final climax.

The Harpagon-Valere exchange is based upon repetition. This is frequently employed in farce verbal structure, as are those other standbys of comic form—exaggeration and incongruity. Farce requires as great a variety of verbal as of physical manner. It will not be the subtle pointing of comedy, the ability to ease through the labyrinths of epigram, or the coloring of poetic images. It is more the use of a wide range of vocal sounds in an endless number of ways. In farce the tongue is not so much a sword or scalpel as a slapstick. A quick glance at the stage directions in a Feydeau farce shows the following words: "hoarse"; "apoplectic"; "with hollow laugh"; "screaming"; "outraged"; "babbling." The gamut of human vocal capacity is called upon—and at the extreme edges of the range. Cries of anguish, pain, hysterical laughter—everything from the deepest stomach bellow to the highest headnote shriek punctuates farce acting. The voices of the characters form an orchestral percussion section, building the action, underlining the responses of characters, and giving a resounding impact to climaxes. Farce is as full of sound as of fury—both, in the end, signifying little.

Character Mask.   Character in farce is not a psychological construct; it is made up of essentially physical qualities. Farce doesn't concern itself with motivation sinisterly rooted in Oedipal or Electra complexes. The audience hasn't come to see why the characters act the way they do, but to see what happens to them when they do—that is where the interest lies. Characters do not change and reveal subtleties or hidden depths. It is the situations that change, while the characters go right on—crashing into them, plunging through them, or bouncing off them. The character is like a pinball in a machine: It is fired into the game and everyone watches excitedly to see what hole it falls into, what lights it turns on, how many points it scores before it returns, after a bruising circuit, back to the starting point.

The problem for an actor with a farce character is not finding out what mixture of parental genetic structure or what environmental influence makes the character act in a particular way. It's a lot simpler: Why does the playwright want the character to act this way, and what absolutely basic and universal human drives has the character been given to make sure it does? In other words, to revert to the pinball metaphor, the actor needs to know what kind of pinball, what kind of machine, and how hard he or she is fired. The actor finds the answers in the play's structure—which shows what the situations are, and what part the character plays in those situations—and also the actor's own imagination, based upon observance of human action, which shows the actor how many ways he or she can make the character fulfill the role the playwright has given it. Put simplistically, if the playwright wants the character to bump into the furniture, the actor must find various amusing ways of doing this within the reality of the mask. The actor needs to discover what information the playwright gives about the character: He is a lawyer, a lecher, a would-be seducer of his friends' wives; he has a great belief in rationality, as befits his profession, yet he cannot control his sexual drive; he has a public position to keep up, befitting a prosperous Parisian of the late nineteenth century; he would have himself seen as a man of precise distinction and cultivated taste. One could go on, but there is already enough for the imaginative actor to go to work. What are the physical rhythms of such an individual—how might he walk, carry his head, look down his nose, adjust his pince-nez, brush off his coat sleeves, swagger his cane? Would he have a long, sharp legal nose; stoop shoulders; lascivious lips that he moistens with his tongue; an eye for female rather than legal forms? Rhythms, mannerisms, deformities, physical quirks—all of these form part of the mask of the farce character. Groucho Marx, Charlie Chaplin, and Jacques Tatti all had distinctive walks and bodily rhythms, just as W. C. Fields and Laurel and Hardy had their mannerisms with cigars, fingers, and bowler hats.[6]

[6]Monty Python—almost a modern *commedia* troupe—had a sketch called "Department of Funny Walks."

The mask is based upon a selected and heightened physical reality. It is then brought into confrontation with the plot situations that have been specifically created by the playwright to reveal it in the most ridiculous light. In the case of our lawyer/lecher the situations will encourage the mechanistic impulses of his sexual lusts and, by frustrating them, exaggerate the inherent conflict in his mask between the propriety of the rational, legal scion of society and the primitive instincts of the lecherous old goat.

So the actor, having determined what the character would be like, then discovers what it would do when confronted with the traps and snares of the situation. The rigid mental attitudes, automatic responses, and impulsive reactions to primitive drives show the mask

A carefully constructed character mask in Ayckbourn's *A Small Family Business.* *British National Theatre. Photo by Nobby Clark.*

in action. While attempting to keep up the mask of rationality and upholding the law, our lawyer character will be seen leaping into beds that collapse on top of him, falling over furniture in his haste to escape, tiptoeing from bedrooms with his trousers in his hand. How he does all this, what his responses are in physical terms, is for the actor to create from his imagination and physical agility. The responses will be consistent with the mask built by the actor—for they are the mask in action. The mask of a farce character may be improbable, but it is consistent. It will be consistently improbable in its reaction to situations. Once built, the mask is recognized by the audience in terms of its external manner and physical reactions. It will create certain expectations in the audience—even if these are expectations of improbability—which must then be fulfilled. If Chaplin or Fields had reacted differently from the associations of their masks, the audience would have felt cheated, would not have believed them, and the humor would have been lost. (Chaplin was less successful in his later movies, when he tried to move away from the mask associated with him.) Once the level of truth of an event has been established, the audience will believe it—however improbable—as long as it is consistently carried through.

In a sense the actor in farce will have two objectives to play. There will be the very simple one-dimensional objective of the character: "I want to seduce my neighbor's wife"; "I want to hide the fact I am wealthy"; "I want everyone to think I am a sick person." Then there will be the actor's objective: "I want to reveal the rigidity, the one-dimensionality, the impulsive response of my character's mask as amusingly as possible within the situations the playwright has given me."

The playwright has done most of the work for the actor, if only he or she will recognize the clues. Not only has the playwright set up situations so that they will be in direct con-

Strongly delineated character mask, a production of *Engaged* directed by Sabin Epstein. A Noise Within.

frontation with the character masks, but has also given the strong, simple outlines of the mask itself. In some instances this goes as far as giving the character a mask name. Many of Plautus's characters bear names that indicate their mask responses. *Commedia* is not only based upon the set of physical masks with consistent names but also the responses expected of these masks are completely conventionalized. Shakespeare and Molière, with their Malvolios, Aguecheeks, Belchs, Fleurants, Dorantes, De Bonnefois, and Jourdains, used the eponymous principle. Even a modern playwright such as Tom Stoppard names Miss Gotobed as a very obvious indication of the lady's function in his play *Dirty Linen;* and in his farce about a farce, *Noises Off,* Michael Frayn gives his young leading man the name Gary Lejeune.

The farce actor must approach performance with absolute seriousness. He or she must never show awareness of how ridiculously the character is acting. Be willing to make a fool of yourself as an actor, but don't show that you know your character is a fool. There is a desperate gravity behind the mask—an attempt to keep the situation normal despite the chaos happening all around. Farce characters are not self-critical or aware. Farce characters believe the audience to be on their side, sympathizing with their predicament.

Farce is a constant struggle, doomed to inevitable defeat, to maintain balance of normality. The more the characters get involved with a situation, the more erratic, childlike, and primitive they become. The civilized adult mask cannot withstand the intensity of the situation. Farce characters are never more appealing to an audience than when they behave like children. It is a wish fulfillment, a release from restrictive adult responsibilities. An actor must be able to cope with the erratic behavior, the swiftly changing moods of farce: Childlike tantrums and sunny charm follow rapidly upon each other. There is no time for change of motivation, only for change of physical response—an immediate reaction to a changing situation. As with everything in farce, this must be done with a delicacy that heightens the effect of the chaos. The farce actor must have a delicacy of touch without which his or her clockwork toy of a character would either smash itself to pieces or go spinning off into space.

Playing for Real.   One of the problems in playing farce—especially for an actor brought up on psychological realism—is the very degree of improbability of the situation and the character reactions. The solution to playing farce is the same as for any theatrical style—learning to play the play and not to impose the actor's own idea of outside reality upon it. Discovering and communicating the inherent reality of the text will communicate the believable truth of the event. If an actor plays his or her mask at the level of exaggeration demanded by the plot situations, and does this consistently, the audience will totally accept

the level of improbability and will not question it in terms of reality outside the play. In other words, the audience is quite prepared to play its part in the theatrical game if the actor shows the audience what that part is.

Farce masks and situations are based in truth. However exaggerated, the roots of farce action go down into the deepest part of the human self and feed upon the most fundamental drives and instincts. Even *commedia*, which is almost entirely a game today, with no patina of surface reality, is based upon those intrigues and desires that have been motivating humans ever since the temptation of Eve. *Commedia* is, of course, distanced by costume, mask, and historicity, and it has the modern function of a kind of live puppet or Punch and Judy show. Just as puppets and Punch and Judy work for young children, so modern farces still have an appeal for young adults. One might think that the social freedom and sexual sophistication of young adults would have defused, or rendered simply stupid, many of the situations upon which farce is based. What is all the fuss about sex? Such urgency and difficulty about getting into someone's bed might seem curious or trivial to a "liberated" generation. But they are still subject to those fundamental human frustrations and instincts that are the eternal stuff of farce.

The idea of distance is important to the acceptance of the farce effect. The improbability of the situations and the exaggeration of the responses add to that distance. The audience operates on two levels: It accepts what is taking place on stage—the truth of the event—but removes itself from the consequences. It therefore permits itself to laugh, because the pain and discomfort are not "really" real. The high level of pace, energy, and exaggeration in farce contributes to this necessary abstraction of effect. We know no human being could withstand such knocking about and come up smiling—so it's a big joke. In farce there is no time for reflection. Coincidences, however unlikely, are never questioned. It is all somewhat improbable and exaggerated, but it is, finally, based upon observed human truth, upon man's attempted inhumanity to man, which is accepted, laughed at, and reconciled to the everyday necessities of living.

The degree of improbability, external energy, physical aggression, and exaggeration will determine the farcical level of a performance. The right level of exaggerated response is important. In *The Miser*, the scene in which Harpagon discovers his money box is stolen must be done with enormous manic energy and exaggeration of gesture. Harpagon's miserliness is so great that he catches and arrests himself in his frenzy. If the actor's manner is less than extreme the scene can become too dark, too painful, and consequently not funny. It has been done that way, and the entire effect of the play is altered. It was not Molière's intention to show the agonized psyche of an unfortunate victim of theft, but rather the comic responses of a miserly old pantaloon who had brought the well-deserved disaster upon himself. How do we know this? From the text. The exaggerated reactions of Harpagon—arresting himself, then the whole audience, and finally hanging himself—and the hysterical rhythms of the speech tell the actor how it should be played.

A game, a joke, a structure of exaggerations and improbabilities farce may be, but it is entirely serious for the actor. No matter how ludicrous the situation, it must be played with total absorption, concentration, and commitment. The hell-bent desperation of the character about things that finally aren't all that important must be absolutely total. Farce must never be self-conscious or aware of itself. When the laughs come, don't milk them. Don't overelaborate, nudge the audience in the ribs, show it you know how funny you are. Play the ridiculous seriously—play for real.

Sense of Occasion. This really brings us full circle, back to the roots we spoke of at the beginning of the chapter. For those roots inform the whole sensibility of farce. It is not souls or psyches that are at risk in farce, but bellies and backsides—human relationship at a very basic level. Deriving from orgiastic celebration, farce has an essentially popular appeal at a simple physical level. Farce is above all alive—at the

Exuberance and physical playfulness in the "festival of fools" that farce is. *British National Theatre. Photo by John Haynes.*

cost of crudity, improbability, indecency. It is the life force having a holiday from reason, restraint, and moral structure. Eat, drink, be merry; fornicate; smash up the furniture; unpin society's hair—for tomorrow it's back to the same spouse and the nine-to-five routine.

The actor makes a compact with the audience to be ridiculous and play the fool. It is a festival of fools in which no one gets hurt or loses more than a little face, and possibly their pants. The actors play out the audience's fantasies for it, while the audience cheers them on and laughs at this surrogate for its own fallible humanity. Although playing the part entirely seriously, the actor must be aware of the fun of the occasion. He or she is playing a game with and for the audience: testing it, pulling the rug out from under it, letting it teeter, deliciously, on the brink of disaster. In farce, above all theatrical occasions, the actor is aware of the audience's presence through the strong, physical response of laughter. Accepting this, riding on it while not being carried away by it, helps the actor to sustain the energy, exuberance, and physical playfulness that is such a crucial part of farce performance—and connects modern shenanigans in bourgeois drawing rooms directly with the earliest wellsprings of the comic spirit.

EXERCISES, GAMES, TECHNIQUES

Slapping and Falling Techniques.   Ideally, a farce actor should take some instruction in tumbling and falling. Short of that, we offer a few techniques that will help the actor with the physical-contact part of farce performance.

Slapping.   The first technique requires the receiver of the slap to be closed to the audience. The slapper sets up the hit, which he pulls just on contact. The receiver times his reaction with the blow, moving his head (say) sharply and at the same time clapping his hands together, in the closed position, to make the sound of contact. The second technique is pos-

sibly better, as it doesn't require the glapper to pull his blow. The receiver should again be turned away from the audience, with his right palm (for a right-handed slap) placed open at the point of contact, say, beneath the jaw. The slapper takes a good swing and hits the open palm of the receiver. At this moment the receiver takes a physical reaction. Timing and trust in the partner are all-important, and slapping requires a lot of rehearsal.

Falling.   An introduction to falling that also serves as an ensemble/trust exercise is to have a group of catchers at the side of a table. Each player in turn falls off the table into the catchers' arms. This should first be done falling forward so that confidence can be gained, but finally it should be a backwards fall into the group. Individual falls can be practiced with two partners. It is best to use a tumbling mat in the first instance. A good introduction to individual falls is to have a catcher standing behind the faller. The faller begins with short falls, being caught under the shoulders by the catcher. Gradually, the fall distance is increased until the faller is caught just short of the ground. Finally, the faller goes solo, breaking the fall with backside and forearms just as he touches the ground.

Pratfalls.   This is the most common and comic form of farce fall. The backside is the most cushioned part of the body on which to fall, and most undignified human associations are centered in it. Thus, a pratfall is the technically safest way of achieving the greatest undercutting of human dignity. The fall should be practiced as suggested above, and highly controlled. However, the effect of the fall must be exaggerated—the arms flung up and the legs flung out much more than the dynamics of the fall require. The best ratio is the smallest actual fall done with the largest possible effect.

Heel Slips.   A controlled way of falling down a stair or off a level is to place the tip of a heel on the edge of the step and put on weight until the heel slips and a stumbling effect is achieved.

Toe Trip.   This is perhaps the oldest technical stumble in the farce book, which is induced by catching the toe of the rear foot against the heel of the leading foot during a walk. The resulting forward falling momentum can be a simple stumble; an actual fall on the face; a clinging on to someone for support; knocking that someone over; both persons falling over a chair, and so on depending on how far the gag is to be taken.

Takes.   *Takes* are a physical way of topping—showing surprise. They are based upon a non-immediate realization that both adds to the observer's anticipation and increases the degree of surprise. A double take is a delayed recognition in passing: A look is taken at what should be surprising, but there is no immediate reaction; there is a return to normal focus; then the realization hits like a thunderbolt with a double-quick return to take another look, followed by surprise. A double take may be made into a triple take by splitting the suddenness of realization: The first look brings no reaction; somewhat quicker second look, some reaction; lightning-quick third look as realization finally hits. The take is a technique for building up extra comic tension—the audience gets to enjoy the same situation twice or three times, and is titillated by the anticipated realization of surprise.

As opposed to the quickness of the *take,* the *slow burn* extends the dawning of realization and shares it with the audience. It is usually a response to some kind of put-down—like a balloon deflation. When he worked with Gracie Allen, George Burns used the slow burn to suggest: "What can you do?" "Would you believe that?" Jack Benny's slow burn usually meant "How did I come to fall for that again?" The *deadpan* is a slow burn without the burn—it lets the audience do all the filling in,

taking the reaction the deadpan consciously refuses to reveal. The subtler the reaction, the less of a physical sign given to the audience, the more difficult is the technique. The deadpan is the most extreme form of "playing against" or "doing less," a technique that gives great focus and clarity to an action but treads a fine line between highly comic emotionlessness and simple lack of reaction.

Exercises

High-Energy Games.   It is useful to begin any workshop or rehearsal for farce with games that require high energy, agility, maneuverability, such as the variants of tag.

Tag.   It is always best to begin with the familiar, so start with a game of basic tag: One player is IT while the other players have to avoid being tagged. Once tagged, a player becomes IT. The game can then be played with everyone having to adopt a funny walk or run—some exaggerated movement rhythm different from the norm. While the basic tag game is going on, players can be required to change their rhythm on a drumbeat or handclap. For farce purposes the space in which tag is played can be complicated by putting obstacles—chairs, boxes, tables—within it. Players have to maneuver around these while playing the game—anyone who touches an obstacle immediately becomes IT.

Three Deep.   This is another good high-energy, physical-control game. Players form two circles, one immediately behind the other, so that players are standing two deep. Two players are outside the circle. One chases the other around the outside of the circle until caught, when the situation is reversed—the chaser becomes the chasee—or the chasee moves into the circle and stands in front of one of the twosomes, making it three deep. When this happens the rear member of the group becomes the chasee and must immediately set off around the outside of the circle either until he or she is tagged, or darts into the circle and stands in front of a twosome when the rear member becomes chasee, and so on.

Dropping the Handkerchief.   This is a somewhat similar game. Players form one circle. One player walks around the outside of the circle with a handkerchief. At some juncture he or she drops this at the heels of one of the players in the circle. This player must pick up the handkerchief and chase the other player around the circle, attempting to tag before the player who dropped the handkerchief can get back into the space of the chaser. If tagged, the handkerchief dropper continues, dropping the handkerchief at another pair of heels. If he or she gets to the empty space the game continues with the new dropper. The trick to this game is nonchalance on the part of the dropper and alertness on the part of the players in the circle. It can lead to a lot of amusement at the expense of players who don't realize the handkerchief is at their heels.

Spin the Platter.   Players sit in a large circle and number off. One player is in the middle with a tin plate (plastic will do). He or she spins the plate, and before it stops spinning calls out a number. The player called has to catch the plate before it starts to fall. If the player fails to do so, he or she pays a forfeit. Forfeits are either removing a piece of clothing, taking a swat on the backside with a slapstick, or performing a funny action named by the group. Whoever paid the forfeit continues as the spinner, and so the game goes on. This is a good ensemble, getting-to-know-you game, as well as one that encourages alertness, precision in handling props, and that willingness to make a fool of oneself that is so important to the farce actor.

Touch-Me-Not.   Players stand in a circle about the size of a boxing ring. Two players are in the middle. Each has to try to touch the other's back. They may use the whole of the circle, but they may not leave it, nor may they touch any other part of their opponent's body (some arm contact is inevitable). Play best of three "hits." Whoever wins takes on the next player. This is a good game for alertness, physical imagination, agility, and finesse. It also encourages concentration on, and response to, every move made by the person with whom you are playing.

Slapstick Games.   Hitting and physical contact is a fundamental part of the farce sensibility. In all the games set out below, the slapstick is a rolled-up newspaper, which produces no real pain but great effect.

Slapstick Tag.   This is a simple introduction to slapstick activity. Any tag game may be played using the slapstick instead of the hand for tagging.

Slap in the Bucket.   Players sit in a circle. One player has a slapstick. In the middle of the circle is a bucket. The player with the slapstick walks around the outside of the circle, gently tapping players with the slapstick. Finally, he or she gives one player a hearty swat, then runs to the center of the circle to put the slapstick in the bucket. The player who has been hit tries to get the slapstick out of the bucket and swat the assailant in return before the assailant can reach the smitten player's place. If successful, the player must return the slapstick to the bucket and return to his or her place before the original assailant can get the slapstick and use it once more. This continues until one player reaches the empty place without being hit. The player left with the slapstick goes around the circle tapping players, finally hitting one, and so the game goes on. This, again, is a game that produces a high level of energy and amusement. It is also good for quick reactions and physical control. There will be a tendency for players to toss the slapstick carelessly into the bucket, whereupon it will fall out and they will be in physical jeopardy, having to put it back in with the smitten player standing on top of them ready to grab and strike. Players learn that haste is not the same as quickness with control.

Master-Slave.   This is a slapstick game that calls for a simple situation in which a slave or servant is given instructions by a master to perform a task, such as cleaning up a room. While appearing to perform the task, the slave finds various ways to make fun of the master. Pulling faces, making obscene gestures, hiding the dust under the carpet; the possibilities for this are endless. However, the slave mustn't be caught joking; if he or she is, the player gets beaten with the slapstick. The game may be elaborated by having a series of masters, or supervisors, come in, each superior to the one before. The game now is for all subordinates to poke fun at or score points off those above them—with resultant beatings if they are caught. This game lets the players explore the structures of repression as well as the double mask of being both oppressor and victim.

Pecking Order.   This is a sophisticated counterpart of the master-slave game and explores the playing of dominance or submission—which is present in all comic relationships. Set up a situation between two players, such as a librarian and book borrower. Ask them to improvise a conversation in which each tries to be superior to the other. For example:

A: I see you're taking out *The Idiot.*
B: Yes. I've read the rest of Dostoevski.
A: Yes. *The Idiot* is my favorite; I've read it several times.
B: In Russian?
A: No-German, French, Spanish, and Italian are my best languages.
B: Oh yes? My brother is professor of romance languages at Harvard.

And so on. Now reverse the aim so that each tries to be submissive:

A: Gosh, I see you're reading Dostoevski.

B: Only in translation.
A: I couldn't get through that.
B: Well, I only really look at the pictures.

And so on.

Many relationships can be explored in this way: man and wife; manager and secretary; student and professor; waiter and customer. One of the oldest known gags is:

CUSTOMER: Waiter, there's a fly in my soup.
WAITER: Well, it can't drink much.

Here the waiter, who is a low-status character, plays dominance. This is often the case with servants in comedy: There is humor in the contrast between the social status of the character and the status he presumes to play. (Chaplin played low status and brought everyone down to his level). The game shows the strong connection between the assumption of status and the assumption of body attitudes. The player portraying dominance will stand or sit straighter, maintain eye contact, keep the body still. The submissive player will tend to small movements, weak gestures, and stooped postures. An understanding of these physical responses is valuable in the creation of character mask. An amusing variation of this exercise is to have players insult each other while playing the scenes. For example:

COP: You went through that light, dummy.
DRIVER: Dummy! It isn't working, jerk.
COP: Jerk! That means an extra ticket, crud-eyes.
DRIVER: Crud-eyes! I bet you wish you could write, meat-face.

It is important for each insult to be repeated with a sense of outrage and incredulity; this involves players totally in the scene. Coach players to concentrate on the action of the scene so that the insults add to it but do not dominate. This exercise, again, helps players to accept being made a fool of on stage, keeps energy flow at a high level between players, and often helps "bound" or uptight players to relax and play with greater freedom.

Chase and Obstacle Games.   The function of chase and obstacle games is to gain expertise in swift movement with control and agility. The ability to move quickly and precisely through a cluttered or convoluted space must become second nature to a farceur, so that concentration in performance may be upon the action being played—not upon moving around the set. The following games and exercises should be played within increasingly more sophisticated spaces; start with a simple slalom made of chairs and make this into a maze; create a less formal obstacle course with objects to go over and under, as well as around; add furniture and freestanding doors if available, finally creating a complete dummy set.

Skipping.   This is a simple but excellent exercise for keeping players light on their feet. It may be done through the slalom individually, then as a team competition.

Musical Maze.   Players move through the maze to different musical rhythms and speeds: march tunes, jazz, disco, waltzes, minuets. Ask players to do this in double time and with different body rhythms and walks. To do this as if wearing ballet toeshoes is a good exercise.

Obstacle Slap.   One player pursues another through the slalom, maze, or obstacle course with a slapstick. If either player touches any of the obstacles, the other player gets a free slap at him or her. Reverse the players.

Silent Movies.   Using the maze, obstacle course, or dummy set, one player is the thief, the others (up to whatever number is reasonable in the available space) are the cops. All have slapsticks, and the object is for the cops to catch and beat up the thief.

The thief, in turn, tries to avoid, outwit, and hit back at the cops. The cops should have hats—papier-mâché derbies are good—that are too small for them and that they must keep on at all times. No one is allowed to catch hold of anyone; nor must it become a simple beating match—the thief must try to avoid the cops, not slug it out with them. This can be done with different rhythms, including the stiff-legged, double-time movement of the silent movies—the Keystone Kops. This game can become as elaborate as space and props will allow.

Attacking Space.   This takes place within a dummy set containing as much household paraphernalia as possible. Within the set are two players. One is entertaining the other to tea or cocktails, with the ultimate objective of seduction. However, an air or propriety must be maintained at all times. Three or four other players cause chaos. They move chairs from under the two players, pull carpets from beneath their feet; bang them with doors; knock over glasses; hit them with cushions; even walk in on them as unexpected visitors. The would-be seducer must try to restore order and maintain his or her mask of unconcerned politeness throughout all this—while tidying cushions, closing doors, cleaning off tea spills, and so forth. The chaos-causing players must be ignored, unless they actually enter the scene as a visitor—someone coming to read the gas meter, for example. This is an excellent exercise for developing imagination with properties and maintaining the mask under pressure. Care must be taken that the chaos is organized—just enough disruption happening at any one time.

Clothing and Property Games.   The maintaining of the physical mask of clothing under pressure or the use of costume and properties for comic business is an important part of the farce player's technique.

Difficulty with Objects.   Players should sit in a circle. In the middle is a heap of everyday objects: cigarette lighter, can opener, corkscrew, compact, zipped handbag, and so on. Players in turn take one of the objects, perform a short activity illustrating its normal use, then redo the activity, this time having a problem that leads to a comic reaction.

Funny Dressing.   Players are again in a circle. In the middle is a pile of clothing. Players, in turn, take two or three articles and dress with them as comically as their imagination allows, producing misbuttoned clothes; zippers that won't work or catch parts of the body; both legs in one trouser legs; shoes on the wrong feet; jackets inside out or back to front; arms that can't find sleeves. This is an exercise for physical skill and imagination.

Ruining an Entrance.   Players sit in a semicircle with a freestanding door facing them. In turn, the players make an entrance through the door, and then redo the entrance to make it as physically comic as possible: The door hits them in the back and sends them on their faces; clothes catch in the door; the doorknob comes off; they drop their handbag, which spills. Again, a practice in physical imagination.

Keeping Face.   A set of clothing put together with Velcro is required for this exercise. One player dresses in the clothes, which, whether male or female, should be a full set: None of the clothing or chase exercises can validly be played in jeans and a T-shirt. The player is put in a social situation—a cocktail party, tea party, giving a public lecture. While playing his or her part in this, two or three other players try to remove parts of his or her clothing: a tie, a vest, unbuttoning the trousers, pulling off the skirt, blouse, etc. The first player must continue with the social action while repairing the clothing mask and maintaining a straight face and composure. This can be done as a competition with two players. Points are taken off for breaking composure or losing concentration, and points are added for the most respectable clothing mask at the end of, say, three minutes. The player with the most points wins.

Amazing Dressing.   One player is given several articles of clothing: shoes, shirt, tie, pants, skirts, women's stockings, underskirts, and so on. This player has to put these on while being chased through a maze, or obstacle course, by another player with a slapstick— this second player is handicapped by having the ankles tied together with a one-foot piece of rope. Anytime the dresser hits the obstacles or fails to get a piece of clothing on he or she gets an extra slap from the pursuer.

Character/Mask Exercises.

Animal Attitudes.   This is a very basic and widely used exercise in actor training. It is especially useful for farce and particularly for *commedia* characterization. Players are asked to pick any animal. They then walk around the workshop space, keeping the image of the animal in mind and exploring the basic rhythms and movements of the animal. Players should be coached to take their time and explore the possibilities fully: "Where is the center of energy?" "How does it hold its head?" "Does it dart? Flow? Trot?" The idea is not to imitate the animal but to assume its essential movement qualities.

Players are then coached to take the essential qualities and to build the mask of a human character from this, using the rhythms, energy centers, and patterns of movement. Players should not get too sophisticated—two or three absolutely basic characteristics are all that is required. Players are then coached to play with these masks, exaggerating rhythms and movements, to discover the comic possibilities in physical action. The mask will finally be simply and clearly defined—recognizably human, but with exaggerated qualities deriving from its animal base. When the character mask is set, games can be played in character: frisbee, tumbling, or any of the chase games given above.

Exaggerated Essences.   This exercise has a structure similar to that of the previous exercise, but the starting point is a quality or attitude. Players are asked to take a quality such as miserliness, gluttony, or pomposity and work with it to discover what physical response they find in their body, what rhythms, what physical attitudes, what disposal of energies are suggested by these qualities. Again, players should be coached to take their time, repeating the idea to themselves and using whatever images come to mind, until the body gradually takes the quality upon itself. Having discovered the outline of the mask, players are coached to play with it, exaggerating aspects of movements, gestures, rhythms, and so forth, to explore the comic possibilities. What will be achieved is a series of gestures and physical attitudes that illustrate the particular quality the player started with, and at the same time give a broadly defined character.

Deformities.   This is another exercise based upon the use of physical qualities to create character masks. Players should walk about the workshop space with an easy consciousness of their own physical rhythms and energy center, achieving a comfortable neutrality. Players are then coached to adopt various abnormalities: Their legs become two feet longer; their feet double in size; their arms touch the floor; their nose is a foot long. Each time they adopt the physical deformity they are coached to explore what it does to their body rhythm, posture, energy center, etc. Players should return to neutral between each abnormality. After exploring various abnormalities and the rhythms associated with them, players are coached to build a character mask by adopting two or three of the physical attributes they discovered when exploring the deformities. This should be done gradually, one at a time, until a strong, integrated physical outline of character is created.

Mechanical Toys.   Players work in pairs. One player decides what toy he or she wishes to make of the partner. The choices should be distinctive—for example, a clown, trapeze artist, tin soldier, witch, circus strongman, or lion tamer. The toy maker then "whitewashes" the partner with his or her hands to remove all traces of real self, and proceeds to "paint" with the hands the characteristics of the toy upon the partner's body. This should be done slowly, carefully, and precisely. The partner who is being painted should close the eyes and follow very carefully the brush strokes of the toy maker, assimilating the feel of what is being done. In about 85 percent of the cases in which concentration is good by both partners, the partner being painted gains a correct impression of what is being done to him or her. When the toy maker is finished he or she winds up the toy, which then walks about in a mechanical fashion and performs the actions its nature would suggest. The toy maker can alter the speed of the toy by the way in which it is wound up. Finally, he or she should overwind it, and the toy can go berserk, performing its actions in a highly exaggerated manner at a crazy speed. Partners then change places.

Id and Ego.   Players work in threes. One player is placed in some social situation of temptation. Food, money, fulfillment of sexual desire are the basic aims of this player. The other two players follow him or her around, one at either ear. One of these players is the *superego,* or conscience; the other is the *id,* or primitive drive. Throughout the acting out of the improvised scene, the id encourages the player in his or her desires while the superego points out the consequences of any act. This game is also easily applicable to work on a text, and it sets up the tension between the mask of propriety a character may wish to keep up, and the pursuit of his or her desires in any situation. The player achieves an experience of the opposing pulls from which all farce characters suffer: what I should like to do versus what I am supposed to do. It is this conflict that creates much of the compressed hyperenergy of farce playing.

Slapstick Shakespeare. This exercise can be used to pull all the techniques of the farce player together. A player, or players, take any well-known scene or soliloquy from Shakespeare and make it farcical. The scene should be from a tragedy—the balcony scene in *Romeo and Juliet*, Lady Macbeth sleepwalking, Hamlet and the gravediggers. It is first done straight. Then the players employ all the tricks at their disposal to make it farcical: awkward entrances, problems with props and clothing, the use of chases and beatings. Players should not get away from the action of the scene; it should be played through, but changed in style to create the farce effect. This exercise provides a good basis for discussion, in hard and direct terms, as to what precise elements of playing made the scene farcical—what succeeded, what failed, and why.

PLAYING THE STYLE

It is difficult to deal on paper with the creation of the mask of a farce character because it is essentially an act of physical imagination that will develop as the situations of the play are confronted by the actor. The actor will probably have very little "character information" given in biographical or psychological terms and will have to make some basic physical choices that will then be developed into a character by the way in which they respond to the challenges of the situations into which the playwright has thrown the character. It is how the character responds to a situation in physical terms, not why the character responds in psychological terms, that is the actor's task in farce. We are going to suggest some ways in which physical business can be developed and how it can be given specific character definition. We are then going to look at the character of Brooke Ashton in Michael Frayn's

farce *Noises Off*[7] to see how a playwright gives an actor very few, very simple, but very direct clues as to approaching a character mask.

Physical Imagination. However exaggerated and improbable, physical business should always have a connection to, rather than being imposed upon, the action of the play. *Commedia* is occasionally an exception to this as there are some set-piece gags that, while they don't further the situation or illustrate character, are conventions of behavior associated with certain masks. These are called *Lazzi*. Many of them are associated with the Arlecchino: Using a false arm, Arlecchino is caught by thieves who hold him and start beating him up, when he runs off leaving them with the arm. Another *Lazzo* (singular of *Lazzi*) is the water held in the cheeks that inevitably gets spat upon someone. Charlie Chaplin had a version of this in which he was standing on a hose so no water could come out; he then moves to look down the spout and, inevitably, gets the water in the face. Many modern farce jokes derive from the traditional farce routines. The modern equivalent of the slapstick is the pie in the face: It is a basic human release of aggression that doesn't cause any serious harm but does undermine the dignity of the authority figure that receives it.

Modern technology and the world of "things" that we inhabit provide great opportunities for the farceur: Impedimenta have always been the stuff of farce. If there is a step, the farceur will trip over it; the comedian probably won't, and the tragedian mustn't. The more uncontrollable the technology the better the opportunity: The electric beater can cover you with egg; the vacuum cleaner can suck off your shorts. In his film *Play It Again, Sam*, Woody Allen has a bathroom cabinet that spews its content all over him, and records

---

[7]Michael Frayn, *Noises Off* (London: Methuen, 1982).

that jump out of their covers. While Allen is trying to appear suave and Bogart-like, all the "things" that surround him conspire to undermine his act—as does the sofa that he attempts blithely to vault into, only to end up on his backside on the floor. The mask of flair is undermined by the situation and ends up showing the reality of gaucherie underneath. It is in this manner that the farceur uses physical business to create a character by illustrating and defining it in action.

The farce actor mustn't be tentative; the mask drive must be played for all it is worth, confronting the obstacles in the situation as strongly and variously as possible. For example, in the basic "getting your clothes off to commit adultery" farce situation, the character mask can be given definition by the way in which the character goes about creating comic business. Is the character nervous, arrogant, careless? Are the fingers too nervous to undo the zip on the pants so they are stuck on the hips? Does the zip break half-way down under the sexual urgency? Does the zip get caught in the shirt so everything has to come off over the head? *Noises Off* has a situation in which a man and woman in their haste to get re-dressed get their zips caught in each other's clothing. Being a farce about a farce, the play also exploits the falling trousers at every opportunity. In one classic illustration of character in action, a drunk of an actor is coming out of the bathroom holding his trousers up when someone passes carrying a whiskey bottle; the drunk grabs for the bottle and, of course, drops his pants and is left to hobble in pursuit. The whiskey bottle, which keeps getting into the wrong hands, then hidden in strange places, is a basic convention of *Noises Off*, as is a bouquet of flowers that suffers the same fate as the whiskey, and a cactus plant that, of course, someone sits on and has to drop his pants and have the nearest woman pull the spikes out of the backside, just as his girlfriend appears.

All of the above business, naturally, loses tremendously in the telling: Farce has to be experienced and explored physically. We are simply trying to underline the fact that all of the costumes and all the properties are fuel for the actor's imagination in developing business out of situations, business that is both funny in itself and that illustrates an aspect of the character's mask. The willingness to risk, to take a situation to its extremity, is a necessary part of the farce actor's technique. But however brilliantly imagined the business is, it should be based upon these principles: It must have some connection, however tenuous, with the action; it should be as simple as possible; it should be consistent with the character mask so that the audience immediately understands the situation.

Building the Mask.   To see how an actor can make use of the few and simple clues a playwright gives the farceur, we are going to look at the character of Brooke Ashton in *Noises Off.* Briefly, *Noises Off* is a farce about playing a farce: a cast getting a farce called *Nothing On* through a technical rehearsal and then through a couple of performances, one of which, in the second act, is seen from backstage. The play is a brilliant excuse for setting up farce situations in which actor/characters have all kinds of farcical problems in trying to play farce/characters, in a play in which all kinds of farcical situations are set up. In his play, Michael Frayn puts a definitive definition of farce into the mouth of his Director character: "If we can just get through the play once tonight for doors and sardines. That's what it's all about. Doors and sardines. Getting on—getting off. . . . That's farce. That's the theatre. That's life. . . . So just keep going. Bang, bang, bang. Bang you're on. Bang you've said it. Bang you're off."

In the middle of all this, not to make a bad joke, the function of Brooke Ashton's character (Vicki in the play within the play) is that she is there to be banged: both literally to bump into things, and in the terms of the sexual metaphor. At her entrance, Brooke's Vicki is described as "a desirable property in her early twenties, well-built and beautifully maintained throughout." She is a realtor's secretary, and she and the realtor are taking the opportunity of visiting one of their rental houses to get into bed together. Brooke's main action, her character mask, is to be beautiful. She is like the character Lovely in *A Funny Thing Happened on the Way to the Forum* (based on Plautine farces): "Lovely is the only thing I do." Apart from the physical description we have of Brooke, we have virtually no other information except that she is short-sighted and wears contacts—which, of course, get lost in the second act to set up all manner of business.

Virtually all that Brooke says, outside of the script within the play, is "Sorry," used in the sense of "What did you say?" This is her response to practically everything that is said to her, the strong indication being that she is not terribly bright and rather self-absorbed. This is confirmed by two stage directions: She can't deviate a hairbreadth from the script; and she does her relaxation exercises everywhere.

So what has the actor to build on? The physical mask must be cosmetic—physically beautiful in a programmed, somewhat self-conscious way: the somewhat plastically attractive quality of the clothes model. Body, hair, nails are terribly important to Brooke, which afford the opportunity for business. There is a sense that in her spare moments she is repairing any of these or doing mini-aerobic routines. There is also a sense of inflexibility about Brooke—she can't deviate from the script—which suggests an uprightness, again of the fashion model, and a vaguely pleasant, hopeful smile. Any of the exercises such as *Exaggerated Essences, Deformities,* and *Mechanical Toys,* will help the actor to explore this clearly defined but rather fixed and cosmetic quality of the character mask.

The vaguely hopeful smile is consistent with Brooke's intention, which is to be admired and to move through life in such a way as not to disturb the pleasant, smooth, self-absorbed mask of beauty that has got her where she is. There is a sense of not being dirtied or touched by life, physically or emotionally, and that having sex is simply a part of the admiration owing to her beauty.

The obstacles to Brooke's achievement of her intention are her somewhat dimness of intellect and unexceptional talent, which limits her success as actress to this rather second-rate company, and makes her subject to the problems it has in putting on the play: Because of her inflexibility she bumps into the problems rather than avoiding them. This is reinforced by the dimness of her eyesight, which obliges her to use contacts, which she loses, and again leads her to bump into things. The poor eyesight is a very important part of the physical mask—it will lead to a peering attitude with the head—and it reinforces the whole sense that she can't quite see or understand things well: the physical giving a strong

The vague, self-absorbed cosmetic mask of Brooke Ashton's "desirable property" in *Noises Off. Ahmanson Theatre, Los Angeles. Photo by Martha Swope.*

indication of the somewhat pleasantly vague, not very bright, hopeful nature of her personality as a whole.

Given all of this—a physical mask she doesn't want disturbed; an inflexibility in the face of difficulty; and a dimness both of intellect and eyesight—being a farce the play conspires to put Brooke into situations in which these qualities are played upon to the best comic effect. She loses her clothes; she wanders into closets she mistakes for bathrooms; she gets into wrong bedrooms with the wrong partner. She loses her contacts and bumps into things; in looking for the contacts she misses her entrance; when she comes on she plays the wrong scene; part of her missing clothes land on her head and blind her further. She continues hopefully, blindly through all of this, trying to keep up her mask and not deviating from either the script or her intention to move beautifully and self-contained through life. It is for the actor to get as much comedic mileage as possible out of the confusion and the contrast between Brooke's mask and the situations it runs into. Here the various chase games such as *Obstacle Slap* and *Attacking*

Space, and the clothing games such as *Keeping Face, Difficulty with Objects,* and *Amazing Dressing,* will enable the actor to explore the many possibilities for farce business which situations afford.

In sum, what the farce actor needs is a strong, simple sense of character mask; a strong drive or intention; obstacles to this intention and situations for comic exploitation. The actor must avoid the twin traps of farce playing: playing the action realistically in the sense of taking thought-pauses and trying to discover and reveal subtext; or playing the comedic business mechanically without any connection to the action of a scene. The character mask is based upon simple truths that are played out and illustrated upon the trampoline of action. These may be any combination of a rigid attitude toward life; a particular set of physical rhythms; a speech mannerism; a physical quirk; a specific costume detail; an uncontrollable prop. Comic business is the tricks that the farce gymnast plays upon the trampoline: quickly, lightly, strongly within the physical range of the character and the demands of the action.

SUGGESTED READINGS

Bentley, Eric, "The Psychology of Farce," in *Let's Get a Divorce and Other Plays.* New York: Hill & Wang, 1958.

Bermel, Albert, *Farce.* New York: Simon & Schuster, 1982.

Blitstein, Elmer, *Comedy in Action.* Durham, N.C.: Duke University Press, 1964.

Davis, Jessica Milner, *Farce.* New York: Methuen, 1978.

Ducharte, Pierre Louis, *The Italian Comedy.* New York: Dover, 1966.

Duckworth, George, *The Nature of Roman Comedy.* Princeton, N.J.: Princeton University Press, 1962.

Gordon, Mel, *Lazzi.* New York: Performing Arts Journal, 1983.

Huberman, Jeffrey, H., *Late Victorian Farce.* Ann Arbor, Mich.: U.M.I. Research Press, 1986.

Madden, David, *Harlequin's Stick, Charlie's Cane.* Bowling Green, Ohio: Popular Press, 1975.

Moore, Will, G., *Molière.* Oxford: Oxford University Press, 1949.

Oreglia, Giacomo, *The Commedia del l'Arte.* New York: Hill & Wang, 1968.

The books by Ducharte and Oreglia cited above are also excellent visual sources. For *commedia* the paintings of Callot and Watteau are useful, and for character illustrations of the nineteenth and early twentieth centuries the following may be referred to: the sketches of Max Beerbohm, and the cartoons of Spy to be found in *Vanity Fair.*

III
Playing Realism

In the introduction to "Playing Comedy" we said that comedy deals with humankind in its more mundane circumstances. This is true and was a valid distinction between comedy and tragedy or drama through much of dramatic history up until the later nineteenth century. At that time a combination of social and political trends produced a drama that mirrored everyday existence, not merely for the comedic purpose of displaying human ridiculousness when betrayed by fundamental appetites but also for the serious purpose of examining men and women in their full relationship to the social order. This form of drama, which is often, conveniently, said to have begun with the work of Henrik Ibsen, has come to be generically called *Realism.*

The basic distinction and focus of Realism, which, over a hundred years, has come to be not only a genre but also a way of approaching modern drama, is the representation of the manners, language, and problems of "the man in the street." Whereas much of the noncomedic drama of the previous two thousand years had dealt with the concerns of kings and queens, military heroes, members of an aristocratic or ruling class, and those in political and economic power, Realism purported to be an illustration of slices of life taken from the streets where average people lived, or from the rooms of their houses from which the fourth wall had been removed to reveal on the stage the normal everyday life within: reality, what we see when we look at life. We must allow here that, for the dramatic critic, Realism is distinguished from Naturalism—a "warts and all" form of realism that deliberately sought to examine the lower social stratum and darker purposes of human action. This is not a distinction that we need to dwell on for our purpose of setting out a basic approach for the actor, which will give him and her the tools for playing the varying degrees of realism that the great majority of playwrights over the past century have written. Since Ibsen, the more successful playwrights include Strindberg, Chekhov, Eugene O'Neill, Lillian Hellman, Tennessee Williams, Arthur Miller, and John Osborne. Or, more recently, August Wilson, Tina Howe, and Terence McNally.

Given that one of the basic precepts of Realism is the recapitulation of a contemporary life style, and that the physical detail of that life style has changed over a hundred years—from the Victorian clothing and living spaces of Ibsen to the blue jeans and casual furnishings of Lanford Wilson—the actor will need to make adjustments in level of formality as he or she moves along this spectrum. What is consistent, however, is the perception of character in realistic drama. In the late nineteenth century there was a qualitative change in the perception and self-consciousness of the individual. This was attributable to the concept of democracy—every individual was uniquely significant—and to scientific psychology: that unique individual was motivated from within in ways that he or she may not even be aware of. The predominance of individualism required that the mirror that theatre holds up to nature should now reflect the everyday actions and concerns of the common man or woman. And the character of this common man or woman had to be individualistic and discovered and revealed through the examination of the inner self. This approach to character connects an unhappy wife in an Ibsen drama with a patient in an AIDS play of the late twentieth century. It also distinguishes Realism from earlier than nineteenth century approaches to character: As we have suggested, a Restoration comedy may have been dealing with a reality of its day; but the way character was dealt with was still much closer to the structure of the medieval humors.

In Realism the actor's task is to create the dynamics of this "individual" who has, at the same time, to resemble the "person next door," with all the economic and social problems that impinge upon an individual within the particular context of his or her time. The specific nature of these problems will change, but they are the constant concerns of Realism from Ibsen's examination of the problem of trying to be an honest politician in *An Enemy of the People,* through Arthur Miller's description of the illusions of the capitalist ethos in *Death of a Salesman,* to the discussion of the issue of AIDS by several playwrights in the late 1980s.

The actor can then take a consistent approach to working in a realistic form whether it be on stage or, as so much of an actor's work today, in film and television. Whether it be in an Ibsen drama or a soap opera, the actor's task will be to adjust the basic approach to the differing technological demands of the medium, or the different social sensibility of the period.

6 | Realism

A Lie of the Mind.   *American Conservatory Theatre, San Francisco. Photo by Larry Merkle.*

BACKGROUND

Historical. While Realism as a form developed in the latter part of the nineteenth century, its roots go back a hundred years to the Romanticism of the late eighteenth century. Romanticism, based upon subjectivity of feelings rather than classical objectivity of form, had its concomitants of the desire to free the individual from oppressive forms, and to focus upon individual desires and feelings as the essential dynamic of human action. Both the French and American revolutions were an expression of this desire for the freedom of the individual. Further revolutions during the nineteenth century led to the breakup of large empires and the overthrowing of aristocratic and hierarchically structured forms of government in favor of more democratic forms: governments of, for, and by the people.

This focus upon the democratic individual as the basic unit of political and social life was reinforced by the development of scientific inquiry with its motto that "the proper study of Mankind is Man." So the focus of this inquiry came more and more to be on the individual, culminating at the end of the nineteenth century in the development of psychology and the placing of human motives for action deep within an inner self. Realism was, then, the response, at this particular moment of history, to the desire of individuals in a democratic society to understand themselves in terms of both motivation for action and relationship to the social and economic limitations and opportunities of that society.

Intellectual and Social Concerns. The focus upon the individual went hand in hand with a sense of human equality and uniqueness. This led to an antiauthoritarian sensibility opposed to restrictions, codes of behavior, formality, or evident distinctions in terms of birth or class. This sensibility also led to a disbelief in powers that were beyond human control. A sense of awe for fate or godhead tended to be re-

placed by a belief in human possibility to change circumstances either through the ever-increasing bounty of industrial capitalism, with its power to change human environment, or the power of psychoanalysis to understand, control, and improve the human psyche. The sense of life was a rational, linear, vertical progression toward an inevitable improvement in the human material condition, and therefore in human happiness: progress.

The attitude toward society was ambivalent. When it provided opportunity and structure for human self-improvement it was a positive force, but where it impinged upon individual self-expression it was negative. Society was seen as having to conform to the individual and not to destroy his or her uniqueness. The distinction rather than the similarity of people was emphasized. Social groups were at best a convenience. Where earlier societies had identified themselves in creed, class, profession, or other stratified terms (individuals belonging to such groups were seen to behave in typical terms: Heroes, old men, warriors, virgins, scholars shared identifiable traits), now uniqueness was prized and group identity accepted only insofar as it could be of utility to the individual. It is interesting to note that this stress upon individualism was most fervent in the United States of America, which was essentially the first artificially created country made up of heterogeneous individuals rather than evolving from an ethnic social group. Realistic drama also had its most dynamic expression in the United States. Finally, even if society was a necessary restriction upon the individual, it too could be changed, being a human creation.

Here is a quite different intellectual position from that in which drama had operated for much of its prior history. No longer do we have the person seen as partaking of the sensibility of a whole; there is no sense of a broadly accepted set of ideas and values mosaically imposed upon society by an immutable fate or godhead. We have moved from the Greek sense that one cannot alter one's destiny toward the behaviorist posture that one can create oneself. Thus, the way is clear for Willy Loman, the "hero" of Arthur Miller's *Death of a Salesman:* The protagonist is no longer the nonconformist who stands alone against the gods, but now is the conformist who sells himself (to sell his capitalist goods) and becomes the victim of Society.

INTRINSIC DEMANDS

Form.   The focus upon the individual and the removal of all restrictions upon his or her freedom of self-expression—one of the main factors producing Realism—also had a significant effect upon the structure of the plays. The concept of freedom extended to what was seen as the restrictions of earlier theatrical forms and conventions. Some of the more famous theatres in the forefront of producing realistic theatre included the term "free" in their names: *Théâtre Libre* in France and *Freie Bühne* in Germany. Plays tended to be written in the more "scientifically" constructed three-act form of what was originally called the "well-made" play, rather than the extravagant, rhetorical structures of the Romantic theatre of the earlier nineteenth century. This three-act form had a very logical and rational structure that befitted the sense of scientific progress and, in keeping with the idea of progress, was problem-specific and moved toward solutions. It also tended to be horizontal and earthbound, dealing with the issues of the individual in society, without the poetical sweeps of fantasy and soaring aspirations of earlier tragedy or Romantic forms.

The three-act form of the "well-made" play, while being geared to the reality of human rhythms, was, in the first instance, equally geared to the needs of theatrical time and space and tended to replace one set of extravagant and "unreal" conventions with an equally artificial mechanistic structure. However, as Realism strove more and more to recapitulate the actuality of human existence, and to deal more with character exploration in relation to events rather than the mechanical necessities of event plotting, so the "well-made" form was adapted to give a greater sense of unstructured rhythms. The "strong" curtain at the close of each act—to keep the audience hooked into an excitement and anticipation of what was to come—gave way to a more open-ended division of theatrical time, recapitulating a "natural" sense of life flow. Exposition, which had tended to be rather heavily set up at the beginning of a play—to provide the skittles that the action would go ahead and knock down—became more distributed throughout the play. This both recaptured a more "natural" sense of how human events worked and also underlined the fact that Realism tended to become more and more concerned with the development and exploration of character, that is, the individual, rather than how a fixed character was affected by the trials heaped upon it by circumstances.

Somewhat ironically, although the structure of Realism was based upon a desire to reject earlier forms and conventions, the nature of Realism's focus upon life tended to make it a more closed form than the wider, more metaphysical sweep of tragedy and Romantic drama. With its focus upon the average human individual (what used to be called the "common man"), the social structure of the plays tended to be private and familial rather than public and universal.

Relationships operated within the concerns of the family unit rather than within palace halls or atop Mount Olympus. In earlier, less democratic forms of drama, when a king might ask about his son it is not because he wants his company or that the family isn't complete without him, but rather that he is concerned for how the prince is doing abroad fighting his country's enemies; or to make sure that he isn't plotting to overthrow the crown. Even in comedy, the father is probably concerned because the boy is off chasing the woman the father has his eye upon, or is out somewhere spending the father's money. In realistic drama the relationships took place within the dynamics of an essentially patriarchal family unit. This unit began to change in the 1970s and 1980s as Realism continued to fulfill its role of reflecting changing social patterns, where fractured families and female-focused units became more visible. But here, still, the emphasis is upon the individual struggling to throw off any repressive form—the logical outcome of which is, finally, to leave him or her locked within the solitude of self. It took another form of drama to deal with this problem and try to connect humankind to a larger sense of purposes, and this form we deal with in the final section of this book.

Space.   A closed, inward-looking form, involved with the private concerns of the individual might be expected to inhabit enclosed spaces; and that is the case with Realism. Here there are no epic battlefields, no palaces, no mansions, but a range that takes us from the Victorian parlors of Ibsen through the cramped New Orleans apartments of Tennessee Williams to the kitchen sink conversations of John Osborne. Although the forms of the furnishings may change, the cluttered informality of the space tends to be constant. The basic design principle of Realism was that the stage should resemble a room with the fourth wall removed to allow the audience to, as it were, accidentally look in upon the action. As we will see in the performance demands section, this sense of the audience not being participants in a theatrical event but simply observers of a life happening had great consequences for the nature of the actors' approach. It is not coincidental that the camera had been invented in the early nineteenth century, and the later invention of gas lighting followed by electricity enabled auditoriums to

be darkened during performance. The combination of these factors led the theatrical event to take on the image of early photography: The photographer with a dark cloth over his or her head was in the position of the audience, pointing a peep-hole mechanism at the subject—the actors—in order to make an exactly "real" copy of the everyday event being looked at. Little wonder that the ultimate extension of Realism was the cinema.

What the stage space attempted to give the audience, looking on through the removed fourth wall, was the environment that would be appropriate to the social circumstances of the characters. This sense that Realism must recreate everyday reality was reinforced by the scientific belief, developed in the late nineteenth century, that environment had a great influence upon the nature and actions of the individual. Thus detail, the filling of the stage space not just with the furniture or properties that might be immediately necessary to the action, but also with all the clutter of the minutiae that the character had surrounded himself or herself with throughout life, became an important aspect of the realistic stage.

In this period the descriptions of environments, and even of character motivations, began to be minutely detailed in stage directions. The actor has, therefore, many more resources available for small business than had previously been the case. Before Realism it had not been thought necessary or important to show a character brushing teeth, unless the toothbrush had been poisoned and was crucial to the plot. Indeed, for kings, queens, aristocrats, etc., there had been something of a conspiracy among playwrights that such characters did not use the bathroom, for whatever reason; it was beneath their dignity or formality. Now, however, it was necessary to show this kind of activity because it was done in "real life." Fully realized rooms with ceilings enclosing the detailed, cluttered, informal, irregular appearance of living in everyday life

(a)

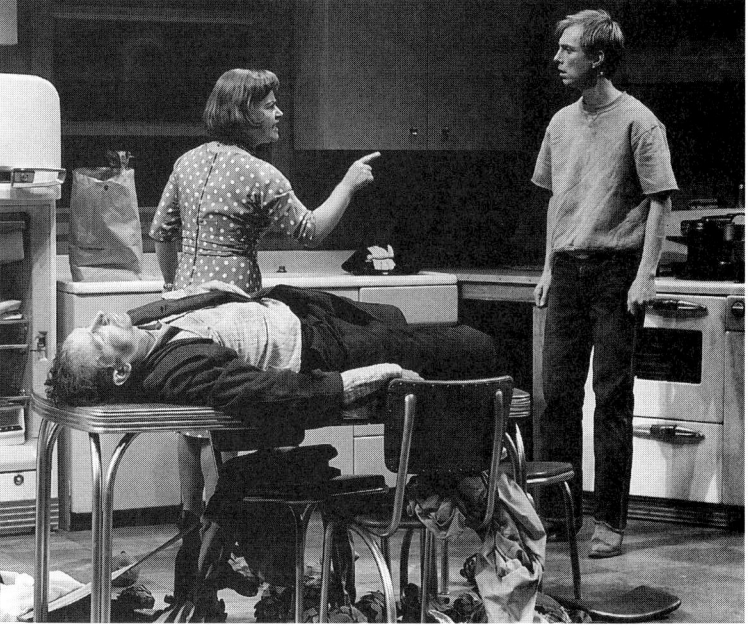

(b)

The spatial range of Realism from Victorian parlor to contemporary kitchen sink seen in productions of (a) *Ghosts* and (b) *The Curse of the Starving Class* by the Oregon Shakespeare Festival.   *Photos by Christopher Briscoe.*

Naturalistic space in a production of *The Lower Depths*, 1903.   *Theatre-Museum, Munich.*

now became the design models for the stages of realistic theatre.

Clothes and Manners.   We are taking these two aspects of social living together because, consistently since the beginnings of Realism, the way in which individuals related to one another went hand in hand with the way in which they presented themselves to society, that is, how they dressed. And, not surprisingly, the trend was toward increasing informality both in manner and dress. There were essentially two watersheds in this progression: World Wars I and II. Wars not only lead to a rethinking of how the survivors should renew life, but they also lead to a breakdown of rigid social conventions and restrictions under the pressure of the emergency of survival. Before World War I, Victorian mores still tended to dominate social life, male clothing was stiffly tailored, stiff collars were worn, and changes

of clothing were made for the time of day: morning dress, evening dress, Sunday "go to church" dress were the rule. Women suffered even more from the prevailing "stiffness" than did men, being corseted into rigid and erect postures and contrived body silhouettes. All of this necessitated, for both men and women, an uprightness, precision, and unrelated (in today's terms, although people adapted to their clothing and learned to be comfortable in them) manner of sitting or standing that went together with a still rigidly adhered to code of social behavior. That code required men to raise their hats to women out of doors and to remove their hats indoors. Women wore hats at all times indoors and out. Men always walked on the outside of women in the street and stood to offer their seats when a woman entered a room. Women would always offer their hands first upon being introduced, and shaking hands had replaced the curtsys and bows of earlier and less "informal" times. Young people at all times showed "respect" for their elders by raising their hats, offering their seats, and generally being as self-effacing as possible. This was the early Realism of Ibsen, still socially hierarchical although concerned with the place of the individual. World War I broke down hierarchies further and led to a period of greater freedom both in social manners and clothing. Women stepped out of their corsets and suffocating layers of clothing into both shorter and easier-fitting clothes. Men left off their starched collars and formal changes of attire and adopted the simpler business suit and "sports" jacket for leisure wear.[1] This allowed both men and women to lounge more comfortably in their seats and to cross their legs in a hitherto unacceptable fashion. Though handshakes and short nods of the head were "formal" greetings, and women were still regarded as "weaker vessels" to be given seats and allowed first through doors, men and women mixed on a much more casual basis, and some of the dances on social occasions—the Charleston, for example—could suggest downright uninhibited relationships, even compared with the waltz of pre-World War I days.

World War II was the greatest leveler, both in terms of the mixing of classes in the military, and the great influx of women both into the military and the general working structure of Western society. In face of a general emergency that brought together people from all aspects of society and all walks of life, social niceties and distinctions crumbled still further. Women adopted slacks and the freedom of movement that went with them. Both men's and women's clothing tended to be functional and geared toward a workaday world in which similarity of function led to similarity of form. Adherence to social codes

and dressing in conformity with social ceremony gave way to an individualistic response to occasion. Both manner and clothing became personal expressions and reactions to impulse rather than conventions. This movement was probably completed by the events of the 1960s: an attempt upon the part of essentially young people finally to remove all remaining social and moral restrictions standing in the way of equality and the personal freedom of expression of the individual. And that freedom of expression extended to clothing and comportment as much as political and economic welfare. Dress tended to become eclectic and unisexual, and essentially comfortable. The universality of jeans—originally worn by miners and cowboys—illustrated both the classlessness of clothing (the status of an individual could not be immediately recognized) and the emphasis upon ease. As clothing became less restricting so did posture become more relaxed. Not only could legs be crossed but sitting on the floor, leaning, slouching, whatever the individual felt like doing became appropriate to whatever situation. If the Charleston had been thought uninhibited, the jitterbug, followed by rock and roll, could not be subscribed to definition.

The post-1960s saw the triumph of democratic individualism, toward which political, social, and moral instincts had been moving throughout the period of Realism. Instinct and personal feeling, reflected in eclecticism and casualness, are the order of the day in the late twentieth century and are reflected in the clothes and manners of individualistic society in which self-fulfillment is the ultimate good.

For the actor dealing with the spectrum of Realism from Ibsen through O'Neill, Williams, Miller, Wilson, and Henley, the task is not an adjustment of technique as it would be from Shakespeare to Ibsen, but an acceptance of what clothing and furnishings along the spectrum of Realism tell him or her about how they were worn. The degree of formality

---

[1]Toward the end of the twentieth century this produced the "natural" shoulder and "unconstructed" look.

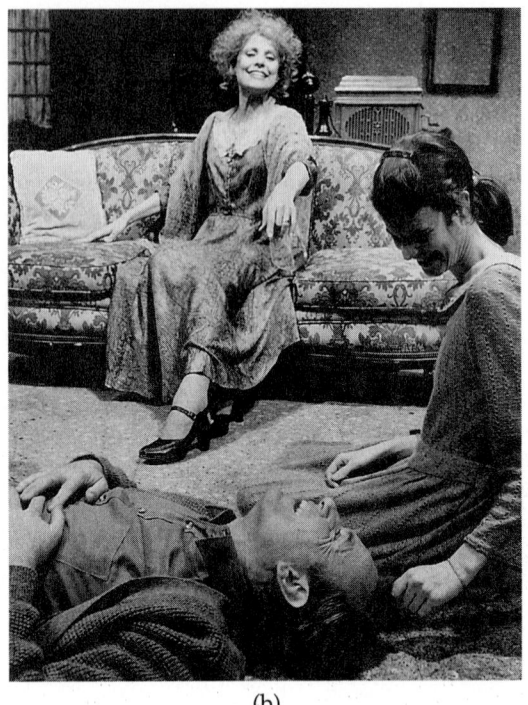

(a)

(b)

(c)

Relaxation of clothing and manners seen through productions of Ibsen, Tennessee Williams, and Beth Henley. *(a) Hedda Gabler, Old Globe Theatre, San Diego. Photo by Ken Howard. (b) The Glass Menagerie, Los Angeles Theatre Center; (c) Crimes of the Heart, Center Theatre Group, Los Angeles. Photo by Martha Swope.*

they dictate at any time suggests how individuals presented themselves in a particular society, as the move toward greater individualism gradually threw off restrictions of clothing and social manner during the next hundred years. Again, it is a feel for the sensibility of a period that will help the actor shape the appropriate mask for the time and communicate how the larger drive for individual self-expression was manifested through the mores of a moment.

Language. Just as one of the major functions of Realism was to capture the quality of everyday life, as opposed to aristocratic or superior social forms and spaces, so it will use everyday speech rather than elevated linguistic forms. It is the language of the streets and living rooms, not of the parliaments or palaces. If, as we have suggested, the eye of Realism is photographic, then its ear might be said to be microphonic. Again, the appropriate level of speech will depend upon the circumstances and will range from the classic "Dear, Highly Esteemed Bookcase, I salute you," of Chekhov's Gaev, through the "Hello, nice to meet you," of the 1940s and 1950s to the "Hi! How ya doin?" of some contemporary drama. The level of formality of speech will match the level of formality of costume and living space—a consistent clue to the actor of what his or her approach should be—but the intention at all levels will be to recapitulate the appropriate vernacular for the character using the language: If one were to meet that character in the street, he or she would sound that way.

There is no deliberate use of verbal music—that quality of Greek, Shakespearean, and other forms of poetic drama whereby, as in opera, the sounds and rhythms of the language, not just the content of the speech, are intended to have an emotional affect upon the audience. As we have suggested, kings and queens in Shakespeare's time no more

spoke in verse than did the average individual, but the size and scope of Shakespeare's style required the music of verse to carry a larger emotional impact than the language in which it was couched. Nor does Realism use witty epigrammatic verbal structures such as are found in Restoration comedy, Noel Coward, and Bernard Shaw; a fact that distinguishes Shaw from the genre of Realism to which chronologically, and by dint of his social theses, he otherwise belongs.

What then are the particular qualities of the vernacular language that Realism employs? Primarily, and prosaically, it is to discover and impart information. This informational aspect, which goes hand in hand with the scientific and technological attitude of the period, is also illustrated by the greater use of stage directions in the plays. Many Realist playwrights, especially Ibsen and Shaw, made significant use of stage directions, both to describe the environment in which their characters lived and to detail the inner dimensions of those characters. This was a very precise and scientific approach to playwriting. One aspect of the science of the day did, however, give an ambivalence to the fact of information: the Freudian idea that human beings were motivated by desires and drives that were subconscious. This led to the concept of subtext—one of the principles of Stanislavski's system, to which we will return—that the character was concealing his true intentions as much as revealing them through the language he or she uses. Character self-examination, a search for true motivations, became one of the structural elements of Realism. That language in Realism does not quite say what it means, or mean what it says, is not the same as character inarticulateness or incoherence, another aspect of the form. Broken speech patterns, pauses, and staccato outbursts are part of Realism's attempt to capture the quality of everyday speech, in which many individuals are not fluent or articulate.

The language of Realism will not then confront the actor with the task of dealing with verse structures, self-conscious rhythmical devices, verbal colorings, epigrammatical deliveries, or other rhetorical devices of non-Realistic theatre. For the most part the actor's task will be the discovery of the "natural" vocal manner appropriate to the character in its situation: a conversational form geared to the exchange of information, and including whatever mannerisms, dialects, and inarticulate responses the quality of everyday speech may demand.

Character and Self.   One of the major influences that Realism had upon acting technique was the development of the concept of playing oneself. As we have suggested, Realism propagated the idea of the primacy of the individual, free from all restraints and conventions. This came to mean that the actor too must be free from any technical restraints; the only way in which the actor could respond freely, and therefore honestly, to the impulses of action was to do whatever the dictates of his or her own emotional feeling produced at that moment. The argument ran: If I am to play freely and honestly, what have I to draw upon but my *own* experience, my emotional memories, my storehouse of inner responses and motivations. Anything else was seen to be an external imposition, an artificial social mask and, as such, dishonest technical trickery.

This gave rise to an unfortunate fallacy of realistic acting. Stanislavski, the great mentor of twentieth-century acting, who created a scientific system to guide a scientific age, was looking to create a reality on stage to match the reality offstage. This reality required of the actor an honesty of response—the support of stage action by truthful human emotion. Stanislavski called for this in contrast to the Romantic rant and melodramatic cliche that he saw in so much theatre of his day. Unfortunately, Stanislavski's emphasis upon re-ality and individual feeling was quickly parlayed into a method that suggested that all an actor had to do on stage was to play oneself. This seemed to be consonant with the idea that the individual is unique and all-important, and that what is interesting about the individual is his or her personal feelings. Thus, the feeling of the moment became the touchstone of theatrical truth: The self of the actor and the self of the character were perceived to have a one-to-one relationship.

This led to the domination of the actor's process by such techniques as emotion memory—the actor's own emotional past becoming the guide to action; the private moment—the exploration of the actor's own private responses to emotional problems; substitution—the replacement of the character the actor is playing against (or with) by someone from the actor's own experience; the Magic If—this was one of Stanislavski's techniques that came to be understood as "What would I do if I were in this situation?" rather than Stanislavski's intention of "What would I do if I were the character in this situation?"

What was ignored in all of this was the character that the playwright had written and the action he or she had been given to play. The pure inner process might occasionally produce bravura performance and displays of self on stage, but it did as much of a disservice to drama as the imitation of surface events that Stanislavski had sought to replace. We have noted that there was a qualitative change in self-consciousness at this time, which became part of the playwright's structure of character, but the character is still a construct meant to serve the play's action, not the feeling of the actor. The missing element of process was precisely the given circumstances of the play's action. The playwright creates a logical consistency between the wishes, wants, needs, and intentions of the character and the events of the play's action, in which the character is involved. An understanding of the given circumstances allows the actor to make choices among his or her feelings and responses that would be appropriate for the character the playwright had created, and then to channel those responses according to the demands of the play's action.

Such techniques as emotion memory, private moment, and substitution can be useful studio exercises to help the actor to tune up his or her instrument, or part of a rehearsal process to explore an actor's response, but the final choice must be in the play's terms, not that of the actor's ego. Stanislavski, later in his career, came to the conclusion that the engendering of feeling was not the prime aim of the actor, or the basis of a realistic process. Stanislavski's final belief, and one to which we subscribe and is the foundation of our approach in this book, is that the actor discovers the appropriate physical action for the needs of his or her character in the given circumstances of the dramatic moment. The playing of this action will draw valid supporting emotion from the actor who will be playing from himself or herself, but not of the self. This has been simply put as "play the action and the feeling will follow." Although actors do not simply play themselves, the actor's self is important: The wider the palette, the more vivid the choices. As human beings we all have a wide range of experiences that are there to be tapped and will respond to physical stimulus; as actors we must select from this and order reality according to the necessary choice of the moment—this is the function of art. Realism, despite its avowed aim of recapitulating reality, is as much an art form as any other theatrical genre and must be approached as such: It is the art that disguises art to create the appearance of reality.

Summary.   Before we move on to show how the concepts of Realism we have described lead to particular physical responses from the actor, which create the style of Realism we are going to try to pull these concepts together to show how they are manifested in one of the classical works of the realistic period: Tennessee Williams's *A Streetcar Named Desire.*

Inevitably when dealing with even the structural elements of a play, aspects of interpretation will arise. We hope our readers will focus on the utility of the discussion that follows rather than on any differences they may have in interpretation.

To be aware of the structure of the whole play, not just the scenes in which he or she appears, is useful to the actor, not simply because an awareness of the crises and climax helps an actor to pace a performance, but also because it allows one to understand how each of a character's individual actions contributes at any moment to the overall pattern of the play. While *A Streetcar Named Desire* is seemingly untypical in that it is written in eleven scenes, it does, in terms of its action and chronological structure, break conveniently and fairly equally into three acts: scenes 1–3, scenes 4–6, scenes 7–11. What the scenic structure does is to give the play a very logical and linear form in the shape of a rite of passage: entrance, trial, and casting out. Scene 1 is mostly exposition, with quite a lot contained in stage directions situating both environment and character. This typically Realistic convention continues throughout the play. Scenes 2 and 3 contain rising action: conflict between Stanley and Blanche; Blanche's potential relationship with Mitch; the strength of the Stanley/Stella relationship. Scenes 4, 5, and 6 are a plateau with hopeful possibilities for Blanche, establishing a springboard for the action to move toward the climax. This movement takes place in scenes 7, 8, 9, and 10, each of which has Blanche confronting a crisis: Stanley tells Mitch of Blanche's sexual exploits; Stanley gives Blanche bus tickets out of town; Mitch rejects Blanche. Scene 10 contains the climax—the rape and defeat of Blanche by Stanley. Scenes 7, 8, 9, and 10 are the shortest in the play, giving a compressed and urgent sense of moving to the climax. In this play the structural climax is also a sexual climax. The dramatic structure of Realistic plays has been compared to the sexual act; but it is also the shape of human effort per se: the way the breath works in strenuous activity; the heartbeat when excited; a strong relationship to basic human rhythms. In scene 11 of the play we have the "denouement," the untying of the complications, a resolution of the action that in human terms is a returning to rest.

The action of the play also takes place within a highly compressed space—Stanley and Stella's two-room apartment. The local environment is basically working class, with the manners and speech patterns of that class manifested by Stanley and his friends. Into this environment comes Blanche with the speech and manner of a different background.

It is a brilliant structural integration on the part of Tennessee Williams, that the individual conflicts within the play are also illustrated in class/manner terms. Blanche, from a much more spacious background, could not fit within the limits of Stanley's space—literally and spiritually. For Stanley the expulsion of Blanche from his space is both a territorial act—protection of wife and property—and confirmation of his individuality, his democratic selfhood. It can also be seen, metaphorically, as a revolutionary act—the defeat of the old aristocratic class structure by the rising proletariat. The victory of the North—industrialized, scientific, urban, and future oriented—over the South—landed, traditional, decadent.

A Streetcar Named Desire is a "classic"; it is a classic because, while it typifies all the structural elements of Realism that we have discussed above, it is greater than the sum of its

The busy, cluttered realistic environment of the Kowalski home, seen in the film of *A Streetcar Named Desire.* *Courtesy of the Academy of Motion Picture Arts & Sciences.*

parts. Its larger sensibility goes back to the very social roots of Realism: a focus on the individual's desire for a unique selfhood, and the overthrowing of all repressive forms. Blanche's rite of passage is also that from an old social structure to a new democratic structure, which itself gave rise to the dramatic form of Realism. This is a classic play because Tennessee Williams achieved a marvelous marriage of realistic form and content, with an all-embracing humanistic vision.

PERFORMANCE DEMANDS

Scenic Form.   Just as we saw above that a play has an overall structure that integrates all aspects of its form, so will each scene within the play have an equivalent structure. While the overall realization of a play's form is the concern of a director, at any given moment within the playing of a scene it is the actor who is producing its dynamics, and an understanding of how a scene is built is an important part of an actor's technique.

A legacy of Stanislavski's scientific approach to the theatre is the breaking down of the dramatic action into small segments of action: units and beats. A *unit* will contain a complete element of intention, which is smaller than a scene, but where the playwright moves the action forward in a specific and particular way. *Beats* occur within units and demark smaller elements of character intention, the tactics or ways in which the actor may choose to achieve his or her main intention in a unit. A change from one tactic or response to another will be a beat. Units and beats, like acts and scenes, are all a part of the rhythmical phrasing of the action. Breaking a text into units and beats gives an actor a much stronger and clearer sense of the moment-to-moment action in which he or she is involved. This leads to the more detailed playing associated with the texture of Realism.

We are now going to look at how this works in the first scene of *A Streetcar Named Desire.* Again, this will involve us in some interpretation, which we ask the reader to bear with if he or she disagrees with our choices.

The main action of the opening scene is to situate Blanche in an alien environment, which includes the close relationship of Stella and Stanley. The scene breaks down into four units, each determined by the entrance or exit of a character—such units are sometimes called *French scenes.* Entrances or exits of major characters nearly always determine a change in the pulse of action, and therefore a unit.

The first unit is from the opening of the play—the set is visual exposition—until the entrance of Blanche, p. 14.[2] The action of the unit is expositional in environment and character terms, creating an intense, informal, sexually charged atmosphere and relationship between Stanley and Stella.

The second unit goes to Eunice's exit on p. 18. The action of the unit is again essentially expositional—environmental as we see the apartment in which Stella and Stanley live, and character as we get to hear details of Blanche's background.

The third unit goes to Stanley's entrance on p. 27. It establishes the relationship between Blanche and Stella, and it has the quickening pulse of rising action based upon Blanche's distaste for where Stella lives and her implicit superiority toward Stella's husband, Stanley. This begins to develop the future conflict between Stanley and Blanche. There are several beats within this unit:

Beat 1 continues until Stella's entrance on p. 18. The action reveals Blanche's fragile and nervous emotional condition. Her attempt to conceal the fact that she had a drink suggests a dependence and a need to deny reality.

Beat 2 goes to the pause and change of subject on p. 20 after Stella's line "Thanks." The action confirms not only Blanche's need

---

[2]All page references are to the Signet paperback edition of *A Streetcar Named Desire,* published by The New American Library.

for liquor and her dissembling nature but also her distaste for the manner in which Stella is living. Stella is accommodated to her life style, which is an obstacle for Blanche in her desire to live under Stella's protection. Blanche also reveals a certain intellectual pretentiousness, which is a further obstacle for her in this environment.

Beat 3 to beat 7 is a series of short beats created by quick changes of subject illustrating the erratic and nervous rhythm of Blanche, who is trying to come to terms with Stella and the new situation. The beat changes occur at the bottom of p. 20: a change of subject, two quick beats in the middle of p. 21 when Blanche quickly changes the subject to the drink and then to her appearance. There is a beat at the top of p. 22 at "Stella you have a maid," then back to the drink in the middle of p. 22, and an immediate switch back to her appearance by Blanche. Again on p. 22, Blanche returns to the subject of the apartment.

Even if the actor did not know the content of this sequence, the quick changing, erratic rhythm would give a strong sense of Blanche's emotionally unstable and nervous condition. In content terms the beats reaffirm Blanche's main character concerns: keeping up appearances; establishing herself in the apartment; finding support from Stella. Stella's essentially short responses suggest a more static rhythm, comfortable in the space, trying to be a stabilizing factor in the situation.

Beat 8 is a much longer beat to the middle of p. 25. The action is a discussion of Stanley, background exposition, and revelation of the strength of the sexual attraction between Stella and Stanley. It is a further indication that Blanche's manner and superiority are likely to be a complication for her in the context of Stanley and his social group.

Beat 9 is the final beat in the unit. It begins with Blanche's tentative "Stella" in the middle of p. 25 and goes down to Stanley's entrance at the bottom of p. 27. The action is exposi-

tional in terms of the loss of *Belle Reve* and Blanche's response to it. There is the possibility of two other beats in the section: when Stella asks, "But how did it go?" in the middle of p. 26, and again when Stella says, "Blanche! You be still" in the middle of p. 27. It would be for the actor to decide if at these moments there is a change in the emotional rhythm of the scene which, in content terms, is consistent from the middle of p. 25 to the bottom of p. 27.

The fourth and last unit in the scene, which we are not going to break into beats, goes from Stanley's entrance at the bottom of p. 28 to the end of the scene on p. 31. The basic action of the scene is to confront Stanley and Blanche for the first time. The scene also provides further social exposition in the nature of Stanley's friends and reveals character exposition about Stanley—a lot of this is carried in stage directions on p. 29; the playwright wants to be quite sure that the actor is aware of some of Stanley's fundamental life motivations. There is a great deal of information for the actor in this scene, which contains the seeds of future complications in the relationship between Blanche and Stanley: Stanley doesn't care about appearances; he was never very good at English, which Blanche teaches—metaphorically they don't speak the same language; Stanley is aware of Blanche's deceit about the whiskey. The rhythm of the language in the unit is stichomythic, suggesting conflict or lack of communication.

Scene analysis is not an exact science: As we have suggested, there were possible beats in unit 3 that depended upon the actor's sense of character. It is, however, for the most part, a very accurate method of determining the emotional/rhythmical structure or, to use a musical term, score of a scene. In this sense the emotional dynamics of a scene could be plotted by tracing the units and beats on a graph. And in this sense too, an actor will feel the musical pulse of a scene if he or she opens up to its rhythm. The added virtue of analysis is

The varied and irregular movement typical of realism. *Balm in Gilead.*   *Circle Repertory Company, New York. Photo by Gerry Goodstein.*

to give the actor a support for his or her instinct. A clear understanding of a character's intention and tactics in a beat, and how that beat relates to intentions and tactics in the whole role, will lead the actor to a much greater variety and interest in character choices. It should further help the actor to appreciate the total structure of the play and the part his or her character plays in it. For, however realistically one is working, and however much of a real person the actor wishes the character to become, this must be achieved within the understanding that the character serves the play's purposes, not the actor's. It is for the actor to make each moment as personal and exciting as possible, but this must be within the context of the fact that beat fits into unit, unit fits into scene, scene fits into act, act fits

into play, and it is the actor's task to discover and perform consistently the tasks that the play requires of the character in order to fulfill the dramatic action of its whole.

Space and Movement.   Just as the life styles and social settings of Realism were less socially formal and hierarchical, so the patterns and shapes of acting movement within the stage space were equally less formal and hierarchical. The tendency of the proscenium stage, which predominated through the eighteenth and nineteenth centuries and which Realism inherited, was to pull the action down center where the major focus was, and to deal in static tableaux and somewhat horizontal relationships in space. The actor would tend to gravitate toward center stage for major

(a)

Increasingly casual physical relationship seen in productions of (a) *Ghosts*, Oregon Shakespeare Festival; (b) *Talley's Folly*, Circle Repertory Company, New York; (c) *Division Street*, Mark Taper Forum, Los Angeles.   *(a) Photo by Christopher Briscoe; (b) Photo by Gerry Goodstein; (c) Mark Taper Forum, Los Angeles.*

(b)

(c)

speeches and when "sharing" the scene would sit or stand in formally balanced relationships to one's fellow actors. The classic furniture situation was a sofa, set stage center and parallel with the proscenium arch, and two chairs equidistant from the sofa, one on either side. The classic standing position was three-quarters open to the audience, and about six feet upstage from the footlights. Realism gradually broke down the formal balance of staging with asymmetrically placed furniture and much more flexible use of body positions, both individually and in relationship to the other actors. The famous *Théâtre Libre*, one of the earliest realistic theatres, was nicknamed the "theatre of Antoine's back," after the name of its founder and his radically new sense of what acting positions were tolerable, and indeed desirable, in the service of imitating everyday events and manners.

Casual movement in more irregular space and a tendency toward more frequent minor movement; the great use of stage properties to fill out the detail of everyday existence, and the movement away from carefully furnished drawing rooms toward what came to be called in England in the 1950s "kitchen sink" drama, with all its clutter of paraphernalia, gave more opportunity to actors to create character detail with small business, and demanded a "busyness" of activity that became one of the hallmarks of realistic style. A glance at any living situation in "real" life will reveal a variety of small activity and physical postures. If Ibsen's and Strindberg's characters—albeit now facing each other when they spoke and adopting less formal positions in sets that had some asymmetricality and reference to a lived-in room—were still locked by clothing and social conventions into a somewhat rigid and inflexible manner, by the time we had reached the 1950s sitting on the floor, lolling in a sofa, sitting on the arms of chairs, and putting one's feet on tables had all become part of the realistic imitation of life on stage. More than this, drinking coffee, smoking, combing one's hair, picking teeth—the almost unconscious behavior of the average person in an average situation—had become part of the texture of the realistic stage.

Thus, one of the tasks of the actor in realistic drama will be to discover a variety of interesting ways of doing the same thing: that is, sitting; as well as the use of stage properties, both in a casual manner that creates the normal rhythms of everyday life, and in a way that is at least appropriate to the character and that may also add a dimensionality to that character. One of the traps of this facet of realistic acting is that the actor will fall into an overly busy, mannered way of performing that can become distracting to the audience and thus obscure depth of character creation with surface mannerisms.

If overly busy playing can be one trap for the actor in realism, unduly small playing can be another. That the performance style of Realism should be smaller than earlier forms of drama should be no surprise. The concerns are more social and private—the physical embracement of the gods or the large authoritarian gestures of monarchs are not called for. The spaces are smaller—living rooms, bedrooms, kitchens—and the relationships are closer physically, all of which calls for less physical histrionics, for the smaller gestures and more casual manner of the intimate and informal. One of the ideas Stanislavski presented in *An Actor Prepares* was that of "circle of attention." This was essentially a focus and concentration exercise geared to ensuring that the actor did no more than was necessary for the action of the moment: The first circle included the actor's self; the second, his or her immediate surroundings; the third embraced the actor being related to. Stanislavski's quite

proper intention was to stop the actor from simply playing to the audience and ignoring the private and interpersonal demands of human relationships. There is, however, a difference between playing to the audience and being aware of the fact of the audience's presence. One of the dangers of private moments on stage, and playing that extends only to one's fellow actors, is that the dramatic action will not carry to the back of the auditorium where an audience member is sitting expecting to be included in the theatrical event. The circle of attention is a fine reminder that action must emanate from the actor's self and that dynamics should be no larger than the emotional response demands; but the final circle must include the audience—the other half of the theatrical performance.

One of the tricks of playing Realism is to use both movement and gesture that are not only natural to the environment but also appropriate to the emotional circumstances; but at the same time these must be articulated so that they will read at the back of the house— whatever size that may be. One of the first things actors do when on tour is get on stage to test the resonance of the house and just how "big" their performance will have to be to just reach the back of the auditorium. One of the best ways of judging this is simply to talk from the stage to a fellow actor standing at the back of the house. A danger of the intimacy of realistic acting is that it will feel fine on stage but simply not engage the audience. As an actor you must still claim your space, have the inner energy that reaches out, and embrace the audience: Truthfulness must be supported by physical presence.

Speech.   As we suggested in the section in this chapter dealing with language, the aim of speech in Realism is whatever level of everyday conversation the environment requires. Techniques that, depending upon the level of formality of the situation, may be employed are the use of whistling, humming,

(a)

Range of intimate physical relationship in productions of (a) *The Glass Menagerie*, The Guthrie Theater; (b) *A Lie of the Mind*, American Conservatory Theatre; (c) *Fool for Love*, Los Angeles Theatre Center.   *(a) Photo by Michal Daniel, (b) Photo by Larry Merkle, (c) Photo by Meridian.*

(b)

(b)

and interjections that give a personal texture to the speech. Language may also be broken up, as there is no poetic structure to observe, and pauses taken in the middle of speeches. The danger here is that the pace may be slowed down if the audience does not continue to be engaged in the dialogue during the pauses; pauses should be related to some necessary thought process of the character, or be related to subtext.

Subtext is, in itself, one of the properties of Realism that affects language. It is usually a hidden intention that is covered by oblique or indirect speech: A character says one thing while intending or trying to achieve another. This can be conscious on the part of the character: The character is deliberately trying to obscure his or her intentions. It can also be unconscious as when the character is unaware of the true motivations of his or her action: Sometimes this is revealed in action by what has come to be called "Freudian slips." An example of subtext in *A Streetcar Named Desire* would be Stanley's remark that, "Liquor goes fast in hot weather." (scene 1). Here he is letting Blanche know that despite her denial he is aware that she has had a drink.

Intentional subtext will have been written into the action by the playwright, and the actor should not play the speech in such a way as to reveal that the character is aware of the subtext: The speech should be played as if the surface intention were the real one. Nor does the audience need to be given a dig in the ribs, for the playwright will have set up the total action in such a way that the audience is aware of the double meaning.

Overlapping is another technique of Realism, especially in its mid-twentieth-century forms; before that time the somewhat greater formality of social relationships would have proscribed it: People were too polite to jump in on another person's speech. This is what overlapping means. A character starts to speak before another character finishes his or her line. This happens all the time in everyday dialogue. It can be used to show familiarity—especially among young people—or it can build the dynamics of a scene as in some kind of excitement or altercation. In this instance it serves the same function as sticomythia in verse. The actor must beware, however, not to obscure totally the other actor's line or to allow crucial words to go unheard by the audience. Speaking of the audience, a final caveat: The actor must be heard. Just as in size of gesture, which must be geared to the size of the house, so in size of voice: The "stage whisper" must be heard at the back of the house, and the softest endearments of "real" love, or the most intimate responses to sorrow, must equally be shared with all members of the audience, no matter how far they may be from the stage.

Character Mask.   Basically, character in Realism will tend to have more dimensions, detail, and nuances than character in other genres. This will be the case even if somewhat distanced in time, as are characters in Ibsen, Strindberg, and other early Realistic writers. As the character gets closer to our own time so will the mask be more directly aligned, verbally and physically, with a recognizable contemporary manner. This will include all the necessary social and personal detail that Realism uses in its attempt to create the closest possible illusion of the "Me acting in the Now." Because of Realism's focus upon the individual operating in his or her environment and its concern for the inner motivations of the individual, the actor is likely to be called upon to show a wider emotional range, more psychological shading, and more moment-to-moment detail. In other forms of drama intentions and motivations may be more direct, less complicated; language will do more of the character formulations. In Realism the language must be consistent with a character but will not contain so much of the character as in more poetic forms. In farce and broader forms of comedy, situations will be more contrived and require less subtle approaches from characters. Typology will also be less rigid in Realism and will give the actor more scope for originality: Old men, for example, who in many forms are seen as some permutation of impotence, miserliness, and irritability, may in Realism be played against this expectation and with a wider range of traits. *In Realism the actor's task is not how interesting one can make a type within the bounds prescribed by convention, but how unique can one make an individual whose character must remain within the demands of the dramatic situation.* This will, of course, allow the actor to make a broader use of his or her self in character creation: a much wider use of the actor's physical, emotional, and psychological palette.

But the character is still a mask, created by choice and selectivity; it is not the simple revelation of the actor's self, although it may make more use of it. The truth of Realism is still the truth of the dramatic action written by the playwright. Character grows out of this action: It is based upon information in the text and is motivated by impulses from the text. Emotional and psychological responses must be made tangible, must be communicated to the audience; it is what the audience feels and experiences that is important in the theatrical event. The actor is the vehicle for communicating the action in such a way that the audience has the appropriate response. This is done by what the semioticians call a "sign," and actors call a "move" or a physical activity. This can range from the smallest movement of the eyebrow (but big enough to reach the back of the house), to the longest diagonal cross. As we have suggested, in Realism the pattern or score of actions played by the actor is likely to be more subtle and detailed.

As communication comes through physical actions, so our approach to the creation of character mask is essentially physical, based upon the gestalt premise that physical actions and emotional responses are mutually supporting: Do the act and the feeling will follow. And physical actions are much more concrete and give an actor more purchase and structure for the creation of character than the intangibility of feelings or psychological responses. In the next section we set out a whole scheme of physical exercises that will give the actor ways of using his or her own experience, in physical terms, to turn the impulses of a text into uniquely interesting characters consistent with the needs of that text. But before we do this we are going to show how actors listen to the information the text is giving them and how to use these impulses to make the choices from which the character mask is built.

The character dimension that usually makes the most impact is the physical. It is the most evident; it is what the audience sees first, and physical activity is the vehicle by which the audience is informed of a character's responses. Usually the actor will find a lot of basic physical information in the text. This will be contained in stage directions and descriptions of the character given by the playwright directly: either self-description, which the character offers, or description of the character by other characters. Age, gender, possibly height and weight, race, and color are usually basic givens, as will be any unusual physical attributes such as large feet, large stomach, or missing limbs. Beyond this the nature and content of the character's speech can provide a lot of information. Is it quick or slow, assertive or recessive, dogmatic or flexible, sexually oriented, orally oriented, head oriented? From this the actor can gain a sense of where the character carries his or her basic center of energy: in the head, in the chest, in the stomach, groin, legs. This will affect the way in which the character moves, thinks, and feels. Our outlook on life is very often indicated by the way in which we physically approach life. Chest and shoulder thrusting can suggest aggressiveness, as can a rigid posture suggest dogmatism or inflexibility. Stomach predominance can suggest softness, sensuality, jolliness—the Falstaffian or Santa Claus syndrome. If all of this sounds like we are back to humors or typology characterization (which we have suggested was more appropriate to a basic Elizabethan and comedy of manners approach to character) we are, but without the rigidly conventional use which both set up and then responded to audience expectations. The story is told of the early days of Realism in which an actor, smitten by the individualistic approach, died in a melodrama by collapsing his legs and crumpling to the ground. Whereupon he was heartily booed by the audience until he got back up and with his legs and arms rigidly together fell stiffly back from his heels in a perpendicular manner—the expected way of dying in the melodramas of the time.

The actor in Realism will make use of the responses and judgments we make of individuals in everyday life. We do tend to make general associations between bodily types and psychological responses, but these are more of a first impression than an ultimate expectation, and we have infinitely more latitude in the way in which the individual may or may not match our expectation. This is particularly true today when, for social and political reasons, cross-gender and cross-racial casting is putting an entirely different perspective upon what is realistic—black parents of white children, for example.

Apart from physical information, the actor will find a lot of information in the text about environmental influences: childhood background, education, social interests, job or profession, class and economic level. All of these may be used to add dimensions to the basic physical attributes, as if they were a prism to give colors and shadings to the way in which the character is perceived by the audience. Similarly, indications about the character's

Strong physical playing in *Fool for Love.*   *British National Theatre. Photo by John Haynes.*

psychological makeup may be gathered from the way in which the character is seen to react to stimulus. Is the attitude toward the world generally positive or negative? Is the character flexible in approaching people and goals? Is there a consistent pattern of choices? Is this informed by a clear value system? This information may come directly as content of dialogue or be seen in the physical manner and actions of the character. In gestalt terms, the psychological and physical choices should support each other and create an integrated character. In fact, the physical sense of character the actor gains from the impulses in the text will lead him or her to expect the psychological choices of the character to be consistent with this. The information the actor derives from the text will lead him or her to what may be termed *functional choices of character,* those based upon textual givens. As we have suggested, however, one of the distinguishing features of Realism is its use of subtext and what might be called *subtexture,* the small pulses and minor details that are woven in and around the major action and events. The use of props, the small business, and personal activity that are not specified in the text will come out of the life lived by the actor in the character's circumstances and the play's environment. These might be called *personal* or *imaginable* choices, deriving from the impulses felt by the actor as he or she lives the character's life: that use of the imagination, that revelation of uniqueness which distinguishes fine acting. What also distinguishes fine acting is *selection* and *economy.* And while living fully the life of the character the actor must take care not to obscure the focus and action of the play with irrelevant detail. However "real" it may be drawn, a character is not a real person but a function of the dramatic action of the play. As actors we are guided in our choices by our experience and the reality in which we live, but we should take care not to impose more behavior upon the play than the demands of *its* reality require. Reality is the palette; it is the background; it is the sociocultural circumstances; but its exact description is not the basic function of the play.[3]

EXERCISES, GAMES, TECHNIQUES

Face-to-Face I.   This exercise focuses the actor strongly upon the facts of his or her body: the basic instrument from which he or she plays. Two actors sit closely facing each other and, taking turns, tell each other exactly what they see in the smallest detail: "Your hair grows strongly on your forehead"; "You have fine blond hair on your cheekbones." The exercise can take anything up to twenty minutes. It both acquaints the actor with details of his or her self of which he or she may not be aware, and it makes the actor look equally closely at another person. The exercise may be repeated with the actors now sitting back to back and telling each other what they have heard about themselves, partly to reinforce the impression upon the actor and partly to check how well the actor was listening. Actors tend not to look and listen well enough. They tend not to look because after a certain time in rehearsal the situation, including the fellow actor, becomes too familiar. They tend not to listen because of a concern with their own lines—they listen for cues but not always to the sense of the other character's line.

Face-to-Face II.   This is a further exercise in listening and responding spontaneously. Two actors are again facing each other. One makes any statement that arises: "It's hot today." The partner repeats, "It's hot today," colored by whatever feeling he or she may have about

---

[3]The director, Jose Quintero, has said that he had grown toward greater simplicity. He no longer feels the need to lard his productions with props and detailed activity to prove it is "real life." Explore, then reduce, is probably the byword for the actor.

the statement, and adds a statement of his or her own. The first actor repeats this and adds a further statement, and so on as a dialogue develops. If at any time no spontaneous added statement comes to an actor, participants may simply repeat the last phrase, testing it until some response arises.

Face-to-Face III.   This is another exercise in looking. Two actors face each other. One chooses a simple everyday activity such as shaving, painting the toenails, making an omelet and, for about a minute, mimes the activity. The partner has then to repeat the activity in the absolute detail performed by the first actor. When this is completed the two actors discuss what may have been omitted. The exercise is repeated with the second actor now performing an activity. This is not only a good exercise in which actors learn how little attention they pay to the small detail of everyday life, but it also leads to a more precise performance of detail that carries over to the handling of props.

Face-to-Face IV.   Two players set up a small improvisation. One player has a full set of circumstances—who, where, and what—and the other player only has an intention. This latter player must discover how to play the scene by discovering the circumstances: by looking, listening, and adapting to what he or she discovers from the other player's actions. This exercise demands great concentration in looking and listening; it also requires the player to relax and pick up the rhythms of a scene, not to impose upon it: to allow the scene to play the player.

Positive-Negative.   Here is an exercise in which the players get to explore the way they feel about themselves in a purely physical way. Players scatter through a space and on a handclap or drumbeat act out a physical response to the first good attribute of themselves that comes to mind. For example, a player may feel

that he or she is very open and accepting of people and may perform a large embracing gesture with the arms. On another handclap or drumbeat, players then express physically a quality they wish they didn't have. Again, players may feel they talk too much and patter through the space making gobbling gestures with their hands. The exercise continues for several minutes until players have had a good opportunity to explore several positive and negative feelings. Player are then asked to work out a complete physical pattern of activities consisting of positive and negative in which they may go quickly from one to another, or extend certain attributes for a longer time. If the exercise is being done in a group that has worked together for a while, each player can then perform the "dance of self" for the group. This usually brings some fascinating and amusing reactions. It can even be taken further with players performing for the group certain aspects of other players they feel may have been left out. Without any indulgence in psychological discussion this exercise can give a player a strong sense of what he or she has to work with and what tendencies may limit that work.

Cloning I.   Write each player's name on a card. Players pick a card and then have ten minutes (say) to clone the player written upon it; this is done by assuming body rhythms and balance—walk, carriage of the head, and so on. When the players are ready, each participant in turn presents his or her clone to the group by performing a simple everyday activity: washing up, making the bed, etc.; the activity shouldn't be static. The group has to identify the player being cloned. A successful clone will lead to an immediate and unanimous identification. After each presentation the group should discuss the qualities that made the clone identifiable. The exercise is usually great fun for the group, and it not only allows practice in the physical creation of a character but also helps players identify their own specific physicality and therefore the better to use and control it.

Cloning II.   Two players set up a short improvisation with clearly conflicting objectives for the two players. One of the players is then told to play his or her objective by aping the physical manner of the other character and performing similar physical actions. The other player has to respond and adapt to this without losing his or her own physicality, objective or "cool." It becomes a status game in which one character is attempting to take over the space and identity of the other. The exercise can be repeated with the situation reversed. The exercise affirms the necessity in realistic acting of playing strongly, of protecting one's own space and status while trying to take over that of one's antagonist in a scene.

ProPositions I.   Set up a small scene with at least three times as many props as there are players; that is, three players, nine or more props. The props should be of the everyday kind, and two-thirds of them should be appropriate to the circumstances of the scene; the other third should be more unusual. For example, if the scene were set in an office there could be the usual files, pens, paper, typewriters, rulers, etc., but there might also be an egg beater, a garden hoe, a hockey stick. During the improvisation players are required to use at least three props and justify the use. The props must not become the focus of any player's action; they must be incidental to the action but seem perfectly natural in their use. The exercise can be made into a game in which the first player to use and justify all of the props wins. There can be a referee who blows a whistle any time a prop is not validly used or justified.

ProPositions II.   This exercise requires a sofa or a chair and two players. Set up a small scene such as two friends studying; boy and girlfriend having coffee after a movie. The players have to find and justify as many ways as possible of using the sofa or chair, while playing their objectives in the scene—studying, making a sexual advance, etc. Imaginative players will find innumerable variations of arms, backs, lying, sitting, heads in laps, backs against legs, backs on floor, legs on chair arms, etc. Try different combinations of men and women: Players will find that, even in this androgynous age, differences in codes of behavior still exist, and they make different statements.

ProPositions III.   Draw a chalk circle of, say, twenty feet in diameter. Have a player standing outside that circle at about six feet from its circumference. Another player has a speech—this may be improvised or can be scripted and memorized—which he or she makes while walking around the inner circumference of the circle. The speech is made to the player outside the circle, and contact must be maintained at all times. This is an excellent exercise for the fluidity and full body use of realistic acting. The moving player, while walking toward, away from, with back to, will be obliged to make over-the-shoulder contact, or contact while walking backwards or sideways. Not only does it break an actor out of needing to work full front, and gives body flexibility, but it is also a good exercise for defining beats in the speech with changes of footwork and head and body turns.

ProPositions IV.   This is a combination of ProPositions II and III. Set up a small scene with chairs, sofa, table, desk, etc. Have one player permanently situated, the other moving around the set with a speech. The moving player has to use all of the furniture on the set in as varied a manner as possible while justifying the moves in the context of the speech. This can also be done as a dialogue between players who take moves in turn. Finally, props can be added so that players are obliged to both move and justify a variety of physical positions and the use of a variety of props. The scene is likely to become very busy, and it is a useful exercise to discuss afterwards what moves were necessary, what unnecessary, and why.

Subtext I.   Have a small realistic set, and a table in the middle of the set that has a number of props not circumstantial to the scene: balls, skipping rope, bat, cuddly toy, feather duster. Set up a short improvisation in which the players are unable to express with words their real feelings and intentions: first date, boy wants to kiss girl goodnight but can't get to it. The players, while keeping up a realistic conversation, would express the subtext with one of the "nonrealistic" props: for example, playing with the ball with their feet, caressing cuddly toy, etc.

Subtext II.   Set up a small improvisation in which players know their circumstances and intentions/objectives. Players are then given scripts made up of snippets from newspapers or unrelated lines from different plays. The players, while using the script, have to achieve their objectives both by physical means and the rhythms they set up with the lines and pauses.

Subtext III.   Players pair off and agree on circumstances and intentions. One player now plays the surface reality of the scene while the other shadows him or her and reminds the player of the subtextual feelings or circumstances of the situation. For example, the player could be calling someone he or she saw in a class with the aim of setting up a date. The player already has a boyfriend or girlfriend. The subtext player will comment on the truth of the conversation and remind the other player of the underlying truth of the situation. For example, "Hi, I'm Bill/Debbie. I saw you in class today and thought you asked a really interesting question." Subtext: "Hi, I'm Bill/Debbie. I saw you in class today and

thought you have a really great body." The exercise can be extended into couples in dialogue situations.

The following exercises deal with the physical creation of character. They are based upon the principle that we can identify and create body types by their physical rhythms and energy centers. Further, on the gestalt principle of psychophysical reciprocation, physical identities will then create supporting psychological features.[4]

Centers I.   For our purpose the body may be divided into five centers: head, chest, stomach, groin, legs. It is hoped that players will have discovered their own actor's working "center," which is where the spine, pelvis, and breath all come together in what is termed the *solar plexus.* In this exercise players experiment with moving their focus of energy into the various parts of body determined as character centers. Players should focus upon how their sense of relationship in space changes as the energy is moved from one center to another. Energy centered in the head, for example, will be inclined to make a character less grounded, possibly physically off-balance. The energy may be contained either in the front or back of a center. Energy at the back of the head may produce a recessive, academic individual; energy at the front may give a curious and intellectually assertive person. Energy in the stomach may suggest softness and self-indulgence. Responses will be individual to each player within the broader context of probabilities and will vary male to female: Chest energy focus in the woman may be more nurturing and less aggressive than in a man. The important factors are that refocusing the center of energy will affect the total body balance and rhythms of the player and will produce a supporting psychological sense of self.

[4]Basic Acting: The Modular Acting Process by the authors (Allyn & Bacon, 1996) uses similar terminology.

There are an infinite number of permutations on this system—there will be secondary centers of energy that will combine with primary centers to produce variations, and some unique individuals may completely vary from type. All of this is available to stimulate an actor's creativity and imagination based upon the physical vocabulary of energy centers for approaching the creation of a character.

Centers II.   Players choose one of the energy centers from the previous exercise and develop the body balances and rhythms that result from this. When the player has a strong sense of the new way he or she is relating to space the player will now set the physical character simple tasks: sitting down, reading a newspaper, etc., When comfortable with having moved into an everyday reality, the player can make the tasks more complex by moving into complete activities such as getting dressed, making breakfast, etc.

Centers III.   The previous exercise will already have involved the player in making choices consistent with the nature of the character evolving: For dressing, one needs to know what kinds of clothes; for breakfast, what food this person eats. This process can now be taken further and developed into what sort of a place does this person live in; what kind of a job does he or she have. The player will find that all of this will develop instinctively from the original choice of energy center. The physical rhythms act upon the player's imagination and creativity in such an instinctive way that the ultimate sense of having developed a complete person seems to be effortless. Finally, two players can set up a small scene for an improvisation in which only the environmental circumstances are known. The players each have an intention for their newly created character, and by playing this in the scene will discover what feelings and responses are evoked when confronting another character. In this way a functional psychological profile will be developed. There will be nothing superfluous, for all choices will have come from actions determined by physical given circumstances.

What follows are further exercises in physical approaches to character. They have a similar function to centers of energy but are based upon the way in which a person moves through space; this is what Stanislavski called *tempo-rhythms* in *Building a Character*, Chapter 2. We are also indebted to the work of Rudolf Laban in *The Mastery of Movement*, Chapter 3.[5]

Tempo-Rhythms I.   When we perform an action we are moving weight in time through space. Basically our movement will either be assertive/contending, or indulgent/yielding.

> The power or weight of our movement can be either strong or gentle.
> The time of the movement can be quick or sustained.
> The focus of the movement in space can be direct or flexible.
> In this context the basic action of contending is strong, quick, direct.
> The basic action of yielding is gentle, sustained, flexible.

This structure can be set out in a table:

	Motion		
Effort	*Weight*	*Time*	*Focus in Space*
Contend	Strong	Quick	Direct
Yield	Gentle	Sustained	Flexible

These factors may also all be permutated against each other to describe the nature of any movement; and this can be defined in everyday terms:

Strong	Quick	Direct	to Punch
Strong	Sustained	Direct	to Press
Gentle	Quick	Direct	to Dab

[5]See Suggested Readings at end of this chapter.

Gentle	Quick	Flexible	to Flick
Strong	Quick	Flexible	to Slash
Strong	Sustained	Flexible	to Wring
Gentle	Sustained	Flexible	to Float
Gentle	Sustained	Direct	to Glide

Basic character movement may be determined in this way. Is the character a Puncher, Presser, Dabber, Flicker, Slasher, Wringer, Floater, Glider? Players should move freely through space, changing the variables to experience in character terms the physical manner resulting from the changes.

Tempo-Rhythms II. Players should now agree upon a set of variables; for example, gentle, sustained, direct: a Glider, and develop a character from these physical characteristics. This character is then taken into various everyday activities—washing up, typing, changing a tire—to confirm the physical structure of the character and discover its everyday rhythms.

Tempo-Rhythms III. Centers and tempo-rhythms are complementary ways of approaching a character physically. Tempo-rhythms have more permutations and therefore more flexibility of detail. A character that is basically a Puncher may, in a given situation, make an adjustment to one of his or her effort factors as a tactical way of dealing with the situation. For example, a Puncher who needs a hotel room late at night and meets a strong resistance may decide to change the weight of his movement, to yield somewhat, which will change his gestures into a dab; he will knock gently upon the reception desk rather than bang forcefully. Putting this the other way around, if a Puncher adopts a dabbing gesture at anytime it will bring a yielding response emotionally: All movement reveals some feature of inner life. Players should explore numerous situations where a change of the weight/time/space focus factor produces tactical adaptations of the character's approach. These changes are especially useful in discovering the smaller character mannerisms that

can fill out the larger physical qualities determined by centers: how a character holds a cigarette, plays with his or her glasses, bites fingernails, smoothes hair, etc.

Essences I. Players pair off and compile a list of their sense of response to each other. The list of descriptions is in objective terms of things that the person *is* like: that is, reminds the partner of, not *would* like. Categories such as the following should be used: jewel, cloth or texture, food or dish, fruit, flower, book, movie, color, vegetable, car, musical instrument, game/sport, pop tune, animal, bird, drink, etc. It should be emphasized that the qualities are what the person reminds the partner of, not what the partner knows or thinks the person would like: The person may like pizza but remind the partner of French onion soup; the person may have blue eyes or black skin but remind the partner of amber or deep yellow. What the exercise does is to deal with the psychological shadings of a person without using psychological jargon or introspection.

Essences II. The theatrical application of the above exercise is in terms of the character one is playing. The exercise should be done when players have gained some familiarity with their characters, possibly toward the end of the first week of rehearsal, or after a couple of readings and rehearsals if it is a scene-work exercise. Players should compile a list describing their own characters in the categories listed in Essence I above; they should also compile a list of the other major characters they relate to in the play or scene. Players should compare lists and discuss any major discrepancies: This should not be in terms of wrong or right but merely giving simple reasons for choices. This is a useful exercise for gaining internal and external perceptions of a character: Remember that in a play what a character perceives about itself and what other characters perceive it to be may be quite different.

Essences III.   This moves the exercise into a more specifically biographical mode but keeps the dynamics within the performing group and the context of the play. Again, after a short acquaintance with the play, characters should be "interviewed" as if they were famous persons. The interviewers or reporters are the other members of the cast. Questions should be asked about the character's personal preferences—very much as in Essences I—but this time what the character likes, *not is like.* Questions will be: "What is your favorite food; favorite movie star; city?" "What kind of car do you drive; clothes do you wear?" etc. Questions and answers should be rapid-fire so that thinking is not involved as much as immediate, instinctive responses. Do not get into specifics of the text at this time.

Essences IV.   This final exercise does deal more specifically with the text of a play or scene. Characters are again interviewed by other players, but this time they are suspects being interviewed by detectives. The character being interviewed will make a short statement of very basic personal details as given in the text—a statement of the part the character plays in the action and his or her intention: for example, I am this . . . , I do this . . . , and I want this. . . . The detectives will now ask any personal, biographical questions, or questions about motives and relationships that are useful and significant to them as characters within the play: They will not question as characters but as detectives. Questions that have no relevance to the text should be avoided. It can be useful to have the director as moderator, not asking questions but making detectives justify any questions that seem not to be relevant to the text. The combination of the Essence exercises leads to a multidimensional understanding of character as it relates to other characters and to the play as a whole, without getting into psychological abstractions or extratextual irrelevancies.

Grock I.   This is an exercise combining centers, tempo-rhythms, and essences. Players should pick someone off the street with quite specific physical characteristics, and within their own age range. They should attempt an immediate clone of the chosen individual by imitating and assimilating physical balance, walk, rhythms, etc. Having done this, players should take the character apart piece by piece to identify its centers and tempo-rhythms. As these become specific in each player's mind, a strong sense of the individual's inner profile will develop, and players should try to establish "who" the person is and what sort of job he or she does. Players should now bring their "Grocks" into the group, and create them for the group by starting from the major center and adding tempo-rhythms and details until the character is fully realized. The player should now create a short improvisation with the character, showing it performing some simple activity in an appropriate environment: drinking coffee in a cafe, writing a letter, shaving, putting on lipstick, etc. After this, the player should be interviewed as in *Essences III* above. When all players have gone through this process, small improvisational situations can be set up in which the characters can confront each other with specific intentions and develop a stronger sense of their inner profiles by the responses played in the situations.

Grock II.   This is a quick character-mask-adjustment exercise that makes use of all the factors practiced above. Set up an improvisation with a specific situation that calls for discussion or debate: a PTA meeting; a Young Chamber of Commerce meeting; a student political group meeting. Have about six specific types of character:

> the Chairperson: wishes to organize and
>   reach conclusions;
> the Oppressed: any discussion seems to his
>   or her disadvantage;
> the Thinker: tends to generalize and speak of
>   larger human values;

the Asserter: rejects all ideas but his or
 her own;
the Arguer: can speak on both sides of
 any issue;
the Ameliorator:tends to agree with
 everyone.

Begin the meeting and change roles every 3 minutes with a 30-second break for character adjustments. The quick-change aspect keeps a strong energy flowing and obliges players to find essential outlines that are often surprisingly well fleshed out during the game. Players will find some characters to be more comfortable and immediate for them; but aspects of them all are available within all players' palettes. At the end of the exercise players should discuss the differences and similarities that occurred in the creation of the characters. What players will discover is that similar character qualities can be revealed in many different ways. This is one of the significant differences between Realism and early dramatic forms in which types would have been expected, indeed required, to act in a certain recognizable fashion. Today we are dealing with a similar spectrum of human types but expect them to be highly individualistic at the same time. This exercise shows the dimensions of that possibility.

Find the Feeling I.   At some juncture when rehearsing a scene with a partner do absolutely anything you feel like doing. This should be agreed with the partner beforehand so he or she can respond in a similar way. The text and the scene objectives should not be changed, but other than that there are no-holds-barred moves short of physically hurting your partner. This has nothing to do with what you "think" your character may or may not do within the realistic context of the scene; it is geared to what your body wants or tells you to do, such as jump on your partner's back, throw furniture around, attack your partner with the pillows from the sofa, etc. This exer-

cise will achieve several things: It opens up choices that didn't occur because you were too tied to the text; it strengthens the sense of subtext, which is beneath the surface of the realistic action; it plugs into the storehouse of emotions your body has through its experience of living—but it doesn't do this in a calculated way by trying to remember the emotion; rather, it lets the emotion react to a strong physical action and is thus present and immediate. When the player returns to the realistic performance of the scene some appropriate discoveries may be incorporated, but, more importantly, players will have a much stronger sense of the emotional structure of the scene.

Find the Feeling II.   This is a one-player exercise that is also geared to the discovery of emotionally charged images. Let us say the player is working on a unit in a scene in which his or her objective is to forget the memory of a boyfriend/girlfriend who has left. The player should choose and perform a very strong physical action such as throwing out or breaking up the friend's things, tearing up photographs, etc. Whatever the action it has to strongly involve the body. While this is happening some image will present itself. It may simply be a vague feeling but it should not be dismissed; when it occurs it should be concentrated upon until it becomes more concrete. Let us suppose, for the man, it was a recollection of the woman's perfume. When the physical action has become strongly charged with this, the player should lie down, relax, and let other images occur. Let us say that one of the strongest images was a serpent. The player now has a sense of perfume combined with a serpent. His objective in the scene was to forget she's gone; this can now become "to drag off the perfumed serpent." It is much stronger and less intellectual image, much more connected with the physical senses, more playable than to forget she's gone. Even without going through this exercise, it will help the player if his or her intention in a scene is expressed in a strong vernacular phrase: "to help her" can become "to get her through this goddamned situation"; "to get my revenge" can be "to get even with those bastards!" All of these exercises will bring a greater dynamic and sense of color to the everyday surface of a realistic scene.

PLAYING THE STYLE

How then does an actor make use of all this in developing a role? We are going to examine this through the character of Blanche Dubois in *A Streetcar Named Desire*.

The first thing an actor does is to read the play, without any specific analytic intention, but rather to get a feel for the rhythms, the environment, and the plot as a texture in which the characters are the threads of action. The next thing an actor does is to read the play again, this time to develop a clearer sense of the plot structure. Not in detail of beats and units but generally what the main action seems to be; where the climax and crises are; what complications lead to rising action, and how character development plays its part in this plot structure. During these two readings the actor will have gained an increasing acquaintance with the character of Blanche, and in a third reading the actor should make specific note of as much information about the character as the play provides. This information will be found in stage directions, in what other characters say of Blanche (bearing in mind this is opinion, not objective truth), what information she provides about herself, and almost more importantly than any of the above, what impression we gain from Blanche's actions as to how she relates to both the world and to the other characters. Collecting information as we move through the play we find the following:

Blanche is thirtyish, delicately beautiful, daintily dressed, quite out of place in the environment.

She has a nervous manner, possibly has a drinking habit, which she tries to hide.

She calls her sister by her unmarried name, suggesting that Blanche lives in the past. This is confirmed by Blanche asking her sister if she has a maid; subtext: "We are the kind of people who always had maids in the good old days." She has a fixation upon external appearance and in keeping up appearances. This is confirmed by Blanche asking her sister to turn off the light: She is concerned about her fading beauty, and the lights show a reality that is too harsh to deal with. Blanche later puts a colored lantern over her own light.

The delicate, freshly-bathed quality of Blanche Dubois is contrasted with the animal sweat of Stanley Kowalski in the film of *A Streetcar Named Desire*. *Courtesy of the Academy of Motion Picture Arts & Sciences.*

Blanche and her sister, Stella, are part of the old antebellum Southern aristocracy. They used to live in a plantation home that is now decayed and lost to the family—the home was called Belle Reve, significantly "beautiful dream," another nonreality.

Blanche teaches English and has a tendency to use unnecessarily important words ("heterogeneous") and to use French phrases that give a sense of cultural superiority. Her speech is also peppered by words such as "pretty," "dainty," "little," "tiny"; delicate words that imply how a lady is supposed to be.

Blanche has been the victim of unhappy love affairs, and, although attracted by the purity and innocence of youth (one aspect of the newsboy scene), she has become sexually promiscuous in her need for comfort, protection, and a recapturing of a lost innocence.

Her immediate response to men is to be flirtatious and to adopt a delicate "need to be helped" manner. She asks Stanley to help with her dress buttons and talks about "you men with your big clumsy fingers." Subtext: "I am a fragile woman who needs to be helped." She is from a culture in which a woman's power was in her sexual attraction, her femininity, her woman's wiles; she squirts Stanley with the scent bottle.

Blanche spends a great deal of time bathing. Not only is this a response to the old Southern upbringing where a lady should always be fresh and sweet-smelling, "glow" but never sweat, it is another retreat from reality into a womblike environment of comfort and security where all one's troubles and sins can be purified and washed away along with the dirt of the real world. She bathes, not showers; Stanley showers: the quick-splash and ready-for-action of the workaday industrial world.

Blanche's relationship with Mitch confirms many of her attributes. He seems "superior"; she calls him "Sir," the flirtatious courtesy of the Old South. She can make believe she is in a world of gentlemen who will

Blanche attempts a brave resistance to the brute reality of Stanley in the film of *A Streetcar Named Desire.*   *Courtesy of the Academy of Motion Picture Arts & Sciences.*

afford her protection. She speaks of Mitch's mother dying: "You will be lonely"; subtext: "You will need a wife."

There is more information to be gleaned but it will essentially serve to show that the actor is dealing with a character who is locked into a social and cultural tradition that is decadent in itself and completely inimical to the environment in which she now lives.

Blanche cannot rid herself of her inherited values—unlike her sister, Stella, who has accommodated herself to a new world. Blanche's behavior patterns will always operate within the "Ladylike" tradition. It is important to her sense of self to maintain this appearance and also her physical attraction; as the Lady tradition dictated that happiness, security, and protection were to be found through a man. The tradition worked in the nineteenth century and afforded a woman a sense of worth, a special place; but it no longer works in a world without gentlemen. But Blanche must believe it, for it is herself; however, it leaves her isolated and unprotected.

Equally, Blanche can't face her true physical needs. The Lady tradition dictated virginity; thus, she calls sex "brutal desire." But she is forced by loneliness to give into it; it affords the illusion of protection; and at the same time she turns to young men in search of a lost innocence.

Blanche is looking for what no longer exists, a gentleman who will treat her like a lady and a virgin, marry her, protect her, and defend her honor.

The play finds Blanche in the last crumbling days of this decaying edifice. She has retreated into a fantasy world to reconcile reality with her ideal, and she is trying to go home again through her sister. When her last hope, Mitch, fails, and brute reality (Stanley) finally crushes her, she makes the ultimate retreat into her own mind, insanity.

If Blanche's main objective is to find protection, preferably through a man, but, if not, a haven with her sister, the main obstacle to this is, of course, Stanley. Stanley is animal and territorial. He doesn't want his life style altered, his territory impinged upon, his wife's loyalty threatened, his sexual activity curtailed. He is not a gentleman. He reacts sensually and directly to women. He is not susceptible to the games of flirtation; he doesn't care about appearances or manners. He is master in his own house and binds Stella to him with his energy and virility and need of her. This is a further obstacle to Blanche who cannot use her sister's influence as a protection from Stanley.

The actor playing Blanche must, then, be able to assume the Ladylike manner and sensibility—the style, grace, manner; this will entail some research into social history, biography, books on etiquette, paintings, photographs of antebellum houses and their owners.

Even the service still practiced today in a few older hotels of the 1920s and 1930s will give a physical sense of manner and rhythms. Costumes especially, both of the antebellum period and of the 1930s—Blanche's young womanhood—will help the actor enormously with the feel of the physical manner.

Within this, the actor will need to discover the physical manner that her confrontation with the real world has forced upon Blanche: What does her "nervous" manner consist of?

The actor will also need to find the courage in Blanche that helped to sustain her through the trials she has suffered, and leads to the dignity, however misplaced, that is present at the end.

Some problems the actor may have to address are: What is the reason for Blanche's promiscuity? Did she lead Stanley on? How superficial is she? She claims that a woman's charm is 50 percent illusionary, but that she has always told the truth about important things. How honest is she? What does her intrinsic worth reside in? She espouses certain values that the playwright probably believed in himself. What we see is a character in disintegration; what the actor must find is the good and the positive elements which have disintegrated.

A problem for the actor in the 1940s and 1950s was that the audience's sympathies tended to be against Blanche as a symbol of a racist, socially decadent South. A problem today may be for the actor to find the worth and positive sense of the Lady tradition Blanche believed in. In a feminist, liberated society, the actor should avoid commenting upon the false values Blanche was addicted to, but should simply play them as sympathetically as possible. Thus, Blanche is a misplaced or misguided woman of intrinsic worth, not a stupid woman who hasn't had her consciousness raised.

Armed with this information we are now going to suggest a process by which the actor may physically approach the character of Blanche Dubois.

Face-to-Face I.   A good getting-to-know you exercise while actors are still reading the text.

Positive Negative.   A physical orientation exercise that is also good for getting to be confident with the other cast members. It is an exercise that can be repeated in character later in rehearsal.

Cloning II.   Another ensemble-cementing exercise that can be repeated later in character. Good for Blanche and Stanley in their status/domination confrontations.

ProPositions IV.   This can be useful as a first introduction to the ground plan. A simple copy of the final plan can be set up. It gives actors a feel of what possibilities they have. It can be repeated later with the actual set and text from the play.

Subtext I.   Can be played as an introduction to a scene before more detailed work upon it. Leads to the discovery of physical choices and stronger physical feeling of scenic action.

Centers II and III.   Based upon the information discovered in the text, and the development of physical responses through the above exercises, the actor will now be ready to experiment with choices as to where Blanche Dubois carries her energy and how that affects her physical carriage, balance, rhythms, and walk. Play all choices broadly and strongly at first until something starts to feel right—to fit with the sense of character that is developing—then gradually reduce to fit the size of the space being used.

Tempo-Rhythms I and II.   With the physical outline discovered in the centers exercise, now work for more detailed and specific responses to tempo-rhythms. The center structure will

suggest a basic character quality: Is Blanche a Dabber, a Floater, a Glider? The tempo-rhythms can then be used with props—we know Blanche uses cigarettes, glasses, spectacles, cosmetics—to discover how these may be used. It will also be useful as the actor gets further into the rehearsal period to discover how the tempo-rhythm can change as the character uses tactics, that is, makes adjustments to situations.

Preening and Plumage.   With this sense of a basic physical character it will be useful to do a couple of exercises described in the comedy of manners section. In some ways, of course, Blanche is a character displaced from a drawing room. The exercises deal with the wearing and display of costume. Blanche should become acquainted with the costumes she is to wear in the production as soon as possible as they will help her strongly with the idea of appearance. In the preening exercise she could be played as trying to impress Stanley with changes of costume; Stanley can play his negative reactions. In the plumage exercise, again, both Stanley, whom Williams describes as a "richly feathered male bird," and Blanche with her flirtatious manner, could explore each other's response to their physicality.

Essences II, III, and IV.   These exercises will fill out the texture of the physical character of Blanche that has been developed and add a rich and varied coloring that will connect the physicality to its psychological base. They are also excellent group exercises that re-energize group dynamics at a time in rehearsal when interest may be flagging. Some possible category suggestions for Blanche are: cloth—chiffon; animal—deer; jewel—opal; bird—flamingo; color—faded pink; car—1930s tourer; food—vichysoisse. These are only our responses; yours will be your own.

Find the Feeling I and II.   Both exercises may be done at any time at both the director's and actor's discretion. The first is a good exercise for loosening up a scene that has gotten tight and is going nowhere—if you are lucky you may not need it. The second is useful to an actor who may not be connecting strongly enough with the intention of a scene.

What follows are a few more exercises and improvisations that can be useful to the development of character during the rehearsal process.

Gibberish.   Play one or two of the scenes between Stanley and Blanche in gibberish. This will emphasize the total lack of communication between them: It could be done in Polish gibberish and French gibberish as well as English, to find levels of response in the ethnic terms that are implicit in the play.

Hide-and-Seek.   One of the basic conflicts in the play is Blanche's desire for protection, a haven in the home of Stella and Stanley, as opposed to Stanley's desire to get rid of her. This can be expressed physically in the game of hide-and-seek in which Blanche finds hiding places and Stanley discovers and destroys them. This may be played both in a rehearsal room and on the actual set; another version of the game can be played in a darkened space in which Blanche tries to hide while Stanley looks for her with a flashlight to shine in her face. In the play Blanche has a constant fear of exposure to harsh light. This exercise will give a powerful experience of that to the actor.

Dance of the Seven Veils.   This game is geared to Blanche's concern for clothes and outward appearances and her instinctive flirtatiousness. Blanche does a dance around Stanley, gradually removing either some light frothy material or parts of the clothes Stanley finds in her trunk—furs, rhinestone beads, etc. This may be played with both the actors playing Stanley and Mitch present for Blanche to find her manner of attracting each, and for both to find their responses. This game can also be played in the context of the rape scene with Stanley finally ripping the clothes off Blanche.

Napoleonic Code.   This is an improvisation in which Stanley as a legal prosecutor cross-examines Blanche both on the loss of Belle Reve, and on the sexual activities that got her banned from Laurel.

Belle of the Ball.   Blanche, beautifully dressed, is at her Coming Out Ball; all the men in the cast play her suitors. Use waltzes, foxtrots, music from the thirties.

Tea Party.   Blanche and Stella have tea in an elegant restaurant with Stanley as a reluctant waiter. This is a dominance/status game that speaks to Blanche's sense of how things ought to be.

All of the above games and exercises are part of a process geared to getting at action and its supporting emotional response by concrete physical means within the stylistic requirements of a scene. Character choices arise organically from the color, structure, rhythms, and content of the language the character speaks and are thus physical, appropriate, evolved within a scenic context, and connected to the emotional rhythm of the action.

SUGGESTED READINGS

Benedetti, Robert, *The Actor at Work.* Englewood Cliffs, N.J.: Prentice-Hall, 1986.

Bentley, Eric, *In Search of Theater,* New York: Alfred A. Knopf, 1953.

Chekhov, Michael, *To the Actor,* New York: Harper & Row, 1953.

Furst, Lilian R., and Skrine, Peter N., *Naturalism.* London: Methuen, 1971.

Grant, Damian, *Realism*. London: Methuen, 1974.

Laban, Rudolf, *The Mastery of Movement*. London: MacDonald and Evans, 1960.

Lewis, Robert, *Method or Madness*. New York: Samuel French, 1958.

Moore, Sonia, *The Stanislavski System*. New York: Viking Press, 1965.

Parke, Laurence, *Since Stanislavski and Vakhtangov*. Los Angeles: Acting World Books, 1985.

Spolin, Viola, *Improvisation for the Theater*. Evanston, Ill.: Northwestern University Press, 1963.

Stanislavski, Constantin, *Building a Character*. New York: Theatre Arts Books, 1949.

Williams, Raymond, *Drama in Performance*. New York: Basic Books, 1968.

7 Chekhov

Stanislavski as Vershinin in *The Three Sisters.* *Foreign Languages Publishing House, Moscow.*

BACKGROUND

While much that we have said in the previous chapter about Realism will apply to Anton Chekhov, the Russian playwright does hold a very particular place in the litany of Realism, and in this short chapter we are going to suggest how the actor may adjust to the unique demands of Chekhov's work. While Chekhov's name is immediately associated with Stanislavski and the highly naturalistic work of the Moscow Art Theatre, his sensibility places him somewhat outside of the main Realistic tradition, stretching from Ibsen to Arthur Miller and beyond, and even partakes of the post-Realistic quality of the mid-twentieth century in such playwrights as Samuel Beckett and Harold Pinter.

Historical Situation.   Chekhov is known for his four major plays: *The Seagull,* which launched the success of the Moscow Art Theatre (MAT) in 1898; *Uncle Vanya,* performed by the MAT in 1899; *The Three Sisters,* performed in 1901; and *The Cherry Orchard,* performed in 1904, the year Chekhov died of tuberculosis. Chekhov's short life—he was forty-four at his death—occurred at an interesting time of Russian history: He was born one year before the freeing of the serfs in 1860 (note the ending of slavery in the United States at the same time), and died just thirteen years before the Bolshevik Revolution in 1917. His lifetime saw the decline of the old Russian landowning class whose estates, no longer supported by slave labor, fell into economic decline and decay; and he heard the murmurings of the revolutionary rhetoric that was to lead to the final overthrow of the aristocracy.

Chekhov himself was descended from serfs and grew up amongst petty merchants. Professionally, he was scientifically trained as a physician. A writer by avocation, he worked within the theatrical form he inherited. An important part of this tradition was the nineteenth-century Russian comic writing

of Griboyedov and Gogol, a tradition that stretched back through the *commedia del l'arte* to the Roman Comedy. As did Molière, Chekhov humanized and adapted this form to his own purposes; but it is important to an understanding of his work to recognize the comic strain and be aware that the character Vanya, for example, can be traced back through Pantalone to the Roman comic Senex, and the character Gaev, in *The Cherry Orchard,* contains elements of the Dottore.

Sensibility.   Though a little too neat to be entirely sufficient, Chekhov's sense of life might be said to have been determined by a series of dialectics. He was born between the old aristocratic Russia and the new Marxist Soviet Union, between a landed and a technological age. He partook of a broad comedic tradition of drama and a subtler realistic one; and he was writing when nineteenth-century Romanticism was giving way to twentieth-century scientific beliefs. Chekhov himself was a poet, a spiritual romantic educated as a scientist. The attempt to reconcile and balance these opposing drives both lends his work its dynamic and tension, but can also be mistaken for vacuum and stasis.

Where Chekhov is in company with the Realists—and in some ways he was the most naturalistic of all—was in his observation and portrayal of the small details of everyday life. Where he parted company with them was that his main concern was not with the contingent world of things and the inevitability of material progress, but with the existential world of being. Chekhov's reality was in the spaces within the human soul, where we silently question our purposes without really expecting any answers.

Chekhov, unlike most of the Realists, tried not to impose dramatic rhythms upon everyday events in order to give them a more exciting structure for theatrical purposes. It was Chekhov's perception that "people do

The comic tradition of Gogol, part of Chekhov's inheritance, seen here in a production of *The Inspector General.*   *British National Theatre. Photo by John Haynes.*

problems could be bettered by improving social conditions: sadness, hopeless love, frustrated ambition, unattainable beauty, and the unkindness of fate will forever remain the human condition. It is not that Chekhov is against social change—he constantly refers to the need to work—he just doesn't think it is a sufficient answer. But, then, he doesn't try to supply answers. He feels no obligation to explain life but, as a true naturalist, simply to represent it truly as it is. Nor does he draw moral conclusions: Life can be beautiful and full of wonder, but it is not full of significance. Life's deepest meaning may lie in its lack of meaning—for that is what we are faced with. The world is unrea-

not spend most of their lives in highly dramatic or threatening situations, but eat, drink, sleep and, if they can get up the energy, chase after other men and women." His form of realism did not deal with the average person as a hero, but with, to quote Thoreau, "the quiet desperation in which most people live their lives," and the nonheroic courage it takes to support this existence.

The Realistic hero tends to be pitted against the social and environmental forces that rule life—he or she must change them and make progress. Realism's energy tends to be goal directed: examine problems; find answers. Unlike the Realists, Chekhov didn't necessarily believe that the deepest human

sonable, inexplicable, so all desires are ultimately unfulfillable, but we are condemned by being here to try to find a reasonable answer. Hope and expectation blend with hopelessness and despair. Yet even if life is to end in death, it is still there to be seen, felt, and tasted. We constantly break out into comic enthusiasms and bang our heads against the inevitable. This stops us from taking ourselves and our lives too seriously, and it gives Chekhov's work its sense of playful whimsical absurdity, taking it beyond the confines of Realism's material pursuit of social progress, to juggle with the uncertain purposes of Being itself, for which logic holds no answers. Chekhov's characters were aware of

The yearning solitude of *Uncle Vanya*. *McCarter Theatre, Princeton. Photo by Andrea Kane.*

Andrey faces his existential vacuum at the end of *The Three Sisters*. *Oregon Shakespeare Festival. Photo by Henry Kranzler.*

the existential vacuum that Beckett and Pinter's characters were later to try to deal with.

INTRINSIC DEMANDS

Structure. As we have suggested, the typical Realistic play has a three-act structure. This tends to give a strong sense of through-line of action: a rising energy of complications leading to crises and climax. Chekhov used a four-act structure, which tends to give a more undulating or harmonic sense of rhythm—a rising and falling action, an even pulse dis-

turbed by outbursts of excitement and then returns to the normal beat. Plot also tends to have this nonclimactic outcome. In *Uncle Vanya* and *The Three Sisters* the main action is circular in form, ending exactly where it began with Vanya and the three sisters locked into the same situation in which they were discovered at the start of the action. *The Cherry Orchard* is very similar; the main change being that the estate has been sold and the cherry orchard destroyed at the end of the play. But in one sense this was inevitable from the start of the play, and the family—Ranevskya and

The Three Sisters locked into their directionless stasis at the end of the play. *Arena Stage, Washington.*

peripetia and gives the plays an uncomplicated, almost static, structure. But this is, of course, only a surface appearance, and the characters are going through constant struggle within themselves. However, if this ferment boils over into hyperbole, melodramatic action, or attempts at heroics, Chekhov constantly undercuts this by showing the characters as inept, clumsy, pompous, and finally comic in their futile attempts to act upon or change the inevitability of essential human circumstances. This, indeed, is an essential part of the comedic element of Chekhov's structure. Uncle Vanya's great outburst at Serebriakov ends with him shooting at but missing him. Not only does this deflate the action but it also provides sadly comic proof of Vanya's inability to take effective action, which is responsible for his ineffectuality in the first place. Similarly, in *The Cherry Orchard*, Lopakhin's triumphant entry after having bought the cherry orchard is undercut by being hit with a broom by Varya. Such undercutting was not only consistent with Chekhov's personal distaste for pretentiousness of any kind but also part of the rhythmical structure of his work and its comedic energy.

Gaev—only returned to preside over this dissolution before leaving again in a somewhat circular manner. The only play in which any real change takes place in character circumstance is *The Seagull*, Chekhov's earlier and self-avowedly most melodramatic play.

This structural circularity, quite apart from its foreshadowing of Samuel Beckett and the Absurdists, gives a sense of indirection to the action of the play. Like the Impressionists, with whom he is contemporary, there is an unforced orchestration of a myriad of small responses. Action is not moved forward by direct revelation of character in conflict with other characters, but more obliquely by avoidances and inability to directly express the nature of the inner action taking place within the characters. What is created is a network of intertwined lives with little contrivance or direction. There is in Chekhov a strong sense that people do not change, but can grow to understand and accept. This lack of personal change means a lack of structural

Space. Unlike the compressed space of Realism, Chekhov gives a sense of endless space; yet this is not an openness but in many ways more oppressive because of the difficulty of filling it with meaning. *Uncle Vanya* has an atmosphere of suffocation and claustrophobia,

(a)

(b)

The oppressiveness of space seen in two productions of *The Cherry Orchard*.   *(a) Goodman Theatre. © 1989, Brigitte Lacombe. (b) British National Theatre.*

yet it is set in a house with twenty-seven rooms. But none of them are seen to be leading anywhere; they are a maze through which lives drift, coming out, if lucky, at the point of entry. A sense of distance, a universal perspective, is always present as if to suggest an infinite possibility which, because it is impervious to human action, represents impossibility at the same time. All of Chekhov's plays have outdoor scenes, and *Uncle Vanya* contains a further marvelous symbol of the unattainable—a map of Africa on the wall of Vanya's study. Vanya has not been outside Russia; he has not been outside his estate for more than twenty years, yet on the wall of his most personal room is the dead image of the most distant, most unknown, most impossible continent.

While less compressed but more oppressive than Realism, Chekhov's space is equally less cluttered but more filled with the past. Chekhov's is not a useful space where things get done, but more of a ceremonial space where rituals take place: everyday rituals of sitting, talking, eating, and drinking. And there is a strong sense that it has been this way for a long time—many scenes start with seated tableaux—and will continue this way for a long time. Chekhov places a sense of existential absurdity not in T. S. Eliot's "Waste Land," not at Samuel Beckett's undefined crossroads, but before them, in the very home of Realism itself—the houses in which we live.

Time.   As with space so with time, a sense of an unfulfilled present is set against an ungraspable past and future. The landowners look to the good old days of the past, while the scientists and students look to the better days of the future; the present works for no one, and yet the present was the future and will become the past. As suggested above, the undifferentiated present is demarked by small ceremonies: arrivals, meals, parties, departures. At the same time Chekhov makes

us very aware of the inexorable passage of time by the progression of the seasons in his work. There is always change between acts, usually a movement toward fall or winter, which emphasizes a sense of dwindling into a future. The characters themselves are affected (infected?) by this, having a sense of over-ripeness or withering in the bud.

In Realism, time is compressed and expectant. The plot is dependent upon human whims, hatreds, stupidities for its crises and climaxes. The space is filled with actors on the edge of their seats listening or speaking with intention, or filled with curiosity. Not so in Chekhov. Whatever we do, time passes indifferent to us. No gods are angered by our actions; nature is undisturbed by our follies. There is no real expectation; characters seem to grow in their chairs, to be rooted in their space. The infinite time scale shows how, in reality, truly insignificant are the issues that appear so important to us in the present. Thus, denied the panacea of true comedy, and refused the significance of tragedy, Chekhov's characters cannot alter the painfulness of reality; and thus they constantly stumble through their circular dance of oblique and thwarted contact. Their effort becomes slightly comic, ridiculous, or "absurd" as it was to be called in the 1950s.

Language and Rhythm.   If rhythm can be said to be the attempt of time to impose a pattern on space, then given the nature of time and space in Chekhov we will expect to find a somewhat impassive rhythm, which will respond to but finally absorb all attempts to change it and act upon it. The pulse in Chekhov neither stops nor fundamentally alters. It is the flow of the future into the past, punctuated by occasional brushes against the present: a waking dream interspersed with blinks of reality and the flutterings of "rapid eye motions." The rhythm is all-embracing and includes dialogue, human action and inactivity, objects, comic outbursts, and silences in its steady sweep.

Dialogue cannot change the rhythm because the characters who utter it cannot individually alter it. Dialogue is not so much a direct exchange as an interplay of disconnected speeches, full of irrelevances or trivia. Characters are unable to say what they would wish to say, so communication slips away through the net of self-absorbed nonsequiturs, and the bursts of rhetorical activity lead to no change in direction or purpose and are absorbed back into the impassive flow.

Much of Chekhov's rhetorical structure is geared either toward anticlimax or collapses back into the norm. In all of the plays there are long monologues in which characters appear to be revealing their innermost thoughts or reflecting upon their lives. But these monologues are self-defeating. They are usually self-exculpatory in content: "If only I had done this; if only I hadn't been obligated to do that." They tend to be full of repeated phrases as if the character is trying to bolster up or convince himself or herself of the argument, and the repetitions have the effect of revealing the frustration of the character—the very inability to move beyond the rhetoric that has kept the character from positive action. Because of being locked into these repetitions the speeches never reach a climax; they gradually fizzle out and dwindle into anticlimax, with nothing having changed and the character left looking somewhat foolish. Repetition is, of course, a major comedic structure, and while Chekhov uses it consciously, he attenuates the joke, makes the skittle fall gently, so that it achieves not a belly laugh but a sympathetic smile of recognition at "what fools these mortals be."

Emotional separation by space inhibits communication.   *American Conservatory Theatre. Photo by Larry Merkle.*

There is an example of this rhetorical structure used for comic effect in act 1 of *Uncle Vanya* when Vanya launches on a tirade about Serebryakov's lack of achievement. Vanya repeats "for twenty-five years," five times in about ten lines, which both makes it lose its force and reminds us that Vanya has himself done nothing for the same period of time. Repetition is also used for anticlimactic, though less evidently, comic effect at the end of *Uncle Vanya* in Sonia's long final speech in which "We shall rest" finally loses its force and the rhetorical steam fizzles out of Sonia's brave rhetoric, letting it collapse into the unchanging rhythm of the characters' lives. As he not infrequently does, Chekhov reaffirms his statement by the rhythms of the total *mise-en-scène*. While Sonia is making her final speech the Watchman is tapping with his stick (almost like a warder reaffirming a sense of imprisonment), Marina is knitting (a neverending task), Marya is making notes on the border of her pamphlet (a constant and futile occupation), and Telygin is playing elegiacally on his guitar. The gradually fading music of the band and Chebutykin's humming at the end of *The Three Sisters* achieve similar effects, as does the sound of a breaking string and an ax striking a tree at the end of *The Cherry Orchard*.

This orchestration of all the sights and sounds of the scene is a crucial part of Chekhov's rhythm, and it lends the constant small pauses and broken actions a sense of life and variety to his work. An actor has to be very aware of this totality and his or her part in it. Listening to the orchestration will sustain an actor through the long pauses and moments of apparent inactivity, and it will keep him or her connected to the constant pulse of rhythm into which all the myriad of smaller responses flow.

PERFORMANCE DEMANDS

It is not our intention here to set out a completely separate process for Chekhov, but to suggest to the actor where adjustments should be made to the Realistic process set out in the previous chapter, in order to accommodate Chekhov's particular demands.

In terms of space and movement, Realism tends to demand a busier, closer, quicker style of activity than will Chekhov's work. This is because Realism is geared to the pursuit of goals and the possibility of action. As we have seen, in Chekhov all of this is inexpressible or frustrated; it requires less determined movement—no one is really going anywhere, and less direct movement—no one is really going to do anything. This will mean more oblique and circular movement, with occasional bursts across the space when characters' repressed energies break out in spurts of frustrated action.

As there is more space per se in the Chekhov environment, characters will tend to keep more space between them. This is to avoid direct contact. Chekhov's characters don't really know how to talk to each other; therefore,

Even in closer physical relationship characters are involved in their own private worlds in *Uncle Vanya*. *American Conservatory Theatre. Photo by Tom Chargin.*

face-to-face contact, which demands direct communication, is too hard for them. Direct contact is often a prelude to some form of ineptitude or physical clumsiness deriving from a hurried or embarrassed attempt to break off contact. Much of Chekhov's humor comes from the consequences of face-to-face contact, the literal or metaphorical tripping over feet in haste to get away.

When they are involved in their own inner worlds, characters are relaxed and comfortable in that well-known space; they are part of the furniture. At the same time, they are trapped and their energies frustrated by the weight of familiarity. But things, objects, furniture are familiar and easier to deal with than are people. The classic example of this is Gaev's address to the bookcase in act 1 of *The Cherry Orchard*. This sense of objects having a history, of being part of relationships, is important to the actor. It might be useful to

think of one of Stanislavski's "circles of attention" as being missing. There is the circle around the character's self and familiar objects, an inner absorption that is mostly rooted in the past. Then there is the circle that reaches out to a distant and unknown future. What tends to be missing is the circle that includes the other characters. This is not to say that they are ignored; it is just that they are taken for granted and not seriously given attention as having any function, being able to effect any change, in the present.

It would be wrong to think of the characters as trying not to communicate; they want desperately to communicate, but they do not know how to express what they feel. They are blocked by too much hope and too little expectation. It is important for the actor to understand this sense of repressed energy. Playing boredom must be avoided at all costs. The characters are bursting inside, but they

(a)

(b)

The desperate need for and difficulty of communication seen in (a) *Uncle Vanya* at American Conservatory Theatre; and (b) *The Seagull*, Los Angeles Theatre Center.   *(a) Photo by Tom Chargin; (b) Photo by Chris Gulker.*

don't know how to get it out or where to put the energy. What comes out is nonsequiturs and trivial remarks; but these are attempts at giving significance to the present and must be played as if they were significant. Every now and again the frustrated energy erupts in rhetorical tirades of self-dramatization, which, as we suggested above, finally deflate themselves and fizzle out because they can't be turned into action. It is too difficult to take action, too difficult to change despite all the desires, because there is no real belief that the deepest human problems can be changed; even work is but a temporary placebo. By talking of wishes and ideas the characters both reaffirm their aims and escape action by deluding themselves with a verbal sense of future purpose.

Because Chekhov lacks this strong structure of action and narrative, which engages the audience by its dramaturgical energies, the actor needs a strong physical definition for his or her character, which becomes the main focus of audience interest. This must be supported by an inner energy to sustain connection with the action through long periods when the character may not be directly in stage focus but still be an important part of the rhythm and texture of the scene. Much depends upon the vitality of the playing, finding the comedic aspects of the character, the foibles, ineptitudes, self-conceits, the ironic self-deprecation that lends humor to what would otherwise be the pathetic moments of clumsiness, *faux pas*, and inflated rhetoric. In a way, all the characters have some aspects of Charlotta, the Governess in *The Cherry Orchard* who does parlor tricks. With their own bag of human tricks and verbal games they are trying to charm, placate, or simply exist in the empty but unforgiving minute. These are sad clowns, yet fully realized human beings, all of whose tricks cannot put off the final curtain, and they are not sure how or why to fill the time they have on stage.

EXERCISES, GAMES, TECHNIQUES

Many of the basic Realism exercises will be useful here; what follows are exercises especially adapted to the particular qualities of Chekhov that we have thus far discussed.

Stasis I.   Players sit around a space with their eyes closed and:

a. silently say the alphabet backwards to themselves;
b. count silently backwards from a hundred;
c. listen to the environment and identify individual sounds;
d. try to remember where they were and what they were doing on an arbitrary date in the past: for example, November 7, 1992.

Stasis II.   Players sit around a space with their eyes open and:

a. perform a small task such as reading a dictionary and making notes on unknown words;
b. looking at a piece of furniture and trying to remember/understand why it is there and what it means to them;
c. play solo chess or solitaire.

Stasis III.   Players do the following:

a. sit in a neutral mask and try to find meaning in the other players (also in neutral masks). What does that blank stare mean to you?
b. in a neutral mask, players walk around the space in time to a metronome (the speed of this should be altered during the exercise). They may look at other players in passing but avoid any contact. Players may sit at any time and listen to the metronome or look at other players before walking around the space again.

Stasis IV.   The space should be darkened and lit only by candlelight. Players move around the space, making no direct contact with other players, but trying to clarify the half world of shadows and dimly lit people. At any time players may sit and perform any of the activities in the above exercises. When bored with the activity they should move around again.

Contact I.   Players sit in chairs, all of which are facing in a different direction in the space. Players have something they want to say about themselves. They must decide when they want to say this and to whom. All players may speak at once; players may speak generally or to one particular player. Players should not look directly at another player when speaking unless the compulsion becomes overpowering.

Contact II.   Players sit in chairs arranged so that none is facing directly at another.

  a. Players may look at another player if they are not speaking; when speaking they may not look.
  b. Players may look at each other if saying something trivial, not if saying something personal.

Contact III.   Players are tied into a chair. They must try to make physical contact with artifacts and people so arranged as to be just out of reach. Players should be tied at different times by different body parts: leg, arm, waist, neck. This should give players an experience of both frustration and discovery of where the point of tension, or energy gap, is in their character.

Contact IV.   Players reach out to other players but cannot quite touch. If they are seen to be reaching by the other player they must turn the gesture into some small ceremony or nonemotional activity.

Distance I.   Players sit around the space. One player makes a move toward another. No player may come within six feet, so the second player has to move away, justify the move, and find a new position of stasis. All players should take it in turn to move toward and away.

Distance II.   All players are moving around the space and must keep an equal distance from each other at all times. Speeds may be varied. On a handclap, players must stop, adjust their distance from other players, and justify the move. On a handclap, all players begin to move again.

Distance III.   Players move around the space keeping an equal distance from each other. Speeds are varied considerably from slow to a canter. On a handclap, players must begin a children's game: hopscotch, ball bounce, skipping, juggling, etc. On a handclap, they must sit and begin a stasis activity. On a handclap, they move around the space again, etc.

Bursting I.   Players sit around a space; each has a balloon.

  a. One of the players makes one of the more flatulent speeches from the plays and blows up a balloon while doing so. The player then makes the speech again while letting the balloon deflate. The speech is made a third time, both inflating the balloon as the speech is puffing itself up, and then letting the air out as it collapses. This is a good way of demarking beats.
  b. A player makes a speech while the other players blow up and let down their balloons as a comment upon it. *Note:* A deflating balloon can make an extremely vulgar sound.

Bursting II.   One player has a balloon that he or she is trying to blow up. The other players are trying to distract him or her from this.

The disruptions must be justified. The player with the balloon must respond and adjust to the disruptions, but must keep a calm equilibrium and continue to blow up the balloon.

Bursting III.   All players but one are seated around a space performing calm activities: reading, writing, knitting, drinking, playing cards. The one player must attract attention in any way that he or she can, short of physically touching. This may be done by performing tricks, telling silly stories, or having something very serious and compelling to say. The occupied players may respond or ignore as they feel acted upon by the central player.

Bursting IV.   This is a text-based exercise. Chekhov's characters are constantly frustrated by their inability to do what they would like to do. If an actor can gain a physical sense of this frustrated energy, it will then be there to create a strong tension within the actor when he or she has to deal with the inactive or indirect expression of frustration that Chekhov gives his characters. For example, in *The Cherry Orchard* there is a scene at the end of act 3 in which Lopakhin returns to tell Ranevskya that he has bought the cherry orchard and that she and her family must leave for it is to be cut down to build worker's *dashas*. The stage direction here is "Ranevskya collapses into a chair, weeping." What is happening is that her home is being broken up and Lopakhin is doing it. A rehearsal exercise would be to have Lopakhin physically overturning the room and Ranevskya trying to put it to rights again. This allows Lopakhin to get out the triumphant energy he feels at the moment, and finally reduces Ranevskya to a frustrated ineptitude. Both actors will thereby experience the feelings that are bound, bursting within them in the actual scene.

Contradiction I.   Players make a short speech giving reasons for following a course of action. They then make a short speech giving reasons for not following the same course of action. Find a physical image for the positive action; play it going forward. Find a physical image for the negating of the action; play it moving backwards. Play each image against the other. This will produce an uncertain rhythm and a sense of inner tension. Players may now sit and sublimate this into small activity.

Contradiction II.   Take an idea that might be found in Chekhov: "The future will be wonderful"; "We must work"; "life will be better in Moscow." Players should find the serious response to this and express it with a physical image. Now find a comic response to it and express this with a physical image. Alternate the images; play them against each other until an image and an emotional response are created that contain both of the contradictory elements. This will produce a positive point of tension and energy.

Orchestra I.

   a. Players sit around a space and decide upon a simple tune known to all. Each player decides upon an instrument: flute, violin, clarinet, oboe. Use strings and woodwinds; avoid too much brass and percussion. With no conductor, the players now "play" the tune, letting the listening to each other determine the rhythm and tempo.

   b. Players decide upon an instrument but no tune. Again with no conductor, players start their own tune and, by holding their motif while listening to the whole, produce a musical score.

   c. Repeat the score created above and this time add small activities and moves in rhythm to the "music." For example, rocking movements, turning over the pages of a book, playing with a thread on a coat, smoothing a beard, etc.

Orchestra II.   Players sit around a space and decide upon a small noise: whisper, sobbing, laughter, hissing, sucking of the teeth. With no conductor, but with a metronome to establish a rhythm, players create a piece of "music" with their sounds, again by playing their sound and being aware of the rhythm of the whole. This may be played without the metronome, when players are adept, and with the addition of such sounds as the clicking of knitting needles, tapping of a stick, drumming of the fingertips, etc.

Orchestra III.   This places the above exercises within a specific situation. Players again choose an everyday sound appropriate to a time and environment: Sunday breakfast; afternoon tea; a doctor's office; a train or bus station; at a dull lecture. Players establish a rhythm for the occasion by listening to the "music" of the situation. Finally, players can change tempo and activity and move from one place to another in the situation while keeping in touch with the basic rhythm of the entire event.

Character Mask I.   We suggested the use of neutral mask in *Stasis III* to encourage a strong sense of ensemble rhythm. The use of character mask will give the player a strong physical character outline. The basic process for working with masks was detailed in Chapter Two. For this exercise a series of character masks is needed. A rule of thumb is to have twice as many masks as players in the exercise. The masks should not be subtle, but have strongly delineated features in a variety of physical types: bucolic, pudgy, goodhumored, sensual, curmudgeonly, inquisitive. Strong features exercise a strong pull toward activity on the part of the wearer. Players should go through the process of finding a response to several masks. Some will exercise a stronger impulse than others. Masks will encourage physical responses: ways of holding the head; a walk; particular gestures. During the exercise the players should return constantly to

the mirror to recatalyze the mask, absorb the emerging character, and discover further impulses. With solid work and concentration, players will evolve a complete posture, sets of body rhythms, and a strong sense of character outline and energy centers.

Character Mask II.   The above process is followed, but with the direct intention of discovering characteristics that respond to an actor's early intuitions of a specific Chekhov role. As part of a rehearsal structure the best time to begin mask work is when the actor has gained enough information from working on the text to begin to make choices, but not so much detailed information as to limit the imagination. The process of discovery is as given in the above exercise with the distinction that, as the actor tries various masks, sooner or later some particular response from a mask will feel right in the context of what the actor already knows/intuits about his or her character. Ultimately each actor will discover a basic physical composite comprised of two or three strong but economical physical characteristics, which will form a strong outline but do not limit the character in terms of detail. More than this, the physical characteristics induced by the mask encourage supporting psychical and emotional responses so that the actor is on the way to achieving an inner structure that corresponds to the physical outline.

As this stage of rehearsal the exercise may be extended in various ways. An appropriate range of props and costume pieces can be introduced from which the actor can choose to develop further his or her character design. Lines from the part can be introduced that can be explored in the developing character. Two or three of the masked characters may be introduced into a small situation that enables them to explore a part of the play's action without resorting directly to the text. At the end of a mask exercise actors may discuss their discoveries together. This gets actors in contact with the play based upon actual experienced character choices in physical terms, not through intellectual discussion about psychological responses or emotional feelings.

Mask work in this context is essentially a rehearsal tool. The mask will be discarded as detailed work on the action proceeds. But the actor will have gained a great deal of concrete knowledge of his or her character, a highly charged personal connection with the inner world of the play, and a base for more sophisticated understanding of character and text. There is a particular danger with Chekhov, due to historical association, that the actor will engage in passive introspection, maudlin emotion, and sentimentality—qualities that mask work inhibits. Work in the mask will give the actor a clear, tensile physical outline and substructure of resources for the character: a sense of the ironic detachment and humor that go with Chekhov's compassion, and a heightened energy that produces a potential excitement in the character, a feeling that it wishes to burst out of its apparently inactive state.

Green Room. This is an improvisation exercise that puts a lot of the Chekhov characteristics together. The exercise should be undertaken by a group of players that know each other fairly well. Set up a space as a Green Room, with old chairs, sofa, books, magazines, photographs, all the paraphernalia of a company that has been in existence for some time. The premise is that the players are a company performing a play. The play may be changed from improvisation to improvisation, but it should be one that all players are familiar with, and parts should be given out. The improvisation is in three stages: opening night, middle of a long run, closing night after the curtain. The improvisation potentially catalyzes all the qualities of Chekhov's work. There is a basic, routine, and ongoing rhythm that is modulated by the excitement and tensions of opening night, the tedium of the middle of the run, and the revitalized but sad and nervous energy of the final performance. The possibility exists of exploring the secret alliances, private jokes, and latent hostilities that develop in a company. The activities used to pass the time between entrances such as playing cards, reading, wondering about notices or the next job—the small ceremonies of theatrical life, the arrivals, and the departures with some company members leaving and some staying on for the next production. In the Green Room, players are in a suspended state waiting to enter an unchanging world whose plot is always the same. In many ways the Green Room is a perfect metaphor for the world of Chekhov, which, as a metatheatrical experience, is well within the experiental compass of young actors.

SUGGESTED READINGS

Gilman, Richard, *The Making of Modern Drama.* New York: Farrar, Straus and Giroux, 1974.

Magarshack, David, *Chekhov the Dramatist.* New York: Hill & Wang, 1960.

Styan, J. L., *Chekhov in Performance.* Cambridge: Cambridge University Press, 1971.

Valery, Maurice, *The Breaking String: The Plays of Anton Chekhov.* New York: Oxford University Press, 1966.

IV   Playing Postrealistic Drama

Art forms share the ebb and flow of all human rhythms: To every action there is an equal and opposite reaction. In these very terms a reaction to realistic theatre would have been expected; as a mature form it would inevitably give way to an avant garde. But the very nature of Realism guaranteed a reaction. Its minute focus upon the social and psychological problems of the individual inevitably brought it to a dead end. Finally, Realism could not answer the questions raised by its own self-examination. The focus upon "cup and saucer" issues has limited returns, and scientific progress was unable to achieve satisfactory material answers, let alone deal with larger human values. Microscopic focus upon the individual had exhausted the humanistic tradition but had found nothing to replace it. Humankind had examined itself out of all beliefs and achieved a world devoid of purpose.

By the mid-twentieth century, God, science, material progress all seemed to have failed, leaving a world filled with existential angst. What humanity seemed to be lacking was an authenticity, a sense of deep human purpose—something to fill the vacuum of self in a sterile, materialist universe. It was a task for which Realism was not equipped. As Brecht put it, "Reality needs not only to be recognized, but also to be understood." Realism had been too busy with the material minutiae of the individual's life to take time out to listen to the silences in which the larger questions reverberate. It became necessary to break out of Realism's dense material core and to let the stage once again deal with space and time in which the existential answers may be found. The theatre's response took three major forms: the philosophical/intellectual, associated with Samuel Beckett and Absurd theatre; the sociological/political, associated with Bertolt Brecht; and the romantic/sensual, associated with Antonin Artaud and Jerzy Grotowski.

We are dealing first of all with the Absurd in the persons of Samuel Beckett, David Mamet, and Harold Pinter. We are placing Pinter here essentially as a bridge between Realism and postrealistic forms. Pinter has the apparent form of a realist but the existential sensibility of the absurdists. As such he forms a link back to Chekhov and forward (not chronologically but in sensibility) to Beckett. We are including Mamet in this category as the American equivalent of Pinter in his use of post-realistic language within the guise of a naturalistic, though quasi-surrealistic setting. Beckett, Brecht, and Artaud were all born within ten years of each other at the turn of the century, just, in fact, as

Chekhov was dying. As we suggested in the last chapter, Chekhov was instinctively aware of the gap between an old system of values, which was passing with the cherry orchard, and a new system that had yet to come into being. Chekhov deals with individuals caught at a moment of spiritual vacuum, locked in a dead past and without the energy to reach to a future. In this he intuited the vacuum of values that was to be the concern of the absurdists but, unlike Beckett and Pinter, he died too soon to look directly into the abyss that was left behind by two world wars that witnessed the death of the God-oriented, stable, and determined value system that had been the inheritance of the humanist tradition. It was left to Beckett to create a form of theatre that could reflect the harsh realities of the modern world, and call for an end to all placebos, an accommodation to the truth of *le néant* (Nothingness) so that humanity could live truthfully and positively with it.

Post-modernism in a production of *Hamlet*.   *Glasgow Citizens' Theatre. Photo by John Vere Brown.*

Brecht's answer to the wasted self of postromantic disillusionment was a new definition of humankind in its socioeconomic identity. He hoped to give purpose and meaning to life by changing human nature through the highly rational and scientific process of the Marxist dialectic. His theatre sought to clear the stage both of illusion and realistic trivia, and to concentrate starkly upon its didactic potential.

Artaud was a neoromantic who wished to cleanse the discontents of materialistic bourgeois society by cutting through the barriers of intellectual ideas and the strictures of authoritarian capitalism. He wished to return humankind to a truer sense of life, in touch with the myths that were inspired by our basic human instincts; an embracement of life's sensuality and a rediscovery and confrontation of humanity's deepest nature.

While each form evinced a particular response to the existential problem, they are all connected by an underlying similarity in theatrical approach. Breaking away from realistic effects and the concern with individual psychology and character minutiae of the naturalistic acting process, they returned emphasis to a broader conception of dramatic action. Actors once again acknowledged themselves as performers who could deal directly with an audience, rather than pretend it wasn't there. Starker theatrical spaces uncluttered by trivial everyday artifacts, and more structured, poetic use of dialogue allowed time and space to make their presence felt upon the stage, encouraging audiences to face their own eternities once again. Mask and play, eternal qualities of theatre, returned to the stage its birthright of illusion.

One of the problems in dealing with a contemporary time span is identifying the significant from the ephemeral. We are aware that less theatre directly in the style of Artaud is now performed; but we believe the influence of his aesthetic to be still highly significant: The total use of the body as a gestural artifact goes to the deepest well-springs of theatre. Nor do we believe that more recent experimental forms yet have a definable aesthetic. The term "postmodern" theatre covers various experimentations with form, allied on the one hand to performance art and on the other to dance. It seems to be informed by a high-tech dispassion that uses actors as part of its visual iconography—a display of plastic physical metaphors, for which an acting methodology would be hard to determine.

It may well be that eclecticism will be the style of the future—an overlay of styles that will require a discontinuous form of acting to match the fragmentary, "byte-sized" nature of a high-tech society. In whatever terms, it is our belief that an actor who has become adept with all the styles discussed in this book will be well-prepared to follow wherever a future eclecticism may lead.

8 The Absurd

Guernica. Picasso's nightmare impression of the twentieth-century human condition. *Copyright 1989 ARS N.Y./SPADEM.*

BACKGROUND

Historical.   In the two thousand or more years since the Greeks had, through the agency of theatre, opened a public dialogue between humanity and the gods upon the nature and ethical purposes of existence, humankind had embarked upon a journey to put itself at least on a par with the gods for mastery over the universe. Christianity had humankind saved by God's own son with a divine purpose on this earth. Descartes then showed that the human being lived in a world of essential truths knowable by reason, and that by exercise of the mind humankind—originally created in its maker's image—could understand and re-create the world in its own image. From the Enlightenment to the twentieth century, religion, philosophy, and science joined hands in pursuit of human self-knowledge and perfectibility. This pursuit was called "progress," and progress was inevitable and progress was good. And theatre, rather than being a dialogue with the gods upon the nature and ethical purposes of existence, became a reflection of the problems and virtues of humankind's scientific and material earthbound progress: realism.

However, even while humanity was achieving its self-proclaimed perfection and superiority as the chosen ruler of the universe, events were conspiring to undermine the inevitable truths upon which this claim was founded and, in the middle of the twentieth century, to bring humanity face-to-face with itself in a religious, philosophical, and scientific impasse. The paring away of certitudes was begun by Copernicus and Galileo who showed that Earth, far from being the center of the universe, was an insignificant planet going nowhere in particular in an undefined space. Darwin then destroyed the lovely thought that we were a special race, created by divinity and ordained to rule over lesser species with whom we had no biological connection. Suddenly we were second cousin to the orangutan.

Shortly after humanity had its comeuppance, God got his (or hers). Nietzsche baldly stated that God was dead, and, with all due acknowledgment to believers, functionally we live today in a world without a godhead. But if not divinely guided, at least we had reason—until Freud. Rather than creatures who could know all and control our universe by exercise of mind, we now see ourselves as driven by deeply subconscious desires and sexual urges, of which we are but dimly aware and find hard to control: Man's knowable self is no more a fixed or certain place

than is the earth or, indeed, the universe itself. Einstein, whose theories further contributed to humankind's disillusionment, showed that everything is relative. The universe is not rationally organized; there are no "hitching posts in space." Everything around us, including ourselves, is volatile.[1]

The upshot of this is that by the mid-twentieth century we had neither God-given truths nor man-given truths. Scientists who had replaced God as the truth-giver now admit that they can at best *describe* phenomena— not *understand* them. Neither causality nor determination is inherent in nature; what we have is the "ultimate unpredictability of things." We no longer live in a meaningful, explicable world. In 1883 Nietzsche's Zarathustra officially proclaimed that God was dead. For a long time before that, however, God's function was gradually being taken over by the substitute religions of nationalism, Marxism, and scientific progress. Then came World War I, and shortly afterwards World War II. We finally discovered that man's scientific achievements and patent religions meant the gassing of six million Jews, the destruction of human life with metallic, technological efficiency, and, of course, the final achievement, the possibility of total destruction—the nuclear bomb.

For all of humanity's strivings, all its achievements, all its romantic hopes and belief in ultimate freedom and perfectibility— nothing works. Not God, humanism, or science. Man exists in a metaphysical void. Ionesco, one of the absurdist playwrights of the mid-twentieth century, said, "I really have the feeling that life is nightmarish, that it is painful, unendurable as a bad dream. Just glance around you: wars, catastrophes, disas-

---

[1]We are indebted to Robert Cohen for some of the images in the foregoing discussion.

ters, hatreds and persecutions, death awaiting on every side. It is horrible, it is Absurd."[2]

In the midst of the material wealth accumulated and the technological triumphs of space travel, television, and computers, humankind feels estranged from God, nature, and its own self. The questions are still there but the answers have failed. In this situation the search for ultimate meaning turned in upon humanity itself. Not any attributes or essences, but the fact of existence was to define humankind.

This is basically the drift of existentialism—a philosophy evolved in France in the 1940s and associated with the names of Sartre and Camus. Underlying this philosophy is the idea that nothing has a fixed, determined, and knowable existence. Even if existence were knowable the knowledge would be incommunicable. There is no objective "human nature": Humankind is what it makes of itself, defined by actions and choices as it goes along. There is no fixed character: In itself, humankind is nothing. Our sense of being is informed by our experience of an alien, inexplicable world in which we live in isolation from other beings. Aware that life has no larger meaning, humanity exists in a void. This emptiness, this meaninglessness, is the experience of the absurd.

"Absurd" means out of harmony with reason and propriety. What humankind seeks is some measure of happiness in a reasonable and predictable world. What it seems to get is unhappiness in a chaotic and unpredictable one. Devoid of purpose, cut off from religious,

metaphysical, and spiritual roots, and betrayed by reason, humankind is lost—all its actions become useless, senseless, absurd. At the root of all consciousness is *le néant:* the void. Humankind cannot know itself, yet is doomed to dwell upon that lack of knowledge. Descartes has come full circle: "I am not—therefore I think."

Aesthetic.   In a world where it was possible to know moral laws, to perceive ultimate values, where there was certainty about the place and purpose of man, the function of art was scientific: to portray events and objects as they existed in external reality. But with the bankruptcy of reason and logic, and the admission by science that all is relative and finally inexplicable, the logic of Realism with its rational structure no longer reflected the true, logicless, irrational, discontinuous, noncoherent reality of the human condition. So, from the end of the nineteenth century the search in art was to break out of the limitations of Realism and discover new forms more nearly representing the situation of the human spirit in this logicless world.

Cubism, futurism, surrealism, Dada were all part of the attempt to discover the true nature of existence in a world in which traditional values had disintegrated and from which the light of reason is missing, a world where people are left groping around in the ruins—in the dark. The surrealists looked for a reality beyond or deeper than the surface reality of external forms. They believed that the artist's vision—the artist's evocative imagination—brought humankind closer to the fundamental truth of existence than did the realists' "slice of life." They used the grotesque, the fantastical, the nonsensical—the stuff of dreams—to liberate the human mind from its dependence upon rational forms and social conventions.

Dada went even further than surrealism. It took the logic of an illogical, formless,

[2]Eugene Ionesco, *Fragments of a Journal,* trans. Jean Stewart (New York: Grove Press, 1968), p. 35. Martin Esslin is credited with giving the name "absurd" to the existential drama as a whole that evolved in this period. The title may in time be seen as inappropriate, as the existential sensibility becomes accepted as the truth of the human condition, and no longer "absurd" in contrast with previously held ideas.

meaningless world to its anarchistic ultimate: "Our symbol was nothingness, a vacuum, a void," said George Grosz. While Dada was theoretically constructive—in destroying all old forms so that new forms more truly representative of humanity's contemporary condition might be discovered—in practice it was closer to a series of childish pranks played among the ruins of nineteenth-century values. Dada was not willing to face the void that its anarchy revealed; this was left to Samuel Beckett and the absurdist playwrights of the mid-twentieth century.

However, theatre as a practical, cooperative and social form tends to be influenced more slowly than other art forms by aesthetic forces, and the movement away from Realism was gradual. Strindberg in his dream plays with Jarry and his *Ubu* cycle prepared the way, undermining Realism with grotesquerie and disregard for logic and verisimilitude in character and setting. The questioning of the nature of reality was carried forward in the 1920s by Luigi Pirandello. His plays had a realistic patina, but they made use of the fact that theatre is an illusion of reality: They asked, what was reality and what was illusion? With this question Pirandello reinforced the idea that truth was endlessly relative, and character endlessly unknowable.

This essentially existentialist idea was also the basis for the plays of Jean-Paul Sartre and Albert Camus, who in the 1940s propounded the tenets of existential philosophy in plays with basically traditional forms. Although the philosophical ideas and sensibility of Sartre and Camus have been highly influential in the development of absurdist theatre, their plays are less significant, in that they use essentially rational forms and knowable characters to deny the validity of rationality or the possibility of knowledge.

It was the 1950s that saw the development of a dramatic form capable of giving an audience a true experience of the absurd condition of humankind: The theatre of the absurd showed it as having no large purpose in life. Habit and material possessions limit freedom; the inadequacy of lan-

Robert Morgan's costumes for *Ubu Roi*. Note grotesqueness and clown-like facial mask combined with military costume pieces and weaponry.

guage prevents communication of inner reality. Humankind no longer has a nature proper to itself. It is, at best, the sum of its actions, confronting the ethical and spiritual void in which humanity is doomed to pass its trivial existence.

Theatre of the absurd did not use traditional plot structure with conflict and vertical progression. It is not a theatre of events, nor does it attempt logically to describe or explain any philosophical position—this would be a contradiction in terms. It gives its audience an "experience" of the absurd condition. It dethrones verisimilitude and logic to get at a truer reality beneath. One should not ask of absurd theatre, "What is it about?" or, "What is going to happen?" The question more properly is, "What is the felt experience communicated through rhythms, sounds, and images?"

While the dramatists of the absurd recognize that the confrontation of the true human condition is a bitter and despairing prospect, they believe that such a recognition is essential if we are to live with this situation and not surround ourselves with pretended answers, pretended purposes. Ironically, absurdity is the only ground upon which humanity's understanding can be secure. One of Samuel Beckett's favorite expressions is that "nothing is more real than nothing." There is also a Zen proverb that claims:

> The denying of reality is the asserting of it;
> And the asserting of emptiness is the
>   denying of it.

Although the acceptance of *le néant*, nothingness, is a seemingly negative experience, the approach of the dramatists of the absurd is, finally, positive. The playwright confronts the audience with the experience of absurdity in order that they may be freed from dogma, illusion, and superstition; that they come to terms with their true reality, and thus find the power to act through acceptance in a positive way of the great absolutes of time and death. Or, as a contemporary man with an acute

sense of the absurd, Woody Allen, put it in his movie *Sleeper:* "Solutions don't work. I believe in sex and death—two experiences that come once in a lifetime!"

Absurd theatre is to some degree a catch-all category. The playwrights included under the heading used a variety of approaches to communicate their sense of the absurd condition of life.[3] Not all the attributes of absurd style are to be found at all times in all of the playwrights.

Samuel Beckett is the classic exponent of the absurd with the most perfect integration of form, content, and sensibility. His play *Waiting for Godot* has already entered the permanent classical repertory and is likely to become the *Everyman* of the twentieth century. This play together with *Endgame, Happy Days,* and *Krapp's Last Tape* make up a corpus of work of lasting significance. Beckett, together with Harold Pinter, will be the prime focus of our discussion under this heading. Although Pinter chronologically follows Beckett and, indeed, follows him in the sense that he is a distant disciple, we are discussing Pinter first because, although he is a product of and reflects the existential sensibility that informs Beckett, he employs this within an apparently realistic form. He thus continues the progression away from Realism, which we suggested began with Chekhov, and connects the Russian playwright with the classical absurdism of Beckett in the importance of time and space that informs the work of three of the classic stylistic playwright's of the twentieth century. It is in the interstices of time and space that the three playwrights operate, and it is in those intervals that meaning or lack of meaning resides. It is in the pauses and the silences that the larger questions appear, when they are no longer filled by the "busyness" of everyday chatter, or obscured by the detailed clutter of "real" life.

---

[3]Apart from Beckett and Harold Pinter, with whom we shall deal at some length, and Ionesco, whom we shall touch upon, these included Adamov, Albee, and Genet.

9 Pinter

John Harrop as Davies in *The Caretaker*.

BACKGROUND

Born in 1930, Harold Pinter's boyhood included the economic disaster of the Great Depression and the social and political disaster of World War II. Although the son of a lower-middle-class family in the East End of London, Pinter benefited from the educational reforms of the 1940s, which enabled him to receive a good secondary education and encouraged, apart from himself, the successful crop of British playwrights of the 1950s: John Osborne, Arnold Wesker, John Arden.

At school Pinter distinguished himself as both actor and athlete, and he also published poetry at the age of nineteen. After briefly attending the Royal Academy of Dramatic Art, Pinter worked as a professional actor for five years before writing his first play, *The Room*, in 1957. *The Room* was given a successful nonprofessional production by the Drama Department of Bristol University and, encouraged, Pinter wrote his second play, *The Birthday Party*, in 1958. This was not an immediate success. Reviewers dismissed the play for the very qualities that were later to become a hallmark of Pinter's work: "Characters are unable to explain their actions, thoughts or feelings"; "The third act studiously refrains from the slightest hint of what the other two were about." Only one reviewer, Harold Hobson, understood that, although Pinter seemed to be writing in the realistic tradition, his vision of life belonged to the existential sensibility that was to inform the most interesting artistic work of the post-World War II period. As Hobson wrote: "Mr. Pinter has got hold of a primary fact of existence. We live on the verge of disaster. . . . The fact that no one can say precisely what [the play] is about . . . is one of its greatest merits."

From that somewhat unpromising start, Harold Pinter has produced a repertory of plays that have become acknowledged classics of the modern theatre. *The Caretaker, The Homecoming, Old Times, No Man's Land*, and *Betrayal*, together with numerous smaller pieces, show every likelihood of assuring Pinter's place among those playwrights whose work has become part of the permanent repertory of the theatre. The plays are an expression of Harold Pinter's response to his time; of an actor, athlete, and poet; of a Jewish man confronted in his boyhood by the pervasive Fascism of the 1930s and the Holocaust of the 1940s; and in his maturity by the possibility of nonbeing, the "atmosfear" of total annihilation that is the legacy of the atomic bomb.

Sensibility and Premises. Within his distinctive personal style Pinter bridges the modern movement from the early existential naturalism of Chekhov to the existential absurdity of Samuel Beckett, with whom we shall deal in Chapter 11. In speaking of himself, Pinter has paraphrased the fatalism of Chekhov: "I'm stuck in my own tracks, whatever they are—for so long. Forever." And in his poetry he has expressed the sense of vacuum and futility in a world that makes no sense—is absurd.

> Only the deaf can hear and the blind
> understand
> The miles I gabble.
> Through these my dances of dunce and devil,
> It's only the dumb can speak through
> The rubble.

Beneath the seemingly realistic surface of Pinter's plays yawns the existential vacuum that is filled with the crucial problems of modern philosophy: identity, purposes, verification. In a godless world within which we stand on the brink of annihilation, we can never know who we are, let alone why we are, with any certainty. Realistic theatre has presumed that, given certain expositional background and biographical details, a character would conform to and act reasonably from these premises. Judge Brack's response to Hedda Gabler's suicide—"But people don't do such things"—suggests that within the bourgeois world of Realism there is a set of expectations that can normally be relied upon. Pinter refutes the possibility of knowing these premises or the logic of expectations. The world is an uncertain place in which not only the future but also the past is unreliable. Nor can we hide from life, not even within our own rooms—a constant spatial metaphor in Pinter—for somehow, in the most innocuous or unexpected way, the intangible threat that hovers in the very air we breathe will find a way in; for it is simply a fact of modern existence. But if there is no safety in staying within our rooms, there is equally no reason or purpose for taking action in the outside world. Here, again, Pinter joins hands with Chekhov and Beckett: Davies in *The Caretaker* is no more likely to get to Sidcup than are the Three Sisters to get to Moscow, or Beckett's tramps to take any action whatsoever—"'Let's go.' They don't move."

The titles of Pinter's plays may be seen as a progressive illustration of his concerns. The earliest, *The Room,* is the space in which we try to define ourselves and find security in some kind of fixed entity that is known. *Old Times* is the play in which Pinter leaves the confines of rooms, which have no security in the present, and looks to the past, to memory, to events that have taken place, to provide some meaning and structure. But the past is equally as dangerous as the present, for we have no means of proving its truths; it may be reinterpreted at will and used in evidence against us. Which leaves Pinter in *No Man's Land*—by definition, emptiness, space, lack of connection or meaning. After that comes *Betrayal,* which suggests the result when connection or commitment is attempted in a world that lacks existential meaning or purpose. The very emotional betrayals, which should be passionate and significant, are infected by the boredom of the existential vacuum and become casual and trivial. His stance is, in fact, the ironically comedic one, which he has in common with the great mentor of the absurdists, Samuel Beckett. But there is, in Pinter, a

very strong sense that having confronted the loneliness, the uncertainty, the lack of meaning and the trepidation of modern existence, he is finally suggesting that without some commitment to some commitment, all of life is a betrayal.

INTRINSIC DEMANDS

Structure.   One of the problems for an actor in confronting a Pinter text is that the surface details of the play seem realistic. We are in real, modern, recognizable spaces, with the kind of furniture real people sit on, the clothes real people wear, and real people from a variety of very specific British social backgrounds doing the sitting, wearing, and talking. It is only when we get to the talking, the language—which we shall deal with below—that the actor gets the first clue that, although the words are perfectly normal, vernacular, and fit the circumstances of the characters speaking them, the way in which they are arranged is, perhaps, not quite the same as with Ibsen, O'Neill, Williams, or even Chekhov. But the dramatic structure, in many ways, could well be that of Ibsen, who was using the basic well-made play form of the nineteenth century, which we dealt with earlier. Pinter's early plays have a basic three-act form, have a series of character conflicts with crises and climaxes, and favor strong endings to scenes to keep the audience expectantly upon the edge of its seats.

However, if this surface appearance of the realistic well-made play is examined more closely, significant differences appear. The exposition—such detail about the characters, or circumstances that have taken place before or outside of the play's events, which is needed to help us make sense of what is going on, is either omitted or unhelpful, because it is often uncertain or downright contradictory. Nor do we find the psychological development of character, the self-exploration or revelation of the character under the pressure of circumstances that is one of the features of realistic drama. Pinter's characters in psychological terms don't change; they are caught up in a pattern of events that may alter their circumstances, but they don't change. Nor does the action of the play reach any resolution. The plays do not resolve tensions, achieve solutions, or create a significant change in circumstances, which is the usual outcome of the realistic structure. Pinter's plays end in moments of stasis, usually achieved by motionless tableau at the end of the final scene. The tableaux themselves suggest an uncertain balance with an intangible sense of potential for further action that, at the same time, would seem only able to be a repetition of what has taken place: possibly a series of different patterns but with the same outcome. Pinter's work does not have the circular form of such absurdist plays as Beckett's *Waiting for Godot*, but neither does it have the vertical movement toward a resolution of Realism. The plays have more the quality of a failed orgasm: Some stimulation has occurred, tension is aroused, but no release takes place and one isn't quite sure why; yet there is the awful sense that another attempt would achieve the same lack of result, after the same gruelling effort. We are in T. S. Eliot's world, which ends not with a bang but a whimper.

While frustrating the purpose of the well-made play structure in his earlier works by giving his audience nothing but uncertainty to hold on to, Pinter moves away from this structure in his later plays to deal with the unstructured form of memory in *Old Times*, and the conscious lack of signposts in *No Man's Land*. Finally, in *Betrayal*, he turns the form against itself, reversing the time and narrative structure so that we begin at the end and move back toward the beginning. Pinter thus sets up the uncertainty of our knowing what the outcome is, but not knowing why— how we got there. And the essential questions

The unresolved stasis of Pinter, in a production of *Old Times.   Arena Stage, Washington. Photo by Joan Marcus.*

of not knowing Why; how we got Here; or Where we are going are, as we saw in the previous section, the concerns of Pinter's work.

By this technique of using a structure without fulfilling its demands to frustrate the expectations of his audience, Pinter prepares the audience for that estrangement of the apparently normal, which is one of the main energies of his work. In place of a narrative through-line we have the delaying of the unfolding of events until the need for action becomes irrelevant as it would serve no purpose in the scene. The scene seems to be filled with nonsequiturs and unverifiable assertions that tend not to move the action forward, but to create a pattern of events out of a series of conversations or "agons" between characters. These have an apparently trivial or ordinary subject matter, but they are in fact serious contests for territory or dominance between characters.

Pinter is basically not a narrator, a storyteller, but a poet whose plays are carefully constructed patterns of relationships illustrating the nature of our existence. Psychology and story are replaced by structure of images, moods, and insights—never arguments or explanations—which the audience experiences through an overall, not moment-by-moment, apprehension of the form. The achievement, the uniqueness of Pinter, is that within a realistic patina of dialogue and character he creates an overall effect of poetic ambiguity and mysterious metaphor.

By careful plotting, by absence of that form of plot which moves logically forward and takes the audience along with it, Pinter creates the sense of uncertainty, or what has been called the *menace* in his work. Setting up a structure of unfulfilled expectations, Pinter then proceeds to fill the gaps by techniques that make the situation even more strange and uncertain. One of these techniques is to make the mundane strange and give the ordinary great significance. In *The Homecoming*, for example, the ticking of a clock, the drinking of a glass of water, the moving of legs during a speech by Ruth all take on an implied threat that the simple facts of the action would not merit. By contrast, again in *The Homecoming*, a man spending two hours seducing his brother's wife and a man lying dead upon the floor are treated as perfectly normal occurrences.

Pinter, having "menaced" his audience by upsetting the moral and emotional balance of their expectations, goes on to make life more threatening for them by undermining the reliability of what information they are given. Eighty percent of *The Homecoming* is made up of description of past events; yet the audience cannot rely upon the truth of any of them. Pinter himself does not believe in the reliability of

"reality." In a note to the audience at a production of *The Room* in 1960 he wrote: "There are no hard distinctions between what is real and what is unreal, nor between what is true and what is false. The thing . . . can be both true and false. The assumption that to verify what has happened and what is happening presents few problems I take to be inaccurate." Pinter uses this principle as a basic technique in structuring his character relationships. If we cannot be certain of the past, a whole range of possibilities—none of them necessarily true—is opened up, and new pasts can be constantly re-created in the present. Pinter's characters do this. They use the reconstruction of different versions of the past as strategies in the present to gain territorial supremacy and dominance over other characters. We, as audience, never know what is "true"; we are only aware of the patterns created by the strategy. While used to their own advantage by characters, the strategy is also used against them. They are constantly faced by the fact that their version of the past, their attempt to control the reality of the present, may or may not succeed. All are struggling in the void at the center, the lack of fixed points in a relativistic, constantly changing world. As the poet Yeats saw the modern condition:

> Things fall apart, the centre cannot hold
> Mere anarchy is loosed upon the world.

This anarchy, lack of certitude, constantly teetering at the edge of disaster is very threatening to the human spirit. So the idea of menace as applied to Pinter's work can be understood. But why "comedy of menace"? Well, we have mentioned Pinter's ironical stance, but structurally he is dealing with specific social groups and their bodily appetites, especially sexual: Marital infidelity is a major theme running through his work. Such issues have long been regarded as the stuff of comedy. But, more than this, Pinter makes his uncertain, menacing world funny. He is, again structurally, in the long tradition of the comedy of manners running from the Restoration through Oscar Wilde to Noel Coward. He starts off as a mannerist of the lower classes, and as he makes his own successful upward progression through the British class system, he turns his eyes and ears on the middle and upper middle class, from *Old Times* onward. His characters, under the patina of contemporary realistic dress and manner, may be seen as descended from the stock types of comedy: Davies in *The Caretaker* is part cunning servant, part braggart warrior; Max in *The Homecoming* is a Pantalone; Deeley in *Old Times* is part Pantalone part Dottore; Spooner in *No Man's Land* has clear elements of the Dottore. And Pinter's women are almost all a combination of the nagging wife and sexually devouring female.

As a true mannerist, much of Pinter's humor is through use of language. In his plays dealing with the lower class, the routines of the music hall, which he uses, are a source of his humor, with the straight man and the banana going through their verbal struggles. As the class level rises, so does the refinement of the wit, but the verbal dueling is constant. Pinter cleverly fits the structures of comedy of manners within the nonnarrative structure of his plotting. Comedy normally requires some resolution, some Hymen pointing to procreation and the future. But the structures of comic convention, the verbal duels, the fights for sexual supremacy are, in fact, ends in themselves. A convention used as a convention requires no verification from an outside source to create its laughter; but when that laughter creates no release of tension, admits no resolution, it becomes threatening. And it is by the interweaving of the unresolved conventions of comedy of manners within the patterns of unverifiable actions and relationships of his characters that Pinter creates the structure of his comedies of menace.

Space. Pinter uses the artifacts and environments of everyday life for his settings. His first play was titled *The Room*, and some form of room or enclosed living space with furniture and domestic props suited to the social level of the occupants is a feature of all his work. A room suits Pinter's purposes very well; it is recognizably realistic and sets up the audience with certain expectations, many of which are associated with hearth, home, comfort, and security. But, once again, Pinter denies the expectations that his realistic

The spare domesticity of Pinter's space, *The Birthday Party.*   *Los Angeles Theatre Center.*

Assorted junk and silent menace in *The Caretaker*.
Theatre Artist's Group.

patina suggests. A room is basically an enclosed space, which can also suggest confinement and entrapment; Harold Pinter's rooms, while containing the recognizable trivia of domestic life, are never entirely comfortable. They are not deliberately uncomfortable, but there is a spareness about them; the cheerfully cluttered aggregation of full lives is missing. Just as silence and pause, that is, space, are important elements of Pinter's language, as we will see below, so physical space is an important part of his settings. Space, while empty, is also filled with potential, and in Pinter's work that potential is threatening. Rooms are not safe havens of relaxation; they are boxing rings, or rather lairs in which animals struggle for territory and dominance. There are areas of territorial control demarked by beds in *The Caretaker*, chairs in *The Homecoming*, divans in *Old Times*, and then spaces between them, no man's lands, in which the maneu-

vering for control takes place. As we saw with Chekhov, lack of direct contact is also a feature of Pinter's work. There is always emotional distance, space between in which the strategies of attack and defense may be played out.

Pinter's first images reinforce both the surface of realism and the estrangement of it. In *The Caretaker* we have a room filled with assorted junk but a man sitting silently in it like a coiled spring, looking at each mundane object in turn. *The Homecoming* has Max and his son, Lenny, both ignoring each other and involved in argument over scissors at the same time. Something is missing—the scissors—just as there is obviously something missing—warm contact—between father and son. Scissors are cold, sharp, and cutting just as the relationship seems to be.[1] As *Old Times* opens we see a carefully set up triangulated space and three dimly discernible figures. Clearly it is a room, but at the same time there is a sense of quiet as on a battlefield at dusk. The estrangement of the ordinary to invest it with a quality much larger than the sum of its parts is essential in the use of space in Pinter's work. An excellent example of it occurred in a production of *Betrayal*.[2] This play has nine scenes and moves chronologically backwards to the start of the affair, which is the basis of its plot. The nine scenes create the physical spine of the memory structure, taking place in a series of bedrooms, apartments, hotel rooms, and rooms in restaurants. The production had the insight to leave each set on stage after it had played its direct part in the action, to continue to play an indirect part in reminding the audience at all times of what had been in the affair. The production used very spare settings for each environment, and the accumulation of them created a skeletal image at the end—the bare bones of the dead

---

[1]We recognize that this is a very particular interpretation.
[2]Directed by Robert Cohen, and designed by Doug Goheen.

relationship that, owing to the chronology of the play, was just beginning. Thus, at the end of the play and beginning of the affair the audience could already see the betrayal of hope and love in the physical skeleton on stage. Present yet absent like memory itself, the stage was cluttered and empty at the same time, concrete yet undefined, filled yet a vacuum. This was a splendid physical image of Pinter's sensibility, which itself brought memories of the dead house at the end of *The Cherry Orchard* and which suggests the vision of life that Chekhov and Pinter share.

Language. In *The Homecoming*, in a speech in which she is referring to her legs and lips, Ruth says, "Perhaps the fact that they move is more significant than the words which come through them." This sums up Pinter's approach to and use of language in his work. It is not so much the content of speeches, or the information conveyed by them that is significant, but the shape, size, and rhythmical structure. It is not what other characters hear that affects them so much as the way in which the fact of the speech creates strategies in the verbal games that are being played by the characters. The games are for dominance, and one of the major strategies, if one thought of the game as a boxing match (though the blows are much more subtle), is the undercut. After a series of exchanges a character produces a short line to which there is no immediate reply. The other characters have to stop and reassess their tactics, and the line is followed by a pause, or silence. In *The Homecoming*, Lenny is trying to dominate Ruth by controlling what she is doing; this leads to the following exchange:

LENNY: And now perhaps I'll relieve you of your glass.
RUTH: I haven't quite finished.
LENNY: You've consumed quite enough in my opinion.
RUTH: No, I haven't.

LENNY: Quite sufficient in my own opinion.
RUTH: Not in mine, Leonard.
       Pause.

Ruth undercuts Lenny here by using his full name; as one does when disciplining a child; as Lenny's mother did; a name that threatens Lenny and causes him to stop and regroup.

In *Old Times* Anna and Deeley are vying for control over Kate and discussing her smile:

DEELEY: What did you think of it?
ANNA: It is a very beautiful smile.
DEELEY: Do it again.
KATE: I'm still smiling.
DEELEY: You're not. Not like you were a moment ago, not like you did then.
       (To Anna) You know the smile I'm talking about?
KATE: This coffee's cold.
       Pause.

Here, Kate undercuts both Anna and Deeley at the same time. It is not just a simple avoidance by change of subject; it is an attack on Deeley, who had made the coffee, and Anna, who had given the coffee to Kate. But, as with all of Pinter's verbal strategies, the attack is oblique. Another oblique strategy that is structurally quite different is the long and seemingly pointless monologue or story told by one of the characters, which seems not to respond to any immediate point in the dialogue. In *The Homecoming*, Lenny has a couple of rambling narratives in his first meeting with Ruth, neither of which provide any information that seems remotely relevant to her or seems to arise out of the situation. They are, however, Lenny's way of not giving away anything about himself in direct terms, while letting Ruth know of his sexual attractiveness, his power over women, and the fact that he is physically stronger than she is and is not afraid to resort to violence if necessary. None of this is, however, made directly explicit to Ruth. It is a concealed self-revelation and an oblique threat. Interestingly, the second of

The off-balance, failed assertiveness of Deeley in *Old Times*.   *Los Angeles Theatre Center.*

these speeches leads up to the Ruth/Lenny exchange we described above in which, after all of his verbal effort, Ruth undercuts him quite simply and wins the point.

In *Old Times*, Deeley has a similar series of tales to tell about himself, which seem to be full of inconsistencies and illogicalities. Again, there is seemingly no connection between the action on stage and the stories. But, equally again, the action is the fact that Deeley is trying to avoid the situation by telling a story. He is shifting the focus to himself without giving anything away or making himself more vulnerable. It is a way of facing the situation while avoiding it at the same time. Deeley is a character who is not so much trying to dominate as to protect his territory throughout the play. He is constantly in danger of being undercut, of being off-balance, and his speeches often give the effect of juggling with a disparate set of desires, motives, emotions, and issues in a desperate attempt to keep them from dropping and breaking.

These strategies, while not giving us a great deal of specific information about the characters, tell us a great deal about the motivations and intentions of the characters in the situation, in the struggle for dominance, the game of attack and defense that is continually going on and whose meanings are contained in the structure and rhythms of the verbal game. Game playing is an important metaphor for the rhythms and patterns of Pinter's work. As we pointed out earlier, Pinter was himself an athlete and game player. Squash is an explicit metaphor for the competition between Jerry and Robert in *The Betrayal*. The game of cricket is implicit in *No Man's Land*, in which all the characters are named after famous British cricket players. The rhythms of games, quick and slow moves, hard and soft blows, are a good practical metaphor for the way in which Pinter uses his verbal strategies. And, as we saw in the comedy of manners chapter, verbal dueling is a time-honored British sport, from the sophisticated wit of the upper class to the tougher, coarser "piss-taking" of the London working class, from whom Pinter drew much of the language of his earlier plays.

Piss-taking is the gaining of advantage over someone by identifying a blind spot, usually vanity or egotism, and then building the person up at a point of vulnerability in order to make the person appear ridiculous or to set them up to be punctured at will. There is an excellent example in *The Caretaker*.[3] Mick—probably named such for "taking the Mickey," another term for piss-taking—plays on the fact that Davies is shambling, down-at-the-heels, and obviously incapable of looking after himself or anything at all, yet he has a pathetic vanity.

MICK: It's just that you look a capable sort of man to me.

DAVIES: I am a capable sort of man . . .

MICK: Well, I could see before, when you took out that knife, that you wouldn't let anyone mess you about.

DAVIES: No one messes me about, man.

MICK: I mean you've been in the services, haven't you?

DAVIES: The what?

MICK: You've been in the services. You can tell by your stance.

DAVIES: Oh . . . yes. Spent half my life there, man. Overseas . . . like . . . serving . . . I was.

MICK: In the colonies, weren't you?

DAVIES: I was over there. I was one of the first over there.

MICK: That's it. You're just the man I been looking for.

DAVIES: What for?

MICK: Caretaker.

Piss-taking is, at the very least, very ironical and sometimes cruel. But often, in group terms, it becomes a form of sociability. Playing the game is such a habit of mind, there is such a shared history of jibes and invective that no one is seriously hurt. It is a form of emotional contact on the fine line between friendliness and hostility; part of a daily vying for power in a harsh environment in which the tough survive—it is part of a training for toughness, and if the group balance of piss-taking is maintained, then open hostility doesn't occur. The apparent cruelty and hostility of the language Pinter's characters often use—the exchange between Max and Lenny at the beginning of *The Homecoming*, for example—is tempered by the fact that it is habit, born of familiarity, and although the strategy is to gain dominance in a situation it is not immediately intended to hurt or crush. In the game terminology it is more a puncturing by throwing darts than trying to kill with a baseball bat.

A further strategy Pinter uses is to put seemingly inappropriate words into his characters' mouths. Lower-class characters use words that would slip more easily from the tongues of verbally facile characters with upper-class educations. Mick dwells on the term "penchant"; Lenny asks Ruth if she would like an "aperitif." This is another tactic of dominance, which is at the same time humorous. The word pops out like the blade of a sheath knife, letting the other person know that in the war of words the character has this superior weapon at his or her disposal. The audience finds it amusing because it recognizes the inappropriateness of the word in the situation—incongruity being a basic comic technique. The tactic may or may not succeed. Characters with a lesser vocabulary will be menaced; characters such as Ruth, who understands what Lenny is trying to do, recognize that he is trying too hard and will wait their chance to undercut.

In the same context, Pinter will use language to deflate itself, especially the vacuous hyperinflated language of modern advertising: empty and meaningless claims covering the absence of any true substance. Mick's speech in act 3 of *The Caretaker*, describing how he will decorate the room, uses the hype

[3]Harold Pinter, *The Caretaker* (London: Methuen, 1960), pp. 50–51.

language of interior decorating including the phrase "afromosia teak veneer." There is no such word as "afromosia," but it sounds very chic and interesting. Pinter is doing two things with this language. It is a technique of dominance, a form of sandbagging with words that have little real meaning but sound very impressive to the listener. At the same time the language has broader resonances of lack of meaning. It points to Pinter's larger concern for meaning and verifiability in a world in which language is our major tool of communication but simply cannot be relied upon, or worse, can be manipulated to any purpose the speaker wishes to achieve.

If the structure of language, used tactically, is more important than what the language says, then silence becomes an important part of language, and perhaps the "Pinter pause" is one of the more notorious elements of the playwright's work. A distinctive feature of Pinter's structural rhythm is the use of ellipsis, pause, and silence. Martin Esslin has drawn attention to the line in *The Dwarfs*, one of Pinter's earlier works, in which the discussion is about poets. A character says, "What do they do when they come to a line with no words in it at all?"[4] In the carefully constructed verbal rhythms of Pinter's work, pauses and silences are indeed lines with no words in them at all. In this structure silence can be more powerful than language because of its potential for many meanings. Silence breaks through the surface of realistic speech with its babble of social and psychological concerns, and it creates a space that resists definition, yet leaves open all possibilities.

The ellipsis is the smallest break in the flow of speech; a small hesitation, an uncertainty as to the appropriate word, a groping for the right meaning suggests the character is not quite in emotional control of the situation,

has to be somewhat careful of what he or she is saying in order not to become too vulnerable. In many ways it is a recapitulation of the inarticulateness of vernacular conversation with its "ums" and "ers." What Pinter has done is to replace these interjections with small silences that hint at a concealment of some kind: that the speech may not be communicating the whole truth and lead the audience to wonder at the character's motivation.

The pause is longer than the ellipsis and is Pinter's most frequently used technique of placing meaning in the silence. Pauses are tactical regroupings in the rhythmical patterns of verbal competitions. The character speaking is waiting to see how the last point has been received: Is the tactic working? Will the point have to be pressed further? Is the opponent going to respond or is it a "palpable hit"? Is he or she waiting to see what other ammunition the adversary has? The battle for dominance is contained in the determination as to who will have to speak next. It is threatening precisely because one doesn't know what will happen next, and a whole world of possibilities is present in the space. In a sense, language is a way in which we choose to represent ourselves, to conceal or reveal what we choose; in silence we are potentially stripped naked and vulnerable to all threats. The audience is also left in silence and is both almost obliged to fill in the silence on stage with its own interpretation, or at least to wonder what will come next; and in the silence that fills the theatre the audience is confronted with its own, personal vulnerability in the face of the great uncertainties of life.

Complete "silence" is the least used of Pinter's techniques. It is the longest quietus and usually denotes the end of a verbal skirmish, as at the end of a "movement" in music, after which another motif will be introduced. "Silence" usually denotes a balance of power; a particular situation has been fought over and no final territorial victory has been gained. It

---

[4]Martin Esslin, *Pinter: A Study of His Plays* (London: Methuen, 1977), p. 261.

is also filled with the resonances of what has been said, usually a set of conflicting possibilities, which give no basis for a definition of the situation and leave all future meanings open.

We touched upon Pinter's comic techniques in the section on structure, and the undercuttings and incongruities of his language are part of that technique. Repetition is the other major linguistic device that Pinter employs to achieve comedy. One of the best examples of this comes at the beginning of *The Birthday Party.* Two middle-aged people, Petey and Meg, are at breakfast:

MEG: Petey, is that you?
>Pause.

Petey?
PETEY: What?
MEG: Is that you?
PETEY: Yes, it's me.
MEG: What? Are you back?
PETEY: Yes.
MEG: I've got your cornflakes ready. Here's your cornflakes. Are they nice?
PETEY: Very nice.
MEG: I thought they'd be nice.

And so the conversation goes on in this vein for several lines. The language is comic because it sets in high relief the boring triviality of the everyday; the attempt to make communication when there is nothing to say: Here the treatment of cornflakes is as if it were a gourmet dish, when cornflakes are always cornflakes and Petey probably has them everyday. Again the rhythmical structure tells us a great deal about the relationship between Meg and Petey: the absolute ordinariness; the balance between the two characters; the lack of emotion and yet the connection through the acceptance of the mundane and the attempt to communicate through it. Pinter uses recognizable reality of the everyday both to situate the character and achieve a comic effect.

There is also the structure of the music hall, or vaudeville, double-act routine in the rhythms. This ancestry is even clearer in a sequence from *The Dumb Waiter,* one of Pinter's early pieces:

BEN: A man of eighty-seven wanted to cross the road. But there was a lot of traffic, see? He couldn't see how he was going to squeeze through. So he crawled under a lorry.
GUS: He what?
BEN: He crawled under a lorry. A stationary lorry.
GUS: No?
BEN: The lorry started and ran over him.
GUS: Go On!
BEN: That's what it says here.
GUS: Get away.
BEN: It's enough to make you want to puke isn't it?
GUS: Who advised him to do a thing like that?

This is a classic straight man to banana routine that goes all the way back to Roman comedy and perhaps reaches its classic form in the "Who's on first?" routine of Abbott and Costello.

In all of his techniques with language, by use of rhythms, structures, and patterns that are carefully chosen and precisely interrelated, Pinter invests the patina of reality with potentialities and resonances that are far larger and more significant than the apparent weight of the surface events. In this, his work is closer to poetry, an open form that deals with the inexpressible and unverifiable nature of human experience.

PERFORMANCE DEMANDS

Much of what is the actor's task in realistic performance will be expected of him or her in approaching Pinter. As we have said, the surface of the work has the appearance of everyday reality: The wearing of the costumes, and the use of furniture and properties will all be what a modern audience would expect of the characters in the particular environment. But what makes the actor's task more difficult is that while the productions will have the look of realism, they won't quite have the feel of it. In very simple terms the actor's work will be more spare. Whereas in purely naturalistic playing one of the actor's tasks is to fill out the environment of the play with the "busyness" of everyday life—to create character detail with which to embellish the action he or she is given by the playwright—with Pinter the playwright doesn't want that kind of help. Here the actor's task is to play clearly and precisely what is given, and to allow the spaces created by the structure of the play to do their work.

This is especially true in approaching character psychology. With Realism, the actor will try to create a consistent psychological mask with logical through-line of motivation. This will be supported by biographical detail from the text, and also from the actor's imagination to give a stronger background from which to work. But, as we have seen, Pinter's characters do not offer consistent biographical detail, or logical through-lines of psychological motivation. They are often self-contradictory, arbitrary, and seemingly unmotivated and unfocused. What actors shouldn't do is tie themselves in knots trying to make logical and psychological sense out of this, reconciling biographical contradictions and clarifying obscurities. This would be to defeat the point. What the actor does is to look for the pattern of events; the tactics and strategies of the character in the moment. If the moment is played as real and true, with as much or as little effort as is needed to convince, with that particular action, then it will form part of the total pattern of events that the playwright has created to communicate the sense of life revealed through the play. Once again the actor is a *dramatis persona,* one of the elements of the total *mise-en-scène,* and as long as his or her strategy is consistent with the total pattern of

The spareness, playing away from emotion of Stanley in *The Birthday Party.* *Oregon Shakespeare Festival. Photo by Henry Kranzler.*

strategies woven together by the playwright, whether the character is psychologically consistent or has a logical through-line of action, is irrelevant.

As we have suggested, the strategies are for dominance; verbal battles for territory: sexual, emotional, and physical. And it is the structure of the language, its rhythms, phrasings, punctuation, not any manifest, overt emotional force, which is used to gain the advantage. What we have is a series of jabs and feints, oblique threats and avoidances rather than heavy punching. Except in the very few and brief instances when the balance of the verbal struggle is upset and overt violence takes place, no line should be read so hard that the other character would be defeated or driven out. The strategy of the play requires that characters shrug off the threat and go on, and the actor must accept this emotional distancing.

Characters try to maneuver each other to get the other into a position to be undercut. It is probably not too much to say that the more dangerous the threat the more oblique will be the delivery.

Characters try to give nothing away, not to register when something hits home—they regroup in the pause, and try another tactic. The shifting of ground, the restructuring of past events, the changing of personal details—all are part of the attempt to throw the other character off balance, and in practical terms are consistent with Pinter's sense that nothing can be known, nothing is black or white in an existential world. Therefore, to try to dot *i*'s and cross *t*'s, to want to play emotion directly, is to work against the play's intention; all of the actor's energy goes into the strategy of the line, not the revealing of feelings. Playing away from, playing against the obvious, is part of Pinter's device to keep the balance of emotional tension, and not foreclose on any possibilities.

One of the possibilities that should not be closed off is the pause. Actors sometimes ask, "How do I fill the pause?" The simple answer is—you don't. As we have suggested, the pause is part of the structural punctuation of the action. It is part of the playwright's strategy whereby he creates the sense of uncertainty or menace that is the atmosphere of his work. Pauses are weapons in the struggle that is taking place; they are an implied threat because they are nonexplicit: If you explain a weapon it loses a good deal of its force. The audience will be aware that the character is

regrouping, but will be uncertain of the outcome, and will fill the pause for itself either by its own conclusions or with the electricity of unspecified expectations. If the actor tries to help the audience to understand, to give indications by shrugs or facial gestures or other business, it will blur the moment and take away much of its force. For the actor, the implicit strategy behind the line continues through the pause.

The understatement of the acting, the playing away from emotional hyperbole, together with the silent spaces created by the pause can invest what would normally be perfectly ordinary and simple moves with great significance. Realism attempted to do away with the taking of "dramatic moments." Pauses before strong exits, flourishes, the sweeping of a cloak were all associated with the melodramatic and shunned as not part of the imitation of everyday reality. Pinter, by making his realistic playing even more spare and uncluttered, has reintroduced the dramatic moment, but makes them out of apparently ordinary and everyday actions. In *The Homecoming*, Ruth draws attention to her shoes and legs. It is not blatant, but the moment is so framed by the stillness of the space surrounding it that it is charged with sexual threat. Again, in *The Homecoming*, a glass of water becomes the focus of struggle for dominance between Ruth and Lenny, and the simple action of drinking from the glass becomes the rape and domination of Lenny by Ruth. Similarly in *The Caretaker*, the offering of a saltcellar by Mick to Davies has the force of a threat, while in *The Birthday Party*, the tearing of a newspaper becomes the destruction of one character by another.

Movement and gesture as a whole will be related to character strategy; it will not be arbitrary and concerned with the creation of everyday detail for its own sake. Over-illustration will disturb the careful rhythms of the action and blur the clarity of space between characters in which the struggle for dominance takes

The emotional and spatial distance of Pinter seen in *The Homecoming*. Compare with Chekhov figure, page 213. *CSC Repertory Company, New York. Photo by Gerry Goodstein.*

place. Emotional distance translates into spatial distance, and movement within that space, though seemingly normal, is filled with territorial significance in the understated but emotionally charged strategies of character relationships. The economy, precision, and clarity of movement is consistent with the way in which Pinter uses all his dramatic elements—language and silence, image and space—to create a carefully framed stage picture in which the actor does not dominate but plays his or her part in the integrated *mise-en-scène* with which Pinter creates his effects.

EXERCISES, GAMES, TECHNIQUES

Verbal Punctuation I. Take any piece of dialogue from a Pinter play and speak it, including the punctuation as if it were words: comma, period, ellipsis, pause. Allow one beat for comma, two for a period, three for an ellipsis, and four to six beats for a pause. This will give the actor a very active and concrete sense of the structure of the language.

Verbal Punctuation II. Take any piece of dialogue from a Pinter play and beat out the ellipsis and pauses. This can be done with a director or coach tapping out the rhythm on a drum, or with the actor involved tapping it out on a piece of furniture, or flicking the rhythm with the fingers. This creates a strong sense of the weight and time of the pauses.

Verbal Punctuation III. Take a piece of modern verse—T. S. Eliot does very well—share the lines among two players, and then use them as if they were shots in a tennis game, or punches in a boxing match. In the tennis structure find the weight and time of the lines by whatever shots they indicate: hard drives, drop shots, back spins, lobs, etc. Similarly in the boxing image: Find jabs, feints, counters, coverups, straight punches, etc. A piece of verse taken from Eliot's "Preludes," for example, is not too far removed from Pinter's language:

> The morning comes to consciousness
> Of faint stale smells of beer
> From the sawdust trampled street
> With its muddy feet that press
> To early coffee stands.

Prose Verse I. Restructure Pinter's long, narrative speeches in a verse form—for example, a speech of Deeley's from *Old Times*:

> Yes, but you're here,
> With us.
> He's there,
> Alone,

Lurching up and down the terrace,
Waiting for a speedboat,
Waiting for a speedboat to spill out beautiful
    people,
At least.

This is not the only structure of verse in which this speech may be expressed, and the actor will already be exercising choices of delivery by whatever form he or she chooses. This exercise may be done with all of Pinter's long narratives, and it gives the actor a strong sense of the rhythmical structure of Pinter's putative prose.

Prose Verse II.   Players hold conversations entirely in rhyming slang. This is a classic British lower-class London form of speech. Although Pinter doesn't use it specifically in his work, the quick, lilting rhythms and sharp verbal imagination are a feature of his language. An example of this form would be: "My plates [plates of meat = feet] are killing me, so I am going round the Johnny Horner [corner], up the apples and pears [stairs], to kip [sleep] with my trouble and strife [wife]." Players can have a lot of amusement making up their own slang, which will break them out of prosaic use of language and accustom them to the cadences of Pinter's speech.

Taking the Piss I.   Any number of players can take part in this exercise. Choose one of the group as the person to be set up. The other members of the group start an apparently innocent conversation in which some vulnerability of the victim (we use this word for want of a better term, for "victim" is too harsh for the joshing nature of the game) is established, and the group bandies it about, playing on the vanity of the victim, building him up until they decide it is time to prick the balloon.

Taking the Piss II.   Two players choose an activity they are jointly involved in: discussing boyfriends or girlfriends; making a meal; discussing their success in some sporting activity.

While the discussion takes place the players find ways of insulting each other with the greatest good nature. The worse the insult the more charming it is. Neither player gives any sign that an insult has been received.

Taking the Piss III.   The situation is similar to the above game. Now the players are each armed with a rolled-up newspaper or some soft, harmless kind of weapon. This time when they are verbally insulting they should be as physically kind as possible, stroking, smiling, etc.; but by contradiction, they should now also be verbally very complimentary and pleasant, while beating up on their partner with the weapon. Again, both players treat this as perfectly normal.

Focus I.   Players perform any small activity: lighting a cigarette, drinking a cup of coffee, putting on a pair of shoes. Each necessary movement in the activity is separately focused and the beat counted. For example, the coffee: put out hand 1, take handle in finger and thumb 2, take cup to mouth 3, tilt cup 4, drink 5 6 7, take cup from mouth 8, replace cup on saucer 9, release cup 10, return hand 11. The exercise achieves the removal of extraneous business, and places a strong focus on the prop and on clarity of gesture.

Focus II.   Set up a small domestic environment: chairs, tables, books, ornaments, etc. One player sits on a chair. The player is now given a series of moves:

"Look at your foot." This must be a particular point on the foot.
    Wait a beat.
    "Look at the table." Again, a particular point of focus.
    Wait a beat.
    "Look at the book."
    A beat.

And so the exercise continues. Physical moves can be included, as long as they have a particular focus. The rhythms can be altered by taking more beats between moves. An object can be given significance by the changes in pace and rhythm: "Take three beats to look at the table; take two beats to move to the table; take three beats to pick up the book." This will invest the book with significance.

Many permutations on this theme can be played. It is an exercise in clarity and precision, and it shows how patterns of actions can communicate without necessarily understanding character.

Focus III.   The above situation is extended to include two actors who make their own choices of moves within the context of a situation known to them. The situation should contain an emotional threat to one of the characters. The actors are not to reveal their emotion in any way except through the props they use, or by minor movements of their bodies such as leg crossings, hand claspings, etc.

Territory I.   Set up a simple domestic environment with chairs, tables, props, etc. Now establish areas of territory for two players; it could be a particular chair, or the cocktail cabinet. The object of the game is for each player to try to take over the other player's territory. Players must preserve their own territory while maneuvering the other player out. This must not be done obviously, and certainly not by physical force. Players must discover what tactics are necessary to achieve their aim. A simple exchange of territory doesn't satisfy the object of the game: One player must finally maneuver the other player out of command of territory, while still preserving his or her own territory.

Territory II.   Create a domestic environment, including a sofa or love seat, and two players, one male one female. The object is to take over the other player's territory, which, in this instance, is the body of the player. Again, do not use physical force; no touching of any

kind. A casual conversation takes place while the players employ sexual tactics to seduce the other without being taken over themselves. Body moves of a non-overt kind, that is, the crossing of legs, not the grinding of the pelvis; the use of props and the use of space, distance, and closeness are the tactics the players should explore. There should be no direct sexual invitation by body or look.

Autobiography.   In turn, players relate a story about themselves to the group. Parts of the story will be true, factual; parts will be made up, false. The group must try to identify which parts are which. The aim is to confuse the group. The exercise also gives players a sense of the fine line between truth and falsehood and how the untrue can blend into the truth the more one repeats it and comes to believe in it.

In the Manner Of.   Form into two groups of players. One group gives a situation to the other group: coffee shop, doctor's office, etc. This group sets up the situation and plays out a small scene with a particular adverbial quality as guide to movement; for example, carefully, warily, precisely, comfortably, uncertainly. The other group should be able to determine the nature of the adverb. If not, the players must replay the scene and make adjustments. This can be played with each player having his or her own adverb, and the same test is applied. This is not an exercise in playing a quality; it is an exercise in the precise playing of choices and framing the work in a particular manner.

PLAYING THE STYLE

If, as the review we quoted at the beginning of this chapter suggests, "Characters are unable to explain their actions, thoughts or feelings," how, for example, would an actor go about playing the part of Davies in *The Caretaker*? Even if the surface information contained in the text cannot be taken at face value, it is still the actor's only guide, and the clues must be discovered by careful reading. In fact, as the content information of the language is less reliable, the actor must have a stronger sense of the rhythms and structure of the language as a whole in which the tactics and strategies of the character are contained.

What information on Davies does the actor have? Davies calls himself an old man; although this is part of a strategy to gain sympathy, there is every indication that he is somewhere between fifty and sixty years old. He still retains some vigor, but is nonetheless a shapeless, shambling, down-at-the-heels individual.

He has no fixed abode and is of uncertain identity. He gives himself a variety of names—Jenkins, Davies, MacDavies. This latter name is both a joke on Pinter's part and a deliberate obfuscation, as Davies would indicate Welsh background, while Mac is a Scottish prefix. He also cannot "remember" where he was born or when. He wants to avoid being pinned down. He claims he left his identity papers with a "man" at Sidcup many years ago, but constantly finds reasons for being unable to go back for them. This again is a tactic. It both gives him a potential focus for action, and a reason for not being able to be a part of society with the responsibilities that entails. It also suggests that there may be something he doesn't want known about his past. He is in general suspicious and fearful of the outside world: A bell may ring, there may be a knock on a door, someone might ask him for his papers and he would be "finished." This has the resonances of Pinter's concern, mentioned at the beginning of the chapter, with the unspecified menace of the modern world where, as in Kafka's *The Trial,* a knock may come at four in the morning and one can be taken away, tried, and executed for a crime of which one has no knowledge.

Davies has a pathetic pride and a faded vanity. He asserts that he has known "better days," he has had "dinner with the best," and "keeps himself up." The latter assertion is in comic contrast to the way he looks, but whether indeed he has known better days is irrelevant; the point is, he asserts that he has, and this leads him to reject good shirts because they are checked not striped, and to accept a totally useless and incongruous smoking jacket. He also is choosy about gifts of shoes, although he claims they are "life and death" to him. He affects a superiority to blacks, and he was fired from a job because he believed taking out the garbage was beneath him: the classic need of someone at the bottom of the heap to have someone lower to look down upon.

His main belongings are a knife, a pipe, and a pair of shoes.

His general motivation is to survive on his own terms, which include protecting his meager territory of self, keeping his options open, and giving nothing away. Specifically his motivation in the action of the play is to take the best advantage of the situation he has fallen into.

His obstacles are his lack of power, his lack of flexibility, his lack of judgment, his vanity, and his lack of self-knowledge. Specifically in the action of the play, Mick is his main obstacle, for Mick lacks his brother's charity, sees Davies for what he is, and wants to protect his—Mick's—territory from him.

Little of the above is based upon any extensive biographical or psychological detail, but it is information derived from the play's structure, from the tactics Davies employs to gain his objective. These tactics are to ingratiate himself with the sources of power; to sniff out the best advantage; to find and play off weaknesses; to establish and protect territory; to manipulate all circumstances including his own according to the perceived need of the moment.

How does this rag-bag of half truths, wishes, fears, manipulations, tactics, and pattern of responses translate into a concrete mask of character? Davies is an underdog. And dog becomes a useful physical image for the actor. He is a stray; he is a mongrel of uncertain pedigree; he fawns and cringes, snarls when cornered, and snaps at the hand that feeds him. He has a keen nose for his best advantage—sniffs it out. Nose and head, in which he is calculating his tactics, are probably strong centers of energy for Davies. The other major center of energy is probably his feet. Feet are important to a stray who has to keep moving, while also looking for a place to lie down. Davies has great concern for his feet and shoes. Use of the *Centers I* and *Centers II* exercises on pages 194–195 would be a good starting point for the actor to explore the head and feet energy of Davies. Our sense is that the actor would discover sharp jabbing or thrusting energy with the head—sniffing out, snapping, looking for the best advantage—while the feet will be more plodding, a somewhat sustained and yielding energy that has no real focus.

This would be consistent with the two major possessions that Davies has: a knife and a pipe. A knife is sharp and jabbing, aggressive and self-protective at the same time, and is a useful image for an aspect of Davies' personality. The pipe is more sedentary, a symbol of time passing, unfocused, and slower, as must be the larger part of Davies' existence passed as it is in the empty, purposeless spaces of the social outcast.

If the actor were to take the knife as a clasp knife (or switchblade)—a knife whose blade is contained within its body (handle) and opens through 180 degrees—it could be an image for a *Psychological Gesture* exercise, in which Davies' rhythms of cringing and asserting were explored: the cringing being a concealed and self-protective, closed gesture—the blade within the knife; the assertion a strong, open thrusting gesture as the knife flicks open and the blade is revealed.

Not surprisingly, given the careful consistency with which Pinter constructs his work, if we turn to Davies' speech rhythms, we find a similar pattern of sharp assertiveness, and unfocused, meandering, and rambling narratives. All three of the *Verbal Punctuation* exercises set out above would be useful for work on Davies. Applying the tennis or boxing match image to Davies' speeches would be especially useful in capturing the alternately attacking and concealing rhythms of his speeches.

The *Autobiography* exercise is also particularly applicable to Davies in discovering the blending and manipulation of truth and untruth, which is a basic function of his narratives.

If, for example, Davies were rehearsing the scene with Mick (act 2, pages 48 to 51 Harold Pinter, *The Caretaker,* London: Methuen, 1960.), *Territory I* and all of the *Taking the Piss* exercises would be a good starting point. *Taking the Piss III* would be especially useful for his relationship, because Mick is potentially physically threatening to Davies as, at their first encounter, Mick actually subdued him with physical force, and after that Davies is always aware of that possibility.

All of the exercises we have set out will be applicable to some degree—and at the actor's and director's discretion—to the creation of a highly concrete and playable mask of character for Davies. The fact that one cannot approach Davies from a simply psychological and biographical point of view is no disadvantage to the actor once the tactics, pattern of strategies, verbal rhythms, and structures are understood to be the fabric of the character, and are integrated with the larger meaning that the playwright has woven into the work as a whole.[5]

---

[5]If confirmation of this point were needed, it comes from the playwright's own mouth in a story told by Peter Hall of a rehearsal for *Betrayal* in which the actor playing the publisher asked if he should go and spend some time in a publisher's office to understand the world of his character: "This baffled Harold; 'Its all in the play,' he said." *Peter Hall's Diaries,* edited by John Goodwin, (New York: Harper & Row, 1984), p. 375.

As a final gloss on this point, interpreted as a reflection of human existence, *The Caretaker* can be seen as either humankind's search for identity and purpose in a godless world, or as the fundamental human myth of the Fall from Grace, the casting out of Paradise, the condemnation to wander the world in search of a resting place that human nature in its restless contradictions cannot find. There are other interpretations: resonances for audiences that the playwright can evoke. And, while it is useful for an actor to be aware of this, the play, finally, is about three men in a room; and the actor's task is to take what the playwright has written and create, in the framework of the playwright's style, a consistent and believable character, by approaching the work in the manner that we have tried to suggest in this chapter.

SUGGESTED READINGS

Diamond, Elin, *Pinter's Comic Play.* London: Associated University Presses, 1985.

Esslin, Martin, *Pinter: A Study of His Plays.* London: Methuen, 1977.

Lahr, John (ed.), *A Casebook on Harold Pinter's The Homecoming.* New York: Grove Press, 1971.

Morrison, Kristin, *Canters and Chronicles.* Chicago: University of Chicago Press, 1983.

Thompson, David, *Pinter: The Player's Playwright.* Basingstoke: Macmillan, 1985.

10   **Mamet**

American Buffalo.   *The Goodman Theatre. Photo by Double 00, Inc.*

Just as the plays of Anton Chekhov convey the moral and social uncertainty of life in Russia at the end of the nineteenth Century, so David Mamet's plays offer us a picture of American life at the end of the twentieth century. While writing within the traditions of Realism, with its well-made play structure, his use of language, especially rhythm, his existential dislocation, and his socioeconomic concerns push the boundaries of the style and position him as an American writer allied in spirit with the post-modern absurdists we are discussing in this section.

As we shall see in this brief section, Mamet's work has been greatly influenced by Harold Pinter. Both writers use language as the prime weapons in the hierarchial warfare waged by their characters. When Pinter's characters speak their language seems cognitive and deliberate, whereas Mamet's characters' are more primitive and instinctual. Pinter, writing in the English tradition, uses the rich verbal heritage of the music hall and the comedy of manners to examine questions of existential identity. Mamet, writing in the American tradition, uses the kinetic energy of the streets as he explores issues of cultural and moral integrity. Mamet's salesmen are, in spirit, the direct descendants of America's most famous saleman, Willy Loman, but they think and speak in a distinctly modern, late twentieth century voice, one which bears special scrutiny.

BACKGROUND

Born in 1947 the grandson of Russian-Jewish immigrants and raised in Chicago during the post World War II economic boom, David Mamet has described his early years as a period of rootlessness and isolation: "My father grew up poor but subsequently made a good living. My life was expunged of any tradition at all. The virtues expounded were not creative but remedial; let's stop being Jewish, let's stop being poor."[1] This drive for assimilation and eco-

nomic success at any price was to profoundly influence his vision of American culture—a culture ruled by the whims of the mass media, the dictates of Madison Avenue, and the rampant materialism of the Reagan era.

His early plays were influenced by the "blackout" style of the work he saw at Chicago's famed theatre, Second City Improvisation. He spent at least 10 years, from 1974 to 1984, writing plays in a similar style: multiple short scenes, each no longer than eight minutes, each scene with a punchline at its end. "There's got to be a good payoff since there is no time for narration, only time left for drama," he has said.

His first commercial success as a writer, *Sexual Perversity in Chicago*, premiered in Chicago in 1975, followed that same year by the debut at the Goodman Theatre of *American Buffalo. A Life in the Theatre* and *Edmond* followed in the late 1970s. By the early 1980s, Mamet had begun to write screenplays; the experience profoundly influenced his writing style.

In a play . . . the only way you have to convey the action of the plot is through the action of the characters, what they say to each other. With a movie, the action has to be advanced narratively . . . showing the audience what's happening, narrating to them the state of mind of the protagonist which is the worst kind of playwriting. You . . . are taking out the elements of feeling and sensitivity, so you're relying absolutely on the structure of the script.[2]

Glengarry Glen Ross, a viscous, violent, and dark satire about scheming, avaricious real estate salesmen who stop at nothing to make a sale, was based in part on Mamet's own experiences working in a Chicago real estate office. Unsure of the play's merits, especially its structure, with its episodic first act and a narratively conventional second act, he sent the play to Harold Pinter for comment. Pinter replied that the only thing wrong with the play was that

---

[1] Program note for *Glengarry Glen Ross*.

[2] Vallely. "David Mamet Makes A Play for Hollywood." *Rolling Stone*, 3 April 1980. p. 46.

it was not in production. *Glengarry Glen Ross* opened in London in 1983 and in New York in 1984, where it won the Pulitzer Prize for Drama. Recent plays include *Speed the Plow* (1988), *Oleanna* (1992) and *The Cryptogram* (1995).

Increasingly, Mamet has turned his attention to filmmaking, with, among others, *The Verdict* (Academy Award nomination, screenplay, 1984), *The Untouchables* (screenplay, 1987), *House of Games* (writer/director, 1987), *Wag the Dog* (Academy Award nomination, screenplay, 1997), and *The Spanish Prisoner* (writer/director, 1998). He teaches acting, and as an acting theoretician has written one book, *True and False,* which has provoked enormous controversy with its dismissal of academic theater training and its refutation of the Strasberg approach to "The Method." *A Practical Handbook for the Actor,* a compilation of his teachings, has been published by members of The Atlantic Theater Company, a New York acting company Mamet was instrumental in founding.

Sensibility and Premises. Mamet writes savage satires in which materialism is valued over friendship, intimate communication is almost impossible, and language is seemingly reduced to its lowest, and often most violent, common denominator. He alleges that there are no longer moral laws, only a system of rewards and punishments. He focuses on characters who exist within their own closed societies; in the tradition of Realism, he wants us to examine the nature of society; unlike Brecht, he does not incite us to revolution but rather to discussion and debate. His language is of the theatre; it is distilled, fiercely poetic in rhythm and linguistic structure, yet cloaked within the patina of everyday life—similar in form to Pinter, but with an uniquely American spin. The cumulative experience of a Mamet play is of being bombarded with a barrage of sounds and silences.

Mamet's salesmen, actors, academics, and producers seem suspended between action and inaction—they are either depressed or hyperactive, often incoherent, usually profane. They are living in a Godless universe, without fixed structure or a concrete morality. Everything is relative, and with that relativity comes uncertainty, confusion, isolation, and despair. Note the influence of Beckett and the tradition of the absurdists. But rather than inertia, in Mamet ambition, naked or disguised, is one antidote for the terror of confronting the void. Mamet's character's feel obligated to better their lives but they can't, won't, or don't know how.

In one guise or another, all Mamet's men are salesmen. Their world is about status, position, and power. To admit the possibility of failure is to admit the possibility of death. It is rejected at every turn. There is little or no place for spirituality in this world. When it is present, usually in the form of a woman, it is seen as attractive and alluring but something that must be subjugated and conquered because it is too threatening.

In Mamet's world action exists solely in the present; there is no acknowledged future or readily identifiable past. Now—with all its possibilities—is the only time that matters. Mamet's characters are often incapable of direct communication; they substitute profanity for profundity, violence for vision. Physical, emotional, and verbal violence is the only way characters can express their frustration and rage. The potential for violence is always present, just beneath the surface; it erupts in the most casual, unpremeditated manner. Mamet cites the truthfulness of his character's desperation as the reason his plays cause such violent reactions: "No one can be forced to sit through an hour and a half of meaningless dialogue—they're (the audience) angry because the play was about them."[3]

Mamet's voice is distinctly American. He writes plays filled with the relentless rhythms

[3]Gottlieb, Richard. " 'The Engine' that Drives Playwright David Mamet." *The New York Times.* 15 January 1978. p. D4.

and kinetic energy of big cities. He sees himself in the role of social critic. Business, in Mamet's world, is a metaphor for the corruption of the American spirit—success at any price, friendship and human values be damned. Spiritual redemption and higher purpose are destroyed in the relentless pursuit of money and power.

INTRINSIC DEMANDS

Structure. Mamet has likened a play's structure to that of a joke. In the joke, he says, narrative detail is unimportant—everything is relegated to correctly structuring the joke for maximum impact. You need know only what you need to know to make the joke work. The teller compresses and condenses detail to drive inevitably towards the joke's climax; nothing else matters. The hearer fills in the missing details based on his own experience. This form of empathy sets the audience up for the full emotional impact of the "punchline."

Sexual Perversity in Chicago, Life In the Theater, Edmond, as well as the one acts and radio plays written in the early period are all constructed in his "blackout" style. Short scenes, sometimes only 4 to 8 lines long, are juxtaposed one against another, building the narrative in a linear, sequential fashion. These plays have the rhythm and feel of short stories; incident piles up against incident to create a fragmented yet unified vision. The drama seems to unfold on its own; it does not build in a great sweeping arc to a climax and resolution. Rather, it moves from incident to incident, creating an emerging picture of emotional isolation, so that the gulfs and valleys between the characters slowly reveal themselves.

In 1984 Mamet began writing in a condensed and compressed, narratively linear manner. "I finally had the will to write a second act. I wrote a million episodic plays. I can write them with my left hand. So what? Who

cares? Fortunately, I got sick of it before (the audience) did."[4]

The later plays all share a more conventional, well-made play sensibility: the inciting incident—usually a betrayal of trust—is identified early on and the conflicts are clearly defined and build towards an inevitable climax. Ironically, once the climax is reached, the action does not automatically resolve to leave the audience fulfilled; rather, the play hangs suspended, creating an unsettling, disturbing after-effect. Since Mamet wants to provoke discussion and debate, these unresolved endings seem entirely appropriate.

While building on his early themes, the later plays expand into a deeper examination of the complexities of the American social system and its effect on character. *Glengarry Glen Ross* is a diatribe against the American way of business with its success-driven ethic and the complete lack of compassion and understanding for the human condition. The salesmen in *Glengarry* live only to sell; they have lost touch with their own compassion, their own sense of humanity. This theme is expanded and developed in *Speed the Plow* and *Oleanna*. While individual characters search for spiritual meaning in their lives, their self identity is at the mercy of their social function. They are who they know how to be, nothing more, nothing less.

There is always a strict division between the sexes in Mamet's world. Men exist in the marketplace and play by the rules of the jungle. They have no private lives. In Mamet's world, the male culture is competitive, ruthless, and ruled by the social expectations of manhood. A man lives by an external, culturally condoned image of what one should be or wants to be, but rarely what one is; that is, Mamet men want to be the perfect lover, the successful businessman, the paternalistic and beloved professor, and the "killer producer."

[4]Allen, Jennifer. "David Mamet's Hard Sell." *New York.* 9 April 1984. p. 41.

These men are disconnected and estranged from their softer, vulnerable sides. They have great scorn and contempt for women—just as they have great scorn and contempt for anything which makes them vulnerable, flawed, or exposed.

Mamet's women carry within them a sense of hope, of compassion, and of emotionality. They tend to be more mysterious and enigmatic. Increasingly, as Mamet's theatrical career has progressed, his women have started to enter the marketplace. But equality never exists in a Mamet play, and the women are either outwitted or overpowered.

Unlike Ibsen's famous onion in *Peer Gynt*, the character's do not reveal themselves, layer by layer, until their core is exposed at play's end. Rather, the mystery of motive and unstated intent—Mamet's use of deliberate ambiguity, subjugating all to the play's action and allowing the audience to decide for itself the play's meaning—creates the raw ambiance that infiltrates a Mamet play in production. Physically, due to the text's strong rhythms, each play's impact is immediate and visceral; but long after, intellectually, one has to decipher and decode a Mamet work to get at its meaning. There are no tidy endings in Mamet's world, just unresolved and unsettling action.

Time and Space.   Mamet's spaces are pressure cookers. And in keeping with Mamet's aesthetic philosophy, his stage directions are deliberately spare and to the point. His scenic descriptions read "Don's Resale Shop," "Gould's Office," "John's Office." Mamet provides only what is needed to set the action in motion, nothing more, nothing less. The exact nature of the environment is deliberately ambiguous, left to the imagination of the reader.

In Mamet, the physical world is either spare and fragmented—raw, unformed, awaiting definition, as the characters are in their lives—or filled with the detritus and waste of

Spare, but disheveled office in *Glengarry Glen Ross*. *The Goodman Theatre. Photo by Brigette Lacombe.*

society, a chaotic jumble of discarded artifacts of former times, former lives, and former systems of order and control now deemed useless.

Mamet's rooms are barriers: they keep out the outside world, with its concerns and possibilities, and keep in the status quo. In Mamet, the outside world is always dangerous:

1. In *Oleanna*, the telephone is a constant reminder that John has a life outside his work yet he seems incapable of leaving his office.
2. In *Glengarry Glen Ross*, the windows of the ransacked real estate office are boarded up, making it almost impossible to see out or in.
3. In *Speed the Plow* Karen, the office temp and lone Hollywood "outsider" challenges all of Charlie Fox's beliefs by her mere presence.

As noted above, the early plays are fragmentary and written in a deliberately *cinematic* style. The focus is on creating a theatrical reality between two characters with as little scenically as possible. Action and activity define locale. There are 33 scenes in *Sexual Perversity in Chicago*, each set in "various spots around the North Side of Chicago, a Big City on a

Lake." The play relies on light, sound, and a minimum of objects to create location; the actors must supply the rest. Similarly, in *Life in the Theater,* the action shifts continually from the backstage dressing room to various scenes on stage in performance. These scenes don't require full environments; the space must help create a feeling of confinement which the two actors relish at first, and which becomes more and more of a prison as the play proceeds. The audience, used to film and television, willingly accepts the convention of shifting and changing location; the actor's task is to provide the emotional narrative that propels the story forward from scene to scene.

Fragmentation also creates rhythm with its blackouts and pauses in the action. Mamet has said, in his stage directions to *Duck Variations:* "intervals (space) between the scenes is analogous to the space between movements in musical presentations." Thus, space between the scenes is used as a deliberate device to heighten theatrical effect; its serves as a counterpart to the rhythms within the scenes, creating a cooling off/cooling down period between the action, allowing the audience to reflect on what they've just seen, and the actors to change costumes. In the later plays, Mamet does the opposite; he compresses the action so that there's no time to think or reflect; the stage action is a relentless barrage of language and imagery, pounding away until the full portrait of the waste and despair in the character's lives has been created.

Language/Rhythm.   Mamet characters love to talk and to impress one another with their ability to talk. Every Mamet character is selling something, and as "salesmen," their job is to create a need for whatever it is they have to sell, be it self-image or property. The quintessential Mamet character is a hustler—and as such, he uses all of the tactics of a hustler to gain dominance and control of his "mark." He will praise, belittle, cajole, harangue, twist

words, and deliberately misinterpret in order to control his listener's attention and make his "sell."

When a Mamet character doesn't talk the silence is intentional—omission and evasion are used as tactics of power and create the necessary rests in rhythm for characters to refuel before speaking. These tactics are rarely planned or intellectual; rather, they are instinctual tools used in times of desperation and under great pressure. They exist below the spoken surface of the text and manifest as displays of dominance and claims of emotional territory.

As we mentioned earlier, all Mamet characters live inside pressure cookers. They have a great deal to say, but often they can't say it. Their sense of frustration and impotence only makes them try harder. Characters search for words, for a way to express themselves. They may not have the skill, but they never give up. Here's Charlie Fox in *Speed The Plow* contemplating his future:

> Fox. Okay. The one, the one, the one thing, I was up all night; I'm sorry, I should be better at these things, I don't know how to say it, you know how you do? You stand and think, you think, and, the only thing, one hand you say: "Am I worthy to be rich?" The other hand, you, you know, you feel *greedy;* so, it's hard to know what's rightfully yours . . . Bob: when we said, when we said: *yesterday:* we were talking, when you said "producer;" what we *meant,* what we were talking about was, I understand it, that we were to "share" above-the-title, we would co-produce, because . . . that's right, isn't it? And the other thing; I'm sure you thought of this; to *say* to Ross, to, that we, as a team, you and I, this is only the *beginning,* for, if we brought *this* (I'm sure you thought of this) it's fairly limitless, we can bring more . . . those two things, only, are what I wanted to say to you.[5]

[5]Mamet, David. *Speed The Plow.* New York: Samuel French, Inc. 1985. p. 56.

Glengarry Glen Ross.   The Goodman Theatre. Photo by Brigette Lacombe.

Charlie quite literally hammers away at Bobby Gould. Here, as elsewhere in Mamet, rhythm and character are one. Fox is smart, quick to react, adept in his gamesmanship, overextended, and exhausted yet energized. He can't stop talking. His mind is in overdrive; he can't speak fast enough to complete one thought before he's on to the next, so he continually interrupts himself—another favorite Mamet device.

Fox begins by apologizing for himself— he lowers and debases himself in deference to Gould ("I'm sorry, I should be better at these things"); then he aligns himself in a position of equality (the continued use of "We"); then he tacitly compliments and elevates Gould ("I'm sure you thought of this") and realigns himself ("we, as a team, you and I") until he assumes he's made his point with clarity and precision. At the same time he's oblique in his manipulation, self-serving in his objective, relentless in its pursuit.

Mamet characters speak in one of two contradictory styles: either in short, punchy sentences or in long, pulsing aria's. The short jabs—rapid thoughts which elicit quick responses—create a pulsing, stichomythic rhythm; the characters quite literally try to beat each other into submission. The long aria, in which a character, overripe with feeling, spins out of control, is never lyric; rather, it's a

character's attempt to release internal pressure, a ploy to regain the high ground of dominance and control by impressing the hearer.

Here's Carol in *Oleanna* explaining herself to John, her professor:

> Now. The thing which you find so cruel is the selfsame process of selection I, and my group go through *every day of our lives.* In admittance to school. In our tests, in our class rankings . . . Is it unfair? I can't tell you. But, it is fair. Or even if it is "unfortunately not necessary" for us, then, by God, so must it be for you. (*Pause*) You write of your "responsibility to the young." Treat us with respect, and that will *show* you your responsibility. You write that education is just hazing. (*Pause.*) But we worked to get to this school (*Pause*) And some of us. (*Pause.*) Overcame prejudices. Economic, sexual, you cannot begin to imagine. And endured humiliations I *pray* that you and those you love never will encounter. (*Pause*) To gain admittance here. To pursue the same dream of security *you* pursue. We, who, who are, at any moment, in danger of being deprived of it. By . . .
> John: . . . by . . .
> Carol: By the administration. By the teachers. By you. By, say, one low grade, that keeps us out of graduate school; by one, say, one capricious or inventive answer on your parts, which, perhaps, you don't find amusing. Now you know, do you see? What it is to be subject to that power. (*Pause.*)
> John: I don't understand. (*Pause.*)[6]

Carol, who has always been powerless and, as a result, near mute for most of the play, speaks in full voice for the first time. She is direct and forceful. She speaks with uninterrupted thought; there is clarity and precision in her language. She neither contradicts nor corrects herself. Her pauses are limited. Her intent may be to help John heal—to affect transformation through change of consciousness—or to assert herself and her own newfound sense

[6]Mamet, David. *Oleanna.* New York: Dramtist's Play Service. 1992. p. 44.

Oleanna.   Yale Repertory Theater. Photo by T. Charles Erickson.

of power; Mamet always leaves motive unspecified. There is also a sense of immediacy, of "nowness" to the speech: she can't hold it in any longer; she must spew until she's said all there is to say.

Punctuation is, as in Pinter, crucial in defining rhythms. In Mamet, the parenthicals (used primarily in the early plays) work to intensify or deepen the thought; the comma, Mamet's most frequent means of punctuation, connects fragments of thought; the colon is a way of driving the action forward without break, rest or pause. The only specified rests in the texts are the deliberately marked pauses. Unlike Pinter, Mamet's pause does not create menace or threat; rather, it is a signal for regrouping and a change of direction in thought and action.

Mamet compresses and condenses language. The character's say only what is absolutely necessary. In creating a spare and economic writing style, Mamet deliberately writes elliptical language. The missing word is

implied and further compresses the thought within the line. Like Shakespearean verse, the thoughts are so full they do not need every word for sense and meaning; the overfull line, with its "felt" meaning, carries sufficient impact. The intent of the line is to sound natural, truthful to character—yet it is meticulously crafted to create the effect of spontaneity.

Profanity in a Mamet play is commonplace because words no longer have impact and meaning. It is also the one form of language that cuts across all social barriers; it becomes a shorthand between people. When used repetitively and mindlessly it has no true meaning—it merely creates rhythm, pattern, energy, and movement. Here's Teach in *American Buffalo:*

> Only—and I tell you this, Don. Only, and I'm not, I don't think, casting anything on anyone: from the mouth of a Southern bulldyke asshole ingrate of a vicious nowhere cunt can this trash come. (To Bob.) And I take nothing back, and I know you're close to them.[7]

Teach's anger, frustration, sense of betrayal, viciousness, and desire for revenge are conveyed with great economy, compression, and impact; he's relentless, scatological, infantile, and outrageous, all at the same time. Mamet's writing is consistently invigorated with propulsive speeches in which the characters spew and vent; if we are uncomfortable, then Mamet has succeeded.

PERFORMANCE DEMANDS

Let us restate once again that our intention in focusing on Mamet is to understand and appreciate the post-modern influences on Mamet and to use them to expand and enhance the basic principles of the naturalistic acting style, to define those qualities which

[7]Mamet, David. *American Buffalo.* New York: Samuel French, Inc. 1975. p. 11.

make Mamet's writing unique, and to suggest strategies for realizing them onstage.

Unlike Tennessee Williams or Anton Chekhov, in the Realistic tradition, Mamet is not necessarily concerned with psychological portraiture; rather, like Brecht, his concern is with the social system which creates the psychology rather than the psychology itself. He leaves any discussion of psychological motivation to the audience to decipher. As we have said earlier, Mamet is ambiguous by design. This does not mean that the actor may be ambiguous in approaching the text. Just the opposite—the actor must be extraordinarily clever in ferreting out all the clues buried in the text, expand upon them imaginatively to create actable given circumstances, and then use those givens to qualify and condition the playing of action.

At the same time the actor must edit anything which does not convey information to move the narrative forward, a variation of the Brechtian *gestus* we will be discussing in the Brecht chapter. The actor's first and primary responsibility in Mamet is to tell the story without commentary, editorializing, or making moral judgments of the characters. Mamet wants the characters to stand and speak for themselves. Let the audience judge their relative merits.

Status.   All Mamet plays deal with power and issues of control. For the actor, a thorough understanding of *status*—the moment to moment positioning of one character in relationship with another—is crucial in uncovering the structure of a Mamet scene.[8] Although we have previously discussed status in the context of farce, we wish to return to it now as a tool in defining dramatic action.

Status works on the seesaw principle: when I raise you I automatically lower myself, and conversely, when I lower you I automatically raise myself. We raise and lower through compliments and insults, open or disguised. A "gap"—the psychological, social, and emotional space between characters—exists in every relationship. In a master/servant relationship, the gap is at its widest; due to the extreme nature of the polarities in the relationship, we refer to it as a *master gap*. When characters are closer to one another on the social scale, i.e, intimate friends, colleagues, etc, we refer to the space between them as a *mini gap*. In the course of any transaction, the gap between the characters widens or narrows according to the dictates of the text.

Hierarchies, with their upward and downward mobility, are socialized pecking orders; at any given moment everyone has a defined place in his or her social order. The position may change from group to group, or within the group—that is the nature of the status transaction. The individual adjusts to each new situation, raising or lowering status accordingly. In highly stratified cultures, the pecking order is clear from birth; you are born into your station and most likely remain there for the rest of your life. In highly mobile cultures, the pecking order is uncertain and leads to enormous possibility. Rising and falling depend entirely on gamesmanship, ambition and daring.

As actors we are interested in the character's status, not our own. We acknowledge our own status preferences—we are all experts when it comes to our own status—but we set aside our preferences to embrace the character's position in his or her hierarchy. Once this has been done the actor is free to surrender to the demands of the text.

Movement.   The pressure cooker nature of Mamet's scenes—tight spaces and strict time limits—creates a need for playing with speed

---

[8]For a further and more complete discussion of the process of playing status, we recommend Keith Johnstone's *Impro.* New York: Theatre Arts Books, 1979.

The Cryptogram.   Yale Repertory Theater. Photo by T. Charles Erickson.

and mental dexterity. Mamet's characters quite literally think on their feet. The actor must not only have the technical facility to handle the demands of the text but the mental agility to shift tactics in a heartbeat.

Because the verbal style is spare, compressed, and condensed, the actor's task in Mamet is to create an analogous physical reality, one which keeps the focus on the word and not on extraneous physical movement. While individual movement must have the appearance of spontaneity it needs to be carefully organized and choreographed around a psychological "spine" from which all action—the verbal as well as the physical—springs. The dissemination of information about character is crucial in creating the Mamet mask.

Since Mamet's characters are warriors they carry their history on their backs. They are beleaguered and hassled men who resist the pressure they feel from the outside world. They respond intuitively to one another rather than with preplanned deliberation. In analyzing Mamet's characters as intuitors

rather than thinkers, we are referring to a system of character typology defined by Carl Jung, the noted Swiss psychologist, who categorized personality into basic types:[9]

- The introvert, who is quite often perceived as impenetrable, taciturn, or shy, more at home in the world of ideas than in the world of people and things. Introverts bottle up emotions and guard themselves carefully as high explosives.
- The extrovert, who is perceived as a doer. Extroverts are seen as expansive and less impassioned; they unload their feelings and go on.

Introversion and Extroversion are two generic categories which can be further broken down into four subcategories, or types:

- The *sensing* type, who faces life observantly, craving enjoyment. Sensors are imitative, wanting to have what other people have and do what other people do; they are dependent on their physical surroundings.
- The *intuiting* type, who faces life expectantly, craving inspiration. Intuitors are inventive and original, indifferent to what other people have and do, and independent of their physical surroundings.
- The *thinking* type, who values logic above sentiment. Thinkers are usually stronger in executive ability than in the social arts, and suppress, undervalue and ignore feelings which are incompatible with the thinking judgments.
- The *feeling* type, who values sentiment above logic. Feelers are usually stronger in the social arts than in executive ability, and suppress, undervalue and ignore thinking that is offensive to the feeling judgments.

---

[9]For an in depth discussion on Jung's typology see: Storr, Anthony. *The Essential Jung.* Princeton, NJ: Princeton University Press, 1983.

For Jung, these four functions—thinking and feeling (which he termed "the rational pair") and sensing and intuiting ("the irrational pair") operate interactively. There is a primary, conscious preference on the part of the individual, which dominates behavior, and a secondary preference, which is subconscious and exists in opposition to the primary core. Thus there is an inner core and an outer core; the two exist simultaneously, one being the cover for the other.

Rudolf Laban, the Austrian movement educator and philosopher and a contemporary of Jung's, took Jung's discoveries one step further, finding correlation's between the different personality type's and their effort preferences (for an earlier discussion of Laban's work, see Tempo-Rhythms, pp. 195–196):

> *Sensors,* Laban suggested, are concerned with impact and intention. Sensors ask: What is my impact?—their dominant effort quality is *weight.*
> *Intuitors* are concerned with making decisions. When? they ask; their dominant effort quality is *time.*
> *Thinkers* are concerned with attention and direction of thought. Where? they ask; their dominant effort quality is *space.*
> *Feelers* are concerned with adapting: How do I keep going? they ask; their dominant effort quality is *flow.*

For the actor approaching Mamet, familiarity with Jung and Laban's approach to effort/shape and character typology leads to the creation of a new type of character mask, one which is dependent on the effort factors as an organizing principle and which ties in directly to the psychological patterns as described by the text. We do not mean to suggest that this is an exact or formulaic science; rather, it is one more way of taking information presented by the playwright and translating it into a practicable methodology to be used in rehearsal for exploration and discovery.

Language.   Although Mamet writes in an highly edited manner, the principles of operative speech still apply. In operative speech, the speaker guides the listener's ear through the text by stressing only those words that carry information and meaning, mainly verbs and nouns, along with their qualifying adjectives and adverbs. Avoid stressing verbs of being (is, was, are) and conjunctions (and, but, or); stress pronouns only in comparisons, and never stress negatives. As in all texts, drive through to the end of the thought, which means the second half of the line is more significant than the first. Pitch, intonation, and slight pause become key strategies in giving the text verbal life and color.

EXERCISES, GAMES, TECHNIQUES

The following exercises and games are meant to supplement the naturalistic acting process and to adapt principles and techniques discussed in previous chapters to the demands of the Mamet rhythm and style. They work best when focusing directly on preparing a Mamet text for study or production, although the principles involved are applicable for any play dealing with high language, be it classical or contemporary.

Language.   These first games are useful in discovering the basic principles of compressed, heightened, direct and indirect speech. They can be played with partners or with groups. They serve as good warm-up games.

Tell a Story #1.   This is a variation of Telegram, found in playing Shakespeare. Two players stand facing one another. Both tell the other an anecdote; both talk simultaneously. Players focus on making their partner listen and respond to the story as they are telling it. Tell the story in 90 seconds.

Tell a Story #2.   Repeat. Tell the story in 60 seconds.

Tell a Story #3.   Tell the story in 30 seconds.

Tell a Story #4.   Tell the story in 10 seconds

   Variation: One player tells a story in "telegram" manner to the entire group. The story must be told in 30 seconds. Players then retell the story simultaneously to the original teller, filling in the missing detail, elaborating and adding color without altering the basic spine of the anecdote.

Treasure Hunt.   Two players improvise a short scene, no longer than 3 minutes. Each has a clear-cut objective in mind, a task which they want their partner to perform for them, i.e., get me a cup of coffee, fill the car with gas, do the laundry, etc. Players never speak directly of the task; they may only drop hints and plant clues. Body language may help. The game is over when one player makes the other respond.

I Have A Secret.   This is a variation of Treasure Hunt. Each player has secret information about the other player. Each player wants confirmation of the information and tries to make the other player confess without revealing what he already knows.

Colorful Speech #1.   Two players decide on a where and a who. Each chooses a color to use as a substitute for profanity. Players play the scene and add as much color/profanity as possible. Players do not make a point of it; they make it part of their everyday speech and vocabulary.

   Variation: Score each scene for creative use of "profanity"; the most colorful scene wins.

Colorful Speech #2.   Repeat, using profanity. Play in exactly the same manner. Use the profanity in exactly the same way color was used.

   Variation: Tag Out: every time a player makes a point with the profanity, he is tagged out and replaced with another player. The objective is to make the profanity a part of every-

day speech and not draw attention to it nor throw it away.

Obstacle Course.   Players divide into two teams, A and B. Each player has a partner on the opposing team. Players stand facing their partner on opposite sides of the playing space. Players on Team A close their eyes; players on Team B fill the playing space with objects found in the room: chairs, books, shoes, bags, etc. The A's work with their eyes closed. The B's must verbally guide their partners through the maze until they are standing together. Everyone speaks simultaneously. Players may never refer to one another directly by name, but they may devise code names. If A touches another player or object, he/she must open their eyes, turn around and return to their starting position and begin again. Once all players have successfully crossed the room, reverse the playing; change the positions of the objects in space; B guides A through the maze. Play with a three-minute time limit. This is a wonderful game for discovering the need for precise, concise communication; words cannot be wasted if the players wish to win.

Verbal Mirroring.   This is a variation on a technique developed by Sanford Meisner. Two players play an interrogation scene between lawyer and client or cop and prisoner. The questioner verbally mirrors the last few words of his partner, building the facts of the case. Word mirror the rhythms and cadence of the interviewee to probe for information and detail. Reply upon and use inflection and implication. The interrogator wants to get all the facts but only has a short amount of time to do so.

Use the following exercises to create verbal energy and rhythm.

Changing Tenses.   One player begins a story with "An amazing thing has just happened ..." He tells the story to impress the other players with his good fortune. Each player begins the story in the past; whenever he adds detail and color, he switches to the present. The player continues to switch tenses throughout the entire story. Repeat until everyone in the group has told a story.

Variation: Score the stories for creativity and clarity of narrative even though the tenses move from past to present.

Add a Thought.   Each player is an expert who has just made an important discovery which will change the course of civilization. Each player must tell the others about the discovery. Players continually interrupt themselves with new realizations about the positive effects of their discovery.

Stomp #1.   Players work with a long prose speech. They stomp out the rhythm of the speech as they talk, one beat for each syllable. Vary the intensity of the stomps so they have different weights, some stronger, some lighter, depending on the length of the vowels within each syllable. Players should focus on the forwardness of the rhythm—how it must drive through the end of the line until the thought is resolved.

Players repeat the speech, stomping it without verbalizing. Play the speech through to the end; focus on the phrasing patterns. Does the rhythm carry intent or does the pattern need to be adjusted?

Players repeat a third time, verbalizing as they stomp out the adjusted speech. Repeat one final time, eliminating the stomping. The speech must contain the percussive rhythms and patterns as if stomped.

Stomp #2.   Two players work together on a scene. They speak and stomp out the scene. They repeat the scene, without words, letting the stomps substitute for the spoken dialogue. They continue until the scene has rhythmic flow. Repeat with dialogue and stomping; repeat one last time without stomping.

The following exercises are best used when applied directly to a text.

No Motion.   Two players work on a scene. They exaggerate the body language within the scene, over-gesturing and overreacting, Anything is valid as long as the action of the scene keeps moving forward. They then repeat the scene with no motion, redirecting all of the physical energy into communicating verbally. Players are penalized any time they move, use their hands or shift their weight.

Add Air.   Two players work on a scene. Each adds a pause after every beat. Use the pause to make the transition to the next thought, then launch into the next beat. Players must deliberately slow down the thinking process and work through each speech from thought to thought. Players focus on discovering the structural skeleton of the scene by defining their patterns of thought. Its very important to coach for slow, deliberate, moment-to-moment progression. Players must work against the natural rhythms of the language to find the logic and connection between thoughts.

Go.   Players repeat the same scene. This time they lose the air they just added; they must keep the skeleton and structure of the scene intact but play without pauses. Every time there is a pause yell "Go" as a reminder to lose the air. If players get lost in the course of the scene they must struggle through as best they can. They keep repeating the exercise until they are thinking and speaking in the same tempo.

Players repeat the scene one more time reinstating the pauses as written. They must keep the forwardness in the playing of the pause and not let the scene collapse because they have stopped talking. They must use the pause as an opportunity to act without words.

Trigger Words.   Players work on a scene with a partner. They focus on listening for the trigger words which prompt their next thought. Whenever they hear a trigger word they must speak. If one player is cut off while speaking he must stop speaking and listen for his own trigger word. Players should try and play the game to get in all of their dialogue.

Verbal Tempo-Rhythms.   Players work through a scene using the tempo-rhythms as described in Chapter 6 Tempo-Rhythms I (p. 195). Players must verbally make each line either press, punch, flick, dab, slash, wring, float, or glide. They may vary the action from thought to thought, line to line, as the intent dictates. Players must adjust and adapt their tactics from line to line. Players should focus on the time and weight factors to find the different actions. This is an excellent way to begin to integrate the physical with the verbal to create a central "spine" for the character.

Rants.   Players sit in a circle. Each person in the group writes down a controversial topic on a slip of paper and puts the slip into a hat. First player up draws a slip and rants, non-stop, for 90 seconds, switching between pro and con on the topic. Next player up draws a new slip and rants on his or her topic. Continue, until every player has had an opportunity to rant.

Variation: Second player rants a rebuttal to Player 1, both pro and con. Third Player rebuts Player 2, etc. All rebuttals must be rants—fully impassioned, boldly committed non-stop diatribes.

Raves.   Each player has 90 seconds to tell the most fantastical story about him/herself to impress the rest of the group. The story can be true or fiction—the listener should not be able to tell the difference.

A/B.   This is a language substitution game, and a variation of a classic gibberish exercise. Two players play a scripted scene. They repeat the scene a second time substituting "A," "B," "AB," or "BA" for the dialogue. They play the scene a few times until they are comfortable with the language substitution. They repeat one last time, returning to the scripted dialogue. Players should use A/B to define and specify their thinking patterns in the course of the scene. The focus is on direct communication and triggering their partner's response.

Mask

Inner and Outer.   This exercise focuses on creating the physical mask of the character. Using the tempo-rhythms described earlier, players define the outer core of the mask: They find the time, weight, direction in space, and flow pattern of the character and play them as either a puncher, presser, flicker, dabber, slasher, wringer, floater, or glider. Add to the mask status bodies (see exercise described below), with special attention to eye focus: direct eye contact for high status, indirect, flicking eye contact for low status.

Once players have established the outer mask, they begin to work on the inner core by using opposing effort factors: If they used strong weight, they'll now use light weight, if quick time, sustained time, etc. They must use the opposite eye-focus pattern as well.

Now players walk and merge the two, the outer mask covering the inner. If the inner core is frightened and insecure, cover it with a puffed up, super-confident exterior. Players focus on maintaining the exterior and making others see them as they'd like to be seen. On a hand clap players drop the cover for a second, revealing the inner, then on a second hand clap, cover the inner and move on. There must always be the possibility that the inner mask will break through and destroy the outer cover.

Planes.   These are a series of exercises developed to integrate many related concepts of body shape and physical typology. Players move comfortably around the playing space. As they move they will focus on discovering the three spatial planes, the vertical, horizontal, and sagittal which, when combined, give the body shape and definition. As players move they focus on either extending or collapsing the spine (i.e. rising or sinking). They are now moving on a vertical plane. Next players shift their focus to widening or narrowing and dropping the center of focus into the pelvis to work on a horizontal plane. They shift their focus one more time to the opposition of shoulders and hips, either advancing or withdrawing in space (i.e., moving on the sagittal plane).

Players can now combine two of the three planes to create shape. First, by using a primarily vertical emphasis with a secondary horizontal, players create the *door* type: elongated spine, tendency for the rigid, primarily intellectual in nature. Second, by using a primarily horizontal emphasis with a secondary sagittal, players create the *table* type: pelvis centers, tendency for the instinctual and physical. Third, by using a primarily sagittal emphasis with a secondary vertical, players create the *wheel* type: strong torque in the torso, tendency for aggressive behavior and "go get'em" personality.

Shapes.   These are 4 more body types which may be used in creating the outer mask.

> *Rigid,* with its strong resistance to gravity
> *Burdened,* with the weight of the world piling up on the back or shoulders;
> *Needy,* with its collapsed chest and helpless spine;
> *Disproportionate Upper*—i.e., the expanded chest with its puffed up pride, or
> *Disproportionate Lower,* with its wide hips and tendency for earthiness and nurturing.[10]

Status Bodies.   These physical shapes are good reference points in defining the status mask:

[10]For a more complete discussion of these body types see Kurtz and Prestera, *The Body Reveals,* New York: Harper & Row, 1978.

High Status.   Everything moves away from the center of the body; the player tries to occupy a great deal of space. The spine is vertical, the neck and head are held still, the trunk moves as one solid shape. Eye focus is direct, weight is strong/firm.

Low Status.   Everything moves into the center of the body, collapsing and imploding; the player tries to occupy as little space as possible. Eye focus is indirect, flicking from the floor to eye level and then back down to the floor again.

Create an Image.   Players mix and match the body types to create the physical mask. Players use one of the Tempo-Rhythms to develop the outer core, coupled with the plane shapes—door, table, or wheel—and one of the shapes—rigid, burdened, needy, disproportionate upper or lower, as well as the status body. Extend the mask into its verbal patterns as well, so that the speech is in the same manner as the movement (i.e., as a high-status presser, puncher, etc.). Use the inner to inform the outer, and use the outer as a cover for the inner.

Right Side/Left Side.   In classic body language, the right side of the body is considered the "masculine," or aggressive side; the left the "feminine" or receptive side. Players work on a scene and physically lead with and favor their right side when talking to one another. Repeat, playing the scene leading with the left side, even if it feels "wrong."

Right/Left #2.   Players repeat the scene, this time consciously choosing which side of their partner they are going to play to—right or left. They may vary the side as the need demands, but must find a way to naturally shift from right to left side in the course of the action.

Status.   The following games will help supplement the status exercises described earlier in the chapter on farce.

Seesawing.   Two players begin a short scene. They compliment one another in the course of the scene as often as possible. Repeat, insulting one another as often as possible. Compliments raise, insults lower. Players may work broadly at first to get the feel of the game. Repeat the game, covering the insults and compliments until they are "backhanded" (i.e., present but barely perceptible). Coach to alternate raising and lowering from line to line, so that players can get the feel of jockeying for position with one another. The objective is to disarm and throw the other player off guard.

PLAYING THE STYLE

We are going to look briefly at the character of Carol in *Oleanna* to help us focus and apply the techniques described above to the world of Mamet.

Oleanna is a play about language and power. Or more simply put, a play in which language is power. Time and place are irrelevant and deliberately ambiguous, as is the subject of John's course. All focus is on the interaction between the two characters, John the instructor and Carol the student, and the socio/political/economic/cultural factors, which create behavior and influence perception between the two characters.

In Act 1 John is anticipating the announcement of his tenure at the University and is celebrating by buying a new house. The constantly ringing telephone is his only link to the outside world; otherwise he is in the cloistered, closeted environment of his office—an insulated, academic world without windows or contact with the "life." Carol, who appears to come from a background of economic hardship and sacrifice, is desperate to pass the course, but she "doesn't understand"; she is confused, upset, terrified of failure and seemingly at a loss for words. John, in his attempt to comfort and counsel her, breaks academic rules and speaks of his own experiences and makes physical contact with her.

In Act 2 Carol has brought up John on charges of sexual harassment. In Act 3 John has been denied tenure and has been placed on academic suspension. He meets with Carol to try and negotiate a settlement that she will agree to only if he meets the conditions of her "group." Without every being specific Carol tells John that she speaks for those who have suffered and faced hardship for the privilege of attending a University. She resents academic pretension and privilege; she wants to be understood wants to be heard. She enters John's office with a mission and stays true to that mission throughout. Her actions are deliberately designed to provoke John—and the audience—into a state of shock and outrage and indignation. Mamet's intent is to provoke discussion and he pits his two characters in a mortal combat in order to stoke the fires of debate and outrage.

The specifics of Carol's background are deliberately ambiguous; what is important is what she does, and how she does it, rather than the psychology motivating her action. At first she appears to be needy, unfocused, lost; as the action progresses she becomes increasing rigid and takes on all the attributes of high status: her speech transforms from short fractured fragments of sentences into strong, deliberate rants and raves; she moves from indirect to direct, from light to strong, from quick to sustained and gains the power position through pressing and punching.

Carol's fierce determination, her unbroken focus, her overwhelming desire to be heard suggest that her inner core is needy and that she wears an outer mask of rigid. Since she wants to be understood (her inner) but constantly stresses that she doesn't understand (her outer) she appears to be a sensor: her primary concern is the impact of her actions, so the dominant strategy underlying all her actions involves shifting weight to keep John off guard and make him listen to her.

See-sawing would be extremely helpful in creating a sense of the balance necessary for the moment to moment playing of the conflict with John. Stomps 1 and 2 will help physicalize and internalize the power of the rhythms of the speeches, A/B will increase the personalization of the speeches, as will the Rants and Raves exercises, the Add Air and Go. Throughout, the actor's task is not to judge the character but rather to fulfill Mamet's intent of provoking discussion by playing in a dynamic, spontaneous, fully committed manner.

Hierarchies.   This is a classic Master/Servant Game. Four players. Player #1 is the master/mistress, preparing to go to a ball. Player #2 enters as Servant #1 and helps master/mistress dress. In the course of the scene, Player 3 enters as a servant to Player #2. Player #2 is now low to Player 1 but high to Player #3. Player 4 enters and is servant to Player 3. Player 3 is low to #2 but high to #4. Keep the hierarchy intact. Players may speak only to those people who are appropriate to their station. This game is a wonderful exercise in the need for fluidity and adjustment,

and involves a tremendous release of comic energy.

These last two exercises are wonderful for helping the actor understand the driving dynamics which underlay all of Mamet's plays.

The Squeeze.   Four players sit in chairs arranged in a semicircle. All four know one another. The objective is to squeeze one character out of the conversation. When one player feels he or she is being squeezed out they may do whatever they can to stay in the game. Play with a two-minute time limit.

Sell the Car.   Players form into two groups: salesmen and customers. They are at a car lot. The salesmen want to close a sale—they must create a reason why closing one more sale is crucial for their survival. The customer wants to return a car recently purchased and must ask for a refund. Someone must yield in the course of the scene. Players may use all of the tactics described above in playing the scene.

SUGGESTED READINGS

Cohen, Bonnie Bainbridge. *Sensing, Feeling, and Action: The Experiential Anatomy of Mind-Body Centering.* Contact Editions, Northampton, MA., 1993.

Dean, Anne. *David Mamet: Language as Dramatic Action.* Rutherford: Farleigh Dickinson University Press, 1992.

Epstein, Sabin, and Harrop, John. *Basic Acting: The Modular Acting Process.* Boston: Allyn and Bacon, 1996.

Kane, Leslie, Ed. *David Mamet: A Casebook.* New York: Garland, 1991.

Kurtz, Ron and Prestera, Hector. *The Body Reveals.* New York: Harper & Row, 1978.

Johnstone Keith. *Impro.* New York: Theatre Arts Books, 1979.

Mamet, David. *True and False.* New York: Pantheon Books, 1997.

Newlove, Jean. *Laban for Actors & Dancers.* New York: Routledge Theatre Arts Books, 1993.

Samuels, Andrew, Shorter, Bani, and Plaut, Fred (Eds.). *A Critical Dictionary of Jungian Analysis.* London: Routledge Publ., 1986.

Sharp, Daryl. *Jung Lexicon: A Primer of Terms & Concepts.* Toronto: Inner City Books, 1991.

11 Beckett

Beckett's "immortal inertia." Estragon in the British National Theatre's production of *Waiting for Godot.*   *Photo by Nobby Clark.*

BACKGROUND

Samuel Beckett was born in 1906 just outside of Dublin, in what is now the Republic of Eire, or Southern Ireland. He attended school in Northern Ireland and then studied modern languages at Trinity College, Dublin. Like Harold Pinter he was a fine athlete, excelling in cricket, rugby, and boxing. After graduating first in his class he became a lecturer at the *École Normale Supérieure*, one of Paris's major universities. Here he met and was profoundly influenced by James Joyce, began to write poetry, and published his critical work on Proust—another major influence on his life. Returning to Ireland he wrote his first novel, *Murphy*, which was finally published after forty-two rejections—a significant exercise in the courage and endurance of "waiting." At this time he was introduced to the stage at the Abbey Theatre in Dublin. In 1937 he returned to Paris, which became his permanent home. His reasons for leaving Ireland are instructive: "I didn't like theocracy, censorship of literature." This suggests both a spiritual alienation from the autocracy of unsubstantiated beliefs, and a personal alienation from a homeland, both of which factors are apparent in his work.

He spent World War II in France where he worked for the French Resistance and was awarded the *Croix de Guerre*. Again, the courage and endurance this presumes are clearly present in his dramas. He wrote *En Attendant Godot*, as a "relaxation from the awful prose I was writing at the time." The play premiered in Paris in 1953, then in London in 1955, and in the United States in 1956. The first American production, billed in Miami as the "laugh riot of two continents," predictably flopped but was successfully revived in New York. Of the failure, Beckett said, "Success and failure on the public level never matters to me much." This statement provides a sense of that disregard for the external placebos of life that runs through all of his work.

Beckett had come late both to public recognition and to the theatre. Coming from the novel and poetry, where language and narrative were his fluid materials, he was not locked into a predetermined dramatic form such as Sartre had borrowed; nor did he express himself like a philosopher, but like a poet. Beckett allowed his form to evolve from and express his own sense of human experience, rejecting the restrictions of previous structures that could no longer contain current truths.

From *Waiting for Godot* to the present time, Samuel Beckett has produced a major body of dramatic work including *Endgame, Krapp's Last Tape, Happy Days, Rockaby*, and the *Ohio Impromptu*, as well as twenty other pieces. He has also received major recognition including, in 1969, the Nobel Prize for Literature for "a body of work that, in new forms of fiction and the theatre, has transmuted the destitution of modern man into his exaltation."

Sensibility and Premises.   Basically, Samuel Beckett shares the existential view of the human condition that we described in the introduction to the theater of the absurd. But he has the courage to face existence squarely and to seek personal dignity in the midst of suffering and decay. He has been called a man "who does not believe in permanence yet still wants to record his existence."

In his work Beckett recognizes three sources of human alienation. First is the alienation of the individual from society; his characters are mostly outcasts or at least isolated from human society. Second, his characters are also alienated from themselves; the mind/body split is a constant theme in his work, the difficulty in reconciling the potential beauty of existence, which is revealed through the mind, and the inevitable suffering and decay of the body. And this leads to the final and overarching issue, the alienation of human beings from their destiny: We are born to die, a fact that we can neither explain nor escape from. The inexorable passage of time through an infinite space is the frame for all of Beckett's work.

It is the concern for time that links Beckett with Chekhov. Time is an ungraspable present; the future is illusion and the past is loss. The suffering is ontological in the conflict between the promise of fulfillment and the corrosion of loss. Both Beckett and Chekhov overcome time by refusing to allow it to define them, either to save or damn: While something sought for is not attained, something unknown is preserved.[1]

Loss and the ravages of time are a constant presence in Beckett, and never more so than in his classic *Waiting for Godot,* whose theme is not the nature of Godot, but what one does while waiting. Waiting in the ontological context has always been a presence in human existence as connected with natural rhythms: waiting for the passing of the seasons, waiting for the coming of the harvest, waiting for the dawn of a new day with its promise of new hope. And in the modern world we have formalized waiting; it is a constant presence in our lives: waiting in traffic jams, in restaurants, in doctors' offices, in welfare lines; much of our lives is spent waiting in order to perform a function that allows us to move on (?) and wait somewhere else. Although Beckett expresses this fact in ontological and metaphorical terms, its concrete relevance to the modern world gives it the greater force and necessity in terms of questioning its purposes.

Beckett deals with the constant failure yet constant trying of the human condition, with an ironical remove that discovers humor in the blackest circumstances. There is a dignity in the endurance: Humanity has kept its appointment even if Godot hasn't. There is a perverse religiosity in the acceptance of *le néant;* a purity of belief that elevates and sustains. The balance of Beckett's stasis creates a positive acceptance. Do not despair: One of the thieves was saved. Do not presume: One of the thieves was damned. The thieves are Didi and Gogo, Hamm and Clov, you and I.[2] Finally, conclusions about Beckett's work will arise from the work itself: "Hamm as stated, and Clov as stated, *nec tecum nec sine te,* in such a place, and in such a world, that's all I can manage, more than I could."

INTRINSIC DEMANDS

Form. "Nothing happens, nobody comes, nobody goes, it's awful," says one of Beckett's characters in *Waiting for Godot.* This play has also been described as one in which "nothing happens—twice." The absurd theatre tends not to have any of the structural characteristics of well-made drama. There are no neatly plotted crises and climaxes, no discoveries and reversals to keep the audience on the edge of their seats, hardly any events as such, and no vertical plotting toward a grand climax and denouement. Nor do the plays have the conventional three-act structure, which presumes a beginning, middle, and end. The theater of the absurd is not logical and linear; it does not deal in tidy plots and clockwork formulas. In a formless, relativistic world, drama must reflect the inconclusiveness and lack of solutions that are the pattern of our daily lives.

The problem for the absurdist playwright was how to reconcile the inherently irrational and formless quality of the absurd with the structural requirements of theatre—that is, how not to make the error of Sartre and Camus and contradict the content with the form. The answer was to do away with concentration upon content and detail—not to

---

[1]We are indebted here to Richard Gilman's discussion in *The Making of Modern Drama,* chapter 4.

[2]Ruby Cohn expresses a similar point of view in *Back to Beckett,* p. 13.

discuss or describe, but to embrace the audience with the experience of absurdity. That experience is essentially circular and repetitious. Life without meaning cannot have a focus or move directly toward some objective. It doesn't "go on" so much as repeat itself. A circular structure communicates the lack of real progress or resolution. The circle of the play's action described both the sense of infinity—a circle goes on forever—and circumscription—you get nowhere, and might as well be in a cage. The sensation of nothingness is that of total possibility—no restriction—and total futility at the same time: "Nothing to be done," which is the first line of *Waiting for Godot*. A circle equals 0, which equals nothing.

In a world of no purpose or determined values, everything operates on a flat plane of equal insignificance. As with the flattening of pictorial space in cubist art and the flattening of time in the modern novel, so in absurd drama there is a flattening out of form. Man is no longer an aspiring Creature, moving upwards toward ever greater achievement; he is either chasing his tail on the flat plane of existence or moving downwards toward disintegration and decay. The form of absurd drama tends to be either circular and repetitious, as with Beckett's *Godot* and *Play* and Ionesco's *The Bald Soprano* and *The Lesson,* or a declining spiral into futility and dissolution, as in *Endgame, Krapp's Last Tape,* and *The Chairs.* In a world in which all events are equally meaningless there can be only one climax—and that is the negative one of death. Once again, as we saw with Pinter, we are in T. S. Eliot's world, which "ends, not with a bang but a whimper."

Absurd drama is not concerned with the representation of events, the telling of a story, or the depiction of a character as much as it is the presentation of individuals within a situation in such a way as to communicate their experience of existence. The plays tend to be many-layered poetic images that have to be in-

tuited in depth rather than rationally followed through a linear development in time. The situation is full of activity, none of which, however, changes the situation in the least. The plays are stuffed with the trivia of daily existence and employ theatrical effects in a wholesale manner—circus clowning, music hall backchat, farce, ritual—to show the endless and futile ways in which humans attempt to fill the vacuum of their existence. The case is never argued; it is presented through concrete images of the absurd in action. Humans are seen as an actor in a cosmic farce. With no accepted values all experience is equally serious, equally ludicrous. Ionesco observed: "It all comes to the same thing—comic and tragic are two aspects of the same situation; it is now hard to distinguish one from the other."[3] Laughter tempers the reality of despair and makes comedy the bedfellow of pathos.

Language. The use of circular and repetitious form communicates the lack of ontological meaning in life. The approach to language in absurd theatre both reinforces that quality and, specifically, shows that language is not equipped to express knowledge or to define the meaningless. Language, the supremely rational structure, is often used as the final distinguishing feature between humans and other animals, whose responses are more instinctual than logical. However, the mid-twentieth century saw rational language come to a dead end in logical positivism. Language was seen to have no value in defining the essential properties of existence; it was reduced to such profound assertions as "green is green." To make a "true statement" was to be redundant. By definition, language could not express the inexpressible and was thus reduced to making

---

[3]Quoted by Richard Schechner, *Three Aspects of Ionesco's Theatre.* Unpublished doctoral dissertation. Tulane University, 1962.

trivial statements or, worse, to masking true experience beneath rhetoric.

Beckett, aware of the rational limitations of language, made a virtue of this to return language to a prerational, poetic structure whose meaning lies not in its content as much as in its shape. Beckett used the gamut of melodic, rhythmical, and associative potential—as well as silence—to create a dialogue that was at one with his form in its all-embracing imagistic impact, rather than displaying any logical structure or intellectual force.

Other absurdist playwrights, especially Ionesco, consciously derided language rather than exploring its poetic dynamics. The derision we find in Ionesco takes the form of vacuous discussions about unimportant matters, nonsense phrases, meaningless association of words—the destruction of language; or its use as an automatic response to match the automatic behavior of the characters. Often language breaks down entirely. In *The Lesson* and *The Bald Soprano* there is a climactic paroxysm whose intensity of feeling language cannot convey; in *The Chairs* the "message" that is to be communicated is given to a deaf-mute— there is no meaning, or if there is, it cannot be communicated.

Beckett's dialogue, on the other hand, is almost a dance of words, whose choreography encourages the choreography of his movement. Words are used for the auras of their associations, reaching out toward a vision, and probing down into an emotion beyond the compass of explicit expression. The rhythmic progression of his "canters" is, in miniature, the structure of the whole work: observations, followed by interruptions, followed by observations that make no progress but are a bleaker paraphrase of the premise. Within these canters, in *Waiting for Godot*, Didi and Gogo change roles, contradict each other, show their different perspectives, but finally are mutually supportive parts of the dialogue,

which itself is a self-contained whole, making no logical progression, but taking a different route over the same verbal course to end in the same place. The interdependence of the linguistic structure matches that of the character structure in revealing the ontological stasis of the piece.

GOGO: All the dead voices.
DIDI: They make a noise like wings.
GOGO: Like leaves.
DIDI: Like sand.
GOGO: Like leaves.
     (Silence)
DIDI: They all speak together.
GOGO: Each one to itself.
     (Silence)
DIDI: Rather they whisper.
GOGO: They rustle.
DIDI: They murmur.
GOGO: They rustle.

The above stichomythic exchange is an example of a canter that is a poetic duet, shared as is the suffering. In this exchange Didi has a poetic vision of possible change, while Gogo asserts a more earthbound consistency. Didi's vision loses energy as the exchange continues; he moves from light images of wings and whispers to earthbound images of murmurs and ashes, which finally ends with:

DIDI: Like ashes,
GOGO: Like leaves.
     (Long silence)
DIDI: Say something.
GOGO: I'm trying.
     (Long silence)
DIDI: Say anything at all.
GOGO: What do we do now?
DIDI: Wait for Godot.[4]

The rhythmical effect is achieved by a consistent but tonally varied quality: patterns of

[4]Samuel Beckett, *Waiting for Godot* (New York: Grove Press, 1954), pp. 40–41.

difference that modulate into the same effect, an agreement to disagree, two aspects of the same totality that finally leaves nothing further to say. The stichomythic simplicity of the line, surrounded by empty space, underlines the starkness of the situation. The spareness of the statement gives it a profundity in that it allows many meanings and yet does not define any of them. The frequent use of pauses isolates words, just as space isolates characters. The silences both make the audience aware of infinity (silence is always a felt presence in tragedies—"The rest is silence") and point to where language is useless in expressing the ultimate feeling.

The canter we have just discussed is lyrical in nature, but Beckett also uses the same structure to achieve a comic effect by the use of stichomythia in the form of a vaudevillian cross-talk act—in very much the same manner that we saw in Pinter:

DIDI: No no, after you.
GOGO: No no, you first.
DIDI: I interrupted you.
GOGO: On the contrary.
DIDI: Ceremonious ape.
GOGO: Punctilious pig.
DIDI: Finish your phrase I tell you.
GOGO: Finish your own.
DIDI: Moron.
GOGO: That's the idea let's abuse each other.
DIDI: Moron.
GOGO: Vermin.
DIDI: Abortion.
GOGO: Morpion.
DIDI: Sewer rat.
GOGO: Curate.
DIDI: Cretin.
GOGO: Critic.
DIDI: Oh![5]

Apart from the in-joke of Beckett's that the final, killing shot was "critic," the words

have no particular significance in the exchange, which produces its irrascible effect by the repetition of sounds. R's run all the way through the exchange giving the gritty sound of irritation, and the rhythmical quality is achieved by using o's with the r's and then hardening into c's. Again the parts in the double act are interchangeable; it is not a character statement but a rhythmical dialogue that achieves its effect by the resonances of the alternation of sound.

The alternation of lyrical duets with comic cross-talk is part of the dialectic tone that is an essential part of the nature of the play as a whole: hope and despair, activity and passivity, intellect and instinct, all reflected within the characters of Didi and Gogo to achieve that synthesis and stasis that is Beckett's reflection upon the human condition. The use of rhythms and repetitions also adds a ritualistic quality to Beckett's work, which further removes it from the mundane and reinforces, through religious associations, its connection to ultimate essences.

Finally, language is also used to undercut sentiment, to give an ironic edge to the situation and prevent indulgence in pathos. Beckett does this with the apposition of phrases: "Embrace me"—"You stink of garlic"; "He's crying"—"Then he's living"; "He's bleeding"—"It's a good sign."

Having recognized the limitation of language in conveying intellectual meaning, and the limitation of that meaning itself, the absurdist playwrights used it to express the experience of the absurd in both poetic and practical terms. On the one hand their language communicates by rhythm, shape, and sound; it embraces the audience in an almost lyrical manner. On the other hand it becomes gestural, using the techniques of mime, vaudeville, and slapstick farce. By these means the playwrights, while dethroning the rational and everyday function of language, infinitely expand its capacity to convey meaning.

[5]*Waiting for Godot*, p. 48.

Space.   For absurd theatre the term *space* has more than usual significance. In theatrical terms space is taken to be where the actors perform, but it is usually identified with *setting,* which is how that space has been filled in order to create an identifiable background or environment for the play. Because the theatre of the absurd is occupied with a sense of nothingness, emptiness, and void, space itself becomes a concrete fact: No matter what is put in it, an all-embracing sense of vacuum is the true environment of the play.

For the absurd theatre, the stage, which had been reduced by Realism to a one-to-one representation of a small "slice of life," returned to its earlier image as a metaphor for the world itself. The quintessential absurdist stage is stripped down to its bare minimum, with man reduced to his questioning, existential stance as a "bare, forked animal" in the middle. Simple, stark—this is the stage of

Waiting for Godot. It is a symbol of the naked void that disregards, almost self-consciously, the material paraphernalia of the realistic stage and its presumption that some action of import can take place. The play's space is defined by two axes—the horizontal road and the vertical tree, itself a spatial metaphor for solitary endurance. The rest is empty wasteland, once again recalling T. S. Eliot. It is the simplest possible human definition: We stand on the earth.

The quality of this theatrical image itself conveys the experience of absurdity. Space equals vacuum equals nothingness. All man's attempts—his aimless searches—to define himself by fixing his position in the void are doomed to failure. If he knew who he was, he might discover where he was; if he knew where, he might discover who. We are everywhere and nowhere at the same time—either at the lonely, unspecified crossroads of Beckett,

Winnie, buried in the wasteland, in *Happy Days.*   *British National Theatre.*

or in the isolated rooms of Pinter, whose realistic patina reflects the absurd by its nonreferential character. The world or a room: It is finally the same thing; both are contained spaces, empty of meaning. One of the essential qualities of the theatre of the absurd is a double sense of space as both infinite—nothingness can have no bounds—and totally confining: Nothingness is impenetrable, and man feels small and isolated in the space he himself occupies. The universe is contained within a grain of sand, and it has as much significance.

If Beckett's characters are not in the visible wasteland, they are buried up to their necks in sand, or in coffins, or in the unspecified limbo of the room in *Endgame*. In whatever situation, Beckett's space conveys a sense of oppressive emptiness filled with inexpressible meaning. Ionesco's space is more cluttered but the feeling is the same: impenetrable meaning, created by a wall of "things." When Beckett does employ "things" their choice is instructive. In *Waiting for Godot* he gives Pozzo a stool. Apart from the "lion-tamer" reference, a stool is nonspecific; it relates through 360 degrees to the space, and reinforces the unimpeded sense of space in a way in which a chair, with the obstruction and definition of its back, could not do. A stool is a "thing" but it introduces no realistic effect; it fits metaphorically with the tree and the mound. Whatever the specific setting, it is what the fact of space says rather than what space is made to represent that creates the spatial dynamics of absurdist theatre.

Time.   We in the Western world have a tremendous preoccupation with time. The concern for the temporal is in many ways the disease of modern industrialized people. In the Middle Ages, humanity's horizon was the eternal: Life was a continuous movement toward oneness with an ineffable spirit. For modern humans, time equals money. There is an anecdote about a businessman who was

extremely happy when the supersonic Concorde jet came into service. Extolling this to a Chinese friend, he said, "Now I can fly from New York to London in four less hours." To which the Chinese replied, "How nice. But what do you do with the time saved?"

"What do you do with the time saved?" To the businessman this was a stupid question. The answer was multifold: make more money; make another appointment; see a physician to check out stress. To the Chinese coming from a different tradition, the occupation with time—especially the saving of it—was amusing and absurd. Time is a flow; it cannot be saved; it cannot even be grasped. It simply has to be accepted and lived. But we in the West have not been in the habit of doing this. We have tried to define, rationalize, and harness time to give our lives structure and meaning. We are always looking optimistically toward tomorrow: "I love ya tomorrow, you're always a day away." We defraud ourselves by pretending there is something (better) yet to come and give ourselves hope through this false expectation of futurity. As long as we were locked inside our man-made system, things were reasonably fine—we made money, gave internal significance to the trivia of our lives. But once we stepped outside that system and applied our puny logic to the explanation of larger purposes—to define time and space, to calculate our existence, to assess the sum of things in terms of thought—then we put ourselves in the position of being absurd.

In Beckett's plays there is always an interminable twilight—time is constantly dying, but goes on. Time is a hemorrhage of existence. We dwell in a vague present whose limits can be expanded or contracted without affecting its significance. Time is eternal, yet passes in a flash. One instant contains a life: "We are born above a grave," says Didi, "the light flashes and is extinguished." "What time is it?" asks Hamm. "The same as usual," replies Clov. The double sense of time, a crucial part of the sensibility of the absurd, gives existence its quality of comic pathos. It is pathetic because human striving is directed toward infinity, and attempting to identify man with the infinite is the supreme achievement of pathos. It is comic because such striving is self-contradictory. Seen pathetically, a second has infinite value; comically, ten thousand years is an instant of tomfoolery.

The sense of timelessness, or the logical absurdity of time, is found in the internal repetitiousness and circular structure of many of the plays of the theatre of the absurd—plays that end where they begin, or begin over again. This aimless continuity is the playing out in dramatic terms of the Greek myth of Sisyphus (which Camus used as the subject of one of his existential essays). Sisyphus was condemned to Hades, where he was to spend an interminable afterlife pushing a stone up a hill, only to see it roll back down each time it reached the top. Human purposes are no longer judged by the gods; the absurd now places the afterlife upon this earth—hell has become other people, as Sartre suggested in his play *Huis Clos (No Exit)*. But time is still the oppressive force that both stretches endlessly before us and yet is gone in the very instant we try to live it; the only response to which is " 'Let's go.' They don't move."

Character/Mask.   Beckett's tramps, *clochards*, and down-and-outs represent the inalienable part of man, which transcends social, political, and ideological details. These characters are negligible if identified with any attitudes or class of people less than humankind itself. We are told little about the background of the characters—like human origins, they are shrouded in mystery. Any attempt to treat them as "real" individuals reduces their impact. They are there to "be." They have no future and no past. What they do is what they are. To determine their "character" one looks

to the structure and language of the plays, in which it is deeply imbedded. The plays are not about anyone; they are about Everyman. Everyman can have no "character" in our limited psychological sense—it is a function of the total experience of the play.

As an example: Some critics have suggested that Didi and Gogo in *Waiting for Godot* must be intelligent and educated men because of the literary and biblical references they make. This is to commit the naturalistic fallacy: to look at them as real persons instead of part of the structure of Beckett's play. Beckett (indeed, an educated and intelligent man) uses references because they are part of human mythology and create the kind of texture and feeling he is trying to communicate. Didi and Gogo may or may not be educated—this is irrelevant to the play. Although one of the many layers of meaning in the play may be concerned with the bankruptcy of man's intellect, to play Didi and Gogo simply as intellectuals fallen on hard times reduces the play's size.

One of the features of characters in absurd drama is that they often come in pairs, like vaudeville or music-hall comedians. Ionesco uses this structure in *The Lesson* and *The Chairs*; Genet in *The Maids* and to some degree *The Balcony* where they take the form of master/slave relationships, explored in a fantasy world of sexual games. Most notably, however, it is Beckett who, with Hamm and Clov, Nagg and Nell, Didi and Gogo, and Pozzo and Lucky, uses mutually dependent pairs of characters to make universal statements. The pairs tend to be complementary, making up between them in a kind of yin-yang fashion a total human construct. Didi and Gogo, for example, operate on three levels of relationship. On the comedic level they are a double act, with Didi tending to be the straight man and Gogo the banana. Their cross-talk and a lot of the physical gags have the rhythms of this relationship. On the human level they have the qualities of an old married couple. They have a mutual dependence that they wish they could reject: Like most human relationships they don't quite work together, but neither could they live apart. Third, and embracing the other two levels, they create *one macro-human character—a mask of mankind itself.* Didi tends to be the thinker, representing mind and intellect. Gogo is more prosaic and earthbound, emphasizing body and instinct.

As with the use of space and time in Beckett's work, so with the use of character there is a complete integration of the mask into the structure and atmosphere of the play. Without an awareness of all the levels upon which character operates, and of its function as part of the total construct of absurd theatre, an actor will make the mistake of examining his or her character with a microscope and inevitably reduce its size and the suprahuman impact of the play.

Costume.   Costume reinforces the mask. Obviously all costuming says something about the character wearing it, but the nature of character in absurd theatre means that costume defines not so much the individuals as what the character represents. Costume tends to be either nonspecific or a highly specific cliché. Beckett's characters, being of the Everyman nature, are largely nonspecific in costuming; it is important that they be so, as highly distinctive costuming would reduce universal qualities. Hamm, Clov, Lucky, and Krapp all wear indeterminate clothing that, if suggestive of anything, has the quality of the thrift store in the poorer district of any modern city. Even the generally accepted dress of Didi and Gogo—the tramp's outfit—is said to have been a happy accident, stemming from the mind of Roger Blin, the first director of *Waiting for Godot.* In some respects the tramp is the perfect icon for Beckett's work, carrying as it does overtones of Chaplin and Laurel and Hardy as well as the generalized sense of the lonely wanderer on the brink of decay who is still trying to make a living.

One of the few items of costume that is called for in *Waiting for Godot* is that all four characters wear bowler hats. We have talked about the bourgeois associations of the bowler hat in the section on farce, and those associations carry over here. They also give a unity to the characters—all sufferers in the human comedy—and a certain absurd dignity. There is one further important association. The bowler hat was originally created for protection to horse riders: It also has the function of a hard hat—it protects against random items dropping from above. In *Waiting for Godot* the need for protection from the great pigeon in the sky is not be be missed.

PERFORMANCE DEMANDS

Movement.   We have already suggested that the form and the action of the absurd theatre tend toward the circular, so it will be no surprise to discover that basic movement patterns reinforce this. As there is no forward progress to be made, the only possible movement is circular—around the perimeter of the space—or repetitive—back and forth across the lateral plane. Nothing leads anywhere, but we go about our business just the same, as if there were some purpose. Thus, the actor will move with a purposeful futility. The circular and repetitive patterns are invested with an urgency as if they might achieve something, but always end where they began. Beckett's characters achieve the semblance of variety with repetitive behavior and familiar fictions. In performing these the actor doesn't drag himself around, selfconsciously burdened with despair; he performs the absurdly repetitive rituals of movement with a heightened energy that further underlines their futility. Equally, when the movement ends nowhere and stops, the stillness reinforces the vast emptiness of time and space surrounding the characters.

The heroic ineffectuality of the Absurd, seen in Winnie's attempt to protect herself from the great pigeon in the sky.   *The Royal Court Theatre, London.*

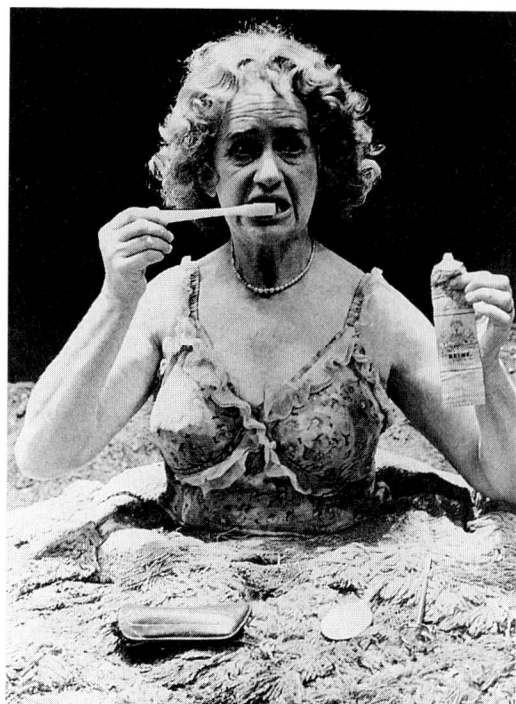

Winnie again, in *Happy Days*, fills the vacuum with the daily busyness of living.   *British National Theatre.*

Stasis is an important characteristic of absurd theatre, which Beckett, especially, uses to the full. "Let's go." They don't move. Where is there to go, and for what reason? Yet at times movement is necessary both to alleviate the boredom and to attempt to prove the fact that one is there—wherever "there" may be. The alternation of movement and stillness in repetitive patterns lends a ritualistic quality to the event, and it gives Beckett his embracing atmosphere of what has been called "immortal inertia."

Although movement in absurd theatre is not extended or exaggerated in size, neither is it naturalistic. Movement has great precision and clarity; it is outlined in such a way as to give it a heightened impact in the frame of space. The effect is achieved by giving every movement a defined beginning, middle, and end—no small, imprecise movements; nothing loose; no blurring of the physical image by swaying and shuffling. When a movement is over, the actor stops, and there is an instant of absolute stillness that allows space and time to make their presence felt. In absurd theatre it is space and time that lie heavily upon the stage, not the action. The action is filled with the trivial "busyness" of our day-to-day lives. There is a briskness and variety of pace and rhythm. The basic rhythm is, of course, the unchanging flow of time, but within this are determined little attacks—Beckett's canters—upon the impassive pace. The actor's basic movement goes against the constant rhythmical flow—not heavy and oppressive, but rather quick and light; not on the toes, like farce, but a flat-footed dexterity.

Pain, decay, and age are part of the atmosphere of the absurd, but more a manifestation of the physical mask of a character than a constant feature of his movement. The bend of the knee, stoop of shoulders, general set of the body will create the necessary image of pain or decreptitude, but it should not be overindulged as a constant obstacle to an actor's movement. The rhythms and total images of the play are the issue, not the physical suffering of any one character. Didi's bladder, Gogo's feet, Clov's inability to sit are all part of the fabric of the play, constants we aren't particularly aware of until the playwright chooses to use them for specific action. The general pattern and quality of movement should manifest the necessary pace and rhythms required by the action. It would, once again, be committing the naturalistic fallacy for an actor to say the old couple are in their nineties, or that Gogo has bad feet, so they can't move briskly—they are often required to by the play. *To belabor character detail is to flatten and reduce the size of the characters.*

Clowning.   If confirmation were needed that actors should not play the decrepit details of old age, but more with a "flat-footed dexterity," the ever-present physical clowning in the absurd would affirm it. Absurd characters have the awkward dignity of the circus clown as he or she parades around the ring before tripping over the feet and falling on the face or backside—and then getting up and carrying on. It is a parody of the average lifetime: There are existential resonances in every fall, every excitement, every brooding silence. It is important for the actor to recognize the elements of clowning, vaudeville, and farce in

absurd drama, to accept the pattern of gags and comic set-pieces for what they are, and not to try to make them "believable" within the context of some character structure or "realistic" conception of action. They are believable within the total metaphor of the play. No one asks if a circus clown is believable. The proper questions are: Is he funny? Is he sad? Does he or she affect you? We accept the structure of the event. On a simple level the clown entertains us; on a deeper level he or she touches us, says something about our humanity in ways of which we are aware but may not be able to define. So with the sensibility of the absurd. The actor must approach each moment of action upon its own terms, recognizing its function in the larger whole that the playwright has conceived. Only in

The existential clowning of Didi and Gogo in a Long Wharf Theatre production of *Waiting for Godot.   Photo by Gerry Goodstein.*

this way will the full dimensions of the absurd be communicated to an audience.

Hyperconcentration.   Concentration is a necessary attribute of all acting. It keeps the actor aware of the action; it creates 100 percent focused energy; it allows immediate reaction; and it has a compelling power that draws the audience's attention. In the absurd it is more than just a necessary technique—it is part of the physical style. In the pauses of Beckett's work the actors do not sit passively—they sit actively. When they look into space it is not a vacant look but an intense stare—at nothing. The time in the pauses is not empty; it is filled by intense concentration that makes the vacuum of space a felt presence for the audience. Effort for no reward; energy wasted in the void; futile activity followed by interminable waiting—this is the essential dichotomy of the absurd.

The inverse ratio of effort to result is clearly illustrated at the beginning of *Waiting for Godot*. Gogo spends several minutes of concentrated effort trying to take off his boot. Beckett gives such directions as "tears at his boot" and "with supreme effort succeeds in pulling off his boot." Having done this he discovers nothing (which could have hurt him) inside, and stares "sightlessly" before him—tremendous effort for no return and in the end an attitude of concentrated stasis. "Sightlessly" is a carefully chosen word. The eyes of a blind person have a great intensity, which comes from the concentration of the person locked within his or her own space. The sense of being trapped within a private space, despite the vastness of the space surrounding him, is a necessary quality of the absurd character, and it is achieved by hyperconcentration.

Intensity of effort, followed by intensity of stillness, produces compression and futility. Concentration makes time appear to stand still, to become a concrete quality, to weigh down upon character and audience alike. There are bursts of intense energy followed by total collapse: Like the labor of an elephant to give birth to a gnat, they create a disparity that is comic, a sense of futility that is absurd. The impossible task is never quite completed—the task that is life itself. As Hamm says, "Moment upon moment, pattering down, like the millet grains of that old Greek, and all life long you wait for that to mount up to a life." Living is like endlessly dividing and subdividing a grain of sand, and the smaller it gets the more concentration it requires. By the use of concentration, by making it an intensely felt force, the actor creates the intangible but absolutely necessary atmosphere surrounding absurd drama.

Business/Gesture.   Intensity of concentration is present in all business and gesture. It lends a heightened energy and clarity to the physical activity that achieves the larger-than-reality effect. Much of the business in Beckett's plays is a form of child's play. If there is no final, objective reality, existence becomes a kind of game, and one way to accept this is to approach existence on its own terms, consciously using games to fill time. Beckett's characters approach their game playing with the innocent enthusiasm of children and with a child's concentration and total commitment to the moment.

The sense of game playing carries over into business, which is derived from the activity and gestures of everyday life. These gestures of normality have a particular manner of presentation, a consciousness of performance that has the effect of ritualizing them and giving them larger significance. Beckett's plays are full of gestures of looking, shaking, tapping, feeling, smelling, embracing, recoiling, brooding, searching with nose to the ground, agitated pacing, bouncing entrances. Each gesture is filled with heightened energy and concentration, which produces an outline in the emptiness of space yet underlines its inadequacy, its ultimate futility. When they think, the characters don't simply sit quietly; they adopt thinking attitudes; they show that they are thinking, as if that will help to give the activity some meaning. They don't simply greet each other; they fall into each other's arms. They don't simply look into hats or boots; they peer with great concentration. All of the energetic occupation with trivia, with moments of glee, hope, and excitement about everyday events, is an attempt to light up an empty existence, to fill the stillness and the vacuum that surrounds them, and to which they always return.

Mask/Character.   The nature of the mask of character is implicit in what has been said about movement and gesture. The physical patterns and images created by the characters in the space define their function. Beckett's plays are not concerned with the lives of individuals or stories about what is happening to them. The plays are conveying an experience of what it is like to be in a particular ontological environment. It is the arrangement of physical patterns, images, rhythms—the sounds and signs in space and time—that communicates this experience to the audience. This is done partly through the agency of the characters, but it is not done through an examination or revelation of individual personalities.

The characters are not discrete individuals; they are parts of the larger metaphor, which has universal, not particular, resonances. The plays tend to take the form of a series of duets—the yin-yang quality we spoke of earlier. Even *Krapp's Last Tape* has this structure: Krapp is involved in a duet with his younger self. All the duets form one mask of relationship with many levels, encompassing the range of human experience: parent/child, husband/wife, master/slave, youth/age, body/mind, comic/pathetic. The characters operate at as many and as different levels as the action demands. The actor must discover

The comic/pathetic double act of Hamm and Clov in *Endgame*. Note hopeless yearning of Clov (on right), and compare with concentration camp survivor.   *American Conservatory Theatre, San Francisco.*

what part of the relationship is his or hers at any one time and respond to this stimulus

Although the character is recognizably human in form, it is not closely defined as a personality: It has metaphysical significance, but little psychological content. Background details are irrelevant to Didi, Gogo, Hamm, Clov, Pozzo, and Ionesco's Smiths, and the Martins (who can't themselves, remember who they are). The very ambivalence and un-

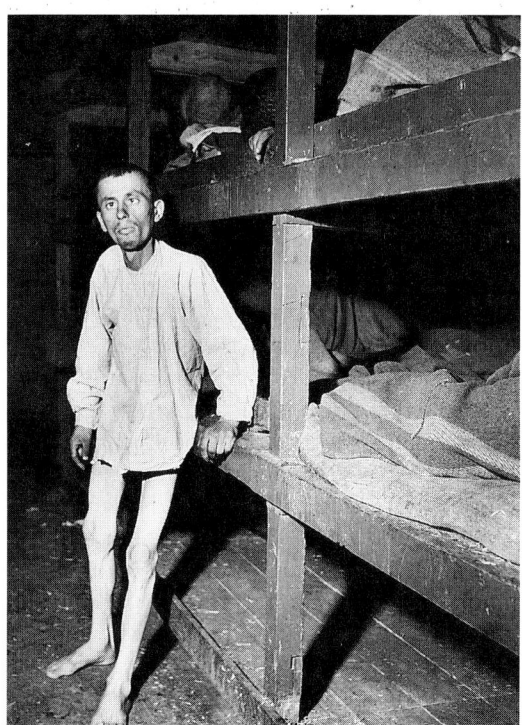

A survivor of the concentration camp at Buchenwald.   *Margaret Bourke-White, LIFE magazine, © 1945, Time, Inc.*

certainty are part of the atmosphere of the absurd theatre. Too many specifics reduce to earth characters who have also to connect with space and time. In a world in which no knowledge is possible, a character cannot have internal definition—the self is in constant flux in the changing flow of time. Didi asks Gogo if the "same lot" beat him. He replies, "The same. I don't know?" In such a world, motives cannot be precise, and responses are arbitrary, determined by the demands of the situation. Characters relate through space, objects, activity, rituals—through the situation rather than directly and emotionally.

In creating the mask, the actor has all the resources of the text: the rhythms, patterns, gestures, and business called for by the playwright. He or she will discover recurrent de-

tails that create a form for the character in the situation. Didi tends mainly to be upright, like the tree; Gogo, who sees it as a bush, tends to sit more, to be lower to the ground. This is further confirmed by Gogo's concern for his feet, while the head-oriented Didi is involved with his hat. The more inquiring Didi also tends to initiate, to move forward more; Gogo, who is more instinctual, is not to be moved unless necessary. Didi's walk, pensive attitudes, and paternal manner toward Gogo; Clov's walk, volatility, bursts of activity, and clowning—all of these qualities and many more are part of the play's givens and are fuel for the actor's imagination. Such particulars may be heightened to form a functional outline for the character—its mask.

Playing the Mask.   The mask is played flexibly and truthfully from moment to moment. Truthfully here means with the necessary value for the communication of the action. It does not mean indulgence in pain, despair, or any of the ongoing properties of the character when they are not the focus of the immediate action. Such elements may represent the outline or form of the mask, but how that outline is fleshed out will depend upon the given demands of the action. Didi's walk (attributable to some kind of prostate problem, if the actor needs to give a name to it) is part of his mask and also of the fabric of the play: It indicates man's decaying functions. The audience accepts Didi's problem and needs to be consciously aware of it only when it directly affects the action, at which time the playwright will have written it into the rhythms. The problem may be used to give a quality of pathos to the play—but Didi is not consistently a pathetic character.

The mask is not a psychologically developed individual, but neither is it a lifeless cardboard construct. It is the selected and heightened outline of the attributes the character must have in order to play its part

Beckett's image of eternal decay seen in *Footfalls.* For the genesis of this sense of the human condition, again compare with World War II concentration camp.   *Royal Court Theatre, London.*

ent sense when we speak, and it is difficult for the actor to accept that the meaning of a play lies in the lack of surface meaning. There is not a cryptic meaning beneath the lines as much as a broader resonance that surrounds it—a supratext, in fact. Lines should not be overexamined, searched for subtext. For example, in *Waiting for Godot* lines such as "I don't know" respond on the surface to a particular question, but the effect of the answer should be existential, and delivery should communicate the broader meaning: "We have never known anything." Again, Gogo constantly responds to Didi's "We're waiting for Godot" with "Ah!" It has been suggested by critics that this exclamation should be given different values as it would be if a normal comic structure were involved—but this seems to work against the function of the lines in conveying the total meaning of the play. Rather than making sense, the "Ah!" is somewhat like a simple expulsion of breath. It does not indicate recognition of the situation, or understanding; it is simply acceptance, unexamined, of Didi's response. The repetition of "Ah!" in the same manner with the same lack of significance reinforces the empty repetitiveness of the situation.

The same lack of true meaning behind the word applies to Ionesco, whose characters use language to fill the vacuum at the core of their existence. There is a surface quality of meaning, a concerned facade, that covers the emptiness beneath.

In the theatre of the absurd the significance of language is not in any meaning, but in the patterns of speech, the rhythms, inflections, and especially the way in which sound is related to silence. The use of builds and undercuts shows unfulfilled expectation; the monotonous circularity of life is evidenced by the verbal repetitions. The patterns of language are not geared to giving significance to any individual. They are part of the construct of the joint masks, and they often take the

in the action at any moment. In this way the particular truth, or style, of the playwright's intention will be communicated to the audience—in this instance, the comic/pathetic sense of life's absurdity.

Playing the Words.   There is a danger that the actor will attempt to force meaning on the meaningless. We are used to making appar-

"Man's inhumanity to Man," as seen in this World War II concentration camp.
World Wide Photos.

form of duets: Didi and Gogo; the Martins with their duet of recognition. The language of the absurd must be approached as a poetic structure—for its function as part of the total statement of the plays rather than for specific content or conversational qualities.

Sense of Occasion.

> Man that is born of woman is of few days,
> And full of trouble.
> He cometh forth like a flower,
> And is cut down.
> He fleeth also as a shadow,
> And continueth not.

There is a strong sense of religiosity about the absurd. Beckett lends a deeply rit-

ualistic quality to his work, and he extrapolates a universal atmosphere from the trivia of the mundane. Even Ionesco—despite his more domestically based concerns and his focus upon language—creates a supervening atmosphere of meaningless absurdity that strongly challenges the audience's sense of existential purpose.

The response to the absurd theatre is not simply didactic, emotional, or psychological; it is an aesthetic totality, an experience that both defies and is reduced by analysis. It is challenging and liberating, bringing the audience face-to-face with its fears, its false hopes, its very existence, in order to produce a new, deeper sense of reality and accommodate to the true nature of life. In this sense the absurd theatre is not negative but optimistic.

It is important for the actor to recognize the positive side of the absurd, to give full rein to the childlike quality of enthusiasm, the humor, and the constant recognition of play. Beckett's characters are conscious of playing, of themselves as acting a part. Hamm's first words are "Me to play." Clov asks what there is to keep him here, to which Hamm responds, "The dialogue." Clov says, "Let's stop playing," to receive the decided answer from Hamm: "Never." That "Never" says much about the attitude of the characters and the general sensibility of absurd theatre. Humankind is trapped in some futile experience, yet it carries on. It is part of its dignity; it defines its selfhood. The human being is an actor in the cosmic farce, just as the actors on the stage form parts of a larger whole, so do the actors and the audience complement each other in sharing not just the theatrical event but the all-embracing experience of what it means to be alive on "this bitch of an earth." To be alive, to share, to commiserate, to laugh at, to accommodate to—actors must be aware of this communion, must realize that while playing the human event they create larger vibrations. The actor is part of the eternal poetry of existence—the messenger of the gods in a godless world.

EXERCISES, GAMES, TECHNIQUES

Because of the basic preoccupation with time and space, workshops in the absurd cannot be hurried. The experience of void and endless time is something the actor must be allowed to develop. The leader of the workshop must be constantly attentive to the actors so that the exploration of both time and waiting is positive, and the actors should not be allowed to become bored with the exercise. Subtle side coaching to maintain the actor's focus and concentration will be necessary in many of the exercises.

Space/Time Exercises.

Blind Faith I.   A well-known "trust" exercise is a good starting point. Players pair off. One is blindfolded and then led around for twenty minutes or so, experiencing the nature of nonvisible space and examining the tactile qualities of any objects that may be encountered. It is important that this exercise not be hurried, so that the blindfolded player develops both an experience of space and confidence in his or her ability to move within it. Partners then change places.

Blind Faith II.   When all the players have experienced being led around blindfolded, all should then be seated, blindfolded, within a large, completely empty indoor space. All are then asked to explore this barren space, at any speed, in any way they wish. They should try to avoid contact with other players. At intervals, coach them to change position: Those who have been walking should sit and shuffle, or crawl; those who have been exploring lower space should become aware of the upper space. Continue the exercise until all players have explored the total perimeter of the space and have moved in several different ways through the inner vacuum.

Blind Faith III.   Players scatter throughout an empty space. One player is blindfolded. All move around the space until the blind player claps hands. All freeze. The blind player is allowed three paces to find another player. If successful, the blindfolded player must try to identify the player by feeling clothing and face. If he or she correctly identifies, they change places. If not, the game continues with the same blind player.

Blind Faith IV.   All players are blindfolded and scatter throughout empty space. The leader of the workshop knocks on certain parts of the walls or floor or ceiling. Players have to make their way toward the knock. Just before any of them reach there, the knock is made elsewhere, and so continues for about fifteen minutes. When some players catch on to what is happening they may simply give up. This is fine; much of the value of the exercise comes from discovering what they do while waiting for it to be over.

Hunt the Thimble. This game is played in a cluttered space with a lot of furniture and props. While the players are outside the space the leader hides a thimble. The players return and search for it. Repeat the game, this time in a darkened space. Then repeat the game in an almost darkened space, but this time don't put the thimble anywhere! When the game is called off, discuss the nature of the frustration felt by players when unable to find the thimble. What did they instinctively feel like doing?

Vacuum. Players sit anywhere in the space. Have them do a deep-breathing exercise for two or three minutes and then "drain" by consciously allowing tension to move to the lower part of the body, where a plug is pulled and all tension drained out. Now ask players to concentrate upon some small object—a stain on the floor, a crack in the wall, the tip of a shoe or foot—until their mind is cleared of all other ideas and finally that object itself loses any meaning and becomes simply an inanimate "thing." This is a difficult exercise. One of the most difficult problems the adult has is just to "be," like a child or an animal. Coach quietly for the maintaining of active concentration, so that the players gain an experience of the meaninglessness of "stain" or "crack"—its complete lack of real connection with the object they are staring at. Ultimately the players will find that they lose all sense of a context and become aware of the isolation of themselves in an undefinable environment.

Effort/Frustration Exercises.

Child's Play. Players scatter throughout a space containing various children's play objects, such as balls, hoops, skipping ropes, and bats, and they use the props to play at children's games (or games that don't need props, such as hopscotch and tumbling). Coach them to put as much energy as possible into their play. Then, on a handclap have them stop dead, drop whatever they are doing, and go into the vacuum exercise. On another handclap they begin another activity at high speed. The rhythm of this exercise alternates between high-energy activity and complete stasis. Coach for total concentration; don't let the playing of the games have a lot of surface energy but little deep concentration: The energy must be highly focused. Repeat the exercise; this time make the game playing take place in pairs and the focus of the stasis some small part of the partner's clothing or body.

Sisyphus I. Players are given small heaps of sand, which they have to move, grain by grain, to another place.

Sisyphus II. Players are given a large piece of paper, which has to be torn into pieces, mixed up. Then players take a break, find a partner, and play hectic children's games. Then they return to their mixed-up paper, which has to be put back together again.

Sisyphus III. Players now put their pieces of paper one by one into a bucket, empty it, and then put the paper piece by piece back in the bucket and so on.

Sisyphus IV. A group of players is given a large jigsaw puzzle to put together—the puzzle will have some pieces missing.

Sisyphus V. Break the players into groups of two or three. Ask a group of players to arrange twenty or thirty chairs in a particular fashion in the space. When they are halfway through their task, have another group begin to rearrange the chairs in a different pattern. When the first group has arranged the chairs, players must go back and put the rearranged chairs into their original pattern—and so on.

No-Sense Exercises.

Roundalay.   Players sit in a circle. One player starts a conversation with the person on the right, making completely trivial or redundant statements, which must be said as if they were of surprising import—for example, "When people fall over they are no longer in an upright position." The person to whom this is said must pick up on it and make a statement to the player on the right, such as "Upright people go to church on Mondays as well as Sunday." This continues around the circle. There will be a tendency at first for some players to giggle or be self-consciously funny—coach for absolute seriousness.

Roundalay II.   Players pair off. Each pair chooses a theme for conversation. The theme is then discussed, but only proverbs or clichés may be used.

Broken Record.   This may be played around a circle or in pairs. Choose a convoluted and opaque paragraph from a textbook on linguistics, psychology, or sociology. A player now reads this mumbo jumbo as if it were part of a course on a record. At intervals the leader of the workshop or the partner claps hands and the previous phrase has to be repeated as if the record were stuck, until a further handclap allows the player to continue. A tape recorder rather than a record player may be used. In this instance it should be played in pairs. One player reads the information as if he or she were a tape recorder. The partner makes adjustments to the recording—changing speeds, stopping and starting, reversing—by pressing or twiddling "knobs" on the player. Partners change places. This is a good exercise for conveying the "disembodied" or potentially mechanical nature of speech.

What Life?   Players tell their life story to an empty auditorium. Make a serious attempt to interest the empty seats in what is being said. A variation on this exercise is to have players seated in a circle. One player is in the center. All lights are turned off. The player in the center now relates his or her life story. At any juncture players in the circle may question the storyteller about the details of what he or she is saying and make the storyteller justify assertions—"prove" that events did in fact take place. The exercise should not be allowed to become chaotic, with interruptions every other second. Coach players to pick significant occurrences to question closely upon. The questions coming from disembodied voices out of the darkness can lead players seriously to doubt "facts" about their past that they have taken for granted. The impossibility of verifying past events is brought strongly home.

Mechanical Men.   Players choose a character with a mechanical attitude or function: TV pitch-man, door-to-door salesman, worker on a production line, supermarket checkout clerk. Each player does a small improvisation illustrating the character and then repeats two or three times, each time performing the function more quickly until it is like a speeded-up film track. The player then performs the improvisation at "normal" speed. This performance will have the quality of a heightened reality as it will retain some of the precision and pace of the preceding performances.

Body and Mind.   Players pair off. Jointly they are one human mask: One player is the body, the other the mind. Choose a number of situations for the mask to respond to: sitting in a cafe noticing a good-looking man/woman—should one approach, and how; on a diet at a party with masses of food; late at night but haven't finished a paper due the following day. The body-and-mind players voice aloud their reactions to the situation: what the body instinctively would do; what reason advises. Try to establish a dialogue, not ignore the other voice. Try to integrate the differing responses; make the dialogue a duet so that finally the mask acts as one person, aware of double consciousness.

Married Couples.   Another joint-mask exercise. Players are paired: man and wife, long-time roommates, or whatever! There has to be a presumption of a long association. A series of domestic problems, situations, are set up. Ultimately the pair has the same interest in achieving a solution, but they can take many different views of the same situation. Coach the players to reminisce about the past, talk in parallel, argue their point of view, and finally come to an acceptable solution to the problem or accept the situation as it stands.

Godot Game.   This is an extended improvisation, pulling together some of the previous exercises. It is particularly useful for rehearsing the techniques and assimilating the atmosphere necessary for the performance of Beckett's work. Required is a large, empty workshop space and light that can be controlled by a dimmer or rheostat. Begin by creating the environment of a children's playground. Coach players to take part in high-energy games, individually and with partners. After some time, when the rhythms of the environment are well established, bring down the lights slightly and suggest to the players that it is beginning to get dark and a little cold, and they should think of going home. Now coach for the idea that they cannot find their way out of the playground; it becomes darker, colder; it begins to rain; they search but cannot find their way home. This is an important part of the exercise because it establishes the atmosphere for much of the rest of it. Take time over it. Coach hard until you feel all of the players are committed to the situation and experiencing the dark, the cold, and the frustration. Bring down the lights to a mere twilight; introduce the concept of hunger—painful hunger. The players are tired, cold, lost, with the pain of hunger in their stomachs. Players will react to this differently. Some will cry,

shout out, thrash around. Let them. Coach that it isn't going to make any difference. Coach the players to accept the situation—not to forget and ignore it, but to accept it. Coach for stillness, awareness of the dark, empty space; no knowledge of how to get out. Take out the lights completely. It is night. Players have to find the best way of passing the night. Most will curl up in a fetal position or try to hide in corners of the space—a very basic, primitive reaction. Let the night be at least fifteen minutes of absolute dark solitude. Occasionally remind the players, quietly, of the hunger, cold, solitariness. Bring up the lights very slowly for morning. Coach the players to examine themselves—they are the only persons they can clearly see—to examine fingers, toes, hair; to determine their own reality. Coach then for discovering ways to pass the endless time. There is no release: They must accept the moment and find ways of filling it. Then, as the light becomes brighter, coach to discover one other person; to relate silently; to find ways to help each other pass the time. Players will rub each other's backs, massage feet, pick lint off one another, play leapfrog. Coach again for hunger, solitude, emptiness, now letting the pairs of players support each other in the situation.

Getting out of the improvisation without breaking the mood is difficult. A good way is to coach for weariness, sleep. Then introduce sunshine, warmth. The players will relax. Go into a deep-breathing exercise and conclude with a vigorous shakeout. The exercise should take up to two hours. When it works completely it gives players a strong sense of an existential angst and void, the importance of basic creature comforts, and the way in which a dependent relationship develops with another person.

PLAYING THE STYLE

As might be expected from a play whose background is *le néant*, *Waiting for Godot* gives virtually nothing biographical about its characters—they might as well have been unchangingly in the same place forever; which, metaphorically, of course, they have. But, as with all nonrealistic works, if we look closely at the structure and rhythms of the play, there is a great deal for the actor to go on.

We get a tremendous amount of information about Didi in the first two pages of the text. The only physical specifics are that he walks with short, stiff strides, legs wide apart. This gives the actor a strong sense of leg energy and rhythms. The shortness of stride suggests a quick, almost scurrying, movement; this is reinforced by stage directions for him such as "feverishly." He is goal-oriented, as we discover in the play, and is indicated in his first speech: "And I resumed the struggle." The leg stiffness may well extend to the rest of the body: We suggested earlier that Didi is not unlike the tree in maintaining his upright posture; he seldom sits.

We are also told in the first two pages that he broods, reflects, and is pensive; he is also later spoken of as musing. All of these are head-oriented qualities. He also peers a great deal, especially into his hat as if in a desperate attempt to discover some answer there. So head focus is added to leg energy, and the peering suggests that he may well lead with his head in posture terms. Didi also makes notes "precisely" and "exactly"; he is the analytic, questing, thinking member of the duo.

Didi is still trying; there is a positive sense about him; "admiringly" and "cheerfully" are used to describe his attitudes. But there is also a very mercurial swing in his manner; he goes from "cheerfully" to "gloomily" in the same sentence. His hearty laugh immediately causes pain in his prostate; his smile ceases as suddenly as it begins. He tells us that he "doesn't know if he is happy or not." All of this, of course, is consistent with the total atmosphere that Beckett is establishing; indeed, it is one of the ways in which he establishes it: the dichotomy of the human situation. Hope and despair, joy and pain, belief and negation, and final uncertainty. The pendulum of the human condition is the rhythm of Beckett's play; and the only fixed point is stasis when the pendulum comes to rest, before the mechanism is wound up to start its perpetual manic motion once again.

It tends to be Didi who rewinds the mechanism. He is the one who initiates: "Will you not play?" he asks. He would like Gogo occasionally to return the ball. All of this is associated with Didi's intention. We suggested that he was still trying: to find out The Answer. As generic as that: What is It about; is there Any purpose; is there Any outcome; is there Anyone there. Gogo's intention is simpler—to survive with as little effort or discomfort as possible.

Didi's obstacles are occasionally Gogo, whose lack of concern or even understanding of the problem is sometimes dispiriting, and the fact that Didi doesn't really know where to look. There is no fixed starting point, no definite premise for his thought process. It cannot be worked out by thought.

So Didi's tactics are to wait it out, to try to keep positive in the belief, like Mr. Micawber, that "something will turn up." He needs to maintain his relationship with Gogo; who is sometimes difficult to live with, but is all Didi has. He wants to keep looking—peering—trying to establish any certitudes—and filling in the rest of the time positively in inventing little games and canters of conviviality.

In pages 46 thorugh 49 of the text we are referring to, Didi and Gogo run the complete gamut of the elements that produce Beckett's style. It begins with a despairing pause, broken by Didi who attacks Gogo for his "whinings" and "lamentations," and then seeing Lucky's hat has a burst of enthusiasm at this "proof" of continuity. Didi tries on the hat, giving his own hat to Gogo, which leads to a classic comic shell game with the hats. It concludes with Didi keeping Lucky's hat on, for his own had "irked" him; that is to say, it had provided him with no solutions. After this highly farcical activity there is a silence. This becomes too much for Didi, who initiates the game of imitating Pozzo and Lucky, which again leads to physical comedy. During the game Gogo runs off, leaving Didi to discover he is alone. He rushes around the stage to find Gogo, punctuated by Gogo returning and leaving again, all of which affords further opportunity for physical bump-and-run shell games—wild erratic activity punctuated by moments of desperate attempted calm by Didi. The final attempt to see "if anyone is coming" leads to a little canter of overly acted politeness, which builds into an insult game. This is formally set up by Gogo, who recognizes that they have discovered a new game. It takes the structure of a *High Noon* confrontation, won by Gogo with the final shot of "critic." Again, this burst of activity is followed by silence, broken by Didi who suggests they could do their exercises. This leads to a joint incantation, very much like ritual church responses, and, in the same spirit of religiosity, the imitating of the tree, which puts both Didi and Gogo into crucifixion images and ends the sequence with cries of "God have pity on me! Pity on me." A return to stasis, pathos, and the ironical Christian iconography that is always present in the play.

The rhythms of excitation and stasis; the farcical activity; the clowning; the mutual irritation and dependency; the verbal duets and incantations, and the attempt by Didi both to initiate and control are all present in this relatively short section that, in true pattern of the circular nature of the play-imitating the pattern of human existence—is repeated with small variations throughout the structure of the play.

The exercises we have suggested here, and in the section on farce, provide an experience for the actors of every element of this structure. The *Vacuum* game and the *Sisyphus* games provide an approach to the silences and the hollow physical presence waiting to be filled. The *Deformities* and *Child's Play* exercises are a starting point for development of physical characterization, and they explore the active physical side of Didi and Gogo's dependency. The further dimensions of the dependency can be discovered through the *Married Couples* and *Body and Mind* exercises, and the *Master-Slave* game from the farce section. What all of these games do is to give the actor a physical experience of the rhythms of waiting and the bursts of childlike release with which they are punctuated. They also allow actors to explore, away from the detailed specifics of the text, and thus discover a broad range of choices, which may then be assimilated into both their characters' masks and the structure of the play's action when the text is confronted.

SUGGESTED READINGS

Barrett, William, *Irrational Man*. New York: Doubleday, 1958.

Bigsby, C. W. E., *Dada and Surrealism*. London: Methuen, 1972.

Cohn, Ruby, *Just Play: Beckett's Theatre*. Princeton, N.J.: Princeton University Press, 1980.

———, ed., *Casebook on Waiting for Godot*. New York: Grove Press, 1967.

Esslin, Martin, *The Theatre of the Absurd*. New York: Doubleday, 1961.

———, ed., *Samuel Beckett*. Englewood Cliffs, N.J.: Prentice-Hall, Spectrum Books, 1965.

Guicharnaud, Jacques, *Modern French Theatre*. New Haven: Yale University Press, 1967.

Hayman, Ronald, *Eugene Ionesco*. New York: Frederick Ungar, 1976.

Morrison, Kristin, *Canters and Chronicles*. Chicago: University of Chicago Press, 1983.

Pronko, Leonard, *Avant-Garde: The Experimental Theatre*. Berkeley: University of California Press, 1965.

12   **Brecht and Epic Theatre**

Helene Weigel as Mother Courage.   *Berliner Ensemble.*

BACKGROUND

Personal.   The character of Bertolt Brecht's theatre reflects the dialectical form that his life itself took: his attempt to balance emotion with reason and poetic instinct with scientific discipline. His traumatic experience as a medical orderly in World War I made him a fanatic pacifist violently opposed to those international political forces—which he identified with capitalism—that for economic profit could send human beings into senseless slaughter. Brecht felt despair at the gap between the romantic sense of human possibility and the brute reality of human actions. It was to be the creed of Marxism that would bring Brecht hope of the possibility of changing human nature and improving social and economic conditions. Before this, however, he wrote a play of cynical romanticism to purge himself before he could begin his journey from poetry and putrefaction, through political didacticism and social mechanics to the dialectical, epic theatre of his mature years.

Baal, written in 1918, has the episodic structure of Brecht's later work but is filled with youthful disgust at man's inability either to control his own lust and greed or to influence the world around him. The play is replete with images of drifting and decay. Man is seen as an excremental creature whose aspirations are mocked by animal instincts and physical decline. Here, as in his play *Edward II,* Brecht identifies human nature with physical nature; these plays are full of savage landscapes, slime, rot, and self-indulgence. We are as little able to change nature as to control our own.

This anarchical, nihilistic Brecht begins to discover a possible solution to the decadent purposelessness of man's condition in his play *Man Is Man,* written in 1925. Here there is still the sense that man is no more than man (with the negative connotations of that fact), but the lack of a defined individuality is now turned to profit: Man can be remade into any model that particular social conditions may require. The possibility of social engineering (with all

that suggests, both in terms of "superman" and brainwashing) was a turning point in Brecht's rejection of his youthful nihilism and his movement toward social awareness and didacticism.

It was after writing *Man Is Man* that Brecht turned to a study of Marxism. This led to the writing of his more overtly political plays: *St. Joan of the Stockyards, The Measures Taken, The Exception and the Rule,* and *The Mother,* all written between 1929 and 1932. In these plays he perfects both the didactic nature and the dialectic structure of his epic theatre. The plays of his maturity—of which the best-known are *Mother Courage, The Good Person of Setzuan,* and *The Caucausian Chalk Circle*—keep the moralistic nature and the epic structure of the earlier plays, but allow his instinctive poetic nature more scope. These later plays are more free-flowing and have less direct didactic impact: Marxism and romanticism, individualism and collectivism, rational skepticism and myth are blended. The pessimism of Brecht's youth is balanced by the optimism he found through the Marxist creed. This dialectic position enabled him to say in the epilogue to one of his last plays—*The Good Person of Setzuan*—"There must, there must, there's got to be a way."

Aesthetic.   The artistic climate of Brecht's early manhood was heavily influenced by expressionism, which used multiple scenes, having no rational connection to recapitulate the fluid, nonlogical sequence of thought and dreams. It was theme- or idea-centered, as opposed to the plot- or conflict-centered nature of the "well-made" play. In its themes, expressionism also shared in the social and political revolt against bourgeois sensibility that was at the root of the artistic avant garde.

Brecht accepted the revolutionary sensibility of the theatre of his time. He rejected the staple diet of nineteenth-century German theatre—bombastic classics, photographic realism, drawing-room comedy—as "culinary"

Two cartoons by George Grosz give strong gestic sense of despair at the human condition which informed Brecht's work.   *Nicholson and Watson.*

theatre, to be consumed for emotional titillation or after-dinner entertainment. Like Stanislavski, he reacted against the empty rant of the romantic acting style and sought after a more "truthful" theatre. But whereas Stanislavski's truth was an emotional and psychological one that led him to become the great exponent of naturalism, Brecht's was a sociopolitical truth that led *him* to reject naturalism and romanticism alike.

A form of theatre that heavily influenced Brecht was that of Erwin Piscator, who regarded the theatre as an instrument for the political education of the masses. It was a theatre of minimal literary content, often compiled simply of newspaper reports or documentary material. Piscator would use graphs, captions, projections, and newsreel and film sequences to convey the political or sociological background to the play. The propaganda inference was drawn by choruses, on stage or in the auditorium, singing or speaking the political point so the audience couldn't miss it.

It was from Piscator that Brecht took the technological structure and political focus of his theatre, and from expressionism he borrowed the episodic form. His themes were not to be the inner-directed and Freudian ones of the expressionists. He rejected these psychological concerns just as he rejected the emotional focus of what he termed the "Aristotelian" theatre of vertical plot progression and cathartic climax. The aesthetic of Brecht's theatre was to show and demonstrate the economic, social, and political condition of humanity.

Political. Brecht's early disillusioned romanticism, which was evident in *Baal,* had left him in an existential void, filled only by despair at a human condition seemingly governed by aimless and irrationally impersonal forces. Brecht needed a core of positive belief, and this was afforded by Marxism. His answer to *le néant* was not to see it as absurd, but to fill it with the vision of a new, progressive man.

To the anarchical side of Brecht, which had seen the world without sense or purpose, the Marxist concept of a dynamic pattern in human history—the inevitability of the class struggle and progress toward the victory of the proletariat—came as both a relief and a worthwhile cause. Life was no longer static and incapable of being influenced by human endeavor. All causes, all effects, all relationships are dynamic and therefore susceptible to improvement. History was not written by an unkind and unknowable fate; it was the outcome of human struggles, and the laws governing these were known. This scientific and rational explanation of life gave Brecht a firm foothold among what had been the shifting sands of an aimless existence. He clung to his new-found belief and determinedly rejected psychological or emotional explanations for man's behavior—a principle that was to have a crucial effect upon the nature of his theatre.

Marxist Dialectic.   It was not only the scientific certitude of Marxism that appealed to Brecht but also the dramatic quality of the Hegelian dialectic upon which it was based. The coexistence of opposites, the merging of thesis and antithesis, the fact that order cannot be conceived without disorder—in a word, dynamic ambiguity—-was for Brecht the ironic essence of drama. The dialectical sense runs throughout his theatre: the actor who impersonates the character, yet remains himself; the stage that represents reality, yet remains a stage; the characters who are themselves, yet can be made into something else.

The dialectic also gave Brecht his integrated form. Following Hegel, Marxism believed that content determined form. Forms are historically determined by the kind of content they have to embody. Thus, the nature of a country's economic structure determines the form of its social, political, and cultural identity. The political intention of Brecht's theatre must, therefore, determine and be dynamically related to its form. More than this, the politically engaged nature of Marxist art (it must be involved in the creation of a socialist society) rejects empathetic illusion (which Brecht associated with Aristotelian theatre), so that the audience will not mistake the symbols and images it receives for realities. Here is the basis for Brecht's objectivity of presentation—or "alienation" effect.

Marxism provided Brecht with a strong sense of purpose—an optimistic political faith susceptible of scientific proof; a political content that matched his theatrical form; and the triumph of rational thought over romantic sentimentality. Yet the poet in Brecht survived. Perhaps the most important dialectic of all, that between the politician and the poet, remained a constant feature of Brecht's life and was to be acknowledged in one of his poems:

> I am the most practical of all my brethren—
> And my head comes first of all!
> My brethren were cruel, I am the cruellest—
> And I weep in the night.[1]

Alienation: Verfremdungs Effect.   It was toward the breaking of empathy that Brecht directed his alienation effect. Brecht did not reject the place of emotion in human life and in theatre. Nor did he exclude pleasure and entertainment as a function of theatre. But the pleasure was not to be gained through meretricious and narcotic emotional self-indulgence. It was to be a more intellectual pleasure, of the kind experienced when one successfully solves a mathematical problem or understands the causes and circumstances of some human event. It was not emotion per

[1]Quoted by Martin Esslin, *Brecht: A Choice of Evils* (London: Methuen, 1965), p. 227.

se that Brecht excluded, but the empathy that it produces. Empathy: giving oneself up to the emotions of a theatrical occasion; sharing the emotional state of the character to the degree that his or her emotions become "real" and erase all consciousness that one is at the theatrical event. It was to this that Brecht objected. For in this condition man has suspended his capacity for critical judgment of the social reality behind the emotional state.

Alienation has the function of freeing socially conditioned phenomena from the stamp of familiarity. To see your mother as "a man's wife" is to achieve an alienation. Alienation draws attention to the familiar by showing it in a new light. It makes something special out of the ordinary.

In the theatre, alienation prevents empathy by breaking the dramatic illusion that what the audience is witnessing is a form of "real" life. The audience must be reminded that it is in a theatre, that the play is not a seamless whole but constructed of many parts, and that those parts must be kept independently visible so the audience may reflect upon the way in which the events are represented. As Brecht put it in the preface to *St. Joan of the Stockyards:* "The intention is to exhibit not only the actions, but the manner in which they are subjected to the processes of theatre."

The theatrical principle of alienation ties in, once again, with Marxist doctrine. *Entfremdung* is the estrangement felt by workers in a capitalist society who can only sell their labor and not participate directly in the economic control of the society. The need Brecht saw for alienation (estrangement) was related to a critical objectivity about the complex social and political ramifications of capitalist society. Rather than accepting conditions as inevitable, they must be viewed with critical remove, a scientific capacity to see beneath the surface of things, or to regain the experience of the

first perception. Brecht was to express this in his poems for the *Messingkauf Dialogues:*

> O joy of beginning. O early morning.
> First grass. O first page of the book,
> Long awaited, the surprise of it.
> And the first spray of water
> on a sweaty face.
> The clean, cool shirt.
> O beginning of work.
> And first puff of smoke,
> filling the lungs. And you too,
> New idea.[2]

Epic versus Dramatic.   The achievement of alienation underlies Brecht's entire theory of epic theatre. Brecht set out the theory, comparing it with dramatic theatre, in a note to his play *Mahagonny*. It will be useful to quote it in full before commenting upon it.

Dramatic Theatre	Epic Theatre
plot	narrative
involves the spectator	makes the spectator an observer
wears down his capacity for action	but arouses his capacity to action
provides him with sensations	forces him to take decisions
experience	view of the world
suggestion	argument
instinctive feeling preserved	brought to the point of recognition
spectator shares the experience	spectator studies the experience
human being is taken for granted	human being subjected to inquiry
he is unalterable	he is able to alter

[2]From *Brecht on Theatre*, edited and translated by John Willett. Copyright © 1957, 1963 and 1964 by Suhrkamp Verlag, Frankfurt am Main. This translation and notes copyright © 1964 by John Willett. Reprinted by permission of Hill & Wang (a division of Farrar, Strauss and Giroux, Inc.).

eyes on the finish	eyes on the course
one scene makes another	each scene for itself
growth	montage
linear development	in curves
evolutionary determinism	jumps
man as a fixed point	man as a process
thought determines being	social being determines thought
feeling	reason[3]

The point here is not the extent to which Brecht was right in his assessment of dramatic or Aristotelian structure, but how the whole theory of epic theatre is geared toward the creation of the alienation effect: the keeping of a critical remove on the part of the audience that enables it to consider the social content of the theatrical action and to make decisions about it in political terms equally in the cause of alienation. Brecht insisted upon the historification of his theatre—the setting of its events in the past. Historification will shut off the conditioning forces of society and allow the audience to sit back and critically consider events placed in the past. However, these events will have significant connections with the audience's present circumstances.

The intention of epic theatre was to create a better human environment—and thus a better human. Marxism, scientific functionalism, and behaviorism all came together to give Brecht's theatre its strong focus on social mechanics. His first really didactic play, *A Man's a Man*, contains these lines:

> You can do with a human being what you will.
> Take him apart like a car, rebuild him bit by bit.[4]

[3]Ibid, p. 37.
[4]From the Grove Press edition, edited by Eric Bentley (New York, 1964), p. 160.

Brecht did not exclude feelings, insights, and impulses from his theatre, but he wished to employ them primarily to change the entire scope of human relationships. For Brecht, the author, actor, and director are producers, like any other maker of a social product, and they operate in a concrete world of abstract creativity. The product—the play—is not a reflection of, but a reflection *on*, social reality. It should show that character and action are historically determined and subject to change. The spectator sees man the way he is, not because fate is the way it is, but because social conditions are the way they are. A new man, not socially or economically oppressed, is needed, and theatre should demonstrate the possibility of his achievement.

The purpose of epic theatre, then, was:

to make the spectator a critical observer who must make decisions.

to present the world as an object and to do this through dialectical demonstration.

to focus on the process, not the outcome of the play.

to explore the social determinism of the individual, showing the historical nature of human misfortune, the changeable order of nature, and the manipulability of man and his environment.

INTRINSIC DEMANDS

Form.   Brecht used the term *epic* in the German sense of the word: a narrative not tied to time. This he opposed to *tragic* or Aristotelian form, which was geared to a strongly focused action and more unified time and place. *Epic* did not necessarily have the connotation of a heroic scale, but simply the idea of a loosely linked series of events. We have already suggested that the episodic form this sense of epic gave to Brecht's theatre was related to expressionism but it also found its sensibility in older forms of theatre. The morality tradition, which saw man as process rather than character, had a similar sense of direct address with a moral theme and abstract use of time and place. Both the Elizabethan drama and the German playwrights Büchner and Wedekind used a dynamic, sequential episodic structure.

The epic form also resembles a Homeric narrative. *Mother Courage* in particular is not unlike the *Odyssey*, with its twelve independent scenes, the journey of its central character, a wagon taking the place of Ulysses' ship, and the battlefields of Sweden and Germany equaling the plains of Troy. Within this form Brecht draws liberally from fairy tales, clown traditions (such as the German Folk figure, Hans Würst), and the British authors Kipling, Gay, and Dickens. Indeed, like Shakespeare, he used whatever suited his needs to create a nuclear form moving on several levels of time, space, and narrative at once. What resulted was a clear, coolly delineated chain of events presenting a body of evidence from which sociopolitical lessons might be drawn in a detached and lucid manner.

The episodic structure, calculated to break the audience's emotional continuity and thus its empathy, had a strongly dialectical basis. The thesis-antithesis structure of an argument was present in the relationship of scenes. This was most evident in Brecht's didactic plays (or *Lehrstücke*), but was also present in his later parables. We are going to look briefly at the structure of a play from the early period.

Epic Form: An Early Example. *The Exception and the Rule* is one of Brecht's most famous didactic plays. It is in nine episodes, and it deals with a German merchant somewhere in Asia who is making a difficult journey through uncharted deserts to beat his competitors to an oil concession. He has with him a guide, and a coolie as porter. The first episode illustrates the merchant's harsh, exploiting attitude toward his companions—his philosophy of winning at all costs. In the second episode the merchant

realizes he can't win on his own, so out of self-interest he appears to change his attitude. He is friendly to the guide in the third episode, but failing to win him over and realizing the coolie can act as guide and carry the goods as well, he dismisses him. A constant dialectic of attitude is taking place, showing the changing faces of self-interest and exploitation.

Episodes four through seven continue the dialectical quality of the play: The more the coolie shows himself intelligent, useful, and willing to serve the merchant, the more the merchant mistrusts and fears him. There is a splendid irony when the coolie pitches a tent for the merchant to sleep in, but the merchant fears he will be attacked in the night and stays awake while the coolie calmly sleeps. Finally, when they have run out of water, the coolie makes a gesture to share his bottle with the merchant, but the merchant's mistrust is such that he believes the coolie is trying to kill him with a stone, and he shoots him. The final scene is in a courtroom—the dramatic yet factual and dispassionate nature of legal proceedings was one of Brecht's favorite models. The merchant is tried for killing the coolie, but the judgment is a neat dialectical irony. The merchant is acquitted because, after all that he had done to the coolie, he had no reason to expect kindness from him, and had every reason to think the coolie would kill him—thus, he acted in self-defense. The didactic moral of the play is that, the way the world is now oriented, kind and humane actions lead to death, and conscious exploitation to success. The audience is asked to recognize this and—the last line of the play—"do something about it."

A Later Example. *The Exception and the Rule,* being geared entirely toward didactic ends, is a highly refined example of the dialectical structure of Brecht's work, to the exclusion of the more sweeping, poetic qualities of his later writing. But running through the broad palette of his mature epic drama is a strong structural spine of a dialectical nature that gives the play a clear sociopolitical focus. *The Good Person of Setzuan* is an example of this. Written in ten episodes, it is a parable *cum* fairy tale about three gods who come down to earth in a Chinese city looking for "good" people. The only person who will give them shelter is the local prostitute Shen Te—an immediate assertion of true goodness being found in a woman regarded as "bad" by society's morality. The play then goes on to explore the dialectic between the attempt to be good and the need to make a living in contemporary social conditions. This is done through the central conceit of the play: Shen Te becomes a split person, pretending to become her cousin, Shui Ta, who is her temperamental opposite—a tough, rational businessman.

A sense of despair at the human condition. *The Good Person of Setzuan.   La Jolla Playhouse. Photo by Ken Howard.*

Each episode of the play gives a different perspective upon this central theme, and the episodes contrast with each other to show the problems Shen Te's "goodness" gets her into, followed by the hard-nosed actions of Shui Ta sorting out the problems.

The dialectical theme of the play is clearly delineated in each episode and constantly brought to the audience's attention. Shen Te, as her own loving, sympathetic self, finds it impossible to operate in the modern world, whereas the somewhat ruthless, hardheaded Shui Ta actually brings about more "good" in the world's terms than she does. Nor are the gods any help. Having found some goodness in the world, they are happy enough to leave things as they are—the implication being, of course, that humankind must change itself. Shen Te is left in pretty much the position she started in—to be good and yet survive tears a person in two. Brecht has stated the thesis and the antithesis; he leaves the audience to find the synthesis, saying, "It is for you to find a way, my friends, you write the happy ending to the play."

Gestus.   In essence, a *gestus* is a refined and firmly outlined physical representation of the thematic idea. Each scene has its gestus, as well as each character—the scenic gestus and character gestus must reinforce each other.

The *Grundgestus* is the basic sociopolitical interpretation of the play. Human action has to be remodeled into gestus: All the events of the text must be considered anew and placed in a larger economic and social context. Within this overview each episode must be examined to discover the gestural expression of the social relationships in the event. Much of this work will be done by the director, whose responsibility it is to create the shape of an episode so that the potential is there for the actor to discover those choices that best reveal the dialectic: This is done by a personal gestus played by the actor. A very famous

Mother Courage's silent scream, in the New York Public Theatre production.   *Photo by Martha Swope.*

Brechtian scenic space in a production of *The Good Person of Setzuan*, directed by John Harrop. Note the spareness, utilitarian props, scaffolding, visible lighting instruments, and slogans.

gestus was that used by Helene Weigel in the title role of *Mother Courage*. The *Grundgestus* of the piece is concerned with criticizing capitalism and the way in which it profits from the horrors of war. Mother Courage represents the dialectic of profit and suffering within her character. She is a businesswoman who makes a living out of war by selling goods to the armies. She is also a mother whose children are potential victims of war. In the particular instance she is asked to pay a bribe to get her son, Swiss Cheese, back from some soldiers. She haggles over the price until too late, and Swiss Cheese is shot. It is at this moment that Weigel played the gestus of the silent scream. Extreme suffering overtook her body but her wide-opened mouth didn't emit a sound. It is a playing against the release of emotion that makes the emotion more powerful. The gestus tells of universal suffering in war, the agony of those who are torn between survival and sacrifice, a pain that is too powerful to express and, equally, is never heard by those who traffic in war.

An extremely interesting gestus was used at the end of the first German production of Peter Weiss's *Marat/Sade*. As the revolutionaries marched, singing, toward the audience, a figure separated from the group and stood with its back to the house. The hat, coat, and posture said Napoleon. The figure then turned to face the house; there was a skull under the tricorn hat. The gestus is clearly saying that the revolutionary aspirations and fervor will end in the death of the revolution through the agency of Napoleon: that revolutionaries, by their actions, are always in danger of putting themselves back in the service of authoritarianism. It is a dialectic in those terms, and a splendid example of alienation: It is an image that will make an audience sit up and think. The skull also has all the metaphoric associations of the medieval *memento mori*, and thus has the power of being one of the most universal of human icons.

Space and Gestus.   Brecht's use of space both accommodates and reinforces the epic qualities of his plays. Being essentially unlocalized and unspecific, after the tradition of the Medieval and Elizabethan stage, it allows for a wide sweep of events and episodic change. In Brecht's own production of *Mother Courage,* the first image was undefined space: a large, empty stage backed by a pale cyclorama. All was open to discussion and definition. On the floor was a large circle within which the scenes were set. The circle was the world of Mother Courage, and the circle turned. Mother Courage's wagon is on this turntable, moving in the opposite direction to the turntable's movement. This appearance of movement on the wagon's part is a neat solution to the changing locations in the play, but it also creates the effect that the wagon is moving but getting nowhere—a gestus of Mother Courage's action. That action is a declining one for, at the end of the play, her children are all lost or dead and she, like an animal, is left to harness herself to the wagon. All of this served the *Grundgestus* or interpretative idea of the play: Mother Courage has stupidly harnessed herself to the warmongering capitalist system that kills off all real value in her life and gives her nothing in return.

The simplicity, spareness, and utilitarian nature of the space in epic theatre emphasizes the play's narrative—or fable—and the actor's didactic function. The space functions as a classroom with the set as teaching aid and the actor as instructor; much of the action in epic theatre will have a downstage focus—it is informing the audience. Brecht did not attempt to disguise any of the theatrical apparatus: The lighting instruments were shown hanging on their pipes and were ungelled; scaffolding was often employed rather than solid scenery. Projections, slides, titles were all used to further the didactic purpose of the theatre and integrate the scenic gestus into the overall function of breaking empathic illusion and producing an audience response that was, in Brecht's own image, like that of the spectator at a sporting event who is judging the quality of the play and the technical expertise of the players, while enjoying the event.

Costume and Properties.   Although Brecht didn't operate on any kind of realistic premise in his use of space, he took extreme care that costumes and properties create the correct socioeconomic impression. Simplicity and selectivity were, again, two principles on which he operated, but to these were added a strong functional and utilitarian sense. His production of *Antigone* used sack-cloth and cotton for the costumes, with inserts of leather—workmanlike materials with tactile qualities. The colors were deep browns, reds, and grays— the colors of earth, blood, and granite. Brecht wished each scene, or episode, of his plays to have a basic tonal gestus. This developed with the play to underscore the *Grundgestus,* or thematic idea. Costumes had to show the evidence of wear, and the props were not realistic but in fact real. Brecht would have them made not by theatre technicians but by actual craftsmen, or he would use objects that had been in daily use in real life. One of his poems shows his sensibility in this area:

> Of all works my favorite
> are those which show usage.
> The Copper vessels with bumps and dented
>   edges.
> The knives and forks whose wooden
>   handles are
> worn down by many hands.[5]

[5]John Willett and Ralph Manheim, eds., in *Bertolt Brecht Poems, 1913–1956,* trans. John Willett. Volumes 3 and 4 of *Gedichte.* © Copyright 1961 Suhrkamp Verlag, Frankfurt am Main. Reproduced by permission of Methuen, Inc. From the estate of Bertold Brecht.

This flowed from Brecht's pragmatic romanticism. The simple, well-worn human artifact appealed to his sense of man's dignity and aspirations seen in a social and historical context. He was as careful over the correct use of properties as he was of the correct performance of work on stage: Scenes of building, cooking, mending, and other basic human tasks had to be done with workmanlike accuracy. Work, the economic product of labor, was, after all, at the basis of Marxist philosophy.

Costume as Gestus.   As props and costumes relate so specifically to character, the way in which they are worn or used can make them part of a character's gestus. The wearing of a cloth cap can be a strong gestus indicating a worker—just as a bowler hat can suggest the bourgeoisie. In *A Man's a Man*, guns denote both military and phallic oppression. In *The Resistible Rise of Arturo Ui*—which transfers to Chicago the story of the rise to power of Adolf Hitler—a mustache and a particular manner of wearing the hair are enough of a gestus to identify the leading character. In this way makeup can play its part in creating both character mask and gestus. In his production of *Edward II*, Brecht asked the question, "What do soldiers do in battle?" Someone suggested, "They are afraid." Brecht gave his soldiers chalk-white faces in a brilliant gestic sense of the scene.

A deathly white face is virtually a mask, and Brecht was given to the use of physical masks, especially in his earlier plays. He was influenced in this by the use of masks in Oriental theatre, which created a broad yet controlled style of playing in which small emotional or psychological detail was discounted. A mask thus becomes an alienation factor and at the same time an absolute indication of character attitude—a strong, simple, if unsubtle gestus. A mask leaves an actor in no doubt of the objective nature of the character he or she is "wearing."

Suit, mustache, hair, and walk create strong, economical character gestus for Arturo Ui in *The Resistible Rise of Arturo Ui.*   *The Guthrie Theatre.*

Music and Song.   Brecht uses music and song—which appear in virtually all of his plays—for the same two basic purposes that underlie the dynamics of the rest of his theatrical form: alienation and gestus. There is never any attempt to disguise the music or use it in an atmospheric or "incidental" way to create emotional mood. The musicians are on stage in full view of the audience, as much a part of the setting as are the lights. The nature of the music is also calculated to break any empathic response from the audience. It is functional music, never lyricism, as in *The Threepenny Opera*, where the most tender love song described the attachment of

Use of masks in a production of *The Good Person of Setzuan*. Note also the simple, worn nature of costumes.

a pimp and his whore—a dialectic between form and content.

The songs punctuate the action of the play and reinforce the theme. There is no pretense—as in musicals or operettas—that the action is continuing from speaking into singing. The action stops for the song—thus reinforcing the alienation effect—and the song passes comment upon the action in a gestic manner. Thus, the song becomes a part of the total gestus of the scene, while adding a perspective to the action that leaves the audience in no doubt as to the correct critical position it should take. The songs range from the most aggressively didactic, as the "Song of the Courts" in *The Exception and the Rule*

> The law courts will give the vultures
> food-aplenty.

> Thither fly the killers. The tormentors
> Will be safe there. And there
> The thieves hide their loot they call profit . . . [6]

to the more ironic song of Mother Courage:

> Sabres and swords are hard to swallow:
> First you must give men beer to drink.
> Then they can face what is to follow—
> But let 'em swim before they sink!

> Christians awake! The winter's gone!
> The snows depart, the dead sleep on.

[6]Bertold Brecht, *The Measures Taken and other Lehrstücke*. From *The Exception and the Rule*, trans. Ralph Manheim (London: Eyre Methuen, Ltd. 1977), p. 52. Translation Copyright © 1977 by Stefan S. Brecht, *Die Ausnähme und die Regel (The Exception and the Rule)*. Copyright 1957 by Suhrkamp Verlag, Berlin. Reprinted by permission of Random House.

And though you may not long survive
Get out of bed and look alive.[7]

To heighten the alienation effect and project the ironic nature of their content, the songs are consciously unmelodic. They are acted rather than sung. The singer is a reporter of the verse, tending not to follow the melody but to speak against the music, setting up a dialectic that creates a strong aural impression on the audience. The audience is not lulled by the music, but made to sit up and take notice of the gestic content.

Language and Gestus.   Brecht was a poet and songwriter before he became a playwright—a poet of the streets and cabarets—whose verse has a light and satirical quality that owes much of its simplicity and directness to the tradition of Anglo-Saxon ballads. This was the basis of his whole sense of language. There was a roughness and irregularity, a carelessness that yet gave a unique sense of character—not unlike the works of Woody Guthrie and Bob Dylan and the folk and protest singers of the 1960s. He drew on street songs, sentimental "pop," the *Barrack-Room Ballads* of Kipling, cabaret lyrics, biblical syntax, and the sweeping unrhymed verses of the Elizabethans. He refined this mixture to the bone, cutting out anything that did not speak to the essence of the theme. The result was a richly textured yet dry, chopped-off linguistic style with a syncopated rhythm—clarity and precision with an inherently dialectical sense of contradiction built into the language. It is full of contrasted half-sentences, parallelisms, inversions. Prose moves into heightened prose or irregular verse. Blank verse and prose alternate. The whole narrative pattern is interspersed with songs.

The language had to do three things: be intelligible to the ears of the proletarian audience; convey the underlying gestus—the essential attitude of the character; and avoid the creation of emotional empathy in the audience. Lyricism, undue embellishment, and rhetorical passion had no part in epic theatre. A narrative style and asymmetrical verse form allowed for both the didactic aim and a poetic impact that kept the audience off balance with its rhythms rather than lulling them to sleep. For Brecht, language was theatrical insofar as it correctly presented the attitude (gestus) of the person speaking it. Everything in his theatre is geared to the presentation of the social theme of the play. The setting makes a thematic statement; the scene/episode has a gestic core; the character has his gestus; and the language—as conveying the theme and used by the characters—will have gestic qualities that fit these purposes.

A simple narrative style; an asymmetrical sense of rhythm; an ironic, dialectic content; a refined poetic eclecticism; and a clear, direct thematic focus—these are the elements the actor must encompass when dealing with the language of Brecht's plays.

Didacticism and Irony.   Didacticism is overtly or implicitly present in all of Brecht's work, and the actor will be unable to understand its sensibility without recognizing this. The *Lehrstücke* contain the most explicit instructions to the audience. The opening of *The Exception and the Rule* states:

> Examine carefully the behaviour of these
>   people.
> Find it surprising though not unusual
> Inexplicable though normal
> . . . .
> For to say that something is natural
> is to regard it as unchangeable.[8]

---

[7]*Mother Courage and Her Children*, trans. Eric Bentley (London: Eyre Methuen Ltd. 1972), p. 4. Translation Copyright © 1955, 1959, 1961, 1962 by Eric Bentley; original work published as *Mutter Courage und ihre Kinder.* Copyright 1949 by Suhrkamp Verlag vormals J. Fischer, Frankfurt/Main.

[8]*The Exception and the Rule*, trans. Manheim, p. 37.

And as we have already noted, the ending to the play asks the audience to "do something about it." Another famous *Lehrstück, The Measures Taken,* specifically sets out the ABC's of communism, both within the play and in the final chorus:

> The ABC of Communism:
> Instructions to the ignorant concerning their
>   condition,
> Class-consciousness to the oppressed
> And to the class-conscious, practical
>   knowledge of the revolution.[9]

While Marxism taught Brecht that society could be changed, and he accepted this because he wanted to believe that life has a positive purpose—that it was not merely absurd—he was still aware that he had to live in the world as he found it. To do this he assumed an attitude of ironic servility: Do not antagonize authority; confuse it with irony, which was the source of much of the humor in his work. The survivors are the antiheroes, those who bend with the wind so as not to break. Enlightened self-interest and peasant cunning will help the oppressed to survive in a world geared against them. One day social revolution will destroy capitalism and preclude war making, so it is important to survive till that day. Like the Good Soldier Schweik, who avoids death by pretending to comply, or Azdak, the corrupt judge who achieves good by playing the world at its own game—two of Brecht's most engaging characters—Brecht's own stance was a pacifistic and antiheroic one.

A strong flavor of the man comes through in his plays, a didactic purpose that not only preaches Marxist philosophy and the need for a revolution in man's socioeconomic condition, but also teaches the importance of playing for time, waiting for the right

moment—and surviving. The grasping of this dialectical and ironic sensibility is important to the actor who wishes to understand Brecht's work: the work of a man who had a Marxist theatre and an Austrian passport; who performed plays in East Germany but published them in West Germany; the anti-capitalist who kept a Swiss bank account—the world-acclaimed theatrical practitioner who liked to speak of himself as "Poor Bert Brecht."

PERFORMANCE DEMANDS

Character and Gestus.   The basis of physical characterization is gestus. This is both a physical attitude and a point of view. The starting point is an external one, not arising from generalized aspects of human behavior, but from those physical elements that will delineate a sociopolitical individual in a specific time, place, and class structure. The actor will build his or her part from a social perspective, and will not look for emotional, psychological, or metaphysical motivations for action, but for the social gist of the part.

The questions an actor must ask are not, Who am I? but What am I? Not, Who does this action? but What is this action? It is the action and the consequences of the action in social and economic terms that concern Brecht, not the nature of the psychical self. The question is not: Is a capitalist a capitalist *because* he or she is anally retentive, or sexually impotent? Rather, it is: What is the social effect of *being* a capitalist? Rather than try to develop an emotional persona for the character, the actor should start with a clear understanding of the *Grundgestus* and how this is reflected in social and economic terms in each episode of the play. The episode is similar to the Stanislavskian unit of action. Brecht broke down the first scene of *Mother Courage* into such episodes as:

> Recruiters roam the country looking for
>   cannon fodder;
> Courage presents her family to a sergeant;

[9]*The Measures Taken,* trans. Carl R. Mueller (London: Eyre Methuen Ltd., 1977), p. 34. Translation Copyright © 1977 by Stefan S. Brecht. *Die Massnähme (The Measures Taken)* Copyright 1955 by Suhrkamp Verlag, Berlin.

Courage defends her sons against recruiters;
Courage bargains and loses one of her sons.

The actor's task is to discover the choices that best illustrate the character's function in each of these episodes. That function is determined in social terms, and no throughline of motivation is required to link the episodes together. Each episode is considered as a separate entity, and apparent contradictions in character attitude are part of the dialectic that Brecht is setting up. The character may be explored in any way the actor believes useful, including emotional responses to the action; but final choices must be made in terms of social, not psychological, behavior, and the demands of the fable—the telling of the narrative of the story—must always supercede any illustration of personal character, as opposed to character in social relationships.

A gestus may be the physical (including costume) attributes of a character that project the essential socioeconomic function of the role, or it may be a particular gesture or moment of action that embodies thematic meaning. To take the example of the dialectical character Shen Te/Shui Ta in *The Good Person of Setzuan:* a change of body rhythm from the shuffling, compliant walk of the exploited woman to the determined stride of the entrepreneur; a change of vocal intonation; plus the change of a *chongsam* dress for a business suit will, in very specific yet simple ways, achieve a complete change of character gestus. Strongly defined body rhythms and centers of energy are fundamental to the delineation of character gestus, which should be done as if using a charcoal pencil with firm, selected, economical strokes.

In her creation of the character of Mother Courage, Helene Weigel constantly used money as a character gestus. Throughout the play every time she was given money she would bite it to make sure it was good. And in the final episode when she is paying peasants to bury her daughter, she took a hand-

Gestus of a capitalist in this cartoon by George Grosz: cigar, paunch containing factory, and stance provide all necessary information.

ful of coins from her purse to give to them, then stopped, put one coin carefully back in the purse before handing them over. Here, at the very last, she sums up in a gestus the dialectical contradiction in her character, between mother and businesswoman, that had destroyed her in the play and reinforced the overall dialectic between humanity and capitalism.

Another good example of gestus from *Mother Courage* was the way in which the old Colonel, who is to pay for the wagon in return for Yvette's sexual favors, used his walking stick. He pushed it into the ground with great sexual force so that it bent and snapped back up again. This was both a piece

Integration of character and scenic gestus illustrate the trapped Macheath in this Oregon Shakespeare Festival production of *The Threepenny Opera*.   *Photo by Henry Kranzler.*

of amusing phallic comedy and a dynamic character gestus.

A good example of the creation of character gestus—although a gestus not consciously made for the purpose of social criticism—may be found in the films of Humphrey Bogart, especially *The Maltese Falcon*. Bogart's character creations were all distinguished by certain gestic features: a walk, a hunch of the shoulders, a curl of the lip, a sibilant, almost lisping speech, a coolly dispassionate manner, a hat, and a trench coat. This was the gestus of the antihero of his time—the outsider, the cynical, warm-hearted, ironical tough guy. Never sparing more effort than was necessary; never emotionally self-indulgent; always coolly in control of himself; seemingly at an intellectual re-move from what he was doing, Humphrey Bogart could well have been a Brechtian actor. Indeed, one of his fellow actors in *The Maltese Falcon* had worked with Brecht: Peter Lorre played the leading role in *A Man's a Man* and other Brecht productions. Lorre's facial mask, peculiar vocal quality, threateningly cringing manner (a dialectic), and dry, restrained style just hinting at emotion are all typically gestic qualities. In the same way, Sydney Green-street's corpulence, panama hat, sweaty fore-head, cigar, and oily politeness created the gestus of the capitalist, gentleman crook. These actors all give the impression of being aware of what they are doing. There is a clarity, economy, and intelligence about their work that suggests they could well be passing social comment upon their characters in the situation.

Whatever form it takes, the gestus should always be related to the total thematic concern of the play. This, as we have suggested, will be embodied by the use of space and the set-ting of the play, and each episode will have its gestus of action that relates to the whole. In working on and presenting his or her charac-ter, an actor must be aware of the group scenic gestus and the part he or she plays in it. The presentation of the total statement of the play is more important than any one character—it is very much an ensemble form of playing.

Playing the Gestus.   The purpose of epic act-ing is to entertain and arouse the critical con-sciousness of the audience, not to create an emotional empathy with the audience and fool audience members into taking a realistic approach to the stage illusion. The epic actor does not look for emotion, pump it up, wal-low in it. He or she accepts what is there, con-trols it, and channels it into the objective playing of the action. Emotion is then exter-nalized and becomes living energy in the pre-sentation of the gestus; it is not held within and subjectively examined. Emotion is thus

The well-known character gestus of Humphrey Bogart, as seen in *The Maltese Falcon*.
Copyright © 1941. Warner Bros. Pictures Inc. Renewed 1969 United Artists Television Inc. All rights
reserved.

subjected to criticism, together with the other elements of action, in terms of the socioeconomic theme. Mother Courage is no Lady of the Sorrows; she is deeply flawed in terms of a pathetic heroine. She has the wrong historical and economic sensibility, and the actor should criticize this in her performance, not seek for emotional empathy. When wrong, emotion must be shown as wrong and *alterable*—not as part of the pitiable human condition.

In rehearsal an actor can discover as much about the character's emotional or psychological makeup as is necessary to enable him or her to build a workable part—to determine the character's actions within the situation and pass valid criticism upon those actions. In performance the actor is presenting a report upon the character's actions, seen in the socioeconomic perspective of the theme.

The uncluttered simplicity of the setting in epic theatre throws the actor into high relief and makes every gesture significant. This makes the observation and selection of gestic detail extremely important, especially in the handling of props and the performance of manual work—elements that give much of the socioeconomic texture to the scenic effect. In rehearsal the actor should listen to and observe the character; should look for new perspective, unique qualities;

Striking relationship of character and scenic gestus in this Goodman Theatre production of *Galileo*.   *Photo by Kevin Horan.*

as if a sculptor were discussing where his or her work should be displayed, not its "meaning" or spirit. There will be an ease that has been achieved through effort, a deliberateness that is the result of conscious choice. Brecht suggested images of achievement through leisurely effort:

> As a river wears
>   down its banks;
> An earthquake
>   shakes the
>   ground with a
>   relaxed hand;
> A fire devours in
>   comfort.[10]

It is important for the actor in epic theatre to know the difference between strong and crude, relaxed and loose, quick and hurried, imaginative and distracting, thought out and concocted, deep-felt and emotional, passionate and uncontrolled. The first set of adjectives apply to Brecht's theatre. There is no indulgence in bombast or intensity, but a basic irony of playing: "quick, light, strong," as Brecht himself reminded his actors in his final note to them, written as they undertook their British tour in 1956.

should be surprised at what he or she discovers and allow that sense to inform the manner of playing.

When the actor's work is presented to the audience, it should have an elegance, dryness, and objectivity—a practical quality

[10]Quoted by John Willett in *The Theatre of Bertolt Brecht* (London: Methuen, 1967), p. 69.

Note irony in this pimp/whore gestus from *The Threepenny Opera*.   *Lincoln Center Theatre.*

The essential qualities of physical presentation will also be found in the vocal manner of epic theatre, with the added demands of the variety of vocal forms Brecht employs. The actor should take each form on its own terms, not try to blur the distinctions among them. Prose, verse, blank verse, chorus speaking, and song are all used by Brecht for consciously rhythmic, gestic, and alienated purposes. The actor must be aware of the purpose of each form and adapt his or her manner of presentation to it. We have already suggested that the singing form is not melody but rather a speaking against the music that almost alienates the rhythm. Similarly, speeches must be examined for their gestic content. Frequently there will be an ironic comment upon the character, as

when in *Mother Courage* the chaplain says: "I was so scared I almost broke out in prayer." And the officer has the line, "I don't trust him; we're friends." An actor must discover where it is necessary to alienate the speech, to achieve a gestic comment by the manner of presentation. We once saw a splendid example of this verbal alienation when an actor performed the raunchy Rolling Stones number "I can't get no satisfaction" in an extremely polite, "frightfully British," plum-in-the-mouth voice with a seeming attempt to explain the situation to the audience. Apart from being hilariously funny it alienated the song, and we saw the Rolling Stones in critical relief.

Sense of Occasion.   There is always the danger in speaking of the necessary didactic purpose and emotional remove of Brecht's theatre that all sense of its function as entertainment—to provide pleasure—will be lost. But Brecht, though holding firm to his desire for raising the political consciousness of his audience, never took himself too seriously. He believed that theatre was a form of game, that it was essentially superfluous—but that the superfluous gave life significance, that nothing needed less justification than pleasure, and that the highest form of pleasure came through learning—expanding one's human horizons. Brecht was not a sober-sided Marxist intellectual. He was poet and playwright before he was politician.

It is true that actors performing Brecht must understand the political intent of Brecht's theatre: It is an exercise in formalism to do a Brecht play without a grasp of the social reality being presented. It is equally true that the classroom is joined by both the sporting arena and the cabaret as formative images in Brecht's work. Music, song, sleight of hand, ironic humor, and conviviality are as much teaching aids as are the posters, placards, filmstrips, and litany of alienation effects. The didactic intention is present; to fulfill this the audience must be able to criticize the social reality being presented to it in a dispassionate manner. But the audience is certainly not to be alienated from the actors or prevented from enjoying itself. Audience and actors are on the same side—that of humanity. They are part of the family of social man—observing and criticizing; sharing ideas, attitudes, feelings, and responses; but above all enjoying a pleasurable, entertaining, and edifying social occasion.

EXERCISES, GAMES, TECHNIQUES

Rehearsal Techniques.   Brecht himself suggested various ways to approach epic acting:

1. transposing the actions and remarks of the character into the third person
2. transposing the action into the past
3. speaking the stage directions.

Thus, a piece of action in rehearsal might go as follows: "Mother Courage slowly got down from her wagon, walked over to the officer, looked at him and said, . . ."

Using the third person and the past tense enables the actor to achieve the right attitude of distance from the action. Putting the action in the past allows the actor to look at the words and make judgments on them. Speaking the stage directions in the third person has the effect of alienating them from the text itself.

These techniques may be varied and elaborated upon. The stage manager can call out the stage directions or narrate the action as the actor moves through it: "So then Mother Courage wearily sat down, took her daughter Kattrin's hand, and waited for the soldiers to bring in the stretcher bearing the body covered with a sheet." The actor may use the third-person alienation technique and add a comment upon the action—the kind of critical comment that the gestus should convey: "He stood up weakly, as, due to the soldiers taking the food, he had not eaten for three days, and, facing the officer with bitterness, said, . . ."

Witness Game I.   This is based on Brecht's own quintessential model for epic acting—the street scene. Set up a situation in which one of the players is relating to the rest of the group an incident he or she has seen. In Brecht's model the incident was an automobile accident at a street corner, but the possibilities are unlimited. The witness describes and acts out the circumstances of the situation and demonstrates the actions of those involved in the incident, so observers are able to form an opinion. There is no attempt to create an illusion, to become emotionally involved. If the witness wants to suggest that someone was angry, the witness will display the actions of the anger, but not assume the emotion. The characters involved in the situation will become known to the observers by their actions, and only by those actions that are absolutely necessary to describe the nature of the event. The witness will demonstrate the actions and talk directly to the observers. If he or she wishes to use props or costume elements it will be for gestic purposes. For example, a crooked hat may suggest that one of the characters was drunk, or a white stick that she was blind.

The object of the witness's demonstration is to show what part each individual played in the incident and to enable the observers to form an opinion and fix responsibility. The player who is the witness must always take an objective standpoint, using the "He did" and "She said" construction, so that the observers are aware of both the witness and the person demonstrated—the actions and opinions are never merged into one, although the witness may have his or her own point of view. The game may be placed in a courtroom environment with witnesses, jury, judge, and lawyers. A certain license will be allowed so that witnesses can demonstrate more physically than they would in a court of law, and the jury should be allowed to ask questions.

Witness Game II. Players now act out a situation in which they themselves have been involved, and which they had at the time accepted uncritically, but may have felt a sense of injustice: being audited by the Internal Revenue Service; being underpaid for one's labor; failing to get a role that was given to the director's boy or girl friend. The player will now narrate and act out the circumstances of the incident, stopping to pass critical comment upon the events and to show how he or she may have acted differently had their social consciousness been raised. Having criticized the situation the player can redo the situation with the "correct" socioeconomic attitude. This exercise accustoms players to analyze episodes in a dialectical manner.

Storytelling. Players should arrange themselves comfortably around the space and focus on the center. One of the players is the storyteller or troubador—if you wish to specify the environment, it can be a medieval hall, a Victorian parlor, a Christmas party, depending upon the nature of the story to be told. The storyteller then narrates the tale, with as much acting out of the actions and demonstration of the characters involved as he or she thinks necessary to entertain and illustrate the theme. Stories from Dickens—such as *The Pickwick Papers* and *A Christmas Carol*—are especially good for this exercise, as are biblical tales such as David and Goliath and the coming of the three wise men.

Players take turns being storyteller, and after each tale the group should discuss the clarity of the narrative: Was there too much detail? Were the stories overelaborated? How effective were the gestic qualities used? This is a good exercise for maintaining thematic focus, direct communication, imagination, and selectivity of gestus.

Roundalay. This is another exercise used by Brecht. Players sit in a circle. One begins a poem, which is picked up by each of the other players in turn so that it becomes a round. As each player joins in, he or she takes a specific vocal character attitude. Brecht's favorite poem was this one:

> A dog went into the kitchen
> And stole an egg from the cook,
> The cook took his cleaver
> And cut the dog in two.
> The other dogs came in
> And dug him a grave,
> And put on it a headstone
> With the following epitaph:
> A dog went into the kitchen
> Etc.

One player would take the vocal attitude of the dog: He was hungry, he had puppies to feed, he was a petty thief; another player the attitude of the cook; another the grave-digging dogs. There are many possibilities. Nursery rhymes or any poems involving many characters can be used for this exercise.

Machine. This is a very basic acting exercise. Players stand in a circle. One goes into the center and begins a simple and repetitive physical movement. The other players join in, one at a time, adding a movement that relates to those that have gone before, until a machine is created by the bodies and their movement. With inexperienced players the first machines will tend to be vertical and have a lot of arm movement. Coach players to use their entire bodies and every plane of the space. The game should be repeated several times, with sounds added to the movements. The game is excellent as a warm-up, and it helps to develop ensemble relationships. Its usefulness for epic acting is that it creates a scenic gestus—the completed machine—out of the sum of the individual gestuses—each player's specific movement. When the players have become adept at the game give them a specific focus for their machine, one having some kind of economic or social significance—a machine for the creation of nuclear energy; a machine for building robots; a machine for political brainwashing. Finally, have the players repeat these machines, asking each player to take a critical attitude toward them, which will be manifested in the way that he or she performs the gestus. Discuss with the players what adjustments were made from performing a simple movement, to performing it with a specific focus, and then with a critical attitude. This is a very good early exercise, for it helps actors get a clear sense of gestus as the embodiment of meaning in a physical attitude.

Common Task.   Players pair off. One of them performs some everyday working task—digging a garden, washing up, changing a tire, replacing bed linen. This should last about a couple of minutes and should focus upon highly specific details. The other player then repeats the partner's performance as accurately as possible. He or she then repeats it a second time with whatever adjustments necessary to clarify the nature of the task. Players may wish to omit some details, add others, change rhythms, and so on. Players then discuss the differences in performance of the task, paying particular attention to accuracy of detail, clarity, and the essential actions. The exercise may be repeated with each player taking a particular social or economic attitude to the task—a trade unionist changing the tire on a Rolls-Royce; an out-of-work engineer digging the garden; an impoverished student changing the linen in an expensive hotel. Taking a critical attitude should not alter the basic detail of the task, only the way in which that detail is performed.

Social Mirror.   Players pair off and begin a simple mirror exercise, establishing good concentration and exchange of rhythms. When the game is well under way suggest broad characters to the players—housewife, model, truck driver—and let them base their mirror movements upon a physical sense of the gestures and rhythms of such a character. Have the players shake out and change partners every few minutes, to keep them relaxed as well as concentrated and to stimulate their imagination. Continue the game, now giving broad socioeconomic situations as the basis for the mirror movements: energy crisis, gas rationing, motherhood, feminism—whatever happens to be topical. Finally, still within the structure of the mirror exercise, give the players a character type and, when it is reflected in the mirror movements, add a socioeconomic situation. The player will now be presenting a movement gestus of a character, and presenting it in such a way as to reflect that character's attitude toward a socioeconomic situation. The exercise must be watched carefully, as there is a fine line between allowing players time to develop their movements validly and tiring them out because of the intense physical concentration the game requires.

Social Critics.   This is an extension of the previous exercise. The players scatter about the space and walk around, focusing upon their own rhythms and energy centers. Coach players to change these rhythms and energies by throwing physical changes at them: They are wearing size-twenty shoes; their ankles are tied together; their head swells to twice its size; their arms become six feet long. When the players are accustomed to making these adjustments, throw them characters who have a specific socioeconomic function in a modern political structure, such as teachers, soldiers, lawyers, police officers, preachers, and physicians. The players now explore the movements, rhythms, and energy centers they associate with these characters, until they achieve a highly selective gestus with which they feel comfortable. Now set up a series of improvisations that allow the players to confront their character gestus with a situation that demands some critical comment from them. For example: a doctor's office with a patient who has a serious problem but no means of paying the physician's fee; an affirmative-action case about a professor denied tenure—this could involve lawyers, educational administrators, judges, and others. Coach players to keep the focus upon both the socioeconomic theme (don't let it wander up emotional blind alleys) and the critical playing of the character gestus.

Social Puppets.   The exercise begins as the previous one. Players explore movements, rhythms, and energy centers until they feel comfortable with a character gestus. Players now pair off, and each in turn gives the other instructions—actions to play in character. The instructions should always by given in the third person past tense: "The soldier was on a route march"; "The soldier was under fire."

This is in keeping with Brecht's own use of the third person in rehearsal and with his demand for the historification of the event. There is a sound logic to this that is crucial to epic acting. In one sense an actor knows he or she is not a soldier and is not under fire. He or she is an actor in a rehearsal room or on a stage. If the actor attempts to *relive* in the present an imaginary event, he or she will constantly come up against that fact and will have a blurred mixture of self and character. What an actor does is *reenact* in the present a past event in which he or she had no part, an event that is historically laid to rest. Rehearsing and performing exercises in the third person past tense will keep the distinction clear between the actor and character. The value of this may be proved in the present exercise. Suppose the situation is that the soldier has taken a position and is to dig in. Let the partner give this instruction in three different ways: "Dig in"; "You were told to dig in"; "The officer told the soldier to dig in." As the order moves from the first person present tense to

the third person past tense, the player/soldier will move from an action that is self-contained to one that is more extroverted and related to a larger scenic environment. The player will be illustrating the action, and the energy will be released outwards into this gestus making it strong and clearer.

Social Masks.   This exercise requires a range of character masks. Players choose a mask and adopt it before a mirror: The technique for this is described on p. 23. When the mask has been absorbed and physical rhythms, energy centers, and gestures developed from it, players unmask and comment upon the nature of the character that has been evolved. This should be done while holding the mask to one side of the body so that a clear sense is gained that the player and the mask/character are separate identities. To illustrate any comment the player may quickly readopt the mask, present an attitude or gestus, then unmask and discuss it. The exercise gives the actor a strong sense of the critical, dialectical nature of developing the Brechtian character.

PLAYING THE STYLE

Summary.   Brecht was concerned with demonstration rather than empathy, with criticism not catharsis. The actor displays the character and demonstrates the incidents. The actor should:

1. Read the play more than usual; don't jump into "living" the part;
2. Have a very clear idea of the *Grundgestus*—the political standpoint of the production;
3. When reading the play take a critical point of view of the character—question the character's actions and motives from a socioeconomic viewpoint;
4. Deal with each episode on its own terms; do not look for psychological consistency

running through the play; look for the contrasts, the dialectic;

5. Look for choices of gestus that illustrate the overall gestus of each episode; the actor is not an individual but a part of a total scenic image;

6. In rehearsal the actor may explore every facet of a character, but must then make the choices of gestus in a socioeconomic context;

7. Keep a cool head in performance; don't be transported by the part or try to cast a spell on the audience—the audience's response should not be: "What a lifelike performance. I was quite carried away";

8. Know what critical response you would like the audience to have. It is the presentation of the character with a critical viewpoint that alienates emotional empathy.

Example.   We are fortunate in having Brecht's Modelbooks as a guide to the performance of his style. Using the *Couragemodell*[11] as a source we are going to look at one of the most famous examples of Brechtian work: the character of Mother Courage as created by Helene Weigel.

In physical terms, Mother Courage's body showed the years of hard labor that the oppression of her class had subjected her to: a lumpy, graceless figure, covered with rough, baggy clothes that left only her hands and feet showing. Her hair was always tightly pushed up on her head; it was never loose, free, and feminine. Her dialectical existence was illustrated by the rapid extremity of her moods, revealed by highly varied facial expressions. Some of these expressions, seen in photographs, are so strong as to almost appear as "mugging"; but that in itself under-

The basic character gestus of Helene Weigel as Mother Courage.   *Berliner Ensemble.*

lines that the gestus was played strongly, and that slight exaggeration was part of the acting technique, to set up a moment in high relief—to ensure that the audience got the point.

The character gives the impression of great energy that kept her in constant motion, and the litany of props that she used all added to the effect of someone constantly working, totally consumed by business and family. This vitality was dialectically contrasted with occasional moments of absolute immobility caused by exhaustion or shock. The switching back and forth from strong energy to totally drained stasis was an illustration of the contradiction

[11]Bertold Brecht, *Couragemodell 1949* (Berlin: Henschelverlag, 1958). We are also indebted to the discussion by David Jones in *Great Directors at Work* (Berkeley: University of California Press, 1986).

Mother Courage with sons and daughter on the way to war. *Berliner Ensemble.*

The drained stasis of Mother Courage as compared with the energy in previous photo. *Oregon Shakespeare Festival. Photo by Henry Kranzler.*

that was the fundamental gestus of the character. And her bouncing back from crushed desolation to cheerful hope had to be seen critically: not as a testament to her resilience but to her failure to learn from her situation and change.

Throughout Weigel's performance as Mother Courage the character was presented as a dialectic, a subject for discussion. There was no attempt at creating an emotional through-line that was played consistently. The character was played scene by scene in consciously dialectic terms: It was this dialectic of oppositions that was the consistent idea.

Weigel's Courage starts with an obvious zest for business, a determined intention to get somewhere—as we say of someone working in a capitalist corporation. In this instance she wanted to get to the war zone to sell her goods to the troops. She is confronted in the first scene by the recruiting sergeant who wants to take her son, Eilif. The sergeant reminds Mother Courage: "You live off the war. How can there be a war without soldiers?" At the end of the scene, Mother Courage has lost her son and gained half a guilder for a belt sold to the sergeant. Weigel played Mother Courage at the end of the scene downcast, dragging her belts on the ground, conscious of what she had lost for half a guilder.

In scene 2, Mother Courage is back up again, still haggling, but now flirtatiously with the cook, the earlier scene apparently forgotten. At the end of the scene she both hugs and slaps her son Eilif, now a heroic soldier. This volatility of emotion, as with her quick change of attitudes between scenes, is part of the dialectic of her character. In scene 3, the character is full of bustling busyness; even when haggling over a ransom for her second son she seems to be paying more attention to organizing her goods than to the threat to her son's life. She haggles over the money too long and the son is shot, which leads to her gestus of the silent scream that we discussed previously.

In scenes 4 and 5, Weigel's Courage changed from bitterness to acceptance with the song of the Great Capitulation: If you want to survive, keep your nose clean. Then she determinedly defends her wagon, her economic being, and all she has left with both her sons gone and only her dumb (literally) daughter at her side. In scene 6, Weigel allowed Courage to be softer and warmer, while calculating how much investment she can put into the war, another dialectic, leading to scene 7, in which Courage has the song "war is a business proposition." In this scene, Brecht and Weigel showed Mother Courage at the height of her business success, walking along by her wagon, bereft of sons but cheerfully draped in jewelry. This was a visual gestus in which the jewelry contrasted with the rough stuff of her clothes, and it set a frame in which the audience could see what she had lost for what she had gained, and that Courage herself appeared not to be aware of the nature of the exchange.

Scene 8 was the middle part of Brecht's production: All was shown as changeable. War changed to peace then back to war again; characters that had appeared earlier reappeared, changed by their experience of the war. It was also the beginning of the final downward curve in Courage's fortune. The scene began with Mother Courage and the cook discussing their losses in the war, and

here Weigel took the cook's hand, an expression that showed her potential even for love, in ironic dialectic contradiction with the loss that surrounds both of them.

The downward curve of Mother Courage's fortune continues through scenes 9 and 10 in which she is dragging her wagon in the wake of the armies, cold and hungry through bitter winter weather until, finally, in scene 11 she loses her last child, Kattrin, who is killed by the soldiers as she is trying to sound an alarm and save the children of a town. This is further dialectical irony: Courage's daughter is killed by the war when she acts in a more maternal manner than Mother Courage herself ever managed to sustain.

Scene 12, the last scene in the play, finds Courage, her head bowed over the body of Kattrin, singing a lullaby and trying to tell herself that her daughter is only sleeping. She is disabused of this by the peasants who accuse her of abandoning her daughter. Weigel played this scene with Courage in a dumb stupor, unable to connect the death of Kattrin with the war and, indeed, only paying interest to the peasants when they tell her she had better be about her business again. It was in this scene that Weigel played another brilliant gestus. When about to give all the money in her purse to the peasants to bury Kattrin, at the last moment she took one coin back, returned it to her purse, and snapped the purse shut. She had used the snapping of the purse as a gestus throughout the production whenever money had been exchanged and here, finally, she connected all those snapping sounds together—a gestic through-line—showing the dialectic that had been a constant issue and, at the very end, the continued triumph of her business sense over her maternal instinct.

Finally, Mother Courage, with the words "I must start up in business again," harnesses herself to the wagon and, like a dumb beast, worn out but still understanding nothing, starts to pull the wagon in circles around the

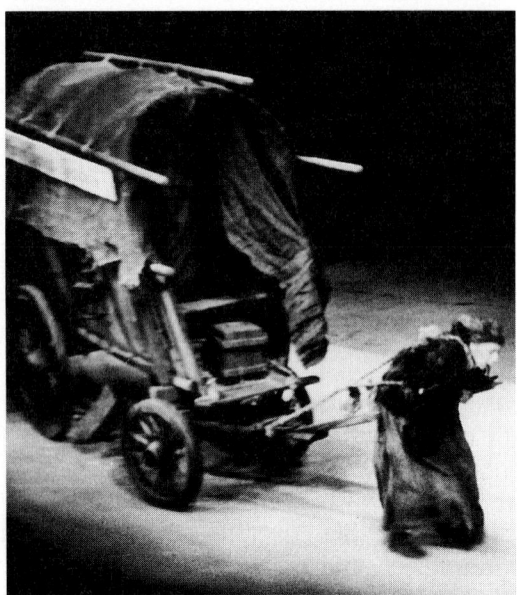

The beast of burden; the final gestus of Mother Courage.   *Berliner Ensemble.*

stage. This last visual image gestically sums up the play: Endurance is a kind of courage, but it is unthinking; Mother Courage is still going on but getting nowhere, still repeating her mistakes; it is a courage of the wrong kind, that of the dray horse or pack animal that allows itself to be exploited for others' gain.

It is interesting to note the implicit circularity of shape of both *Mother Courage* and *Waiting for Godot*. But, whereas Didi and Gogo had the running theme of "Let's go" but don't move, Mother Courage kept on going but essentially in a declining spiral. It was this declining spiral that Brecht wanted the audience to be aware of, to criticize Courage for allowing herself to be trapped in it, and to realize that if she had made other choices and refused to let herself be exploited by the capitalist system then change would be possible. This critical posture is induced by the dialectical playing of the role of Mother Courage. The actor's task is to discover and illustrate the dialectical pattern of the text. Often Brecht has made the dialectic explicit. In scene 6, for example, Courage is bemoaning the death of war heroes while counting socks: "Pity about the Chief—twenty-two pairs of socks—getting killed like that." But even when it is not made explicit by the dialogue, the actor responds to the situation in a dialectical manner, showing Courage to be worthy yet wanting in perception; attracting and repelling the audience at the same time, so that the audience is drawn to her, cares for her situation, but criticizes her behavior in allowing herself to be destroyed as a human being by her subjugation to the capitalist ethic.

SUGGESTED READINGS

Brecht, Bertolt, *Couragemodell 1949*. Berlin: Henschelverlag, 1958.

———, *The Messingkauf Dialogues*, trans. John Willett. London: Methuen, 1972.

Eagleton, Terry, *Marxism and Literary Criticism*. Berkeley: University of California Press, 1976.

Esslin, Martin, *Brecht: A Choice of Evils*. London: Methuen, 1965.

Gray, Ronald, *Brecht*. London: Oliver & Boyd, 1961.

Jones, David, *Great Directors at Work*. Berkeley: University of California Press, 1986.

Willet, John, *The Theatre of Bertolt Brecht*. London: Methuen, 1967.

———, ed., *Brecht on Theatre*. New York: Hill & Wang, 1964.

13 Artaud, Grotowski, and the Theatre of Physical Metaphor

'Tis Pity She's a Whore.   Glasgow Citizens' Theatre. Photo by John Vere Brown.

BACKGROUND

In our chapter on Greek theatre we said that there were four good reasons why it should be the starting point. In this, the final chapter, there are again four good reasons why we are concluding with the highly physically oriented style associated in recent theatre history with Antonin Artaud and Jerzy Grotowski.

First, this style returns us to the metaphysical roots of theatre: a concern for myths and sources that we found in our discussion of Greek tragedy. While doing this it rediscovers a physical approach to the actor's task. Interestingly, here it can trace its aesthetic back to Meyerhold, who was the first of Stanislavski's disciples to reassert the need for the total physical expression of the actor's body. The aesthetic, as such, is also very clear: It is a definite way of responding to the existential problems of life in the late twentieth century. And, in its focus upon the actor's metaphorical potential, it aligns itself with the late-twentieth-century investigations of theatre criticism with its semiotic focus upon theatre as a vocabulary of signs. Finally, although, as we acknowledged with Greek theatre, it is now less frequently performed as a specific style, its influence is felt throughout both the mainstream and areas of experimental theatre that have followed it. Given this, an exposure to and training for its demands is still of enormous value to the actor whose experience of the body as instrument, sign, and sacrifice will prepare him or her for the holistic and eclectic demands of the essential experimental sensibility.

Aesthetic.   Antonin Artaud was the prophet, and Jerzy Grotowski the classic practitioner, of this form of theatre. Artaud set out his aesthetic of what he terms a "theatre of cruelty," in his book *The Theatre and Its Double.*[1] Artaud

wanted a theatre that worked on the nerves and the senses rather than through language working on the intellect. He intuited a response to life of greater hope and intensity than that imprisoned within the logical forms and narrow social structure of twentieth-century society. Artaud was against a theatre that referred simplistically to the realistic world of "things." Artaud deplored the absence of eros, of fantasy, of deep feeling and physical expression in modern life—the price paid for the technological conveniences of bourgeois society. His theatre sought to retrieve a naive perception of true "essence" that existed before language rigidly defined, or "things" concretized, our existence. Myths of the blood, rather than fictions of social behavior, were to be the substance of his work.[2]

The essential function of "cruelty" was to smash through the veneer of bourgeois civilization to express freely the full potentiality of life in all its forms, be that love, charity, pain, or peril. Cruelty has been well described by Charles Marowitz: "The exposure of mind, heart and nerve ends to the gruelling truth behind a social reality that deals in psychological crises when it wants to be honest, and political evils when it wants to be responsible, but rarely, if ever, confronts the existential horror behind all psychological and social facades."[3]

Cruelty is, above all, rigor. It is the passion of the human being confronting destiny at the most intense edge of the senses. In a prescient image that predated the semiotic approach to theatrical communication, Artaud described actors as martyrs, burning alive but still signaling to us through flames. There is a purgation brought about by the intense impact upon the sense made by the

---

[1]Antonin Artaud, *The Theatre and Its Double,* trans. Mary Richards (New York: Grove Press, 1958).

[2]This is well put by Bert States in *Great Reckonings in Little Rooms* (Berkeley: University of California Press, 1985), pp. 108–115.

[3]Charles Marowitz, *The Act of Being,* (London: Secker and Warburg, 1978), p. 147.

physical images discovered by the theatre of cruelty. These images contain sacred truths, signs of the gods, as well as myth and ritual, human beings' earliest responses to the great mysteries of life, which were, for Artaud, a dynamic source for his theatre.

The aesthetic of the theatre of cruelty

> sought to break through the veneer of bourgeois culture by an intense and rigorous impact;
>
> rejected overly literary, psychological, and intellectuary didactic theatre;
>
> wished to return to a theatre of myth and ritual;
>
> emphasized dream, fantasy, and archetype;
>
> demanded a new theatrical language of physical signs and hieroglyphs;
>
> created an all-embracing sensual impact and spectacle;
>
> aimed at a therapeutic purgation in the spectator.

Artaud summed up his intention succinctly in describing his most famous production, *The Cenci:*

> My heroes dwell in the realm of cruelty and must be judged outside of good and evil. They are incestuous and sacrilegious, they are adulterers, rebels, insurgents and blasphemers. And that cruelty in which the entire work is bathed is not a purely corporal cruelty, but a moral one; it goes to the extremity of instinct and forces the actor to plunge right to the roots of his being so that he leaves the stage exhausted. A cruelty which acts as well upon the spectator and should not allow him to leave the theatre intact, but exhausted, involved; perhaps transformed.[4]

The themes that Artaud based his theatre on were the ultimate truths of man's existence: creation, chaos, birth, death, eros. These are the myths humans have inherited through their blood and their religions—the very stuff

[4]Antonin Artaud, *Oeuvres Completes,* Vol. V (Paris: Gallimard, 1964), p. 309; our translation.

of the human collective unconscious. In specific theatrical terms Artaud suggested reinterpretations of Elizabethan and Jacobean plays (*'Tis Pity She's a Whore*), romantic melodramas (*The Cenci*), and the use of biblical stories and those of the Marquis de Sade (note Peter Brook's "theatre of cruelty" production of Peter Weiss's play known in the shortened title as *Marat/Sade*).

Historical Background. As befitting a prophet, Artaud was some thirty years before his time, and only after his death did the heady, revolutionary days of the 1960s and 1970s provide a flashpoint for his instincts, when a new sense of life catalyzed the need for a new sense of theatre. The cultural watershed of that time overturned many of the moral and social structures and strictures that had grown up around both Christianity and capitalism. The existential void seemed to have no worthy hitching posts, no rational paths. A physical theatre responded to the need for physical solutions.

The all-embracing physical demands of Artaud's theatre are reinforced by the perceptions of Marshall McLuhan. In his highly influential sociological theses *Understanding Media* and *The Medium Is the Message,* McLuhan suggested that the worldwide proliferation of media had turned the world into a global village. Post-Renaissance humanity had been rationalized into using but a part of its sensory capacity and had hidden its feeling beneath intellect and the printed word. But now the imagistic world of film, television, and visual immediacy could return to humankind its capacity for a total sensual experience of life in a prerational, multifocused, and many-faceted way. Such a thesis is supported by much of what has happened in the broad world of art. Action painting and collages seek the direct involvement of the artist with his or her work, and the physical impact of op art, pop art, and psychedelic art

Powerful intensity of image in the idea of "cruelty." Note aspects of sacrilege and sexuality.   *Glasgow Citizens' Theatre.*

and, above all, electronic music is designed to arouse, disturb, and possess spectators/listeners and transform them and their perception of the world. Contemporary rock concerts may be the ultimate achievement of the Artaud/McLuhan vision.

Artaud's disciples took his ideas in various directions. His most faithful follower is Jerzy Grotowski, whose Polish Laboratory Theatre developed a series of stringent exercises to support the physical demands of Artaud's theatre, and formulated an aesthetic of the "holy" actor in a "poor" theatre. Grotowski emphasized the self-sacrificing religiosity of Artaud's ethic. Grotowski's actors were the prime focus of his theatre: Everything was stripped away to reveal the actor in an intense

confrontation with the great human myths and legends. Through this confrontation the actor would reveal the modern significance of the myth, touching in the process the actor's own deepest self and that of the audience.

Richard Schechner and his Performance Group emphasized the all-embracing "environment" aspects of Artaud, experimenting with theatrical spaces to include the audience totally as participants in the event. Schechner's theatre was also sensual and tactile, using nudity and physical contact to make moral statements. The Living Theatre was similar to Schechner in its physical stance, but more aggressive in its social statements and highly tribal in life style. Joseph Chaikin's Open Theatre created its own rituals to comment upon

Intense physical and emotional commitment of actor Ryszard Cieslak in Grotowski's *The Constant Prince.*   *Teatr Laboratorium.*

atre, Peter Brook is known for his classically famous production of *Marat/Sade,* and for the introduction of Artaud's ideas into Shakespearean production. French director Ariane Mnouchkine continues the Shakespearean exploration with her *Richard II* and *Henry IV,* productions of intense physical theatricality influenced by Oriental theatre, which, itself, had been one of Artaud's inspirations. With her Shakespearean work, and her chronicle of the holocaust of modern Cambodia, titled *Sinanouk,* Mnouchkine continues in the Artaud/Grotowski tradition of moral theatricality and stringent gestural language. Another French director, Roger Planchon, with productions such as *Gilles de Rais,* a haunting historical nightmare of metaphorical images, works equally in the same tradition.

In the United States, Mabou Mines has been a continuing force of Artaud's disciples; and the Wooster Group, with such productions as *Saint Anthony*—a rebirth and transfiguration piece reminiscent of Grotowski's *Akropolis*—and its 1986 spiritual and political passage through American culture, The *Road to Immortality,* mixes flamboyant theatricality with moral inquiry. Martha Clarke's dance theatre employed, in the mid-1980s, those images of Hieronymus Bosch and Peter Bruegel that had influenced Artaud, in its productions of *The Garden of Earthly Delights, Metamorphosis in Miniature,* and *Vienna: Lusthaus.* Even the poetic metaphors of Richard Foreman despite their dispassionate formalism, bear testament to the continuing influence of Artaud's instincts upon experimental forms of theatre and the need of the complete actor to have an understanding of, and an ability to work within, the sensibility that Artaud represents.

the political and moral problems confronting contemporary society. Chaikin expressed his purpose as "to shake off the sophistication of our time by which we close ourselves up, to become vulnerable again . . . , become naive, innocent, cultivate our deeper climates—our dread. Only then will we be able to express the attitudes we hold in common with the outside world."[5]

Continued Tradition.   Of those disciples of Artaud who are still pursuing his form of the-

[5]Quoted in Robert Pasolli, *A Book on the Open Theatre* (New York: Bobbs-Merrill, 1970), p. 95.

Post-Artaudian imagery in a production of *Philosophy in the Boudoir* by the Marquis de Sade.   *Glasglow Citizens' Theatre. Photo by John Vere Brown.*

INTRINSIC DEMANDS

Form.   This form of theatre is not strictly text-oriented. The form tends to evolve in physical shape during the rehearsal period. Frequently Artaudian theatre is not developed from a text but from themes, impulses, or ideas that concern the participants. The Open Theatre developed its *Terminal* from an exploration of the concept of death. Conversely, their *Serpent* evolved from an interest in the idea of original creation and original sin—the myth of the Garden of Eden, mankind's paradise lost. *The Serpent* became a text in collaboration with Jean-Claude van Itallie—a not infrequent method of working whereby a playwright sets down the sound and shape of the theatrical piece as it is originated by the actors in their exploration of impulses and ideas.

If a text is used, it becomes a pretext—not a literary artifact to be regarded as sacrosanct, but a sounding board or artistic trampoline. Against this the actor tests responses to the text's deepest impulses and creates a physical form that reflects those responses. The actor is not trying to discover and recapitulate the playwright's precise intentions, but is using the playwright's ideas and intuitions to discover and reveal his or her own reaction to the deepest purposes of the play. This was the principle Grotowski employed when working on such texts as *Akropolis* and *The Constant Prince;* it was also Richard Schechner's intention in transforming Euripide's *Bacchae* into *Dionysus in '69.* The term for this process is *confrontation.* In speaking of *Akropolis* Grotowski noted: "One structures the montage so that this confrontation can take place. We eliminate those parts of the text that have no importance for us. We did not wish to write a new play; we wished to confront ourselves."[6]

The creation of *Akropolis* is an example of how the theatrical event develops through confrontation with a text. *Akropolis* was writ-

[6]"Grotowski in interview," *Tulane Drama Review* 13 (Fall 1968), p. 44.

Detail from *The Garden of Earthly Delights* by Hieronymus Bosch, an influence upon Artaud. *Copyright © Museodel Prado, Madrid. All rights reserved.*

ten in 1904 by the Polish symbolist playwright Stanislaw Wyspianski. It was based upon a Polish religious tradition whereby on the night of the Resurrection, characters in a sixteenth-century tapestry in the Cracow royal palace come to life and reenact scenes from the Bible and classical mythology. The intention of the play is to reveal the sum of civilization's contribution to humanity, and confront it with the nature of contemporary experience in an icon of "The Cemetery of the Tribes." To achieve this experience for his late-twentieth-century audience, Grotowski transferred the situation to the Auschwitz concentration camp (a cemetery of at least one tribe) where ancient myths of the Trojan War, Paris and Helen, Jacob and the Angel were played out by the fragments of humanity who were the victims

of our twentieth-century inhumanity: the inmates of Auschwitz. The score of actions was built by an improvisatory confrontation by the actors with the images of Wyspianski's text, creating scenes that were interspersed with the harsh, mechanical rhythms of the reality of the concentration camp. A true confrontation (cf. Brecht's dialectical form) to make the audience both experience and question the values by which it lives.

The form of the event created by the participants' confrontation of the pretext or basic idea is frequently that of a ritual or rite of passage. It is not so much the telling of a story as it is the exploration of a theme, and one that touches the core of human identity. Like the Christian Mass with its smell of incense, its incantations, its symbolic sharing of flesh and blood, and the raising of the host, an Artaudian theatrical event physically and spiritually embraces the participants with an intense experience of deep human significance celebrated within a symbolic form.

Space.   In the earlier chapters our discussion of the demands of space has been determined either by the theatrical givens of a particular period (for example, the architectural nature of the Greek, Elizabethan, or seventeenth-century playhouses), or by the specific form of a play, as in the work of Brecht, Mamet, or Beckett. With theatre of cruelty the space tends not to be either architecturally or textually predetermined, but to be created in accordance with the evolving nature of the event.

Artaud described his sense of staging as "a concrete physical space which asks to be filled and to be given its own concrete language to speak."[7] He suggested that the spectator should be surrounded by the sights, sounds, and concentrated action of the event. Theatre comes completely out of the proscenium and

[7]Antonin Artaud, *The Theatre and Its Double,* trans. Mary Richards (New York: Grove Press, 1958), p. 37.

Akropolis.   Teatr Laboratorium.

returns to a medieval, or even pre-Greek, quality of staging, bringing theatre full circle and back to its physical roots in ritual whereby space is altered and structured to suit the demands of each particular celebration. Because an open space is concrete yet totally flexible, it can be transformed and articulated to match the shapes and rhythms of the events as it evolves from the responses of the actors. Space never becomes simply an architectural backing to the performance. It is fully involved with the action, affecting and being affected by the actors.

For his production of *Akropolis* Grotowski had the audience sit on a form of bleachers raised around the space—a similar feel to the double wooden cots on which inmates of Auschwitz existed. In the center of the space was a huge box of metal junk that included stove pipes, tin tubs, wheelbarrows. Out of

this, as occasion demanded, the actors built the structure of a physical situation, for example, the crematorium. Finally, the entire space was filled with the oppressive, metallic structure of our modern world, in which humanity decays and is destroyed, or sacrificed.

Grotowski was the most sophisticated of Artaud's disciples in his use of audience participation. He found ways of including the audience as members of the event without resorting to the physical embracement engaged in by some of the more self-indulgent groups. In his production of *Faustus*, the audience were Faustus's guests at a last supper, sitting around tables as in a refectory. In a brilliant *coup de theatre*, toward the end of the event, the Emperor's servant goes berserk and dismantles the rostrum tops, under the very noses of the audience but without touching them, leaving only skeletons of table sup-

Actors.

Spectators.

The space for Grotowski's *Kordian*. The room was the interior of a mental hospital with the spectators incorporated as patients.   *Teatr Laboratorium.*

ports: an intense, physical, and poetic image of a world coming apart.

In *The Constant Prince*, Grotowski once again had the audience surrounding the event, as at a bull ring or operating theatre, watching the actor spiritually dismember himself on their behalf; this becomes another act of sacrifice, both for the audience and including the audience in the intensity of the physical metaphor they experience.

Mise-en-Scène.   The intention of this form of theatre is that costume, lighting, sound— all the effects with which the space is filled, will create an integrated impact, the *mise-en-scène*, which will produce a dynamic totality of impression upon the audience. The actor is in the midst of the mise-en-scène, and must be prepared to create sounds, respond to lighting, and wear costumes not as part of the development of a character, but as one of

many artifacts geared to making a total impression that may cohere only in the audience's mind.

Although he rejected the primacy of language, Artaud did not dismiss the effect of sound: groans, roars, liturgical chants, folksong, declamation, babblings—the whole range of human vocal possibility is at the actor's disposal. The effect of Grotowski's use of vocal rhythms, pitch, tonality, and its careful orchestration, rather than destroying the word, did, in fact, restore it from simple intellectual idea to full poetic image.

Costume equally supports the total impact of the *mise-en-scène*, with no necessary restriction in terms of historical accuracy or detail. Although Artaud rejected modern dress because of its limited and specific connotations, costuming has run the gamut from the simplest body coverings, such as T-shirts and leotards, to resplendent and ritualistic dress. The qualities of costuming will be body enhancing, timeless, and symbolic: everything from nakedness—the purest and most ritualistic form of body enhancement—to shamanic masks of paint, animal fur, body ornaments, and feathers.[8]

Grotowski's use of costume in *The Constant Prince* enhanced the visual metaphors. The persecutors wore cloaks, high boots, and a crown—all symbols of power. The Prince, on the other hand, wore a white shirt and loin cloth, symbolizing purity and vulnerability, and a red cloak of martyrdom that was to become his shroud.[9] Similarly, in *Akropolis*, Grotowski wished to create a poetic metaphor of the inmates' experience, not attempt to match a reality that documentary film had already recorded. He used costumes made from potato sacks, which were full of holes and covered naked bodies. The holes themselves were lined with a material suggesting torn flesh. It was a metaphor of degraded, tortured bodies. The function of the costumes, as with all aspects of the *mise-en-scène*, is not to delimit a situation or specifically define a character, but to confront and surround the audience with an intense sensual impact. (See photograph of *Akropolis*, p. 324.)

Actor and Shaman. This form of theatre is avowedly idealistic; it is a search for human identity through the confrontation of myth and rediscovery of ritual. Ritual is both a formal celebration of communal identity and an assertion of faith. Twenty-first-century society lacks faith, and is broken into heterogeneous, individualistic units. The practitioners

of Artaud's theatre want to reexplore the very roots of drama; to bring back commonality and break through alienation. They wish to rediscover both myth and the miraculous, which have been undermined by psychological causations, just as eros has vanished beneath libido to become associated with the dirty, crude, and inelegant instead of the joyfully creative. The earliest human rituals were concerned with hunting and sexual activity—with the main events and the cyclical process of life. Killing and the restoring of life, nakedness and fertility, the passage from boyhood to manhood, from child to warrior—it is from these that drama takes its preoccupation with violence, love, and death. And it is to these fundamental properties of drama that Artaud wished to return. In such a form of theatre the actor takes on the function of the shaman in those early rites of passage, or the priest in the religious ceremonies that followed them. The actor is a form of priest who builds bridges that link the actor to both the past and to the spectators.[10]

The priest's predecessor, the shaman, conducted the earliest religious ceremonies—the initiation rites of boys at puberty. The reaching of the age of fertility was approached both reverently and ecstatically, befitting a central mystery of life. The shaman was priest and witch doctor; he was the good and evil that influenced the community's life. He was the go-between through whom the spirit moved into the audience with the ecstasy and satisfaction of the event. The shaman/actor's performance is the revelation of a truth that stands for all. The actor, as descendant of the shaman, was reviled by the established church, which would accept only half of the shamanistic experience—namely, the sentimental celebration of man's potential goodness. The magic,

---

[8]The symbolic significance of costuming and properties should be explored, as in American Indian culture, where an eagle feather worn by a shaman symbolized the power of flight.

[9]We are indebted here, and in other parts of this section, to Jennifer Kumiega's *The Theatre of Grotowski* (London: Methuen, 1987).

[10]The Latin word for priest is *pontifex,* meaning "he who builds bridges."

the trickery, the sexual ecstasy were dismissed. The priest emasculated the shamanistic spirit and used his spiritual power to whip the Dionysian devil out of humankind.

The Artaudian actor, as true descendant of the shaman, conducts the rite of passage, which is, to quote the Living Theatre, "a voyage from the many to the one and from the one to the many. It is a spiritual voyage and a political voyage. It is an interior voyage and an exterior voyage for the actors and spectators."[11] It takes theatre both beyond and beneath the encrustations of bourgeois commercialization; it returns theatre to itself.

PERFORMANCE DEMANDS

Via Negativa.   Artaud left no details of an acting process; this had to be explored by his disciples, especially Jerzy Grotowski, who originated a basic process he called *via negativa*. This is essentially a process of stripping down; the removal of blocks, resistances, simplistic stereotypes that stand in the way of an actor's true impulses discovered when confronting the role. What Grotowski sought in all his exercises was an organic response rooted in the body. If this "body memory" could be released, then these natural impulses, discovered in confrontation with the text or demands of the role, would create a flow of action, gesture, sound. This organic system of signs is communicable to the audience who will share the intensity of the actor's experience.

The willingness to reveal the self, to get behind politeness, good taste, all the social masks, is a fundamental requirement of the actor in Artaudian theatre. With Yeats, he or she must be willing to reveal the truth, even if it is unattractive:

I must lie down where all the ladders start
In the foul rag and bone shop of the heart.[12]

Too many young actors want to appear "sympathetic" and are unwilling to take risks for fear of failure. If, as actors, we are constantly monitoring ourselves, looking for the right result, then only the mind and not the body works and we are limiting our range of choices. The ability to be still and naked, both literally and metaphorically, is a basic starting point for the actor. To be still at the core of self; to have that balance at the center that allows all impulses to flow freely; to be stripped of all physical masks that might block the full expression of feeling: This is the goal. The revelation of true passion can only be achieved by removal of all blocks that stand in the way of the most direct, simple, and pure response—the *via negativa*.

Confrontation.   Self-revelation is not an egotistical act; it takes place within a focused theatrical context: the confrontation of the text, myth, or whatever the impulse for the event may be. In confronting the Constant Prince, or Hamlet or Ophelia, the actor does not build up attributes or adopt any mask; rather, he or she removes anything that stands in the way of the most intense, organic response to the role. The actor is not trying to find the detailed and specific responses of a character in terms of any biographical detail; but neither is the actor simply performing as him or herself: the responses to the stimulus are in the form of signs, images, and hieroglyphs that are all-encompassing—larger than any individual.

To confront the role is to use it both as trampoline and scalpel. The actor researches the situation with the body, probes for responses, finds associations, contacts, and relationships, and then uses these as a springboard

[11]Julian Beck and Judith Malina, *Paradise Now: A Collective Creation of the Living Theatre* (New York: Random House, 1971), p. 5.

[12]W. B. Yeats, "The Circus Animals' Desertion," in *Last Poems*. New York: The Macmillan Co., 1940, p. 80.

Powerful self confrontation of actor in a work based upon the life of Artaud: *Un Homme à la Rencontre d'Antonin Artaud.*   *French Cultural Services.*

for confronting the spectator with his or her discoveries. In rehearsal the performer selects from among the discoveries those responses that create the shape of the event with the greatest intensity and clarity. These become the score of the event, a series of consistently motivated actions. The score is fixed, but it does not restrict the actor. Performance is not mimetic; it is both "real"—in that the actor reveals his or her deepest self—and highly theatricalized—in that the actor's responses are much larger than "real" life, are hieroglyphic in form and metaphysical in resonance.

Signals and Signs.   The "signals through the flames" of which Artaud speaks when discussing how the actor communicates are of an imagistic or hieroglyphic nature. These hieroglyphs are not psychological or pantomimic; they have a resonance far beyond that of any detailed, realistic gesture. A hieroglyph will have its source in humanity's deepest cultural associations—the "collective unconscious" of which Jung spoke.

Forms of common or natural behavior often mask deeper truths. A hieroglyph is never a common gesture such as might be made over a cup of coffee with a cigarette, or a toss of the head. Anger is not a tic of irritation; it is a body-centered gesture that could disturb the gods. While the hieroglyph played intensely will draw strong supporting emotion from the body, feeling as such has no value unless shaped into a communicative image. Feeling without form can be soft, mawkish, and lie like a leaden pool upon the stage. A gesture, sign, or hieroglyph gives shape to feeling and impacts directly upon the audience's own vocabulary of physical experience.

As physical signs in themselves, the actor will find props useful in this exploration. Not the properties of our everyday life, the bric-a-brac of realism such as cups and saucers, cigarettes, glasses, books—the actor in this form of theatre does not "measure out life in coffee spoons." The properties have less specific identity—colored ribbons, staves, pieces of cloth, nets, ropes, pieces of paper—and may, by the way in which they are used, be given a highly symbolic value, just as the wafer and the wine become the flesh and blood of Christ in the Christian Mass. By the use of gesture the actor can transform a piece of blue silk into a rippling sea, a stool into an altar, a piece of glass into a teardrop.

A poetic hieroglyph, played with intensity will have far more intense an impact than will any literal usage. In his production of *Marat/Sade* Peter Brook had Charlotte Corday flagellate de Sade with her hair. This is an es-

The death of Marat from Peter Brook's Royal Shakespeare Company production. Note the poetic values of the image which is staged after the painting by David.   © *Max Waldman*

sentially Artaudian image, more interesting, more intense in audience impact, and of far broader dramatic significance than any literal whipping of de Sade could be. Actors' bodies may be used to create collective hieroglyphs such as the womb and vaginal passage created by the Performance Group in *Dionysus in '69*. In the image, Dionysus was born through a passageway of naked actors pulsating and groaning in expulsive rhythms. Here the naked body of the mother, the image of birth, and a literal rite of passage are combined in one active hieroglyph compounded of the bodies of many actors who experience the event as individuals and blend their bodies in a group image at the same time. The serpent in the Open Theatre's production of that name was created in a similar manner, a line of actors performing in a serpentine manner to create the image. There was no attempt to imitate a snake, but the qualities of evil and temptation—the serpent's action in the Garden of Eden—were

Birth of Dionysus hieroglyph from *Dionysus in '69*.   *By permission of Richard Schechner.*

blended into a poetic hieroglyph far more interesting and dynamic than any literal imitation.[13]

Process and Score.   The signals, signs, or hieroglyphs discovered by the actors are not played in random fashion, according to the impulse of the moment, but are combined into a score. This process begins with an exercise structure geared to rediscovering access to body memory, and giving the body instrument itself greater balance, plasticity, and extension. Grotowski was the only disciple of Artaud (with the possible exception of Joseph Chaikin) to establish a methodology to support his work, and he located the organic source of the body memory response at the base of the vertebral column where it is joined to and intersects the pelvis. This is the area known as the solar plexus, which is now commonly referred to as the actor's "center." Physiologically, it is an area that contains a complex of nerve endings, and in the yoga tradition it contains a concentration of life energy.

Just as the actor learned through exercises to activate the body memory and release its store of responses, so the actor could use the fact of body memory to encode the score of the event into his or her body. This, of course, is in the mode of Stanislavski's emotion memory whereby inspiration would be aroused by consciously remembering past emotional reactions to situations; but it transfers the source from the mind or psyche to the body: It is our tissue and our nerves that have remembered, and will automatically respond again to similar stimulus. Do the act and the feeling will follow. Grotowski's approach returns to the biomechanical theories of Meyerhold and incorporates those of William James and M. Feldenkrais that memories are always physical reactions: Every emotion, in one way or another, is associated and linked in the cor-

tex with some muscular configuration and attitude that has the power of reinstating the entire situation.

In rehearsal, as an actor discovers the bodily impulses emanating from his or her confrontation with the text these are themselves incarnated in the body memory in association with that moment of action. The score is the complete structure of physical actions inspired by and attached to impulses linked moment-to-moment so that a clear and disciplined set of images is communicated to the audience. And, while the score is fixed, it is not without spontaneity, because the body in revealing its encoded signs is, at the same time, responding to the stimulus of the moment so that the signs will be played by the actor in the context of each specific performance and its given circumstances. That is to say, as in life, each time we repeat something, it is the same, but slightly different.

Vocal Dynamics.   Artaud was not trying to dispense with language per se, but to restructure the way in which it was used in the theatre. It was his perception that all theatrical dynamics had been subordinated to rhetoric and a literary interpretation of text. The actor was locked into words and was inhibited from a true physical expression of the feeling for which words were merely a sign. The actor must explore unaccustomed ways of using the voice to express the powerful forces normally hidden beneath the polite patina of everyday speech. The reserved, word-oriented, literary tradition of the theatre means that ideas remain in and are expressed from the mind. Instead of connecting with the breath deep in the solar plexus (the traditional seat of the emotions), impulses are cut off by the mind and filtered through the intellect to come out in words as a pale imitation of the original inspiration.[14] Ar-

---

[13]Note the relationship to the creation of the dragon in the ancient Chinese dance ritual.

[14]*Inspiration* literally means the taking in of the breath, which shows the original connection among impulse, breath, and creative feeling.

taud wished to use words as a concrete means of expression conveying an emotional content arising from the core of the body and impelled by one of the body's two basic rhythms—the powerful pulsing of the lungs.

In technical terms the actor must develop breathing capacity and control so that he or she may make as full use as possible of the resonating capacity of the body. The actor must be aware of the diaphragmatic rhythms and connect vocal with physical responses (see the sound and movement exercises below), and must stop "thinking" about reactions and learn to respond in a more immediate and visceral manner. The actor must get out of the "academic" habit of prejudging responses because he or she is afraid to make mistakes, and give air to the deepest and most instinctual sounds.

This form of theatre gives language broader and deeper dimensions. The intellectual information of the words is less important than is the poetic feeling the sound conveys. In working on a text the actor will discover where clarity of information is important and where concrete vocal sound best conveys the impact of the moment. The text will be reduced to its most essential elements.

The actor has, in fact, to be hyperverbally aware, must be conscious of the sound beneath the word so that the emotional root may be given full value. A perfect example of this occurred in a workshop in which a young actor was trying to express his feelings at a sunrise he had just encountered (confronted). The feeling was too overwhelming for words, and all the young man could do was to take a deep breath and exhale his emotion. The nearest sound to the exhalation was "Aaaaaaah," which, of course, if verbalized becomes Awe! This was the very nature of the experience the actor was feeling. All the emotive potential of words must

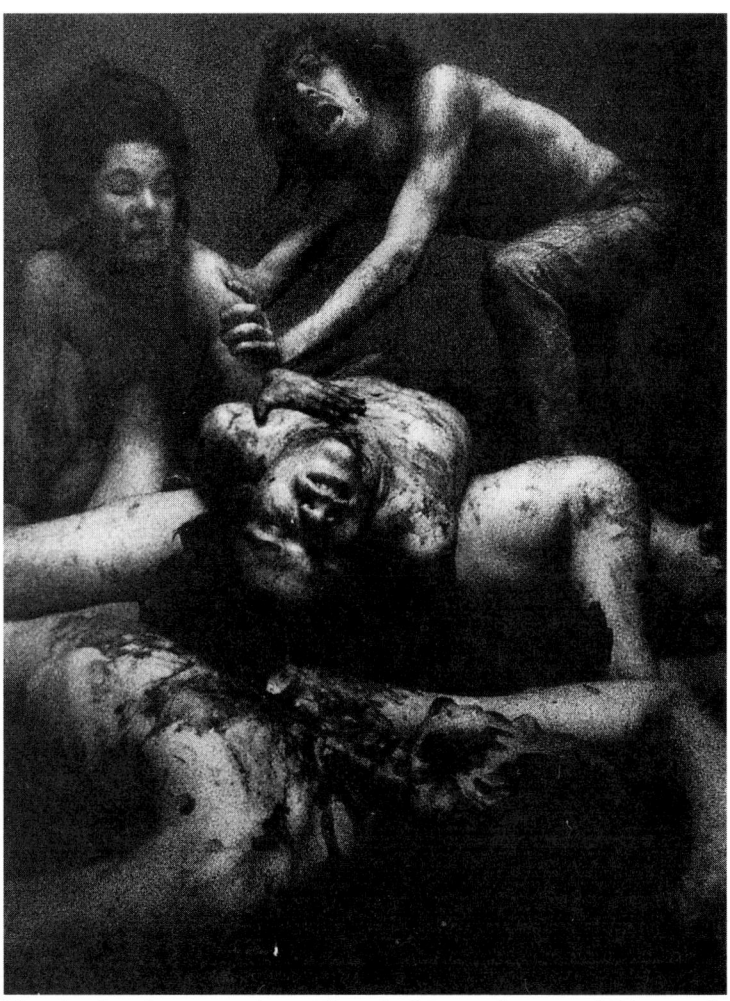

The ritual and communion of "cruelty" in production of *Dionysus in '69.* © *Max Waldman, 1969.*

be discovered in this form of theatre: the fullness of the *a, o,* and *u* vowels, and the piercing quality of *e* and *i*. The onomatopoeic roots and incantatory rhythms from which our verbal language has evolved create the vocal dynamics of this theatre.

Sense of Occasion. The words that come to mind when trying to encapsulate the essential quality of the Artaudian theatrical event have all been used before and are implicit within our discussion: holistic, ritualistic, participatory, intense, all-embracing. The use of total space, the filling of the total space with images and sensations, the tearing away of masks to reach human essences, the confrontation of humankind with itself as represented in its most deeply rooted myths—all of this suggests the physical and spiritual demands of the occasion.

In simply technical terms, the directness of the spatial relationship between actor and audience allows the actor to include the audience members in the event. They may become peasants, soldiers, the dead, the legions of the damned—whatever the focus of the myth or idea the actor is confronting. Thus, the participation can be physically realized, but the true participation happens at a deeper level: It is an embracement of a spiritual kind. In a way the sensibility of this theatre brings us full circle: Aesthetics and ethics meet as they did in the earliest rituals and in the Greek theatre, the starting point of our discussion. The essential sense of community, the sharing of the ideal of citizenship underlying the sensibility of the Greek theatrical event is something Artaud and Grotowski wished to recapture. Call it ritual, communion, mass: The core of the event is the actor's and audience's celebration of their common humanity, a celebration that reveals their deepest selves and shares the catharsis as they touch and act out the grace that lives within us all.

EXERCISES, GAMES, TECHNIQUES

An actor's physical instrument should always be well tuned, but never more so than when confronting the demands of Artaudian theatre. Companies such as Grotowski's and Chaikin's spent years in stringent daily physical and vocal training. We cannot pretend to set down such a program on paper. Rather, we are setting down a core of basic exercises that will cover the range of demands placed upon the performer, while recommending serious attention to extending vocal range and capacity and achieving a freedom and supple, tensile responsiveness in the body.

Free Flow. These are spinal exercises. The spine carries the nervous system, the flow of bodily impulses. The freer the spine, the more fluid the flow and the fuller and more direct will be the physical response to action. When engaged with the pelvis—the body's center of gravity and balance—the free spine allows the actor to respond with a complete instrument—not just the movement of arms and legs for physical expression and the face for feelings.

Solo Stretch. Sit on the floor, well forward on the pelvis, and elongate the spine. Open the legs into as wide a V as possible and place the hands behind the body, fingertips touching the floor. Flex the feet so that the heels come forward. Push the body up off the floor with the fingertips so that it is balanced on fingertips and heels. Point the toes and release the pelvis to the floor. Repeat twice, then return to original position and breathe for one minute. Now walk the hands out in front of the body, stretching forward until the elbows contact the floor and, if possible, the chest contacts the floor between the V of the legs. Sustain this position for one minute. Breathe in, lengthen the spine, and return to original position. Now draw the knees up to the chest and, with the soles of the feet touching each other, let the knees fall to the floor at either side. Take the image of a butterfly for this position. Stretch the knees outwards without bouncing; try to lengthen the chest onto the floor while the knees work outwards at the side. Breathe in, lengthen the spine, and return to original position. Repeat the entire pattern again.

Spinal Float.   Two players matched in height and weight stand back-to-back. One player wraps the elbows under the partner's and bends the knees so that the partner's buttocks rest in the small of his or her back. Straightening the knees, the partner leans forward so that the other player is stretched along his or her back, legs dangling and spine released. Both players breathe for a while in this position—take an image of floating on water. The under player now takes the other's wrists and they straighten up, once more standing back-to-back. Reverse roles and repeat. This is a good activity after the rounding exercises, as it takes the spine in the opposite direction.

Monkey Walk.   Lie on the stomach, head resting on folded arms. Breathe in, lift the head, and curve the spine into the yoga cobra position. From the cobra, lift the pelvis into the air, forming the high point of a triangle with hands on the floor, heels on the floor, and shoulders pulled back to lengthen the spine. Now walk the palms toward the feet, keeping the knees straight. Tap the way up the body with the palms: along thighs, through the stomach, up the chest to the top of the head, and end with arms extended as far as they will go. Reverse the process down the body, into triangle, into cobra, and back to starting position. Accompany the activity with sound—an ascending note to go up, a descending note to come down. Repeat. Players feel foolish doing this exercise. That's fine; players must be willing to make fools of themselves to release the truest impulses. The exercise is a good coordination of pelvis with spine.

Rope Trick.   Sit on the floor with knees drawn to chest and arms around them. Elongate the spine. Now roll the spine down to the floor until it reaches the small of the back. Roll back to a seated position. Repeat, this time rolling down to middle of back and up again. Finally, roll the entire spine down to the floor; then reverse, tucking the head slightly forward and elongating the spine. Repeat the entire process, taking the image of pulling a rope taut with a partner; release to roll down; pull on the rope to sit up.

Groin Grind.   Stand opposite a wall with the arms extended so that the fingertips just touch the wall. Now, place palms on the wall—this will make you lean slightly forward. Now bend the arms so that the chest moves forward to touch the wall; this will make the spine concave. Push off the wall so that the spine becomes convex, and return to beginning position. Repeat, this time trying to touch the wall with the groin. Push into convex position and return to start. Repeat the process several times, trying to make fuller contact with the wall each time.

The Cat.   This is an exercise popularized by Grotowski, but which originated with Stanislavski. Lie face down on floor, head on arms. Move into the cobra position, and from here into a triangle by lifting the pelvis into the air with hands and feet on the floor. Circle the torso to the right. Repeat, circling to the left. Release the pelvis toward the floor, then arch back up to the roof. Now extend left leg as far as it will stretch and shake it out. Repeat for right leg. Repeat for left arm, then right arm. Now release knees to floor and slide back into the cobra, and from there go into a prone position. Do not force this exercise; it should flow. Taking the image of a cat waking and stretching should help achieve the exercise.

The Plastique.   Stand in a neutral position with the legs comfortably apart, knees slightly bent, pelvis released forward. Isolate the head, drop it forward, return center, drop it back, return center. Now drop right, center, left. Make a complete head roll. Now raise right shoulder, drop, and return to center. Drop shoulder down, lift, and return to center. Roll shoulder in a circular pattern. Repeat the process with left shoulder. Isolate the rib cage, bring it forward, return to center; to the right, center; left, center. Isolate the pelvis and repeat the process. Circle with pelvis. Work through the wrists, pulling them in and away as if pulling taffy. Rotate the elbows; stretch them and pull the shoulders forward. The movements should be taken quickly, and each pattern repeated several times.

Sound Concrete I.   Players sit at random around a space. Within the space are numerous objects with which sound can be produced: sticks, stones, tin cans, empty boxes, and so forth. The players explore the sound potential of these nonmusical "instruments," playing them on the floor, in midair, muted against the body. The body may also be used as a sound instrument—by patting air-filled cheeks, slapping parts of the body with hands or solid objects, clicking with the tongue, using exaggerated breathing. The purpose of the exercise is to get players to understand the possibilities of producing different sounds without the voice or musical instruments—the range of the actor's aural imagination can be enormously broadened.

Sound Concrete II.   Players move around a space and attempt to use sound as a physical tool—to make it do things: open a door, cut through wood, heat a metal object; also to change in form such as becoming a lasso and capturing an object; becoming ribbon and tying up a parcel. This exercise enormously broadens the actor's perception of the potency and potentiality of sound.

Zap.   Players form a circle, or two lines opposite each other. One player throws a ball of energy with a particular body movement and sound at another player. The second player

must accept the energy, repeat the movement and sound, transform it into his or her own movement and sound, and zap it at another player. There should be no gap between receiving the energy, performing it, and then transforming it. The game is high-energy and high-pace. Players may need to be coached to use their whole bodies, rather than just arms and legs, in performing the movements. The game is a good warm-up and encourages 360-degree use of physical imagination.

Conductor.   This can be played as an extension of "Zap." Players form a circle with one player in the center. The center player performs any kind of rhythmical movement with his or her body. The other players respond with movements of their own, not imitating the central player but picking up the dynamics of the rhythmical action. He or she is the conductor, and they are the orchestra. He or she can change the rhythm and pace at any time, and they should follow. After a short while the conductor offers his or her rhythm and action to a specific member of the orchestra, who picks it up, moves into the center, and becomes the new conductor. He or she may now create his or her own dynamics. The exercise continues until all the players have a turn as conductor. An elaboration upon the exercise is to add nonmusical sound to the movement, emphasizing the rhythm and connecting physical and vocal impulses.

Tone Poem.   This is an extension of "Conductor." Begin that exercise and allow the rhythmical concentration to develop. When the exercise is under way throw various themes at the conductor as a basis for the "music" he or she is creating. The themes may start simply and allow of imitation—a carousel, an old Ford car, a 767 jet. They should then move into broader essences and abstractions—for example, colors, tastes, and concepts such as imprisonment, revolution, and hatred. Through this exercise the players will find themselves on the way to exploring their basic reactions to metaphysical ideas and to discovering hieroglyphic responses.

Jamming.   Players start by using all kinds of vocal sounds, hisses, tongue clicks, pantings, etc., to improvise a musical piece. This is then extended to individual words that are picked up on by other players and musically extended as in a jazz "jam session." This can be extended to sentences based upon themes. It can also be done progressively: One actor begins a "riff" with a phrase in illustration of a theme, moving with the rhythms, using sound and gesture as the moment dictates. Another actor joins in, picks up and extends the theme, and so on until the group is involved. It is preferable not to have more than a group of six to eight—as there would be in a jazz band—so that an ensemble can be maintained.

Backslapping.   Players form a ring with two players in the center. The center players must try to touch each other's back with their fingertips. They must not make contact with any other part of the body, and must stay within the ring. Whoever first makes three touches is the winner and two other players take over. The game can be played with the winner staying in the ring and taking on all challengers until defeated. The game encourages quickness of response and body flexibility. It can also be used as a warm-up exercise for any highly physical style such as farce. (See Chapter 5.)

Phantom Fighting.   Players pair off and begin a fight, but without touching each other. All the motions of punching, kicking, butting, kneeing, etc., can be gone through, but they must be controlled so that no contact is made. The styles of fighting may be varied: boxing, wrestling, laser swords, street brawling. This is another total-body-involvement game, but it also requires a strong sense of awareness, of playing with another actor. The players can be coached to experience the fight intensely, but

the performance of it takes on a ritualistic quality—it is the essence of a fight that is being created by the participants.

Four-Letter Feelings.   Players find their own space and begin to improvise upon some basic human function, such as eating. They should start with the most polite form they know—possibly a formal banquet or sophisticated restaurant with the paraphernalia of silver and linen napkins. As they go through the improvisation they should murmur appropriate words such as "dining," "entertaining," "banqueting." Gradually reduce the formality of the situation, doing away with knives, forks, and napkins and using the hands and appropriate words such as "eating" and "chewing." Finally, reduce the act to its basic animal idea, using hands and feet and tearing with the mouth—the words will become "gnaw" and "rip" and finally simple animal sounds. This exercise should be done with all the human functions, at the discretion of the coach and group of players. The willingness to deal with such concepts as fucking and shitting will be a test of the group's ability to get below polite masks and strip away taboos. It is not an exercise that should be attempted by an inexperienced coach with a group that has not learned to have mutual trust. It is an exercise that takes the players back to more dynamic and vivid physical responses; it brings their center of response out of their head into the lower, pelvic part of the body, where it should be. We have learned to wrap up subjects that society finds taboo in polite terminology;[15] we talk of "putting to sleep" when we mean "killing." The sex act is perhaps the strongest taboo, and dealing with it in this exercise produces interesting

---

[15]"It is interesting to note that the basic, expressive, simple terms tend to be Anglo-Saxon, closer to the primitive origins of a culture. The complex terms of the English language have mostly a Latin base, brought into the language by the invasion of the more sophisticated Norman culture.

modulations, which will go through flirting, making love, going to bed, having sex, and finally the ultimate four-letter word and the rhythmical, dynamic, total body response the act presumes.

Encounters.   Players pair off and select a simple human relationship such as boyfriend/ girlfriend, teacher/pupil, cop/crook, salesperson/customer. Without further discussion the players move around the space exploring the relationship. No words are used and no realistic props are employed. Players should concentrate on the rhythms of their character, expressing them through space to the partner. A pattern will emerge that expresses the nature of the relationship as both players perceive it. At this stage of the exercise one partner should choose a simple but emotionally strong message to communicate to his or her partner—for example, "The man you shot died!" or "I'm leaving you!" Again, no words are to be used; the message is to be communicated through the body movements in the spatial pattern already developed. When the partner senses the nature of the message, he or she replies in a similar manner—with body movement in spatial patterns. With strong concentration and bodily commitment to the exercise, messages can be understood and dynamic conversations held. Some coaching will be needed to channel players away from small, realistic gestures into more deeply seated, engaged movements of the whole body.

Hieroglyphs.   What follows are games to help the actor discover and then physically communicate the *essential* nature of concepts.

Contrasts.   Players scatter around the space, contacting it in a neutral manner. Within the space are various nonspecific props, such as sticks, ropes, colored ribbons, and pieces of cloth. Number the players and introduce opposing concepts to be explored, such as harmony/discord. Have the odd-numbered

players explore one concept, the even numbers the other. Players should work individually and physically at first, responding to an immediate sense of what the concept means to them. The response should be confronted and refined into a hieroglyph—a series of gestures or movements. When the players seem to have discovered their hieroglyph, call out pairs of numbers—one even, one odd—and have these players reveal their hieroglyph to each other, responding to one another's rhythms, confronting the opposite concept, and adjusting so that the two hieroglyphs become one—a hieroglyph that displays the essence of the dichotomy. While working in pairs, players may use any of the props around the space. There are many pairs of concepts that work for this exercise: goodness/evil, victory/defeat, truth/falsehood, freedom/ restraint, self-interest/sacrifice, and so on. Players should be coached to reject the realistic gestures they first employ and to discover deeper and more meaningful images.

Seven Deadly Sins.   Players begin by contacting space in a neutral manner. Introduce the "sin" concepts (gluttony, lust, avarice, envy, pride, sloth, wrath) one at a time. The players should follow their immediate physical response. At first there will be a certain amount of imitation, pantomime—the sticking out of the belly for gluttony, moving slowly for sloth. Coach for an understanding of the full medieval significance of sin—not contemporary peccadilloes. Coach for strong visceral reactions, a full body response from the feet up, a total physical exploration. When all players seem to be working at this deep level, coach to refine the physical discoveries into a rhythmical, disciplined, repetitive image that retains the intensity of feeling at its core. Between work on each concept have the players shake out and resume a neutral walk in space—this is necessary owing to the intensity of the work involved. When all the sins have been individually explored, throw them all at the group and allow players to work on one they have a particular response to. After a few minutes' work, have the players shake out and sit in a circle. Now each player in turn performs his or her particular hieroglyph in the center of the circle. The other players don't know the concept, but if the hieroglyph is valid they will soon sense it. As they get the idea they begin to whisper the concept: "lust," "envy," "pride," and so on, in time with the center player's rhythm, encouraging the player to a peak of intensity. The exercise is excellent for achieving a visceral response to ideas and a refined, intensified image based in that response. It quickly reveals clichés and weak, realistic gestures.

Fantasies. Players split up into groups of about four. In turn, each of the players arranges the others in a tableau illustrating a fantasy—profane, morbid, heroic, erotic, whatever has some deep meaning for the players. Then the tableaux are wound up and act out the fantasy in a rhythmically repetitive way. Fantasies, as depicted by humans in their art, from the earliest cave drawings, are the wellspring of human imagination and are strongly connected to the ritual roots of drama.

Perfect People. Players improvise a social event—cocktail party, PTA meeting, presidential inauguration, homecoming ball—with the necessary social decorum and the polite conversation appropriate to the situation. When it is established, the players begin to act out impulses that are normally controlled beneath the social mask: They pick noses, smell armpits, unzip pants, look under dresses, pinch bottoms, giving free physical rein to the instinct of the moment. While they are doing this, however, they continue to make the right small talk and register no surprise at what is going on. The exercise shows in strong relief the difference between our social behavior and our basic instinct.

Cruelty. This is an exercise that pulls all the others together: "Encounters" and "Hieroglyphs" are especially good exercises for leading into it. Players choose a five- to ten-minute scene from a play—strong classical texts such as *'Tis Pity She's a Whore, The White Devil,* and *Titus Andronicus* work well—explore the text purely in terms of sound to get at the core of the feeling—a quality sometimes hidden by the words. Players will begin by extending vowel sounds and drawing out the words themselves. Coach them to get more deeply in touch with the essential meanings of the scene and discover sounds that may have no specific reference points in the text. Repeat the exercise, this time adding physical gestures—the sounds and gestures should support each other. Again, players will at first simply extend everyday gestures; coach for stronger confrontation of the ideas in the text, to reject clichés and discover clear, powerful images that encapsulate the essential qualities of the scene. As the other exercises lead up to this, it shouldn't be played until near the end of a fairly extensive workshop exploration of the style.

PLAYING THE STYLE

One of the difficulties in discussing the playing of this form of theatre is its essentially physical nature, which loses all force on the written page, as well as the fact that it evolves in process as a series of images that are not predetermined by any hard-and-fast character facts or given circumstances. Despite this, in an attempt to illustrate the process we are going to describe some workshop experiences that were based upon approaching Greek tragedy, not rhetorically as it is written, but as a source of physical confrontation with its dynamic issues, retaining the power and scale but translating this into physical images. In a sense, therefore, we are concluding where we began, only with the obverse, physical realization of the metaphysical issues at the roots of drama.

The first workshop was based upon the messenger speech near the end of *The Bacchae* (approx., lines 1040 to 1150). The speech describes the death and dismemberment of Pentheus at the hands of the acolytes of Dionysus, the Maenads. The actors were two women and a man. The actors began by inviting the spectators into the darkened stage space. The women then stripped off their street clothes and were revealed in textured tights and leotards, the first image of their transportation from the everyday world into a realm of ritual. This was taken further with the next image where the women raised a chalice of white powder with which they then covered themselves, gradually building into an ecstatic, drug-induced physical frenzy and embracing all the other women in the audience. At the height of this moment a voice from the darkness used Euripides' lines: "Women, I bring you the man who has mocked at you and me and at our holy mysteries. Take vengeance on him." At this moment the man in the group was revealed in a shaft of light watching the women from atop a ladder. The women, picking up the cry of "Take vengeance," shook the ladder intensely until the actor playing Pentheus fell with a dynamic acrobatic leap into the middle of the stage space. Here the women bound him with strips of cloth, and then ritually poured a red dye over this body. This done they declaimed Euripides' lines about the tearing of Pentheus's flesh and tore the now dripping red pieces of cloth from the body. Finally the women, themselves now covered with white powder and red dye, took pieces of the cloth and anointed each member of the audience. This was both a "blooding" and an act of primitive communion, illustrating the sacrifice and guilt that we all share and tying Christian symbology to that of the pagan Dionysian from which it derived.

The actors discovered their score by a process of deciding that for them the piece was about the power and danger of religious fervor and the connection between the Dionysian and the Christian symbology. Then they determined upon the important images that created a score—images such as intoxication, vengeance, sacrifice—and confronted these physically to discover their personal responses. Exercises such as *Hieroglyph Contrasts, Encounters,* and *Four-Letter Feelings* were used as a basis for the explorations. An important aspect of the work was that images were discarded until all actors agreed on their connection to the image, and when these were discovered a process of strong repetition was used to encode them into the actors' bodies.

In another instance, when working on the messenger speech from *Hippolytus,* which describes the destruction of Hippolytus at the hands of his horses maddened by Poseidon, two actors discovered a powerful physical image that was the extension of a simple exercise. Using the *Rope Trick* as a warm-up exercise, the actor extended this by using an actual piece of rope that became the reins of Hippolytus's horses. The actors explored the tensions between them through the rope, and through a process of confrontations discovered a powerful illustration of the bolting horses whereby the actor who had become the horse moved with powerful diagonal dashes back and forth across the stage, while Hippolytus at the other end of the rope was jerked through a series of acrobatic movements until his last gasp: "Curse, Save me, Father, Curse."

Simple, nonspecific, but dramatic props are an important part of the actor's creativity. On occasion we have seen a white sheet used as a connecting symbol throughout a piece. At different times the sheet was a cloak—the removal of which represented a physical stripping and transfer of dominance—a serpent, representing sensuality and threat; a whip tantalizing and punishing; a shroud, creating the image of death, and as both an umbilical cord and, passing through the crotch of one actor to the crotch of another, the passage of semen in the sexual act.

This is, as we have suggested, a theatre of physical metaphor, in which the signs or hieroglyphs created by the actor with his or her own physicality produce the effect upon the audience. The poetic image has much greater force than does naturalistic detail. The actor must be able to distinguish between sensuality and mere salacity: Copulation is much less dramatic than its symbolic enactment—it is pornographic rather than erotic. These crucial distinctions are a function of the level of exploration and discovery achieved by the actor in confrontation with the text or pretext of the event. The deeper the discovery the more authentic the image. The rehearsal process is the selection of the appropriate, the demanding of the right sign; the "signal through the flames" that is itself a metaphor for the burning conviction to destroy and remake anew that is at the heart of all experimental theatre.

SUGGESTED READINGS

Artaud, Antonin, *The Theatre and Its Double*, trans. Mary Richards. New York: Grove Press, 1958.

Blumenthal, Eileen, *Directors in Perspective: Joseph Chaikin*. New York: Cambridge University Press, 1984.

Grotowski, Jerzy, *Towards a Poor Theatre*. London: Methuen, 1969.

Kumiega, Jennifer, *The Theatre of Grotowski*. London: Methuen, 1987.

Malpede, Karen, *Three Works by the Open Theatre*. New York: Drama Book Specialists, 1974. An excellent visual source.

Savrian, David, *The Wooster Group 1975–85: Breaking the Rules*. Ann Arbor, Mich.: U.M.I. Research Press, 1986.

Shank, Theodore, *American Alternative Theatre*. New York: Grove Press, 1982.

Wiles, Timothy, *The Theatre Event: Modern Theories of Performance*. Chicago: University of Chicago Press, 1982.

Index